The Consumer Revolution
in Urban China

This volume and the conference from which it resulted were supported by the Joint Committee on Chinese Studies of the American Council of Learned Societies and the Social Science Research Council.

The
Consumer Revolution
in Urban China

—

EDITED BY

Deborah S. Davis

UNIVERSITY OF CALIFORNIA PRESS

Berkeley · Los Angeles · London

University of California Press
Berkeley and Los Angeles, California
University of California Press, Ltd.
London, England
© 2000 by the Regents of the University of California

Library of Congress Cataloging-in-Publication Data
Davis, Deborah, 1945–.
The consumer revolution in urban China / edited by Deborah S. Davis.
    p.   cm.   (Studies on China; 22)
Includes bibliographical references and index.
ISBN 0-520-21639 (hardcover : alk. paper)
ISBN 0-520-21640-7 (pbk. : alk. paper)
    1. Consumers—China   2. Consumption (Economics)—China   3. Consumer
behavior—China   I. Davis, Deborah, 1945–   .
II. Series.
HC430.C6C66   2000
339.4'7'0951—dc21   98-43811
                                                                        CIP

Manufactured in the United States of America

08   07   06   05   04   03   02   01   00   99   10   9   8   7   6   5   4   3   2   1

The paper used in this publication meets the minimum requirements of ANSI/NISO
Z39.48-1992 (R 1997) (*Permanence of Paper*)

STUDIES ON CHINA

A series of conference volumes sponsored by the American Council of Learned Societies.

18. *Voices of the Song Lyric in China,* edited by Pauline Yu, University of California Press, 1993.

19. *Education and Society in Late Imperial China, 1600–1900,* edited by Benjamin A. Elman and Alexander Woodside, University of California Press, 1994.

20. *Chinese Historical Micro-Demography,* edited by Stevan Harrell, University of California Press, 1994.

21. *The Waning of the Communist State: Economic Origins of Political Decline in China and Hungary,* edited by Andrew G. Walder, University of California Press, 1995.

22. *The Consumer Revolution in Urban China,* edited by Deborah S. Davis, University of California Press, 2000.

CONTENTS

II
SOCIABILITY IN A MORE COMMODIFIED SOCIETY

FIGURES AND TABLES

FIGURES

TABLES

ACKNOWLEDGMENTS

The chapters in this volume were first presented at the conference "Consumers and Consumer Culture in Contemporary Urban China" held at Yale University, January 9–12, 1997. Financial support for the conference and subsequent editorial expenses were provided by a grant from the Joint Committee on Chinese Studies of the American Council of Learned Societies and the Social Science Research Council with funds granted by the Henry Luce Foundation. In addition to the fourteen authors whose revised papers constitute this volume, the editor would like to recognize the intellectual contributions from conference participants: Jean-Christophe Agnew, Yanjie Bian, Sherman Cochran, Joshua Gamson, Thomas Gold, Jun Jing, Eiko Ikegami, William Kelly, and Joseph Soares. Able logistical assistance was provided by Krista Forsgren-Ahdieh, Ken Liu, and Vivian Louie, who worked under the expert guidance of Ann Fitzpatrick. For invaluable help with all stages of manuscript preparation, the editor gives special thanks to Anthony Spires.

—

CHAPTER 1

Introduction

A Revolution in Consumption

Deborah S. Davis

Chairman Mao Zedong was not gone two years when his successors jettisoned core principles of the Communist revolution and assigned private entrepreneurship and consumer demand central roles in a new blueprint for economic growth. Initially these deviations from Maoist orthodoxy were endorsed as short-term compromises to spur efficiency and jump start a stagnant economy.[1] There was no intention of allowing individuals to accumulate significant capital or property rights, and any link between economic and political reform was explicitly rejected. However, by the early 1990s, when the initial reform had produced a decade of double-digit growth and ensconced Chinese industry firmly within the global capitalist economy, the leadership discovered that they could not reverse course. Neither could they control the social consequences of the economy's dependency on market transactions and private entrepreneurship. Millions of daily commercial exchanges not only calibrated the flow of material goods; they also nurtured individual desires and social networks that challenged official discourse and conventions. The political regime remained intact, but relationships between agents of the state and ordinary citizens had changed.

For the urban residents who are the subjects of this volume, the financial gains from post-Mao economic reform have been rapid and impressive.[2] Adjusted for inflation, per capita income doubled between 1978 and 1990, and

In addition to the participants in the ACLS conference who commented on drafts of this introduction, I would like to thank Stevan Harrell and Mark Selden for useful criticism on earlier versions of this chapter.

1. In 1980, chief economist Chen Yun encouraged a focus on the consumer industries both to provide material incentives for higher labor productivity and to prevent the bottlenecks that he expected if there were no new outlets for increased agricultural inputs. Naughton 1995, pp. 77–79.

2. In the 1950s the Chinese government instituted a household registration system that di-

between 1990 and 1994 it increased another 50 percent.[3] Savings of city households rose from $1.85 billion in 1978 to $62.5 billion in 1990 and to $192 billion in 1994.[4] Consumer durables like washing machines and refrigerators that had previously been available to a minority with special connections became routine purchases (see Table 1.1), and a host of previously exotic products became commonplace in retail outlets throughout urban China. In 1990 there were 20,000 cellular phones in China; by 1995 there were 3.4 million.[5] English-Chinese dictionaries had no official translation for greeting card, but by 1995 a street stall in Beijing reportedly sold 80,000 cards in one day.[6] In Shanghai in 1985 there were 52 dance halls and discos; by 1994 there were more than 1,000. In Shenzhen the number of bowling alleys grew by a factor of 40 in one year.[7] When within less than a decade millions of people gained access to new modes of communication, new vocabularies of social discourse, and novel forms of leisure through newly commercialized outlets, it does not seem an exaggeration to claim that there was a revolution of consumption. Moreover as the contributors to this volume explain, this rapid commercialization of consumption did more than simply increase consumer choice and raise the material standard of living. It also broke the monopolies that had previously cast urban consumers in the

---

vided the population into those with agricultural status (*nongye hukou*) and nonagricultural status (*feinongye hukou*). Every person needed police approval to change residence, and migration from rural to urban areas and from small towns to cities was prohibited. These policies were linked to consumption. Those with agricultural registration had to grow their own food and were excluded from the subsidized state grain market. With the creation of the People's Communes in 1958 the registration system became formalized on a national scale, and even after the elimination of the communes in the early 1980s it continued to control rural migration and exclude the rural majority from most government-subsidized goods and services.

In 1993 there were 430 million people living in 570 cities and towns. However, only 177 million had nonagricultural status. It is this group that can best be described as urbanites. *Zhongguo chengshi tongji nianjian 1993–1994*, p. 3. Within this nonagricultural population, there are further distinctions based on the size of a metropolitan area. The consumers described by the authors of this volume come from cities with populations in excess of 2 million where the standard of living is higher than in other cities and the choice of goods and services more diverse. In 1993 they represented 25 percent of all city dwellers. *Zhongguo chengshi tongji nianjian 1987*, p. 1, and *Zhongguo chengshi tongji nianjian 1993–1994*, p.14.

3. In 1978 per capita income was 316 renminbi (rmb), in 1990 it was 1,387 rmb, and in 1994 it was 3,179 rmb. Indexed with 1978 as 100, per capita income had grown to 197 in 1990 and 273 in 1994. *Zhongguo tongji nianjian 1995* (hereafter *ZGTJNJ 1995*), p. 257.

4. These U.S. dollar estimates are based on a rate of 8.3 rmb to the dollar. Household savings totaled 15.45 billion rmb in 1978, 62.5 billion in 1990, and 1.6 trillion in 1994. *ZGTJNJ 1995*, p. 259.

5. See Chapter 7 by Kathleen Erwin.

6. See Chapter 8 by Mary Erbaugh.

7. On dance halls, see Chapter 10 by James Farrer. On Shenzhen bowling, see Chapter 11 by Gan Wang.

role of supplicants to the state. When party and government officials reduced their control over the flow of commodities, they also ceded greater autonomy to everyday sociability. In granting market principles new legitimacy to coordinate economic transactions, the reformers became increasingly indifferent to how citizens used their new commercial freedoms. And in this more lightly censored terrain, urban residents initiated networks of trust, reciprocity, and attachment that differed from the vertical relationship of obedience between subject-citizens and party or government officials. The extent to which these investments in unofficial social relationships threaten the political monopolies claimed by the Leninist state remains open to debate and empirical investigation. No contributor to this volume argues for a triumph of the private over the public. But all agree that the greater affluence and new consumerism of the 1990s have weakened the hegemonic sureties that defined urban life throughout the 1960s and 1970s.

In Part 1, the contributors analyze the implications of new consumer behaviors surrounding domestic spending, the everyday purchases of food, clothing, and transportation and the more unusual expenditures for wedding finery and a special vacation. Part 2 brings together chapters that explore experiences outside the domestic sphere: radio call-in shows, exchanges of greeting cards, feasting, dancing, bowling, and "having a good smoke." No master narrative unites the chapters. There is no central hypothesis that commercialization heralds the triumph of the private over the public. Nevertheless, a common thread ties together each setting and group of consumers analyzed. Each author documents an increasing reliance of urban residents on horizontal ties of friendship, kinship, or informal sociability that challenge the vertical relationship between subject-citizens and state agents. Thus when read as an integrated whole, the volume tells a story of how changing consumer behavior can enlarge the social space for urban residents to invest in nonofficial initiatives. Whether these actions seriously threaten the monopolies claimed by a Leninist state remains unclear. But none of the contributors found Chinese society untouched by consumerism.

A REVOLUTION IN DOMESTIC CONSUMPTION

In the 1970s the resources of the workplace determined a Chinese family's standard of living as much as, or even more than, the wages earned by the household head. Not only did enterprises distribute social welfare benefits that were otherwise unavailable, but they also allocated apartments and provided many consumer items that in capitalist societies were discretionary personal expenditures—a weekly movie, fresh fruit at holidays, plastic sandals for the summer, even the cake to celebrate a baby's birth. Through these noncommercial, redistributive practices urban residents experienced what

TABLE 1.1 Consumer Items Owned per 100 Households
in China's Ten Largest Cities and Shenzhen, 1986–1995

	Washing machine			Refrigerator			Color TV			Camera			Air conditioner		
	1986	1990	1995	1986	1990	1995	1986	1990	1995	1986	1990	1995	1986	1990	1995
National average	65	83	89	18	57	66	29	67	90	17	26	31	0.1	0.4	
Beijing	76	93	100	62	96	98	51	91	102	47	67	87	0	0	12
Chongqing	62	83	92	27	82	93	27	74	98	25	30	38	0	0.7	29
Guangzhou	68	87	105	52	87	102	46	89	111	17	34	66	0	1.3	57
Harbin	61	79	83	6	39	67	25	58	83	16	29	36	0	0	
Nanjing	52	88	98	18	71	95	25	64	99	18	33	52	0	0	
Shanghai	39	72	78	47	88	98	36	77	109	28	44	52	0	0	33
Shenyang	68	84	87	7	62	78	18	80	94	24	42	54	0	0.3	
Shenzhen	73	88	97	77	97	102	83	109	125	34	51	78	0	26	101
Tianjin	69	84	94	23	78	98	33	72	102	25	37	52	0.2	0.5	13
Wuhan	24	90	91	29	81	96	17	58	94	21	30	44	0	0.8	26
Xi'an	72	90	96	14	52	83	33	73	101	29	35	45	0.3	0.7	18

SOURCES: For 1986, State Statistical Bureau and East-West Population Center 1991, pp. 225–28, 293–95; for 1995, Zhongguo chengzhen zhumin jiating shouzhuo diaochaziliao 1991, pp. 242–45; for 1990, Zhongguo chengzhen zhumin jiating shouzhuo diaochaziliao 1991, pp. 225–28, 293–95; for 1995, Beijing tongji nianjian 1996, p. 414; Chongqing tongji nianjian 1996, p. 138; Guangzhou tongji nianjian 1996, p. 383; Harbin tonji nianjian 1996, p. 205; Nanjing tongji nianjian 1996, p. 305; Shanghai tongji nianjian 1996, p. 71; Shenyang tongji nianjian 1996, p. 305; Shenzhen tongji nianjian 1996, p. 434; Tianjin tongji nianjian 1996, p. 185; Wuhan tongji nianjian 1996, p. 305; Xi'an tongji nianjian 1996, p. 205.

Hanlong Lu calls "massified" consumption (Chapter 6). Whether a household was headed by a professional or a blue-collar production worker, their family members lived in comparable homes, took the same buses to work, confronted similar food shortages, and faced an equally limited choice of leisure activities and selection of clothing. Material inequalities existed, and behind the closed doors and high walls of cadre compounds the political elite enjoyed a distinctive lifestyle. Overall, however, living standards were remarkably homogeneous within enterprises, and differences among city families were attributable more to variations in the resources of employers than to individual or family wealth.[8]

Distributing consumer goods and services by bureaucratic fiat rather than through markets also affected social relationships. Politicized ties between subordinates and superiors in the workplace could define the quality of one's personal life, and it was virtually impossible for employees or their family members to prosper without the active support of enterprise leaders.[9] If an employer denied or failed to provide a benefit, there was rarely an alternative source. Even leisure time and venues for socializing were rationed through bureaucratic channels under the supervision of the Chinese Communist Party (CCP).[10]

By the mid-1990s, higher incomes and new retail markets had reduced the obligations on the workplace to satisfy consumer demands. Independent hawkers filled daily markets and sold such previously rationed items as seafood, meat, milk, and grain products. Private restaurateurs or subcontractors (*chengbao*) replaced workplace canteens, and a largely commercialized entertainment industry multiplied opportunities for individuals to relax or conduct business in the unofficial world away from work.

Even during the Cultural Revolution (1966–76), when the Maoist party-state was most intrusive, families retained some autonomy and the domestic sphere provided a modicum of privacy. The law dictated that children and parents be financially responsible for one another, and only the childless elderly or orphans could rely on the state in time of need.[11] Enterprises paid employees' medical costs but only partially reimbursed the expenditures of their dependents. Wedding and funeral expenditures, although modest in comparison with what they would become in the 1990s, required years of saving.[12] Home furnishings usually included workplace-issued desks, tables, and chairs, but the home was also decorated with personal possessions and

8. Bian 1994.

9. This argument is made most strongly for employees of state-owned industrial enterprises, but it applies more generally to most urban adults (see Walder 1986).

10. S. Wang 1995.

11. Davis-Friedmann 1991.

12. Studying Guangdong urban residents in the 1970s, Martin Whyte and William Parish found that grooms and their families spent on average three to five months of family income,

furniture inherited from older relatives or received as personal gifts.[13] According to CCP orthodoxy, families were the cells of society embedded in the matrix of public life. Nevertheless, they retained duties that distinguished one family from another and made kinship roles exclusive. Accelerating marketization and the retreat of state supervision have heightened these distinctions.

Weaker redistributive policies and increased reliance on markets also ended "massified' consumption patterns and widened economic differences between households. Economic reforms ushered in a decade of aggregate growth, but a minority experienced a decline in their absolute as well as relative standard of living. The story of the urban revolution of consumption therefore is how market-based differentiation fostered both new forms of social solidarity and new patterns of inequality. Let me first summarize the gains; a subsequent section will consider the issue of increasing inequality.

Food

In cross-national comparisons, household expenditures on food provide an inflation-proof metric for assessing a population's economic progress. The general assumption is that as real incomes rise consumers spend a lower percentage of their income on food for home cooking and eat more animal protein, fruits, and prepared foods. During the early 1990s, urban Chinese conformed to these expectations.[14] But as Ann Veeck demonstrates in her study of Nanjing food shoppers (Chapter 5) close examination of household expenditures for food reveal much more than the relative share of protein in average diets. China has one of the great cuisines of the world, and buying, preparing, and enjoying food have cultural, medicinal, and ritual meanings that make food shopping a template for a wide range of social attitudes and behaviors. Older residents have searing memories of the near starvation they endured after the failure of the Great Leap Forward, and few adults have forgotten the monotonous diets of the 1970s, when many foodstuffs were distributed to workers at the end of the week or before a holiday, and grain and oil were sold through designated state outlets that required customers to use coupons and a ration book. Throughout the

---

brides and their families two to three months of income, on their weddings. Given that families needed at least 80 percent of their monthly income to meet basic needs, weddings required several years of saving. Whyte and Parish 1984, p.137.

13. Davis 1989.

14. Between 1990 and 1994, per capita purchases of grains fell by 30 percent, while those of seafood and edible oils grew by 10–20 percent. The correlation between income and food choices also conformed to international patterns. In 1994 urban households in the lowest income decile spent 18 percent of their food budget on grains; those in the top decile spent only 11 percent. *ZGTJNJ 1995*, pp. 260–61, 263.

1980s, economic reforms fundamentally changed the experience of shopping and the dynamic of food retailing. The expanded food offerings of the 1990s and the end of rationing, therefore, created an environment in which grocery shopping became a lively social context for observing the consequences of the consumer revolution.

Veeck's Nanjing respondents spent six hours a week shopping for food, and in her community sample, families on average spent 52 percent of their household income on food. Veeck herself focused on the interpersonal dynamic of consumers and retailers, and through extended interviews with shoppers (many of which she recorded verbatim while accompanying respondents on their trips to the market) she probed the impact of marketization on the exercise of personal taste and choice. During the time of her observation, class differences had begun to emerge, and Veeck predicts that over time Chinese food expenditures will follow world trends and become clearly differentiated by household income level. However, to her initial surprise the appearance of thriving, competitive street markets did not foster behaviors common in African and Latin American cities, where families also buy daily from individual food vendors. In those other settings buyers often return to the same vendor for months and even years, and the marketplace creates enduring bonds of social solidarity. In Nanjing, by contrast, customers were extremely mistrustful of food peddlers and routinely carried a scale to market to verify the weight of their purchases. The marketplace was quite atomized and socially unpredictable, in part because of the instability of retail environments in an era of reform. The government repeatedly forced markets to relocate, many salesmen were migrants with no fixed abode or identity as vendors, and—perhaps most important—in 1995–96 during Veeck's observation, vendors did not extend credit.

Based on the policy announcements of the municipal government, Veeck predicts that the turbulence of the retail scene will stabilize. The workplace will withdraw completely from stocking domestic larders, and vendors will lease stalls in large market halls either as agents of state enterprises or as independent hawkers. There are even indicators that supermarket chains may come to dominate the retail sector. However, what is unlikely to change is the cultural code that equates care in food shopping with concern for family members. Thus for Chinese families, shopping for food will always reflect the attachments and intensity of the domestic sphere.

Spending for Children

One of the most radical components of the reforms undertaken by Deng Xiaoping, and quite at variance with the general pattern of a "retreating" party-state, was the one-child campaign launched in 1979. Fifteen years later the campaign had successfully reduced the number of third or higher-order births throughout the nation and made the one-child family the urban norm (see Table 1.2). Against this demographic testimony to the persistence of party-state authority and power, in Chapter 3 Julia Sensenbrenner and I explore the impact of increased commercialization on the character of childhood. Focusing on parental purchases of toys, clothes, and leisure activities for Shanghai's singletons in the summer of 1995, we analyze the multiple ways in which commercialization spurred the separation of work and home and expanded the legitimate realm of the personal and individual. Most parents of Shanghai's singletons came of age during the Cultural Revolution. Their living standard was spartan, and consumption was oriented to the collective. They therefore eagerly examined each new product or service as a means not only of giving their children happier childhoods than their own, but also of allowing them to fully develop their individual talents. China's draconian birth quotas denied young couples the freedom to define family size, but the vast flood of affordable consumer goods enabled Shanghai mothers and fathers to spend money on toys and leisure activities that they believed would cultivate their children's individuality and strengthen attachments to the immediate family.

Housing

In the 1970s most urban housing was a "public" good owned and allocated by enterprises or municipal real estate bureaus. The first decade of economic reforms did little to change the ownership structure and instead concentrated on upgrading the quality and quantity of collectively owned housing. Public funds, primarily from state-owned enterprises, poured into urban housing construction, and between 1978 and 1992 average living space doubled from 3.6 square meters per capita to 7.1 square meters.[15] In the 1990s, however, policy shifted to spur commodification of residential real estate.

At the Second National Housing Reform Conference in October 1991, the leadership announced three initiatives. First, rents were to be raised to cover the costs of maintenance; second, renters were to be encouraged to purchase their flats on the installment plan; and third, an increasing share of new housing was to be offered for direct sale.[16] Within a short time, these policy shifts developed far-reaching consequences. By the summer of 1992, 5 million urban households held twelve-year mortgages from the Chinese Construction Bank, and by December 1994 30.5 percent of urban households held some type of ownership rights.[17] Most home buyers purchased

---

15. *ZGTJNJ 1995*, p. 290.

16. *Renmin ribao* (People's daily), Oct. 12, 1991.

17. Basically, there were three levels of ownership: ownership with right to resell in the marketplace, ownership with obligation to resell to the employer, and ownership of use rights with no right to resell. *Ming bao,* Oct. 6, 1992, p. 9; and *Renmin ribao,* Sept. 14, 1995, p. 1.

TABLE 1.2   Changing Birth Parities in the PRC,
1970–1994

Percentage of births that were	first	second	third or higher
1970	20.7	27.1	62.2
1977	30.8	24.7	44.5
1981	46.5	25.5	28.0
1985	50.2	30.1	19.7
1989	49.5	31.2	19.3
1992	58.0	27.0	14.0
1994	63.0	27.0	10.0

SOURCES: For 1970–81, *Renmin ribao* (hereafter *RMRB*), Oct. 28, 1988, p. 3; for 1985, Whyte and Gu 1987, p. 474; for 1989, *RMRB*, May 21, 1992, p. 3; for 1992, *Zhongguo renkou tongji nianjian* 1993, pp. 24–25; for 1994, *RMRB*, March 5, 1995, p. 3.

the rental units they already occupied at a highly subsidized price, but others bought newly built homes sold by commercial developers. A private real estate market had existed before 1991 but was concentrated in areas where overseas Chinese could purchase homes for themselves or their PRC relatives. In the 1990s, commercial developments appeared throughout the country, and new homes were sold to individuals with no overseas connections.

In part, China's immature financial institutions spurred home ownership. Families were accumulating substantial savings, and in the face of inflationary pressures the purchase of a home was an attractive investment. However, as David Fraser explains in his interpretation of Shanghai real estate advertising (Chapter 2) considerations were not entirely financial. Urban residents also bought their own homes in order to enjoy both greater privacy and a sense of exclusivity.

Given the high price of most commercial real estate, only 5–10 percent of Shanghai residents could actually afford to purchase the accommodations advertised in the evening paper. However, 40–50 percent of city residents could realistically become home owners if they purchased their current apartments. In this way central government policy shifted to commodify a welfare good of the Mao years and allowed a broad cross-section of urban residents to respond positively to the advertisers' exhortations to "buy a home and become a boss!"[18]

Even when home ownership was impossible, urban residents could real-

18. Advertisement for Yongde Homes published in *Xinmin wanbao* (New people's evening news), Shanghai, May 11, 1994, p. 15.

ize dreams for enhanced domesticity by redecorating, and in the mid-1990s home renovation emerged as a mass phenomenon. Publishing houses all over China produced a range of lavishly illustrated home-decorating guides, and bookstore shelves were well stocked with magazines dedicated to installing new floors, elaborate window treatments, and recessed lighting. Television stations broadcast do-it-yourself shows that simultaneously promoted local retailers and demonstrated how best to refurbish a home. Typical was the half-hour program sponsored by a Changzhou wallpaper factory I saw August 30, 1997, at 7 A.M. on Shanghai channel 2. A modestly dressed young man first discussed the practical advantages of wallpaper and then introduced a wide range of designs, commenting on which would be most appropriate for different family members. For elderly parents he recommended muted colors, for newly married couples silky textured bamboo weave, and for children a washable wall covering with patterns of animals or flowers. During the second half of the program he narrated a step-by-step demonstration of a young couple papering a small sitting room.

In 1994, Shanghai's Orient television station introduced a home-decorating contest, and People's Art Publishing House then published the top 100 designs, complete with floor plans and photographs of the winning entries.[19] Some designs were extravagant, but most concentrated on how best to renovate a three-room apartment of less than 300 square feet. Of particular note were renovators' efforts to separate adjoining households and reconfigure interior space to provide more privacy. Even as late at 1992 only 45 percent of urban households lived in self-contained (*chengtau*) flats. Most families shared a bathroom or kitchen with neighbors, and many did not have a separate entrance. By 1996, 62 percent of urban households had achieved this level of privacy, and the goal was to make self-contained apartments universal within ten years.[20]

Family Rituals and Celebrations

Throughout the 1960s and 1970s government and party officials pushed policies to secularize family life and simplify domestic rituals, and even in cities populated by national minorities, official efforts succeeded. The Bureau of Civil Affairs issued marriage licenses, new couples celebrated with simple tea parties or meals in their homes, and there was little wedding finery or elaborate public display. Funerals were similarly frugal. Cremation was nearly universal, and memorial services were often held at the deceased's place of work. After 1978, family rituals, especially those connected to a child's marriage,

19. *Shanghai jiating buzhi yibaili 1995.*
20. *Xinmin wanbao,* August 26, 1997, p. 5.

became increasingly elaborate, expensive, and independent from the work-place.[21] By the mid-1990s many urban couples spent more than 3,000 ren-minbi (rmb) on wedding photos, and expenditures for the banquets, new clothes, and household furnishings routinely surpassed 40,000 rmb, a sum approximately ten times greater than a young man's yearly salary.[22]

In studying Hui weddings in Xi'an (Chapter 4), Maris Gillette was impressed not only by the enormous financial investment but also by the ways in which brides in their new role as savvy consumers served as agents of change. One revealing episode took place just hours before a bride was to leave for her wedding banquet. For that occasion the young woman had rented a floor-length, rose-colored evening gown, but when her sister brought the dress to her home she found stains on the bodice and dirt along the hem. The gowns originated in Taiwan and were sold to PRC bridal shops when no longer fashionable. Xi'an customers knew the gowns were used and would be rented to many brides, but it was expected that they would be cleaned after each use. Discovering the dirt on the hem and stains on the bodice, the bride raced by taxi to the shop and insisted she be given a replacement on the spot. But as Gillette's analysis makes clear, Hui brides were not primarily "free agents." Rather, what Gillette finds most striking in the behavior of these young women was their conformity to the expectations of female relatives, who demanded Western-style wedding gowns and elaborate coiffures as necessary public displays of family wealth and status. Thus even as young Xi'an brides became aggressive consumers and flouted religious leaders' criticism of these purchases, they deferred to the demands of their kin that they be richly dressed brides of whom the family could be proud.

For Xi'an brides, Shanghai parents, and Nanjing shoppers, the expanded role of market transactions multiplied the opportunities to exercise personal choices and to invest in their homes and family celebrations. As the reforms pushed factories and other enterprises to concentrate on production and to shed responsibility for feeding, dressing, and sheltering their employees, the character and resources of a site of production became increasingly distinct from those of a site for consumption. Consequently, as individuals went about their daily routines they could ignore the importuning of state agents in ways that were unthinkable during the first three decades of CCP rule. But increased autonomy in one dimension could mean new or intensified constraints in others. Moreover, as Hanlong Lu illustrates with his Shanghai survey data (Chapter 6), many employees still "ate heartily from the big pot." And one should never forget that high levels of parental spending on sin-

21. Whyte 1993.
22. In 1993, average urban salaries were 3,371 rmb; in 1994, 4,538 rmb. *ZGTJNJ 1995*, p. 113.

gletons was the direct result of the state's extraordinary power to enforce the one-child quota.

By the 1990s the CCP party-state had ceased to closely monitor domestic consumption. As a result urban families were no longer supplicants or clients of the state as they had been in earlier decades. Yet the degree to which the new small freedoms in the domestic realm substantially realigned political power between the state and the people or, in the vocabulary of James Scott, provided "hidden transcripts" of insubordination that might precipitate fundamental political change, is unclear.[23] First, family investments increased in areas from which the party-state had willingly evacuated; thus the increased reliance of individual consumers on lightly regulated commercial transactions well served the self-interest of the party-state. An examination of the ways in which urban consumers have used their new affluence and the multitude of new commercial venues outside the home to socialize, however, suggests that the self-interests of the party-state may have been less well served, and new patterns of consumption may have more clearly challenged the political status quo.

SOCIABILITY IN A MORE COMMODIFIED CHINA

In years when the redistributive economy prevailed, urban social life was highly constrained. People worked six days a week, twelve months a year. Few had more than a week's break at Lunar New Year, and nonofficial travel between cities was expensive and hard to arrange. Personal telephone calls were rare and had to be made in public locations such as the post office, the workplace, or the office of the neighborhood Residents' Committee. Even personal letters sent through the post office were subject to seizure and inspection. City parks provided what little space existed for socializing outside the home or workplace, and even there one did not escape the watchful eye of city employees.

Separating locations of production from locations of consumption in the context of increased affluence has fundamentally altered the experience and consequences of socializing outside the home. When the workplace lost its obligation to provide recreation activities, the commercial sector went into high gear. Whether it was pool tables at the roadside or multilevel discos, entrepreneurs saw profitable niches, and the number of commercial venues where residents could relax beyond the purview of their employers and their relatives grew exponentially.

Chinese society's new access to the outside world also brought a flood of videos and movies. Within a span of just three or four years, urban residents, especially young adults, had a lengthy and ever-changing menu of topics and

23. Scott 1990.

leisure activities to discuss and experience. In the 1970s, personal networks (*guanxiwang*) helped people secure scarce goods and protection, but the explosive growth of new venues and modes for socializing with others expanded and altered the character of social networks. Using the language of Pierre Bourdieu, one could say that the expansion and commercialization of leisure enabled people from all strata to accumulate private caches of "social capital" whose acquisition "presupposes an unceasing effort of sociability."[24] Thus to move ahead in the 1990s one did not necessarily need to have privileged access or control over scarce goods; one could also build capital by forging dense and varied social connections.

In Chapter 7, Kathleen Erwin explores one expression of this new sociability by analyzing the discourse of radio call-in shows and counseling hotlines spawned by the telecommunications revolution. In part, she found what one might expect from the explosive growth of anonymous forms of public speech: when talk of private suffering and desire goes public, it liberates social discourse. Yet the spoken exchanges of Shanghai hotlines and call-in shows were not entirely "free." Counselors were party members, and several programs survived at the sufferance of corporate sponsors. In addition, Erwin detected a clear reassertion of traditional mores and norms of hierarchy that constrained the disembodied exchanges over the telephone wires and radio waves. In general, men talked explicitly about their sexual problems, while women were more inclined to express their dissatisfaction in terms of emotional needs. Erwin also found that when counselors spoke with women rather than men they were more likely to encapsulate the callers' complaints within regimes of traditional family expectations that subordinated individual sexual desire. Thus following Michel Foucault's analysis of "modern discursive power," Erwin interprets the telephone- and radio-mediated dialogues at two levels.[25] At one level, they exemplified greater individual freedom and expansion of social space that was unreachable through old forms of control or punishment. On another level, they facilitated a moral discourse that ultimately constrained listeners by reviving traditional family regimes of hierarchy and power.

In Chapter 8, Mary Erbaugh uses greeting cards she received or purchased over a twelve-month period beginning in November 1995 to look at another innovative form of communication that gained currency during the 1990s. The cards Erbaugh collected celebrated only happy events and were purchased primarily by young urban women to send to other young urban women. Exploring the composite images and happy sentiments engraved on the cards, Erbaugh finds that the cards "reinforce affiliation with an imagined community." Like Erwin, she places her discussion in the context of the changing economy, which challenges previous Communist moral sureties,

24. Bourdieu 1986, p. 250.
25. Foucault 1978.

but unlike Erwin, she does not explore the new discomforts of emergent capitalism. However, as is illustrated by her concluding story about Hong Kong residents who sent boxes of winter-solstice cards to former political prisoner Wei Jingsheng, Erbaugh is aware that new modes of communication are polyvalent. In most exchanges, greeting cards reinforced ties of affection or investment in private relationships; in another context, they could express ideological insubordination and articulate a critique of the state.

Throughout the world, feasting and eating out offer ideal conditions for transforming informal sociability into instrumental economic and political networks. And in the Mao era, China was no exception. However, in those years dining someplace other than the workplace canteen or one's home—not to mention banqueting—was a prerogative largely monopolized by those with political prestige and position. Thus one of the most telling indicators of China's consumer revolution is the rapid proliferation of restaurants and the increasing percentage of household budgets ordinary families spend on eating out (see Chapter 6 by Hanlong Lu). But as Yunxiang Yan demonstrates in his ethnography of McDonald's in Beijing (Chapter 9), consumers do not eat out just for the food or the chance to cement social networks. They also eat out because certain social settings allow diners to realize powerful fantasies, which in the case of McDonald's the producer willingly facilitates. Thus, on one hand McDonald's has succeeded in China because it sells meals more efficiently than local competitors. But McDonald's has also flourished because the chain came to represent an extension of America.[26] Ordering a Big Mac provided a "bridge" to the affluent, industrial West and thereby allowed Beijing customers to realize, if only temporarily, their emergent identities as discerning, modern individuals.

In the Shanghai dance halls where sociologist James Farrer went to observe changing attitudes of city youth toward romance and love, the newly liberated zones for private pleasure forged new identities in an even more sustained fashion (see Chapter 10). Shanghai dancers did not limit themselves to enjoying a quick glimpse into an exotic foreign land; they returned week after week to throw themselves into energetic, erotically charged "play" with partners who enabled them to explore new desires and identities. In the 1990s, Shanghai commercial dance halls appealed to a wide range of consumers. Men and women went out dancing in about equal numbers, and the middle-aged were as likely to be avid dancers as the young. Over the three years Farrer worked in Shanghai, 1993–96, facilities became increasingly differentiated by cost of admission, décor, and music, but at all price levels they offered customers a place of escape where through dancing people could temporarily set aside their everyday lives and personas. Throughout the city,

26. Watson 1997.

dance halls were locations of social flux and emotional complexity where proprietors deliberately distorted everyday appearances and customers searched for intimacy with strangers. Farrer was not in a position to discover whether the dancers he met extended these new social connections to the workplace or their neighborhoods. We therefore have no evidence that dancing functioned as anything more than an escapist fantasy. But as with greeting cards, oppositional intentions remain a latent potential, and it is thus premature to conclude that the dancers' networks of connections had or will have no disruptive social consequences.

THE IMPORTANCE OF LUXURY

Both Shanghai dance halls and Beijing's McDonald's were within the budgets of many residents of metropolitan China in the 1990s. A morning session at a local dance hall cost less than 5 rmb; a small burger, fries, and a coke 10 rmb.[27] Fancy discos on the weekend could cost 50 times as much, and if one wanted a Big Mac, apple pie, and coffee one could spend 40 rmb. But the basic price of admission made dancing and meals at McDonald's items of mass culture. By contrast, a night of bowling in Shenzhen as described by Gan Wang in Chapter 11 could exceed 400 rmb. Bowling therefore did not provide easy access to global mass culture; instead, the bowling alley became a new enclave of luxury.[28]

However when bowling alleys first appeared in Shenzhen and offered an exotic, sophisticated entertainment, those who could afford the exorbitant charges did not use the cost as a means to exclude others. On the contrary, they deliberately used their ability to play host as part of a strategy to advance their careers and gain protection from government bureaucrats. Given the power of state agents to constrain or sponsor commercial activity, ambitious entrepreneurs needed good relations with cadres, and luxury leisure activities provided an ideal opportunity for businessmen to make officials sympathetic to their interests. Historically, established elites have resisted efforts

27. In 1995, residents' per capita daily consumption averaged 18 rmb in Beijing and 21 rmb in Shanghai (see Table 1.3). In May 1997, I paid $1.19 for a meal in the McDonald's adjacent to the Tianjin railroad station.

28. Arjun Appadurai has used the term "enclaving" to explicate the dynamic process of commodification. It refers primarily to the process by which a powerful minority restrict access to certain items—either through sumptuary laws or astronomical prices—to maintain their identity as a self-recruiting elite. Nonelite, particularly enterprising entrepreneurs continuously try to divert the enclaved items into the larger market. Thus, over time, few objects sustain their enclaved status, and the processes of decommodification and recommodification are dynamic and political. The use of bowling alleys by Shenzhen entrepreneurs also speaks directly to their political insecurity in an only partially marketized Communist polity. See Appadurai 1986.

of the nouveaux riches to commodify enclaved goods,[29] but in Shenzhen old and new elites shared the commercialized luxury entertainment to achieve mutually desired ends. The entrepreneurs used their ability to play host to build personal ties to further their own commercial careers. The government officials enjoyed luxury goods beyond their incomes but in accord with their position of authority.

In Chapter 12, David Wank looks closely at another luxury good—high-priced cigarettes. Although by the 1990s premium-brand cigarettes were neither a new commodity nor as costly as an evening of bowling, they remained an extravagance through which private businessmen in Xiamen displayed their status and manipulated social interaction. In the early 1980s when Wank first worked in China, the best cigarettes were unavailable to the ordinary citizen. High-ranking cadres could buy them in special stores, and people with foreign-exchange certificates (FECs) could buy limited quantities at Friendship Stores. A decade later, expensive high-quality cigarettes were being sold by street vendors. Nevertheless, they continued to serve as markers of social distinction that elites used to signal and control their relationships with others. In particular, they were central in rituals entrepreneurs choreographed to send complex social messages both as they negotiated business deals with government officials and as they exercised power over subordinates.

Participants in the exchange of premium cigarettes and in the conspicuous consumption at bowling alleys were cognizant of who stood on the side of the state and who represented the market. But in the commercial cities of southern China such as Shenzhen and Xiamen, the boundaries between the state and the market were deliberately transgressed by new business elites who depended on special favors from state agents to advance their careers. In the process, the state realm was colonized and public resources were subverted. In earlier years, citizens used gifts to obtain scarce goods and services, but in those exchanges government officials had allocated items already designated for public consumption (e.g., a hospital bed for a sick patient). By the 1990s, however, the gifts were used to gain access to items the state should have retained for itself (e.g., tax revenues or confidential information). As a result, state agents not only squandered state resources; they also inadvertently subverted their own positions of domination.

GROWING INEQUALITY IN A MORE MARKETIZED CHINA

When Deng Xiaoping launched the policies of decollectivization and relegitimated private entrepreneurship, he defined success as realizing a relatively comfortable (*xiaokang*) society with a per capita annual income of $800

---

29. Ibid.

by the year 2000. But the connotations of that achievement were broader. As Hanlong Lu explains in Chapter 6, the popular understanding of *xiaokang* derives from its origins in the Confucian Book of Rites, where the appearance of a *xiaokang* society signaled the demise of a society of equality (*datong*) in which "all under heaven is public" (*tianxia wei gong*) and its transformation into a stratified society where "all under heaven belongs to the family" (*tianxia wei jia*). Thus in proclaiming the goal of reform to be the establishment of a *xiaokang* society the CCP leadership legitimated a society stratified by financial inequalities. Moreover, the reform policies to enlarge the cash nexus and increase efficiency virtually guaranteed that gains would be unevenly distributed.

Until 1990 the majority of urban adults worked in state-owned enterprises and enjoyed the "iron rice bowl" of lifetime employment, egalitarian wages, and generous welfare benefits.[30] The introduction of bonuses and piece rates during the 1980s chipped away at workers' security, but most managers still felt obligated to distribute wages and noncash benefits evenly within their enterprises.[31] However, as nonstate employment surged, and especially after the third plenum of the Fourteenth Party Congress in 1993, the iron rice bowl turned to clay. State firms furloughed hundreds of thousands, workers moved quickly to maximize their individual advantages, and income disparities widened.[32]

Not surprisingly, the greatest wealth and some of the greatest inequalities emerged in the Special Economic Zone of Shenzhen, where the export-processing zone established in 1980 attracted thousands of investors from Hong Kong and Taiwan. Subsequently fourteen other coastal cities were given permission to deviate from the plan and allow market forces greater leeway. By the mid-1990s, cities on the coast had moved furthest from the planned economy, and coastal residents enjoyed the highest per capita income, the greatest supply of new consumer goods, and the most improved infrastructure. Cities farther inland and in northeastern China lagged behind, and their residents experienced less dramatic gains in their standard of living (see Table 1.3).

Substantial regional inequality and the advantaged position of such cities as Beijing, Guangzhou, and Shanghai had existed during the Mao era, but the decentralization of the economy and disappearance of redistributive policies exacerbated the differentials. For example, in 1985 per capita consumption expenditures in Shanghai were only 299 rmb higher than the na-

30. Davis 1992.
31. Walder 1991.
32. Li Qiang 1995. Additional studies that document the growing gap include Bian and Logan 1996; Davis 1995; Feng Tongqing 1993; Khan et al. 1992; Li Yongqiao 1995; Li Yu 1994; and Zhou Dengge 1993.

TABLE 1.3   Yearly per Capita Expenditure on Consumption
(*Shenghuo Fei*) in the Ten Largest Cities and Shenzhen,
1985–1995

(in renminbi [rmb])*	1985	1990	1995
Urban Average	685	1,387	3,893
Beijing	907	1,787	5,868
Chongqing	762	1,552	4,053
Guangzhou	1,044	2,592	8,556
Harbin	708	1,264	3,374
Nanjing		1,506	4,658
Shanghai	984	2,050	6,822
Shenyang	721	1,534	3,721
Shenzhen	1,800	3,660	11,028
Tianjin	770	1,440	4,064
Wuhan	726	1,465	4,170
Xi'an	719	1,518	3,914

SOURCES: *Beijing tongji nianjian 1996*, p. 502; *Chongqing tongji nianjian 1996*, p. 137; *Guangzhou tongji nianjian 1991*, p. 324; *Guangzhou tongji nianjian 1996*, p. 374; *Harbin tonji nianjian 1996*, p. 195; *Nanjing tongji nianjian 1996*, p. 311; *Shanghai tongji nianjian 1986*, p. 441; *Shenyang tongji nianjian 1996*, p. 578; *Shenzhen tongji nianjian 1991*, p. 355; *Shenzhen tongji nianjian 1996*, p. 177; *Tianjin tongji nianjian 1990*, p. 372; *Tianjin tongji nianjian 1996*, p. 177; *Wuhan tongji nianjian 1996*, p. 391; *Xi'an tongji nianjian 1994*, p. 318; *Xi'an tongji nianjian 1996*, p. 296; *Zhongguo tongji nianjian 1990*, p. 279; *Zhongguo tongji nianjian 1996*, p. 283.

* 8.3 rmb = one U.S. dollar.

tional urban average, but by 1990 the gap had grown to 663 rmb, and by 1995 it had jumped to 2,929 rmb. In Guangzhou and Shenzhen the 1995 differential reached 4,663 rmb and 7,134 rmb respectively. By contrast, consumption expenditures in inland cities like Nanjing, Wuhan, and Xi'an remained close to the national average, while in the northeastern city of Harbin consumers actually experienced a decline in relative rank (see Table 1.3).

Certainly these financial inequalities affected the extent to which urban residents in different cities owned such consumer durables as color televisions, refrigerators, or cameras (see Table 1.1). Moreover, the mere fact of ownership did not mean that everyone owned items of the same quality and style. For example, by 1995 almost all urban families owned a washing machine, but only a minority of wealthy individuals could purchase a European-made Siemens washer-dryer, which was five times as expensive as the basic model produced by the Jiangsu Province White Swan group.[33]

Since Thorstein Veblen's work on conspicuous consumption and Georg

33. The prices quoted here appeared on items in the Beijing Modern Plaza department store, May 29, 1997.

Simmel's studies of fashion, sociologists have found consumer behavior a rich subject for the study of social emulation and social-class differentiation. In the contemporary period, Pierre Bourdieu has integrated the study of lifestyles with the processes of social-class reproduction.[34] Yet to the extent that the essays in this volume document social differentiation, the distinctions are as much along lines of gender and generation as social class. Shanghai parents of different social classes held similar aspirations for their singletons and often made identical purchases. Among Hui brides in Xi'an generational differences were most striking, while for the diners at McDonald's and the Shanghai dancers variation in gender and age structured consumers' participation as much as differences in monthly income.

Official surveys and observations in urban homes tell us that those with the least income purchased few consumer durables and never engaged in expensive new leisure pursuits unless they were invited as guests. We also know that poorer families spent more of their incomes on food and had simpler diets and fewer housing options. In the cities, even the rich coastal cities visited by the contributors to this volume, millions of rural migrants lived in wretched shacks and worked for months without ever visiting a disco, a McDonald's, or a bowling alley. Moreover, many of these migrants were not short-term sojourners; in Shanghai, Beijing, Guangzhou, and other metropolitan centers they have settled down and created a dual society.[35]

By the mid-1990s urban wealth was far more concentrated than in the 1908s,[36] and both policy makers and Chinese intellectuals feared greater inequality would destabilize urban Chinese society. Yet recent investigations by Beijing sociologist Li Qiang revealed a surprising tolerance of income inequality and even a perception that urban life is less stratified than it was in the more egalitarian 1970s.[37] Li's explanation for this apparent contradiction is that urbanites retained an optimism about the uneven gains because political status was of less consequence in determining an individual's social position and lifestyle than in the past. Thus while increased income inequality certainly suggested increased stratification, the decline in the consequences of political discrimination created the perception of a more open opportunity structure and less oppressive class hierarchies.

On the basis of the observations of consumer behavior presented in this volume, I would suggest that the decline of political stigma and the narrower scope of political repression only partially explain why a minority of Li's respondents were resentful. First, despite the considerable commodification, several core elements of the prereform "public goods regime" survived into the

34. Bourdieu 1984.
35. F. Wang 1997.
36. Kernan and Rocca 1998; Gustafson and Li Shi 1997.
37. Li Qiang 1997.

1990s.[38] As a result, low or stagnant salary did not necessarily exclude individuals from experiencing the consumer revolution. Seventy percent of urban residents continued to rent their apartments from a municipal real estate bureau or from their employer, and even after a decade of government reforms to commercialize rents, tenants rarely paid more than 6 percent of their official income for housing.[39] Canteens at the workplace were routinely subcontracted out, but meals remained subsidized. Similar practices reduced the direct cost of public transportation. Thus, through the mid-1990s, many necessities remained relatively inexpensive, and therefore even low-income families felt able to participate actively in the new consumer markets. As further withdrawal of subsidies raises the price of necessities and an increasing number of state employees lose their jobs, low-income households will likely develop lifestyles more congruent with their incomes, and one may see a "culture of necessity" similar to that which Pierre Bourdieu found to distinguish the French working class from the bourgeoisie. But during the 1990s commodification in urban China was less complete than in postwar France, and therefore income inequality did not consistently predict differences in lifestyle.

A second reason income differences did not immediately segregate consumers by social class was that many of the new goods and services—stylish accessories, fast food, discos, greeting cards, radio call-in shows—were disproportionately targeted at young people and often required only an eagerness to try something new, not high expenditures. When urban men and women called a sex hotline, bought birthday cards for close friends, or danced away a boring Saturday afternoon in a dark disco, they were cultivating an identity that distinguished them from an older generation or someone of the opposite sex. They were not necessarily cultivating a lifestyle tied to a particular financial position or drawing on codes of cultural etiquette tied to positions of social superiority or subordination.

In addition, the high percentage of households in which two adult generations co-reside allowed the younger members more discretionary funds than their incomes might have predicted. Before marriage, very few urban residents lived separately from their parents, and although many reimbursed their parents (usually their mothers) for the cost of their meals, they spent most of their wages on personal discretionary goods and services. Because young workers could spend a third of a month's wage at a disco or on the newest-style shoes, personal income was an imperfect predictor of many consumer choices, and lifestyle distinctions varied as much by generation as by socioeconomic position.

38. The phrase "public goods regime" comes from Solinger 1994.
39. Li Rongxia 1998.

COMMODIFICATION AND THE PUBLIC SPHERE

After June 4, 1989, it was difficult to be sanguine about the emergence of a robust Chinese "public sphere," especially the classic Habermasian version, which requires open critical discourse of the state as well as the ability of citizens to defend individual rights. In fact, in the immediate aftermath of the Beijing massacre some observers even argued that Chinese society was culturally incapable of developing a true public sphere.[40] While not explicitly sharing the pessimistic views of Eastern European intellectuals such as Vaclav Havel, who disdain mass consumer culture as anathema to critical public discourse and active citizenship,[41] some post-Tiananmen pessimists have treated increased autonomy in informal socializing as apolitical escapism with no connection to formal advances in the area of property rights or civil liberties.[42] However, by restricting the field of vision to politically well-institutionalized activities, we may overlook alternative locations of and pathways to structural change and underestimate the ability of increased sociability in nonofficial activities to incubate loyalties that ultimately generate the actions capable of weakening or toppling an authoritarian state.

The failure of the 1989 protesters to create an effective organizational buffer to protect speech and actions critical of the regime undoubtedly delayed political reforms. But that failure did not eliminate the corrosive potential of nonstate market forces. Living in urban China during the 1980s, Mayfair Yang and Thomas Gold observed that unofficial socializing created personal networks that challenged the monopolies of state agents and reduced the earlier domination of ordinary citizens by state agents.[43] However, there is some disagreement among the contributors to this volume about the degree to which market reforms increase the freedom of urban citizens or erode the power of the state. For example, in her analysis of radio call-in shows, Erwin uses Foucauldian theory to reject the linear connection between market choice and antiestablishment behavior. Instead, she finds urban residents repressed and disciplined by emerging bourgeois forms of hierarchy. In an earlier discussion of Xiamen businessmen, Wank also discounted the connection between increased market involvement and antistate ideology or action. Rather, when observing the interaction of wealthy capitalists and state cadres Wank was most impressed by the strength of the

---

40. Barmé 1995; Chamberlain 1993; Wagner 1995; Wakeman 1993.

41. Havel wrote, "A person who has been seduced by the consumer value system, whose identity is dissolved in an amalgam of the accoutrements of mass civilization and who has no roots in the order of being, has no sense of responsibility for anything higher than his or her own personal survival and is a demoralized person." Havel 1985, p. 45.

42. Chamberlain 1993; Wagner 1995; Wakeman 1993.

43. Gold 1993; M. Yang 1994.

"symbiotic clientelism" that bound together agents of the state and representatives of the market.[44]

In the family shopping activities observed by Veeck, Davis, Sensenbrenner, Yan, and Lu one also can not easily trace a causal link between intensified reliance on the cash nexus and heterodox political ideals or antistate action. However, as Richard Kraus demonstrates in his study of public art in Nanjing (Chapter 13), when the CCP leadership redefined the essence of socialism as economic growth, they granted the masses new grounds on which to question party orthodoxy. And by ceding an increasing proportion of public space to personal use and by allowing the disparate desires of urban consumer-citizens to make legitimate claims on societal resources, the CCP inadvertently reduced its own leverage and legitimacy. Therefore when Richard Kraus introduces Nanjing residents who tango in the ruins of the Ming emperor's palace, he rhetorically asks whether it is always possible to distinguish clearly between dancers and demonstrators. The answer provided by this volume is that it is not. Deng Xiaoping knew that a *xiaokang* society would demolish the "massified" conditions of the Mao era, but neither he nor any of his immediate successors could control the attachments and investments spawned by the promotion of commercial mass consumption. Whether or not the millions of apolitical market transactions have realigned institutional power and authority, the multiplicity of horizontal ties and the increased invisibility and privacy of personal life have already created a society for which the past conventions of the authoritarian rule appear ill-suited. Eating a Big Mac will not bring down a dictator, but it can send a million daily messages that old ways have changed.[45]

---

44. "Bureaucratic Patronage and Private Business," p.176 in Walder 1995.

45. In July 1997, less than a year before the resignation of President Suharto, *New York Times* reporter Thomas Friedman interviewed several Indonesian reformers about how Indonesia's integration into the world economy affected the prospects for political reform. Military analyst Jowono Sudarsono emphasized how global markets force "discipline we cannot internally generate." Another reformer told Friedman, "My son and I get our revenge on Suharto everyday by eating at McDonald's" (Friedman 1997). Without a doubt, the international currency and banking crisis played the central role in Suharto's fall from power, but it is of note that among those who actively worked to promote political change, the small freedoms of consumer culture were explicitly linked to toppling an authoritarian regime.

PART 1

—

THE
CONSUMER REVOLUTION
AND THE DOMESTIC SPHERE

———

CHAPTER 2

Inventing Oasis

Luxury Housing Advertisements and Reconfiguring Domestic Space in Shanghai

David Fraser

On May 5, 1994, in despair, apartment dweller Li Lenglu published the following essay in *Xinmin wanbao*, Shanghai's most popular daily newspaper. Because it speaks with an authentic voice and addresses a range of issues at the intersection of housing and consumer society in China—the subject of this chapter—Li's article is worth printing in its entirety.

Apartment Noise (Dalou zaosheng)
By Li Lenglu

I read in the "Yeguangbei" column the January 13 article "The noise has just begun" by Yang Yunhui and feel that she seems to be writing about the situation in the apartment where I live. Is it possible that this is a common failing of apartments? The end of the article conjectured: "After enduring a year of this noise, (residents now) can hope for peace." Her longing is too honest and sincere. I've lived in an apartment building for a full three years, and everyone is still driving everyone else crazy with noise.

The apartment building is home to several hundred families who are always moving in and out; when people move into an empty flat, they want to remodel it (zhuangxiu), and so do those people who are switching apartments.

The title of this chapter borrows from Sherman Cochran's article "Inventing Nanjing Road: Advertising by the British-American Tobacco Company in Early Twentieth-Century China" (1992). Professor Cochran's pioneering work on Chinese advertising and his enthusiastic encouragement have been major stimuli for my research. I thank Deborah Davis for encouraging me in this exploration and for numerous perceptive insights. Richard Madsen, Min Zhou, and Mayfair Yang gave generously of their time in conversations that sharpened my focus. I am very grateful to David Ding for illuminating comments, moral support, and the 1997 newspapers. I also thank Yanjie Bian, Michael Liu, Kaidi Zhan, Jean Han, Jeffrey Kapellas, Lin Hui, Yang Zhaowen, Wang Changcheng, and Tony Mu for their assistance.

Some people like the new and deride the old; they see a popular style and want to imitate it by remodeling yet again. Some people swarm like bees to follow the majority: originally, the balcony served to let in light, wind, and fresh air, and to dry clothes; suddenly they are installing aluminum alloy windows, closing off the balcony, and wanting to redo the whole place . . . some folks want to build a cozy home so they seek to remodel in a big way.

Some people's aesthetic sense is not very developed. They seriously want to reshape the door frame into an arch, and everywhere they hang variegated fringes and install colored lamps . . . making over their homes like coffee shops, private "karaoke rooms," or even brothels . . . is this the warmth of home?

Reinforced concrete integrates an apartment building as one body; people's desire to refurbish will affect everyone within. Remodeling noise sounds as if it's all shooting out from the apartment above. An electric drill making a hole in the wall thrusts in noise like "TU TU TU," vibrating the floor and warping it with a sound like a wild cow's crazy bellow. The noises of sawing wood, cutting water pipe, and sudden poundings on the wall mix together from different directions, blotting out the sky and blanketing the earth, with no end and no finish, no way to hide, no way to endure . . . a cacophony of torment . . . " (P. 11)

Li's desperation expresses one of the central paradoxes of China's urbanization. Government policy, growing household incomes, and the rise of consumerism in cities like Shanghai spurred waves of housing construction by private contractors in the 1990s. This effort has remolded the urban landscape and offered residents who can afford it the chance to buy a spacious apartment. Construction noise, however, permeates the city and, as Li's essay shows, takes its toll on the human environment. There is little tranquillity in the metropolis.

The dream of home ownership is now within grasp of many Shanghainese. Government policy is to encourage housing purchase, and most households that acquired homes in the 1990s decade bought them cheaply from their employers or work units. Many apartments are beyond the means of all but wealthy Shanghainese or their overseas cousins. But because of rising household incomes, the availability of fifteen-year mortgages, and the overconstruction of homes intended for an elite market, even Shanghai's burgeoning middle class can consider buying into the low end of exclusivity.

The impulse to refocus home life around an improved domestic setting is an important indicator of the transformation of Shanghai society. Many chapters in this volume demonstrate the explosion of consumption activities and public venues for personal expression elaborated through commercial purchase. In contrast, this chapter focuses on the symbolic representation of a private domestic life as expressed through advertisements for luxury apartments. Individually, such ads are mere peepholes into the commercialized aspirations of well-off residents. To the extent that they resonate with nonelite imaginations, though, these advertisements, viewed in the aggregate, serve as lenses that offer a refracted vision into ordinary urbanites' dreams of domesticity.

Several important issues emerge from a close reading of the ads. One message is that buying private housing—a major investment in real property—is the first step in creating a domestic lifestyle in which the home is the central site for social interaction and consumption. When people buy private housing, they acquire not merely a domicile but also a personal, private terrain that fosters a greater sense of individual entitlement that is often expressed through consumption. The new lifestyle repudiates the severe constraints on personal life imposed in earlier decades by the Maoist work unit or *danwei*. Such refiguring of social and political relations requires a redefinition and clear delineation of the home as both social and spatial entity and a sense of its conceptual location within social and geographic contexts.

The main mechanism by which these advertisements render private luxury housing desirable and inviting is what I call oasification, the marketing of "oasis" (in Chinese, *lüzhou* or *lühua*). Oasification commodifies green, pleasant aspects of a constructed nature to create a buffer zone between the individual apartment and its larger social and spatial contexts. As I shall show, oasis, as both a conceptual relationship in urban design and a marketing tool, reverberates across social strata with its promise of respite, greenery, and peace.

As such, oasis is the element that seems to conjure privacy, putting a cushion between itself and the clamorous world of commerce and transport—urban life. Yet these are necessary connections for Shanghai families, and oasis should be seen as one focal point on a continuum of personal interaction that ranges from peace and quiet (*ningjing*) to the boisterous entertainment (*renao*) beloved by many of Shanghai's 13 million inhabitants. More abstractly, advertisements portray these concepts in a shifting combination of solitude and connection. The ads commodify consumptive activity with the home at the center, from electronic connections via home communications systems, to engagement with an oasified nature, to public interactions in neighborhood schools, parks, and fast-food outlets.

In this chapter I highlight oasis as a complement to other modes of personal activity. Many of the other chapters provide ample evidence of the options for public consumption available in Shanghai. Here, the focus is on domestic life, seen not in isolation but as an expanding zone of personal or family-centered activity within the boundaries of an oasified structure.

To clarify the overlapping territories of socialization, many ads employ what I call internal and external mapping. The former focuses on the domicile, the latter on the geographic context of the housing. Oasis, as the middle ground between the core home and the peripheral neighborhood, is generally the primary marketing feature and tends to be represented through symbolic conceptions of nature rather than space.

Each advertisement, to a greater or lesser degree, constitutes a visual context for domestic life, a chart for the urban imagination. Each one is a panel of fantasy, within which is embedded the mosaic of commercialized dreams.

To place the advertising in historical and social context, I first discuss the recent development of Shanghai's housing industry. I then present key display (pictorial) advertisements from *Xinmin wanbao* (New people's evening news), Shanghai's premier commercial daily newspaper. (Its daily press run in 1994, the first period researched, was 1.7 million copies.)[1] These ads ran in May 1994, when the notion of buying a newly built apartment at market rates was inconceivable to most residents. I compare those ads with advertisements from May 1997. Finally, I analyze these and other ads in several contexts through which domesticity is being reconceived and conclude with an examination of the broader significance of these transformations.

ADVERTISING LAYOUT

In May 1994, *Xinmin wanbao* devoted specific pages of each edition to different topics—sports, international news, domestic news, and the like. Advertisements appeared on any page, including the front page. Pages dedicated to advertising alone were headed "*guanggao*" (advertisements), "*fenlei guanggao*" (classified ads), and "*guanggao zengkan*" (advertising supplement).

The Shatian Real Estate company's ads, for example, ranged from a quarter-page to a half-page. Housing advertisements (and other sizable pictorial ads) tended to run the full width of the page if they were a quarter-page or larger, emphasizing the horizontal and allowing for placement of text, illustrations, and a map. As is standard practice in the Western media, the newspaper "anchored" the foot of the page with large ads.[2]

1. An inhouse ad for *Xinmin wanbao* on May 27, 1994, stated that this was China's second-highest circulation rate (p. 17).

2. There was little direct correlation between the page designation and the type of advertising that ran there. Housing ads, while often found on the domestic or local news pages, also ran on sports and international pages. However, many issues of *Xinmin wanbao* carry articles that deal with or touch on issues of urban housing. An article published May 3, for example, delineated government efforts to relocate Mr. Liang Guoji, described as a "man of low ability." Liang was labeled an "unmoving squatter" (*dingzi hu*, literally a "nail household") for refusing to vacate the cramped flat he had occupied for years. The article stressed the efforts of various municipal organs to find a suitable new home for Mr. Liang, who eventually was given a 23.4 square-meter flat in Yangpu. In the same issue, Shatian ran a luxury apartment ad with its slogan, "Shatian shows you the road home." The contrast is suggestive of the tension between government and *danwei* roles in providing ordinary housing and the commodification of private elite units. The relationship between newspaper structure and advertising choice is a fertile topic for further research.

ADVERTISING THEMES

Advertisements are about dreams and the construction of alternative realities. In the words of Jackson Lears, they offer "fables of abundance."[3] It is not my concern to argue their suasive power or lack of it. Rather, I take the view that advertisements mediate between the perceptual reality of everyday life and the imagined reality of a better world that offers commodity-based solutions to social dissatisfactions. This process relies on symbolic expression of personal want and relief.

The advertisements surveyed in this chapter may be viewed analytically as an aggregate system of signs. In analyzing advertisements, I have tried to avoid presuming that unilateral meanings can be derived from a symbolic reading. Rather, I have tried to elicit common elements and themes, what Roland Marchand calls "visual cliches," which reflect both conventionalized approaches to marketing and contemporary public or commercial discourse.[4] In interpreting the ads and their meaning, Robert Weller's caveat is useful: "Meaning lies not just in the text, but in socially and historically grounded processes of interpretation."[5] Thus I compare the symbolic construction of the ads with empirical data on the nature of the housing market and the social transformations wrought by economic reform and the consumer revolution. I look for meaning, or reflections of social meaning, in the dynamic relationship between representation and received reality.[6] I hope to derive a picture of the ways in which this commodity is woven into the social relations and consumer behaviors of the city's residents. More broadly, my goal is to provide a complex picture of the shifting map of urban social geography that is being redrawn by the economic reforms of the 1990s.

To broaden the analytical perspective I showed a number of ads to Chinese informants living in the United States and recorded their reactions.[7]

THE HOUSING INDUSTRY

As Zhong Yi Tong and R. Allen Hays have noted, "Housing is the material symbol of having a family and has always been viewed as the source of safety

3. Lears 1994.
4. Marchand 1985.
5. Weller 1994, p. 14.
6. I am grateful to Richard Madsen for suggesting this approach.
7. Informant A is a scholar and businesswoman from Beijing. Informant N is a Chinese student. Informant D is a Shanghainese college student with a background in advertising. All three reside in the San Francisco area. I am very grateful for their assistance and comments.

and happiness in Chinese life."[8] As such, housing is a key element in the social, political, economic, and cultural configurations and discourses that reflect
and shape relations between people and places, goods and power. The rise of
urban private housing markets in the 1990s is an important consequence of
post-Mao reforms; it repudiates the Maoist bias against personal consumption.

During the Maoist period, China's Communist party-state decommodified
housing and made it a state-provided social good under the socialist welfare
system. This eliminated the private housing construction industry.[9] By 1956,
officials had nationalized 95 percent of rental housing and urban land.[10] The
state transformed housing into an element of the redistributive economy,
with individuals' work units providing and allocating accommodations. Population growth far outstripped housing construction, leaving most urban Chinese crammed into tiny flats. By 1976, urban housing provided an average
of only 3 square meters per person.[11] In Shanghai, per capita floor space
dropped from 3.7 square meters in 1949 to 2.2 square meters in 1963.[12]

Beginning in the late 1970s, Deng Xiaoping began to press for housing
reform. The government began encouraging the privatization of urban housing and subsidizing new housing purchases. By 1983, private property rights
were being guaranteed. Banks began to loan money to work units and enterprises for housing construction. The efforts, though inconsistent and incomplete, raised the possibility of private home purchase for the first time
since the Communist revolution.

The 1980s was a period of trial and error for China's housing policy. Several cities were targeted for reform experiments aimed at promoting housing commodification and sales and at rationalizing rents, which had been
held artificially low.

The experiments culminated in a reform plan issued by the city of Shanghai in 1991 that is the basis for the current partial recommodification of
housing. Key provisions included mandatory savings plans and discounts
for housing purchase, ten- to fifteen-year mortgages, and resale options.
These changes spurred nationwide reforms under the State Council's Urban Housing Reform Resolution of 1991, which aimed to restructure the
rental-purchase relationship in favor of purchasing. Another goal—to boost
available floor space to an average 7.5 square meters per person by 1995—
was reached in most cities by the end of 1993.[13]

Shanghai was thus both a spearhead and an early beneficiary of the re-

---

8. Tong and Hays 1996, p. 625.
9. This discussion is based largely on Wang and Murie 1996, p. 972 ff.
10. Chen and Gao 1993, p. 119.
11. Wang and Murie 1996, p. 973.
12. Chen and Gao 1993, p. 120.
13. Wang and Murie 1996, pp. 980, 987.

forms.[14] As the private housing market expanded, relations between state, seller, and buyer grew highly complex. One reason is that, despite the reforms, the state retains the power to appropriate land and relocate people by fiat. More important, latent state power inheres in its continued ownership of urban land.

1994 ADVERTISING

Kangxing Park

Three major marketing elements are brought together in an ad for Kang xing Park: convenience, security, and oasis. Together they suggest an elite lifestyle (see Figure 2.1). At this exclusive complex in southwest Shanghai, an elite lifestyle is explicitly equated with personal privacy and service. These are represented by two popular modes of consumption: shopping and recreation. The enclave—"Shanghai's only duplexes!"[15] says the ad—features an "elegant and luxurious private clubhouse" with shops, billiard room (*danzi fang*), a health center, karaoke dance hall, and sun deck, all "to satisfy the various needs of the enclave's (*xiaoqu*) residents." The designation "private" (*siren*) in China has long connoted selfishness, but here the advertisers have inverted both Confucian and Communist critiques of privacy as antisocial. It is now a virtue that means exclusivity.

Electronic gadgets reinforce this exclusivity, opening links to the outside world while controlling access within. Kangxing Park units have direct international and domestic telephone lines, a closed-circuit television system and satellite dish, and an emergency police call button. Like many such complexes, Kangxing Park features security personnel on duty round the clock. Two security features are unusual: a surrounding wall with an automatic alarm connected to the police and remote-controlled garage doors.

Both printed and visual text reinforce the notion of oasis at Kangxing Park. The illustration depicts landscaped grounds with trees for shade. The advertising copy states that the enclave is "surrounded on all sides by parkland and filled with the rich flavors of the forest and intoxicating fragrances." Skeptics will note that most of the fragrances in the area spew from the congested thoroughfares that border Kangxing Park.[16]

14. Shanghai's housing reform plan was approved by the State Council in March 1991. See Song 1992, pp. 213–22.

15. *Xinmin wanbao*, May 25, 1994, p. 16. According to the ad, 115 square-meter suites run 700,000 rmb, or 6,280 rmb per square meter. The average per capita annual income in 1994 for Shanghai families with a registered household was 4,668 rmb, according to the *Shanghai tongji nianjian 1995* (p. 588).

16. Humin, Guilin, and Hongmei Roads near Huadong University of Science and Engineering. In 1994, Hongmei/Humin was a major bottleneck.

FIGURE 2.1.   Kangxing Park (*Xinmin wanbao*, May 25, 1994, p.16)

The concentration of service features at Kangxing Park recalls Grant McCracken's important study of how people acquire ensembles of goods to match their self-perceived status. McCracken calls these consumption clusters "product complements" and the urge to coordinate purchases the "Diderot effect."[17] In my view, the clustering of facilities and services around a central commodity, the luxury apartment, reinforces the urge to consume at a level appropriate to the surroundings. Advertising provides possible models for consumption and potential configurations of social identity that result from purchase: visions of lifestyle. It is the potential implied by ad-

17. McCracken 1988. Advertisements in *Xinmin wanbao* and elsewhere suggest or define the parameters of ensemble, providing guidelines by which consumers can implement the Diderot effect.

Two types of commodities were widely advertised in *Xinmin wanbao* in 1997: furniture and appliances. While an analysis is beyond the scope of this chapter, it is significant that these types of ads are often clustered around housing ads. The unspoken methodology of advertising is to generate the Diderot effect so that one major purchase will engender others. One simple example is the May 4, 1997, ad for Carrier air conditioners, a quarter-page ad placed directly under two one-eighth-page ads for luxury housing. Carrier's main selling point is a louvered vent to control airflow and the efficient exchange of old for fresh air. The tag line states: "Carrier gives you a lifestyle; it's not simply a machine!" (*Kai Li gei ni yi zhong shenghuo; er bu jinjin shi tai jiqi!*)

vertising that is designed to resonate with readers' imaginations; it is the to-
tality and congruence of both representation and emotive connection that
create a theater of familiarity in which readers may envisage themselves at
home.

In Kangxing's ad, the subjects of the marketing discourse—exclusivity,
security, convenience, consumption, recreation, and communication—
inform a direct appeal to elitism via social function and economic status. A
small caption links success to desirable professions: "At a paradise for successful entrepreneurs, scientists, and artists, the key to the main gate of
Kangxing Park will be the symbol of a successful individual (*chenggong ren-
shi shenfen*)."[18]

Informant A responded positively to the "skillful illustration" of Kangxing's
duplexes. She observed that linking "success" with lifestyle and profession
was itself a "key" to the ad's message. Overall, she found the ad to be of good
quality but too wordy: "The drawing is better than the text."

Taihe New City

Advertising for Taihe New City (*Taihe xincheng*) targets the nonluxury market (see Figure 2.2). At this housing complex in the far northern part of
Shanghai, a professional facilities management team (*zhuanyehua wuye guanli
duiwu*) provides 24-hour security, repairs, and cleaning services.[19] The marketing rhetoric used is a reminder that domestic services, once provided
through the work unit, have shifted to the commercial world. Servants and
service industries in any society function as buffers between manual labor
and elite affairs and also between the potential irritations of the "outside
world" and the home. Within the complex realm of recommodified housing, Shanghainese are acquiring homes, goods, and services that symbolize
and create a "lifestyle apart."

The choice of words in the advertisement is suggestive: "professional management" echoes contemporary business rhetoric aimed at rationalizing operations and establishing performance standards; the word for team, *duiwu*,
is an anachronism recalling the production teams (*shengchan dui*) of the Mao
era. These were symbols of mass mobilization in service of state demands for
(socialist) efficiency and production. Now, "teams" serve the consuming elite.

Or perhaps the not-so-elite. The Taihe ad, executed cartoon-style, depicts

18. By 1997, some advertisements were expanding this commodification of occupation to
include high- and mid-level intellectuals and the children of "intellectual youth" (*zhishi qingnian*) who had been rusticated during the 1966–76 Cultural Revolution. Intellectuals were
promised a discount of Y100 per square meter, and youths whose parents had lost their right
of residence in Shanghai were offered "blue cards" that guaranteed the same discount if they
purchased a luxury apartment.

19. *Xinmin wanbao*, May 26, 1994, p. 3.

FIGURE 2.2.   Taihe New City (*Xinmin wanbao*, May 26, 1994, p.3)

a young housewife holding a suitcase and notes the convenience of planned direct bus service. The boldest typeface in the ad states the date on which direct service is to begin. The ubiquity of bus route listings, in fact, is the best evidence that advertisers in 1994 were targeting the nonelite in society. In Shanghai, the truly wealthy do not take many buses; they drive or are driven or take taxis. Market segmentation is also suggested by the range of six apartment sizes available (50.1 to 100.18 square meters). Although the price for the smallest unit (one bedroom, one living room) is 85,671 renminbi (rmb), the fifteen-year mortgage option puts it within reach of the middle class.

CASE STUDY: THE FLOWERING OF COMMODIFIED HOUSING

Like poetry, print advertising gathers disparate elements and images and if successful unifies them into a symbolic whole. One half-page advertisement that engages many of the theoretical issues addressed in this chapter is for Yongde (Forever Virtuous) New China Homes (see Figure 2.3). The ad combines facts about the new housing within a symbolic discourse that illumi-

FIGURE 2.3. Yongde (*Xinmin wanbao*, May 11, 1994, p. 15)

nates the changing relations of home, work, consumer, and city.[20] This multidimensionality provides a useful case study of the relationships among marketing representation, housing, oasis, and consumption.

Yongde's ad may be seen as a cohesive set of ideas about new ways of life, new expectations, and new behaviors. The ad balances a cartoon illustration of a happy family with four extraordinarily specific lists of services, presented as the "Four Basic Rights of Enclave Residents" (*xiaoqu jumin sixiang jiben quanli*). My informants found this a highly effective presentation; one noted that the rhetoric recalled the "four basic principles" of Communist ideology: adhering to socialism, party primacy, people's democratic dictatorship, and the mass line. The smiling family consists of parents and a boy, echoing urban China's one-child policy and the cultural preference for sons.

A caption says: "Buy a new house, become a boss (*laoban*)!" This term, discredited under Mao as capitalistic, embodies entrepreneurial and manage-

20. *Xinmin wanbao*, May 11, 1994, p. 15. This is the only ad in the group surveyed that gives a specific figure on the amount of space to be developed; the plan calls for 500,000 square meters of housing.

ment aspirations and inspired a lively reaction from one informant, who exclaimed, "Become a boss . . . who doesn't want to be, under the reforms! . . . Why can't I be an owner, too?"

"BASIC RIGHTS"

Oasis

One "basic right" is the right to a "green environment for gentle enjoyment" (*lüse huanjing, youya xiangshou*). The text for the ad in Figure 2.3 reads as follows:

·· The enclave's green ground cover is more than 30 percent (of area), kept green by a specialty firm.
·· More than 30 varieties of flowers and plants, including peonies and Chinese roses, have been planted. All year round there is birdsong and fragrance, with no raw earth showing.
·· Small gardens and green areas (*lüdi*) are provided for residents to plant; they can "adopt and cultivate" famous varieties of trees and flowers.

This discourse provides far more detail on the relationship between residents and oasis than that in other ads surveyed. The notion of "adopting" varietals appealed to one informant; she cited the specificity of the ad as evidence that the property was likely to be well managed. Overall, there is a highly personal quality to the marketing approach that spotlights numerous aspects of Shanghai's changing society. Personalizing the gardens at Yongde seems to be an effective strategy because it personalizes oasis, seeming to suggest that residents will have a functional role in their enclave.

The remaining "rights" discourses focus on key issues for home buyers: they are microcosms of changing social relations in Shanghai:

Time Payments

The "right" to installment purchase symbolically extends the potential home buyers' market to the nonelite classes. Yongde's 64 square-meter two-bedroom apartments require a 40 percent down payment plus installment payments of 900 rmb per month on a total cost of around 100,000 rmb. This is within the upper-middle-class budget. Moreover, the mortgage option is a notable step in China's slow march toward a credit economy.

Transport

The "right" to private transport via a van pool reflects the nightmare of commuting in Shanghai's transportation morass. Services offered under this heading reveal an awareness of the importance of efficient connections between home and office (the father in the illustration wears a tie, hinting at his white-collar status).

Yongde, in the southwest, is some distance from Shanghai's subway. The van pool provides commuter service to the station and to Longhua, Meilong, and Xuhui districts, the Nanpu bridge, and People's Square downtown. The transport section of the ad shows that shifting urban demographics and changes in social relations led to efforts to provide local solutions. These solutions are then commoditized as marketing elements.[21]

Strikingly, the ad invites Yongde residents to "participate in management of the van pool" (*canyu chedui guanli*). Echoing the worker-participation rhetoric of the Mao era, this phrase points to the possibility of a cooperative relationship between residents, property management, and their environment. As with the gardening option above, the advertisers offer readers a means to increase their personal stake in both oasis and local management. Although there are insufficient examples from which to generalize, the Yongde ad at least hints that private housing may provide avenues and sites for the reconfiguration of personal and institutional relations along the lines of homeowners' associations in the United States. This possibility contains the seeds for development of new nonparty institutions that have been developing informally across China, and thus for realignments of the political economy.

Special Services / Saving Time and Energy

Yongde's fourth "right" focuses on residential services, offering further clues to how elite domesticity is imagined. The services include: improved parcel delivery and bigger mailboxes; apartment remodeling (50 percent discount on labor); hospital services including home hospital beds and free annual health examinations for residents over 70 or under seven; early breakfast delivery (again, to facilitate the commute); and school bus service for students at magnet schools (*zhongdian zhongxue*), elite schools whose students are on a fast track to career success. Enrolling a child in one of these schools is a major status marker; thus the transport service is a sign of McCracken's Diderot effect in operation.

The following section examines *Xinmin wanbao* ads from May 1997. Echoing the social scientist Leslie Sklair, Informant D notes that Shanghai consumers are highly selective and have become "more familiar" with the elite

21. Many work units maintain vans or cars for staff use. The Shanghai Academy of Social Sciences, where I worked in 1994–95, had a fleet of air-conditioned minivans and buses on call. Such a system also echoes the dedicated commuter bus networks in Taiwan (more visible before the advent of personal cars) and similar operations in the United States.

housing market. Informant D maintains that housing advertisements are relatively reliable, since "if people go to a housing development and find they
are lying in the ads, how can the company continue?"

1997 ADVERTISING

"If you have a good home, then you don't have a lot of headaches. . . . don't you agree?"

—JIADONG GARDENS AD, *Xinmin wanbao*, MAY 5, 1997, P. 3.

Wutong Gardens

The text for the ads shown in Figure 2.4 depicts a housing enclave so exclusive that price is not mentioned. The marketing conjures opulence and
elegance, a whiff of imagined France: Louis Quatorze invades Xujiahui.

> Every time when you get a taste from television or books of the magnificent
> Louvre Palace, the relaxing murmur of the Seine River, and the romance of
> the Champs Élysées, you always hope that one day you can own a home like
> that, with all the romantic style of France.
>   Today, after you visit the showcase homes in Wutong Gardens, it may be
> that you can find your dream home there: where interior and exterior design
> and construction embody typical French architectural style, with furnished
> rooms decorated in the style of the Middle Ages." (*Xinmin wanbao*, May 7, 1997,
> p. 12)

Tree-shaded Jianguo West Road was a major east-west thoroughfare in the
Republican era (1912–49), when the French occupied a wide swath of central and southern Shanghai. Then, as now, it is a much-coveted residential
district, where Chinese share streets with foreign elites.

The Wutong ads revive and reconceive the link between the foreign and
the fine. Named after the Chinese plane trees that shade much of the city,
Wutong Gardens is presented as a community of "dream homes" (*mengzhong
de jia*), where an unremembered European past of autocrats and elysian
streets is romanticized into a lifestyle striving to recall the vanishing elegance
of 80 years earlier (see Figure 2.5).

This revived French classicism is a variant of a foreign aesthetic currently
in vogue across Shanghai. Strollers on the city's main boulevards like Huaihai Road can spot bas-reliefs of Greco-Roman heroes, whose nude torsos
mock, in a style that jeers at both Confucian and Communist prudery, the
monumental Maoist aesthetic of selfless, rosy-cheeked workers, peasants, and
soldiers striving to "serve the people." Shanghai's style of eclecticism in public art is a decidedly commercial, and currently classicist, aesthetic that contrasts with the state-sponsored art of Nanjing (described in Chapter 13). Yet

FIGURE 2.4.   Wutong 1 (*Xinmin wanbao*, May 7, 1997, p. 12)

both share an underlying playfulness of inversion that thumbs the public nose at the gigantism of the Mao period.

> When you enter the showcase homes of Wutong Gardens, a spacious, bright living room appears before your eyes. There is a French medieval (sic) dining table and chairs, and an antique-style grandfather clock abuts the wall. The slow, steady tick-tock of its pendulum seems to tell tales of romance; there is also an elegant sofa covered in a floral pattern and a coffee table of cherrywood.
>
> When you enter the master bedroom, the furniture, the lamps, the paintings and the curtains all display for you the unique artistic atmosphere (*yishu qixi*) of Wutong Gardens. It automatically imbues you with a primitive and simple, elegant and refined feeling, and you truly wish to own this romantic, artistic home. (*Xinmin wanbao*, May 14, 1997, p. 10)[22]

This rhetoric takes the abstracted expression of dreams in the first ad and commodifies it as a system of objects for consumption: the "Diderot effect" of ensemble purchase is operating at full force and is linked to an anachronistic, imagined France. The interior appears designed, mature, and complete, like Venus's birth. With enough cash, the consumer can acquire not merely a culture, but *une civilisation*!

Wutong, of course, offers a representation of a home, not fully furnished apartments. "No one in Shanghai," says Informant D, "is going to buy a furnished apartment. They are selling atmosphere."

In this choicest of residential locations, what is being marketed is a refracted and incomplete vision of the very culture whose imperialist drive had colonized the district where the Wutong towers were erected. The irony is heightened by the fact that the Republican-era elite residents of the French

22. This channel for consumer appropriation of foreign culture is reminiscent of the eighteenth-century European penchant for chinoiserie. Contemporary Western sinologists are hardly immune: many academic homes support a dining room done in faux Ming, with table and chairs in teak.

FIGURE 2.5. Wutong 2
(*Xinmin wanbao*, May 14, 1997, p. 10)

Concession, whose former homes are at risk of being razed for office buildings and luxury housing towers, imported staggering amounts of European
furnishings like those imitated in the Wutong showrooms: those residents
knew French medieval when they eschewed it.

JIADONG GARDENS

The cartoon-style advertisement for Jiadong Gardens targets a very different audience, for whom consumption of the familiar is central. The ad is a
cogent statement about the symbolic conceptualization of lifestyles and their
relationship to class and place (see Figure 2.6).

Beneath the caption "Hassle-free for housewives" (*zhufu mei fannao*)
stands a young Shanghai mother with a daughter and a dog. Beside them is
a collage of buildings, done as a woodblock, representing *shikumen*, Shanghai's characteristic architectural style of tile-roofed row houses linked in alley complexes. The nostalgic quality of the scene is reinforced by ground-
floor vegetable markets and bicyclists.

The form and content of the housewife's "story" are told in a cartoon
"thought balloon." This rhetorical discourse encapsulates several important
issues resulting from widespread social dislocation due to commercial and
residential construction. The use of Shanghai dialect in the story is notable
(see informant's remarks below). Here is a full translation:

The Story of Jiadong Gardens

The seven crucial needs of a household: fuel, rice, oil, salt, soy sauce, vinegar,
and tea. Although you can say these are all little things, for those of us [Shang-
hai dialect characters: *a-la*] who work as housewives, each of them is a part of
our heart. When we previously lived in the alley apartments (*shikumen*), it was
pretty cramped and crowded. But it was really convenient to buy anything we
wanted. Now we've got a bit of extra cash, and we're getting ready to buy a new
house. We've heard people say that in a new housing estate the apartments are
suitable, but the home accessories (*peitao*) aren't good, and if you want to buy
things you have to walk a very long way. So I was really a bit worried. Last week,
my husband and I went specially to Jiadong Gardens and walked around the
area a bit. In fact it was really pretty good (*bucuo*), with a department store, supermarket, food market, school, hospital—all of them were there, and the transportation is also really convenient.

The housewife's expression of links between housing and the consumption
of household staples is one element in a series of social adaptations and transformations that reforms have required of many urbanites. Suburbanization
has many advantages—larger apartments, less congestion, more oasis—but
it does not provide the familiar interactions of a neighborhood and creates
greater demand for reintegration in the new locale.

FIGURE 2.6.   Jiadong Garden (*Xinmin wanbao*, May 5, 1997, p. 3)

Informant D saw the Jiadong Gardens ad as a successful and creative endeavor. He applauded the cartoon design style and layout: "The ad emphasizes community and convenience. Its target is probably lower middle class because it refers to *shikumen*, where many of that class live. The key appeal is the use of Shanghai dialect, which sounds authentic. The ad is trying to be intimate with ordinary families."[23]

The Jiadong Gardens ad embodies an alternative vision of privatized domesticity. It contrasts sharply with the majority of ads equating success, modernity, and luxury. The ad does not breathlessly list closed-circuit televisions, garages, and other accoutrements of an elite lifestyle. Oasis is virtually absent as a symbol, and the only physical structure highlighted is an aluminum alloy–enclosed balcony, the same improvement being made by essayist Li Lenglu's neighbors. Allusions to class are made through use of dialect and references to a vanishing neighborhood lifestyle. What the protagonist seeks is commodified familiarity, not anomic, isolating modernity. Here, nostalgia is the vehicle for reassurance that moving up in the world does not mean losing the institutional and personal anchors of one's life: they can be constituted anew.

ANALYSIS: HISTORICAL CONTEXT, PRIVACY, OASIS, AND MAPPING

Historical Context

In the Republican era it was the custom of Shanghai elites—like elites everywhere—to build urban villas surrounded by walls and gardens. The more discriminating residents, Chinese and foreign, erected homes in the old

---

23. Informant D also noted that the use of written Shanghai dialect rather than standard Mandarin Chinese has been the topic of debate and official sanction recently, and that "the

French Concession, which stretched along the choicest parts of Shanghai on tree-shaded streets and boulevards named for a parade of French generals. For Huang Jinrong, municipal leader and Green Gang chieftain, power meant the wherewithal to create oasis, and oasis symbolized power: "Adjoining [the Huang mansion] is the Huang garden, where springs flow between [the trees] by layers and layers of stones. . . . This is a place of scenic beauty, reflecting the delight and joy of the master, where his disciples (*dizi*) can hasten forward to received the benefit of his instruction."[24]

In his 1991 study of housing and social strata in Republican-era Shanghai, Hanchao Lu notes that the "Western-style" mansion (*yanghang*) with a front garden was the residential form preferred by the city's foreign and Chinese elites.[25] The mansions of government official and banker Song Ziwen (T. V. Soong) and revolutionary leader Sun Yat-sen still stand in this former French zone, which now comprises Luwan and Xuhui districts. Appropriately enough, the villa of Sun, the father of the Chinese Republic, adjoins a real estate office.

Privacy

After 1949, under Mao Zedong, personal life in urban China was intensely public. The state, through the work unit, closely monitored and directed personal activity and behavior. The post-Mao decline of the work-unit system and the withdrawal of the state from a dominant role in people's daily lives has created opportunities for social interaction beyond the gaze of the state. The rise of a private housing market centered on oasis has carved out domestic spaces in which increased personal autonomy from state control is given a series of relatively private—or more exactly, personal, non-public—venues in which to consume and to act. Domesticity, in short, has been privatized.

In "My Mother's House," an examination of the political and social meaning of home decorating in the 1980s, Deborah Davis found that interior design in Shanghai homes often served as a vehicle for self-expression outside or in opposition to the claustrophobic control of the Communist party-state.[26] But that was shortly before the explosion of the consumer revolution of the 1990s. Now, the combination of oasified private housing and

---

advertisers probably encountered trouble" for using Shanghainese. Television programs that featured local dialects instead of the official Mandarin (*putonghua*) have also faced government sanctions.

24. Quoted in Wakeman 1995, pp. 411–12, fn 57.

25. Lu Hanchao 1991, p. 222.,

26. Davis 1989.

intensive (though uneven) infrastructure and business expansion throughout suburban Shanghai have broadened the array of options for those able
to afford them.

The consumer revolution in Shanghai has spawned numerous fresh
spaces for consumption. As the contributors to this volume show, these include recreational sites like discos and bowling alleys; retail outlets like food
markets, department stores, shopping centers and restaurants; and public
spaces like squares and parks. The growth of private housing has provided
an alternative site for consumption—the modern apartment complex—
which both complements and competes with more public locations. The nature and locus of consumption are in flux, as enhanced domesticity opens
doors to creative uses of time, space, and personal resources.

For example, the revolution in home electronics has expanded opportunities for home consumption of entertainment and information. In the
1980s, according to Shaoguang Wang, scarcity of videotapes and VCRs
spawned commercial "video rooms," which often showed nominally illegal
foreign titles.[27] By the mid-1990s, however, home entertainment, from televisions to laser discs, was flourishing. As Davis and Sensenbrenner point out
in Chapter 3, VCRs and other electronic equipment were frequently found
in Shanghai homes. In one 1997 ad, a housing firm even advertised a free
"home theater" stereo system with the purchase of a home.[28] (Presumably,
as with furniture, most families prefer to choose their own.) This advertisement, for Garden Scene World apartments, also diverged from conventional
marketing approaches by featuring floor plans with furnishings sketched in.
Both plans showed living rooms with seats grouped around a television and
master bedrooms with TVs opposite the bed.

Oasis

Too long I was held within the barred cage.
Now I am able to return again to nature.
—TAO QIAN, *Two Poems on Returning
to Dwell in the Country*[29]

Shanghainese, whether they live in construction sheds or penthouses, usually spend their evenings in their homes. As newly empowered consumers,
they have choices as to how they wish to conjure themselves, their families,
and their place in the overlapping social worlds they inhabit. Advertising
reveals how the shift to a personal, domestic sphere for consumption at-
taches clear economic and social value to the notion of environment. The

27. S. Wang 1995.
28. *Xinmin wanbao*, May 7, 1977, p. 23.
29. Birch 1965, p. 183.

increased use of spatial terms of reference serve as both actual and symbolic means of carving out a place of one's own. Paradoxically, as Shanghai clatters under constant construction, it is also turning to constructed oasis as an antidote.

Macroasis

The domestic urge for oasis expressed in housing advertisements is mirrored in municipal public works policy. I call these complementary appropriations of urban greenery "microoasis" and "macroasis." Between 1978 and 1996, the total area of parks, gardens, and green areas in Shanghai grew almost tenfold, to 7,231 hectares. In 1978, public green areas amounted to less than half a square meter per person; by 1996 the figure was nearly two square meters. And tree planting grew from 352,000 to an astounding 3.54 million.[30]

Another indicator that the government is taking oasification seriously is its inclusion, under the title "Afforestation and Garden Building," in the urban planning section of the Shanghai Economic Yearbook. In 1996, much effort went to creating or refurbishing parks and to planting trees along key thoroughfares. The city is also creating a macroasis, a 97-kilometer greenbelt designed to circle Shanghai along a planned outer beltway, by 2010. By then, according to the yearbook, "the public green area per capita in Shanghai urban district will have reached 4.5 square meters."[31]

Given the size of the greenbelt project, though, and its distance from the core city, it is probable that most residents will still need to seek microoasis close to home—in their backyards, as it were.

Microoasis

No one who has spent time in contemporary Shanghai would suggest that oasis is the dominant social aesthetic there. I am arguing here that oasis is something that city dwellers dream about.

Both before and in the midst of the current economic reforms, Shanghai was and continues to be a vibrant, bustling city. It is also very loud. Car, truck, bus, and motorcycle horns honk constantly (a ban on honking to warn pedestrians was rescinded after the accident rate skyrocketed). Construction noise drowns the chime of bicycle bells (informal estimates in 1994 were that 9,000 legal and illegal construction projects were in progress around

30. *Shanghai tongji nianjian 1997*, p. 109.
31. 1996 Shanghai Economic Yearbook, pp. 213–15. The Shanghai Green Belt construction probably accounts for much of the higher ratio. Its relevance to most residents will depend on ease of access as the belt is carved through Putuo, Jiading, Changning, Xuhui, Minhang, and Pudong districts.

FIGURE 2.7.   Jiaxin City Gardens #1 (*Xinmin wanbao*, May 14, 1997, p. 23)
FIGURE 2.8.   Jiaxin City Gardens #2 (*Xinmin wanbao*, May 14, 1997, p. 23)

the city). It is hardly surprising, then, that urban residents, like those in any major city, seek peace and quiet. The complaints of Li Lenglu, whose essay opens this chapter, are common to many.

Oasis provides an antidote by equating nature with quiet peacefulness. Because these elements are associated with a romanticized ruralism, they convey a sense of placidness among the urban tumult. The omnipresent use of "Gardens" in housing development names is emblematic of this. Formal Chinese gardens are oasified recreations of natural settings: paths are curved, aesthetically pleasing rocks are imported from other regions. These widely reproduced cultural models serve as templates for urban microasis.

Cocooning is part of the commodification of oasis and has its recent roots in both Chinese pastoralism and the commercialized aesthetics of the early twentieth century. Cigarette and insecticide ads from the 1920s frequently were set in elegant homes against a naturalistic background.[32] Oasis meant an elite leisure and freedom from annoyance.

---

32. I discuss cigarettes as icons of leisure and nationalism in Fraser 1994.

FIGURE 2.9.   Great China Gardens (Datang) (*Xinmin wanbao*, May 3, 1997, p. 19)
FIGURE 2.10.   Mingjia Villas (*Xinmin wanbao*, May 4, 1997, p. 3)

Several 1997 ads established a direct perceptual link between purchase and oasis. An ad for New Century Villas, for example, notes that "in the area, greening (*lühua*) is already complete, and greenery and fresh air [literally, oxygen] now encompass the quiet homes. To enjoy them you don't have to spend a lot of money" (*Xinmin wanbao*, May 1, 1997, p. 4).

One housing development, otherwise unremarkable, is in fact called Oasis Apartments (*Lüzhou huayuan*) (*Xinmin wanbao*, May 13, 1997, p. 17). A much livelier ad for Jiaxin City Gardens (*Jiaxin dushi huayuan*) urges: "Spread Green around Shanghai!" (*lübo Shanghai!*) (*Xinmin wanbao*, May 14,

1997, p. 23). The logo is enclosed in a leaf-filled plaque with the company's name formed into a peak-roofed house. Next to an artist's sketch of low-rise and high-rise towers is an architectural plan of the environs, and partly superimposed is an aerial rendering of the grounds. The extensive parkland is represented in pen-and-ink style, with tiny labels indicating rock garden, fountains, lawns, and a "resting pavilion." This focus on oasis is reinforced for readers in the text, which states that the minicity contains 6,000 square meters of green gardens, as well as a shopping center, amusement park, health center, and garage (see Figures 2.7 and 2.8).

Through diverse combinations of artistic and printed texts, housing advertising commodifies nature as a constellation of trees, plants, water, flowers, and birds. While some ads simply feature a "quiet green zone," many others construct more complex messages linking oasis to an elite lifestyle. Illustrations of a fountain, plaza, open space, trees, and shrubbery dominate a 1994 ad for International Gardens (*Guoji huayuan*) (*Xinmin wanbao*, May 7, 1997, p. 7). Even a cartoon-style ad for the relatively downscale Taihe New City (*Taihe xincheng*) features potted flowers on balconies and a Disneyesque bird overhead (*Xinmin wanbao*, May 26, 1994, p. 3).

While the relationship between oasis and elite lifestyle is suggested in many of the 1994 ads surveyed, by 1997 the link had become both explicit and concrete. At Great China Gardens (*Da Tang huayuan*), readers are urged, "Bring sunlight and garden into your lifestyle (*shenghuo*)" (see Figure 2.9). A smaller caption, printed on a background of trees painted in brush-and-ink, says, "Birdsong, flower perfume, peace and quiet for your home" (*Xinmin wanbao*, May 3, 1997, p. 19).

Ratio of Oasis

One of the most notable changes from 1994 to 1997 was increased specificity about the ratio of oasified to residential space. Xingshu Gardens, a high-end luxury tower (top range 6,480–8,000 rmb/square meter) in the crowded Xuhui district, is "more than 35 percent" oasified (*lü hua lü*) (*Xinmin wanbao*, May 4, 1997, p. 24). Haishen Gardens, to the west in a growing suburban district, boasts 60 percent oasified space. Like New Century Villas, the Haishen ad explicitly uses its oasification ratio as a marketing tool, asking: "How much is 60 percent oasis worth?" (*Xinmin wanbao*, May 6, 1997, p. 2).

Ancillary details reinforce the significance of oasis for marketing and suggest that it may be affecting design as well. The Great China Gardens ad also offers a sunroom (*yangguangshi*) for early buyers, and includes a free roof garden for top-floor owners.

In a divergent approach, an ad for Mingjia Villas seeks to link oasis to modernity (see Figure 2.10). A caption next to an illustration of two apartment towers says, "Embodying the whole concept of modern people's residence." The narrative continues: "In beautiful Xujiahui [district], a completely new, lofty garden residence enclave has been brilliantly erected. Besides its modern living concept, it also features the constructed elegance of fresh air, sunlight, and greenery; quiet, peace, and comfort—a picture—a story—a way of life. Here, perhaps, is what you need. . . . " (*Xinmin wanbao*, May 4, 1997, p. 3) What you need also would appear to include alternative uses of space. The second portion of the printed text offers "specially installed" tennis courts and a minigolf course and then returns to the naturalistic theme: central plaza with a fountain, large central green area "constituting a space for enjoyment together done in extremely popular hues."

The naturalistic rhetoric of oasis is conceived in advertising in terms of light and shade. In 1997 advertisements, the phrase "southward facing rooms" is more common than in the previous survey, suggesting that consumer consciousness and customer preference have made their tastes known. What has changed more radically is the degree and intensity of the language of nature. In conjunction with the other advertising elements, nature has become a reified player in the commercialization of oasis.

Oasis neither exists in nor constitutes a vacuum. It is, rather, a central element in the effort by real estate advertisers to capture and shape the dreams of urbanites who want a better place to live. Just as the oasified areas may provide a visual and physical buffer between the housing complex and the surrounding neighborhood, these areas also modulate the movements and roles of people who inhabit the enclaves. They are thus part of the housing arrangement and yet peripheral to it. They constitute the realm where the urban imagination and longing for peacefulness join with the cityscape of dreams for a more pleasant place to live. Oasis is the symbol of peace and the gateway to privacy.

As informant D put it: The nature of the dream is space. . . . The green space is an extension of your living space, yet you don't have to pay for it directly. Shanghai is so polluted, but people are health conscious—they want a good environment, they want to feel like they *own* the living space and something beyond. The greenery makes them feel good. People are so tired of being packed [in dwellings] like animals—they want to breathe.

THE SETTING OF SOCIAL CONSUMPTION

Privatized domesticity and oasis, of course, do not mean isolation. That would be unthinkable in Shanghai, where a vibrant mercantile atmosphere pervades most neighborhoods. Goods and services for home consumption, once provided by employers, must now be obtained through property offices or through ordinary purchase.

This has given housing advertisers an extra marketing tool: the concept of consumer choice. One result has been a high degree of specificity about neighborhoods and institutional locations. Luxury home purchase is becoming socially contextualized. That is, home buyers are offered not merely a domicile, but a home, sited within the nexus of personal and institutional relations of the city. Oasis, it seems, is crucial, but not enough.

Thus, for example, an ad for Xibu (Westside) Apartments lists nearby middle schools and a medical academy, parks, shopping centers, and a department store (*Xinmin wanbao*, May 6, 1997, p. 8). New Century Villas (*Xin shiji huayuan*) is advertised as convenient to (*fangbian*) Kentucky Fried Chicken, as well as banks, restaurants, parks, and food/vegetable markets, and summed up, in the Chinese rhetoric for basic needs, as "convenient to clothes, food, residence, and transport of every sort" (*Xinmin wanbao*, May 1, 1997, p. 4).

In luxury housing advertisements, various modes of mapping help to provide context for the privatization of domestic life. The following section describes this function.

Mapping

The two types of maps provided in luxury housing advertisements reflect advertisers' presumptions about the perceptions of their readership. The maps focus on what might be called internal and external representations of domesticity. The internal maps, consisting of apartment floor plans, as noted above, are skeletal.[33] Occasionally these are the dominant element in the advertisement, but more commonly they are subsidiary or simply show the variety of housing configurations available. External maps locate the housing enclave in its geographic and social contexts within the greater Shanghai area. Their construction and detail indicate how the urban landscape is being redefined by construction of "new cities" and other enclaves.

One approach is to map in small scale, which emphasizes the neighborhood quality of the enclave and focuses attention on local services. The map for Jinyang Apartments in the Pudong district, for example, takes up a third of the advertisement. Its focus is locational and institutional; it shows major

---

33. Eastern Sea Gardens (*Haidong huayuan*) in Pudong is typical (space in square meters): living room 26.72; master bedroom 16.63; bathroom 5.67; bedroom 11.66; bathroom 4.14; kitchen 6.91; balcony 5.94 for a total of 77.67 feet (88.23 architectural [external] feet).

streets, three middle schools, a golf course, supermarket, park, and security police headquarters (*gong an ju*). Clustered across Yanggao Street from Jinyang are a kindergarten, college, language school, and another enclave, the "foreign merchants elite apartment district (*waishang gaoji zhuzhai qu*) (*Xinmin wanbao*, May 14, 1997, p. 7).[34]

The headline reads: "Buying a Jinyang Apartment . . . Is Really Buying Jinyang District" (*mai Jinyang gongyu jiushi mai Jinyang shequ*). While the Jinyang housing enclave is partially oasified, with a waterfall, fountain, and greenery, the ad emphasizes the integration with the surrounding area. This approach makes sense, given Jinyang's distance both from central Pudong and from downtown Shanghai across the river.

A more common approach to external mapping is to sketch on a larger scale, to emphasize the enclave's geographic location within the larger city or at least within a district. This situates the enclave within a network of familiarity—for those who know the district. Thus Dangui Gardens is identified on a reproduced street map that emphasizes its proximity to Hongqiao Airport (*Xinmin wanbao*, May 7, 1997, p. 2). An ad for International Square (*Guoji guangchang*) carries this a step further, superimposing labels of key locations—Yu Gardens, People's Square, the Bund (*waitan*), Nanpu bridge, and Lujiazui in Pudong—on a detailed city map. Only Fuxing and Xizang (Tibet) Roads are marked; the enclave is located at their intersection. The map, set into a circle, looks remarkably like an aerial photograph (*Xinmin wanbao*, May 12, 1997, p. 5).

Labeling key locations reinforces the elite quality of the site: all are landmarks for visitors. By including International Square as one of six labeled sites, the map turns the residential and commercial development into a downtown landmark.[35]

---

34. The sequestering of foreigners is a long-standing cultural tradition in China. In the late Qing and Republican periods, the wealthy created their own oasified enclaves within the zones of occupation known as foreign concessions, although numerous Chinese lived there as well. Since 1949 foreigners have been generally restricted to selected housing as a method of social control, to limit their domestic interactions with Chinese. The Pudong enclave for foreign merchants reflects this history but also is likely to be a means to maintain foreign investment levels by providing enclaved luxury housing. Rents in the most exclusive foreign enclaves run thousands of dollars a month.

35. The International Square ad suggests the extent to which Shanghai's traditional downtown business district still functions as a magnet for finance and trade. The marked locations are, in fact, nearby icons of Shanghai that reflect municipal policy aimed at enticing international capital: the Bund is the precommunist seat of political and financial power; People's Square is the premier large open space; Lujiazui is a major district in Pudong, designated as Shanghai's magnet for investment and development. The Nanpu bridge is a key

CONCLUSION: THE MAPPING OF HOME

"Maps Are Moments in the Process of Decision-Making"
— JACQUES BERTIN[36]

In Shanghai real estate advertisements, maps are significant elements. They show, or purport to show, what readers can expect to find and where to find it. A comparison of internal and external maps in the ads surveyed for this chapter reveals a bifurcation in the way in which housing serves as the subject of commercial discourse on space. The blankness of apartment floor plans in internal maps not only reflects the fact that apartments are generally sold unfurnished. This skeletal mapping also symbolizes the range of consumer choices available and the customer's right to choose.

External maps perform complementary roles. First, they show consumers where the housing estates are located, an increasingly important function in an expanding metropolis. Second, by siting the housing enclave within institutional and geographical parameters, ads focus attention on the social geography of housing acquisition. They help answer questions that a family might ask a real estate agent: Where are the schools? hospitals? swimming pools? police? Is there a McDonald's nearby?

On another level, the advertised discourse on private home life has also shifted from what I see as ownership of home to ownership of lifestyle. In 1994, the phrase "ownership rights in perpetuity" (*yongjiu chanquan*) appeared in virtually every housing advertisement surveyed. By 1997 the phrase had practically disappeared. Similarly, the earlier ads tended to depict people in or near a home setting. In 1997 the setting and its environs, not the inhabitants, were emphasized. The novelty of private ownership of housing—previously a key element in marketing—had yielded to increased specificity about the nature of housing and its surroundings. Against a backdrop of neighborhood services, oasis was moved into the foreground, and became the dominant feature of most ads.

The advertisements in *Xinmin wanbao* can be aggregated into a developing but incomplete system of information about the changing nature of Shanghai as an urban organism and the home as the center of domestic life. Maps, taken in the context of the ads they support, offer both a geography lesson and a symbolic representation of the city's social realignment. They

---

means of access to Pudong; and Yu Gardens, in the old Chinese city, is a must-visit tourist spot and symbol of commercial oasis. (There are numerous shops inside the gardens, built by a Chinese merchant family. Foreign visitors must buy special "souvenir tickets," which are sold at a premium. One of the first stops for foreign delegates transiting Shanghai en route to the 1995 Women's Nongovernmental Conference near Beijing was at Yu Gardens (personal observation).)

36. Quoted in Wood 1992, p. 185.

provide a schematic counterpart to the romanticized discourse of oasification. Oasis, as a means to embody the public longing for a spot of green and quiet, provides a spatial cushion as the urban household redefines itself. The trees and flowers of the urban housing estate also mark the commodified borders of enhanced domesticity and the boundaries of a more private lifestyle for those who can afford it and those who can dream of it.

Perhaps the most poignant statement of this comes from Rainbow Star Park, a complex near Hongqiao Airport. The bold headline of a 1994 advertisement says, "The city's flourishing dream, to live in a home with a gentle, fragrant feeling" (*Xinmin wanbao,* May 7, 1994, p. 12).

CHAPTER 3

Commercializing Childhood

Parental Purchases
for Shanghai's Only Child

Deborah S. Davis and Julia S. Sensenbrenner

During the 1990s, two revolutions transformed childhood in Shanghai, one demographic and one commercial. As a result, the social world of primary-school children bore scant resemblance to that of their parents. First, strict implementation of the 1979 one-child policy guaranteed that almost no Shanghai child under fifteen had a sibling. Second, China's headlong plunge into "market socialism" immersed an entire generation of "singletons" into an increasingly commodified environment deeply engaged with the products and advertising of global capitalism.

When advertising first appeared on Chinese television in the mid-1980s, Shanghai viewers caught a glimpse of Heinz baby foods and Johnson and Johnson baby lotions through the rosy haze of Hong Kong commercial landscapes. However, few department stores sold these accoutrements of modern child-rearing, and milk powder remained expensive and in short supply. Ten years later, parents browsed through entire floors devoted to infant and toddler equipment, and even a state-owned store like Parkson gave discounts on two competing brands of Chinese-made disposable diapers (see Figure 3.1). On commercial thoroughfares like Huaihai Road, product representatives touted the merits of the next generation of Gameboy and Sega video games (see Figure 3.2), while newspapers directly targeted primary-school students as consumers. For example, during the week of the June 1 International Children's Day, the Guomai beeper company took out a half-

Deborah Davis wishes to thank the participants in the 1996 Chinese University of Hong Kong–Yale University summer workshop for sharing their fieldwork observations and the Institute of Sociology at the Shanghai Academy of Social Sciences for its administrative support. Funding for Davis's fieldwork was provided by a grant from the Cheng-Lee Fund of the Council on East Asian Studies, Yale University.

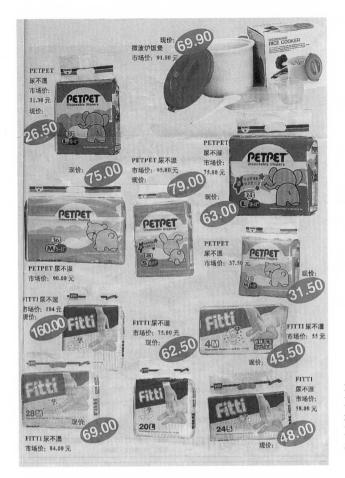

FIGURE 3.1.
Brochure
from Parkson
Department
Store (July 27,
1996)

page advertisement to promote the sale of a 500 renminbi beeper to pre-
teens about to enter junior high.[1] The headline read: " For your very last
Children's Day Festival you need this gift."[2] The text accompanying the advertisement then explained how the beeper would allow the owner (in this
photo a long-haired preteen girl with an enchanting smile) to balance the
competing demands of her academic and extracurricular activities as well

1. In the Soviet world, June 1 was a national holiday in honor of primary-school children,
which was institutionalized in urban China during the 1950s. Even through the mid-1980s it
was primarily a day celebrated with formal performances and speeches by party officials. Five
hundred renminbi represented 80 percent of the average monthly salary in 1994 and 65 percent in 1995. *Shanghai tongji nianjian 1996*, p. 61.

2. *Xinmin wanbao*, June 2, 1994, p.15. Also of note is that when we approached the advertiser in 1997 for permission to reprint this ad, the company refused on the grounds that it had

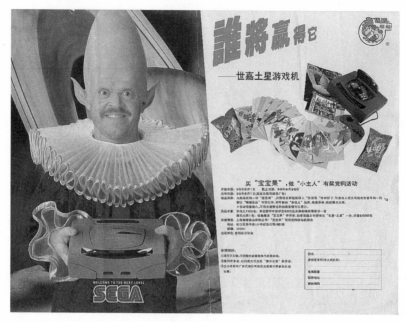

FIGURE 3.2.   Sega Video flyer distributed on Huai Hai Road (July 16, 1996)

as keep track of her friends, all for the small fee of just ten renminbi per month.

But it was not just in the hyped-up world of commercial advertising and retail promotions that Shanghai childhoods had become increasingly commercialized. The new for-profit entertainment sector also invested heavily in child-centered recreation. The Kentucky Fried Chicken menu was familiar to most ten-year-olds, even if the purchase of a KFC meal continued to be reserved for special occasions.[3] The same Spielberg-inspired plastic action figures that clutter the shelves of youngsters in Hong Kong, Tokyo, and San Jose were sold to Shanghai children in stores and street stalls all over the city. Michael Jordan's image was ubiquitous, and Chicago Bulls tank tops were worn by several hundred thousand boys between the ages of eight and

received severe criticism that the ad undermined children's commitment to their studies even though the text of the ad explicitly touted the advantage of beepers to protect study time from social interruptions.

3. Unlike in Beijing, through 1996 Kentucky Fried Chicken remained the most favored location for Shanghai parents to take children for a treat and to celebrate birthdays. As a gift to our interviewees we presented coupons for McDonald's; in every family we had to explain that McDonald's offered the same kind of children's meals that KFC did.

TABLE 3.1   Number of Births and Birth Parities
in Urban Districts of Shanghai, 1978–1995

		Percentage of births that were		
Number of births (in millions)		first	second	third or higher
1978	39,000	77.6	21.8	0.47
1981	75.000	96.9	3.0	0.02
1985	98,600	99.2	0.7	0.02
1989	98.000	98.0	1.8	0.04
1992	48,900	96.9	2.9	0.05
1995	45,400			

SOURCE: *Shanghai tongji nianjian 1993*, p. 72; *Shanghai tongji nianjian 1996*, p. 46.

eighteen. After fifteen years of economic reform, Shanghai children were emerging as members of China's first real generation of consumers, and they were consumers with global tastes.[4]

Rapid commercialization of childhood is not unique to Deng's China. During the commercial revolutions of eighteenth-century England and nineteenth-century America, economic restructuring, new affluence, and innovative retailing practices also produced a surge in the number and variety of products targeted at children, as well as opportunities for children themselves to become consumers.[5] But in those capitalist economies, the process unfolded at a slower pace and was clearly stratified by class, with only a small minority of privileged, urban middle-class children constituting the first generation to experience childhood as consumers. By contrast, in Shanghai during the 1990s the breakneck speed of development and the spectacular success in universalizing a one-child family plunged children and parents from all social strata into a consumer revolution. By 1996 almost every Shanghai child was a singleton who would never share parental resources—or anxieties—with a brother or sister (see Table 3.1). As a result, the proportional claims of Shanghai children on their family's financial resources were both larger *and more uniform* across different economic strata than for children in earlier rapidly commercializing societies.

By contrast, the childhoods of the singletons' parents, men and women born in the 1950s and early 1960s, had been defined by the material shortages and political suffering imposed by the Great Leap Forward and the upheavals of the Cultural Revolution. They grew up in large families with stagnant incomes where providing necessities was a daily challenge. Their parents' place of employment and their school provided what little nonfamily entertainment they

4. Our thanks to Jun Jing for so eloquently making this point.
5. Formanek-Bunnell 1993; McKendrick, Brewer, and Plumb 1982, chap. 7; Zelizer 1987.

experienced. Children were not taken shopping and were not consulted about their preferences or desires. In general, children were dressed in hand-me-downs or adult clothes recut to fit a child; only to celebrate Lunar New Year did parents or relatives purchase new items of clothing. A piece of fruit was a special and rare treat; leather shoes were for adults only.

In this chapter on parental purchases of toys and clothes, the theoretical point of departure is the work of Mary Douglas and Baron Isherwood, who presumed that material goods and everyday consumption practices were not fetishistic ephemera but component parts of "an information system" that "fix(ed) public meaning" and "anchor(ed) human social purposes."[6] Building on these assumptions of Douglas and Isherwood, this study of how parents "consume" for their children directly addresses the larger questions that unite the essays in this book by considering how marketization in a still Communist polity alters personal attachments and social relationships. Pierre Bourdieu's work on lifestyle and habitus is also relevant, and we build on his argument that close study of domestic investments can identify social boundaries and hierarchies.[7] However, because Chinese consumer practices of the 1990s were in such flux, this essay can not as easily draw on Bourdieu's argument about how lifestyle furthers social-class reproduction. Over time, the lifestyles created by Chinese parents for their children may become stratified by class, and one may be able to trace the process of social-class reproduction through variation in the consumer experiences of childhood. But in 1996 the combination of explosive economic growth and unusual demographic uniformities across economic strata made a Bourdieu-type analysis of habitus premature and instead favored the open-ended Douglas-Isherwood mode of inquiry that interprets the flow of material goods and commodities as a language that articulates changes in the meanings and intensities of social relationships.

6. Douglas and Isherwood 1979, pp. 59, 64. The observational and interview materials cited in this chapter were gathered during the summer of 1996 in the central districts of urban Shanghai. During two weeks in July, Davis led a group of twelve students and faculty from Yale, the Chinese University of Hong Kong, the Shanghai Academy of Social Sciences, and Shanghai University in an investigation of parental spending. Working in four teams, the group made structured observations in twelve different stores and shopping arcades, interviewed head teachers at one elite school and one school in a former squatter area, and interviewed a parent and child in twenty families accompanied by one of the teachers. In addition, the group visited three museums and attended a morning matinee of Disney's *Toy Story*, and Davis spent several evenings revisiting large department stores, McDonald's, and Kentucky Fried Chicken on Huaihai Road. Sensenbrenner spent ten weeks in Shanghai caring for her three sons and visiting family. She had copies of the interview and department store observation schedules used by Davis's seminar group but followed a more open-ended research strategy, observing families in child-oriented public spaces and informally interviewing parents she encountered in daily activities.

7. Bourdieu 1984.

TABLE 3.2   Basic Budget for a Primary School Child,
January–June 1996

(in renminbi at 8.3 *renminbi* to one U.S. dollar)

One semester of school fees	150–200 rmb
School lunch (70 rmb x 6 months)	420 rmb
One book bag	75 rmb
One pair gym shoes	7 rmb
Three school uniforms	210 rmb
One pair leather school shoes	100 rmb
One winter coat	300 rmb
Basic meals at home plus one bottle of milk per day	
(230 rmb x 6 months)	1,380 rmb
Daily pocket money (2 rmb/day x 180 days)	360 rmb
Estimated total	3,052 rmb or 508/month

HOUSEHOLD BUDGETING FOR SHANGHAI'S ONLY CHILDREN

When we asked Shanghai parents during the summer of 1996 how much they spent to support their primary-school-age son or daughter, they routinely replied: one parent's basic wage. After reconsidering earnings from all sources and collecting prices on a wide range of products used exclusively by children, we found that parents did in fact spend nearly the equivalent of an average monthly wage or approximately 508 renminbi (hereafter rmb) for basic needs and another 100 rmb for optional but routine purchases, such as new clothes other than school uniforms or an occasional meal at Kentucky Fried Chicken or McDonald's (see Table 3.2). Thus even without considering optional yet not unusual costs such as swimming lessons, after-school tutoring, or a new video game, Shanghai families routinely spent about 600 rmb each month to provide their only son or daughter with the necessities of what was becoming a typical Shanghai childhood. In fact, as will be clear in our discussion of purchases of toys, clothing, entertainment, and educational enrichment activities, a noticeable minority of Shanghai children enjoyed an even more expensive lifestyle as a result of additional expenditures by parents, grandparents, other relatives, and friends.

Another comment parents frequently volunteered when we discussed the rapid change in consumption patterns was their perception that they spent more on their child's discretionary needs than they did on their own small and large pleasures. If one adds to the basic budget items in Table 3.2 expenditures on toys, restaurant meals, and swimming trips, which we knew from observations and interviews were routine for children from all but the poorest families, parental estimates did not immediately seem incorrect. However, after we compared the cost of routine and discretionary expendi-

TABLE 3.3 Cost of Items Purchased for Shanghai Children and Adults in July 1996

For children	For adults	For family
5–10 rmb		
Ice-cream (1–4 rmb)	Red-bean ice drink (6 rmb)	Rent on 26 sq. ft apt (26 rmb)
Lunch at school (2–3 rmb)	Lunch at workplace (3–7 rmb)	Monthly telephone service (24 rmb)
Morning show of Disney movie (8 rmb)	Evening first-run movie (20–30 rmb)	Monthly water service (30 rmb)
Public swimming pool entrance fee (3–10 rmb)	Hotel swimming pool (30–50 rmb)	Monthly newspaper subscription (30 rmb)
Entrance fee for city art museum (8 rmb)	Entrance fee for art museum (10rmb)	
Cotton shorts with Mickey logo (9 rmb)		
20–30 rmb		
KFC/McDonald's special meal (19–23 rmb)	Coffee in three-star hotel (30 rmb)	
Disney figure watch (22 rmb)	Bowling (20–30 rmb per game)	
Imported pencil box (18–22 rmb)		
Boxed set of Disney *Toy Story* heroes (18 rmb)	Women's mesh shoes (20 rmb)	
Ultraman figures (22–28 rmb)	Women's T-shirt (28 rmb)	
Model planes, boats, cars (20–22 rmb)	Women's sleeveless shift (28 rmb)	
Basic leather sandals (30 rmb)		
Shorts and T-shirt with logo (28 rmb)		
Cotton pinafore (28 rmb)		
60–70 rmb		
Eight-inch birthday cake (68 rmb)	Hair ornaments (50–100 rmb)	Monthly gas service (50 rmb)
Imported Italian puzzle (55 rmb)		Monthly electricity without air conditioning (50–80 rmb)

100–120 rmb
Twelve-inch birthday cake (110–116 rmb)
Six jars Play-doh and model (127 rmb)
Video cartridges for TV games (109–123 rmb)
150–200 rmb
Four weeks of piano lessons (4 x 50 rmb)
Barbie doll set (147 rmb)

Men's leather sandals (108–245 rmb)

Custom men's shirt (200 rmb)

Monthly electricity with air conditioning (200 rmb)
Weekly food for three persons (150–200 rmb)

3,500 rmb
Eight-day trip to Xi'an (3,500 rmb)
Banquet for 30th birthday (3,500 rmb)

Installation of phone (3,500 rmb)

8,000 rmb
Straus upright piano (8,000 rmb)
Entry fee for special kindergarten (8,000 rmb)

Italian moped (8,000–12,000 rmb)
Cell phone (8,000–10,000 rmb)

Japanese air conditioner (8,000 rmb)
Purchase of two-room flat (8,000 rmb)*

20,000 rmb
Entry fee to keypoint middle school (20,000 rmb)

Trip for two to Thailand (20,000 rmb)

Refurbishing kitchen and bathroom (20,000 rmb)

* In 1996 most home sales were heavily discounted to current residents. The cost of commercial space was 10–20 times higher.

tures for children with those for the entire household and with those primarily or exclusively for adults (see Tables 3.2 and 3.3), we discovered that the stereotype of China's singletons as indulged little emperors and empresses dictating family expenditures did not hold up to scrutiny. For example, while it was true that Shanghai parents spent heavily on the recreation and entertainment of their children (and astronomically more than their parents had spent on them), the expenditures for children were rarely as costly as many adult "treats." As Table 3.3 shows, a matinee showing of a first-run foreign movie cost 8 rmb for a child; an adult ticket for an evening show cost three to four times as much; similarly, a father's leather sandals cost three to eight times more than a child's.

Although we did not systematically ask respondents to explain the difference between purchases for adults and for children, the spending pattern appeared to conform to that suggested by Table 3.3. That is, parents indulged children with frequent purchases of small treats such as ice cream cones, a new bathing suit, or a box of candy, purchases that previous generations of working-class children rarely if ever had enjoyed. But parents spent more extravagantly on themselves as well, on custom-made clothing, mobile phones, and vacations. Tellingly, the comparable new luxury for a child was piano lessons, a discretionary expenditure that certainly distinguished children of the 1990s from those of the 1950s and 1960s but at the same time reflected the long Chinese tradition of using scarce family resources for advancing a child's education. Affluent adults might display their own success or prestige with designer clothes, Japanese raincoats or ostentatious jewelry, letting their bodies (or those of their wives) signal social standing in the newly materialistic Shanghai society, but they measured the success of their own children and the children of others by educational achievement. Some parents even volunteered that dressing a child in obviously expensive clothing might, in fact, distract the child from working hard enough to succeed in competitive school exams.[8]

After considering more carefully the actual cost of discretionary items for both adults and children, we did not find that the consumer revolution of the 1990s was as child-centered as popular opinion suggested. This misperception is likely rooted in the small share of the monthly budget spent on such heavily subsidized necessities as rent and bus fares (see Table 3.3). As Hanlong Lu points out in Chapter 6, Chinese citizens continued to "eat from the big pot," with government subsidies making the basic cost of maintaining a household relatively cheap. In an economy where a meal at McDon-

8. One mother commented to Sensenbrenner on a neighbor child who wore designer clothes, noting that it was a waste of money to spend so much on clothing that the child would quickly outgrow. She also criticized the child for his poor study habits.

ald's cost the same as a month's water service, and a child's birthday cake cost more than a month's electricity service, it is easy to see why parents perceived their children as the primary recipients of luxury spending. However, by comparing prices of household necessities and discretionary items for both adults and children, we saw more clearly how subsidies for daily expenditures made relatively modest cash outlays appear extravagant.

In the following sections, we examine spending on children's clothing, toys, and recreation in more detail to consider how China's consumer revolution has affected the purchases and attitudes of both parents and children.

CLOTHES

On the basis of work done in the United States, we initially hypothesized that parental purchases of children's clothes could be interpreted as indicators of parental striving for higher social status.[9] Given the changes from earlier visits we observed in the quality and quantity of children's clothing for sale in Shanghai stores, we were confident that there would be a correlation between clothing purchases and aspirations for social prestige. Advertising and store displays, which played to desires for high status, also reinforced this expectation. Windows of the state-owned "June First Children's Store" on Huaihai Road featured an ornately framed photo of Pierre Cardin surrounded by young European children in Cardin-designed creations grouped before one of the vermilion gates of Beijing's Forbidden City. Another photo in the window featured four Chinese children posing as members of a string quartet, also outfitted in Cardin couture. It was not only on Shanghai's premier commercial thoroughfare that children's clothes were presented as glamorous and sophisticated. Department stores all over the city had designer corners featuring famous brand (*ming pai*) children's shoes, sportswear, and dresses. However, we observed very few children wearing clothes with designer labels.

After systematically tracking prices for clothing and noting the daily wear of Shanghai girls and boys, we determined that clothing purchases were poor indicators of social-class distinctions. When asked in interviews about purchases during the previous three months, mothers consistently reported that the most important considerations in purchasing their children's clothes were durability and price. Very few admitted that they bought famous brands or enjoyed receiving expensive clothes for gifts. Several working-class mothers said they still made their daughters' clothes or bought fabric for relatives to sew for them. One woman interviewed in her home proudly explained in great detail how she could make a dress for her daughter for less

9. Seiter 1993, p. 224.

than 20 rmb that looked just as good as one for 200 rmb.[10] Other mothers reported that they shopped for children's clothes at sales or in the off-season to secure cheaper prices and then stored purchases until their children grew into them.

This apparent lack of concern with displaying status through clothing purchases, however, did not mean that the intensified commercialism had not affected sales of children's clothing. On the contrary, there was a much wider range of available styles in a broader range of prices in the summer of 1996 than there had been in the early 1980s. Prices of clothing for primary-school students were about the same as those for women's clothes but lower than prices for adult men.[11] Standard prices for matching shorts and shirt sets worn by boys and girls were 18–38 rmb, as were most girls' pinafores. For 58–68 rmb one could buy play outfits made of higher-grade cotton bearing designer logos. Stores throughout the city also displayed elaborate dresses with appliqués, lace, and covered buttons priced between 128 and 198 rmb.[12]

In general, city boys and girls dressed in T-shirts decorated with the ubiquitous Mickey and Minnie or other cartoon characters, while in the stores, parks, and restaurants Shanghai girls wore sundresses with tie sashes and appliqués of hearts, fruit, or flowers. We often spotted identical articles of clothing sold at comparable prices in a wide range of stores, and even where color or pattern were different, styles generally were the same.[13] To note differences in the clothing children wore, we had to focus on the pictures on their T-shirts or the quality of the fabric. In short, despite the rapid expansion of retail clothing outlets and increased purchasing power, children's dress remained remarkably homogeneous, producing a similarity in summer vacation clothes that almost replicated that achieved by uniforms during the school year.[14]

On the basis of research in the United States, we initially hypothesized that parents of girls would spend more on clothing than on toys and that

10. Interview with Davis on July 22, 1996.

11. For example, the most common summer shoes were leather sandals sold throughout the city for 30 rmb and sneakers priced between 15 and 38 rmb. For school, a standard girl's shoe was a 100 rmb red leather loafer. By contrast, adult women favored plastic sandals for about 15 rmb, mesh flats for 20 rmb, or leather shoes for 50–80 rmb. Men's shoes were noticeably more expensive, ranging from 78 to 200 rmb.

12. We never saw anyone buy the latter, although in almost every store we saw girls from the countryside wearing such finery.

13. For example, in one week in July a cotton blue and white dress with puffed sleeves and white-trimmed pockets (which could easily have been sold to European or American girls) was available for 28 rmb at the joint venture Yaohan in Pudong, in the No. 2 State Department Store, and in the June 1 Children's Store, as well as in several small street stalls near Huaihai Road.

14. One mother noted that the only way to find something original for her daughter was to frequent boutique-type clothing stores in Shanghai or have her husband purchase outfits made in Hong Kong during his business trips to Guangzhou or Shenzhen.

parents of boys would emphasize toys.[15] We assumed that decoration and display would be central concerns to parents outfitting girls and that socializing and training a child for adult roles in the workplace would be perceived to be more critical for boys. We found almost no support for this hypothesis. Working-class parents of both sons and daughters consistently said that they spent more on clothes than on toys. Clothes were considered a necessity for both sexes, and parents of girls seemed to "invest" in toys as much as parents of boys. Parents of both girls and boys believed that educational expenditures for lessons and educational toys were important and legitimate types of parental investment in a child's academic success and future employment. Because girls in Shanghai are usually only children and grow up in families where both mothers and grandmothers have always held full-time jobs outside the home, it should not be a surprise that parents of girls stressed investing in a daughter's preparation for employment and insisted that spending on girls' clothing was not a priority. Unable to trace actual purchases for an extended period of time, we cannot know whether these mothers practiced what they claimed to believe. The public voice of consumers, however, was consistent in its denial of heavy spending on clothing, and there seemed to be a gender-blind parental emphasis on achievement and investment over display and decoration.

This is not to say that gender differences played no role in the style of clothing. We saw very little unisex clothing; even shoes usually had clear "boy styles" and "girl styles." Moreover, although the May 29, 1996 *Xinmin wanbao* (p. 22) featured boys' and girls' hairstyles for parents to copy for celebration of International Children's Day on June 1, dressing up girls was more costly than dressing up boys. Two types of consumption were particularly biased toward girls. First, we observed heavy spending on hair ornaments for and by girls of all ages. The cheapest hair ornaments cost 2 rmb, but many were priced between 20 and 30 rmb, and when we visited girls in their home we often saw a wide selection of plastic, velvet, and beaded hair pins and decorations. There was nothing comparable for boys.

Another type of expensive fashion fad that clearly favored girls was a studio photography session, where a child was made up (with cosmetics imported from the United States), dressed as a "glamour kid," and then photographed with a favorite cartoon character or a huge white rabbit (see Figure 3.3).[16] The basic cost was 300 rmb, or the equivalent of a very fancy

15. This was suggested by Ellen Seiter's finding that in the United States there are more toys and videos aimed exclusively at preteen boys than at preteen girls (Seiter 1993, pp. 74–76).

16. In the one studio Davis visited, she observed a girl between the ages of eight and ten being prepared for a photography session. In the homes we visited, girls, not boys, were featured in large photos on display.

特別為您設計的
卡通背景

兒童天地

★ 由專業化妝師,采用美國進口的
   化妝品,為您創造新形象。

★ 美國進口的時尚飾物,任您配襯。

★ 采用最先進的攝影器材和特別的
   柯達相紙。

★ "好便宜"快來,祇需一瞬間就可
   體現童真魅力。

專業化妝師為您
創造新形象

由本店提供時尚
服裝為您配襯

一流攝影師悉心
教導您擺甫士

童真魅力

"好新奇"有機會可以同
"儷影白兔人"一起拍照

儷 影 卡 通
GLAMOUR
KiDS
PHOTOGRAPHY FOR CHILDREN

FIGURE 3.3.   Photo Corner brochure from Parkson Department Store (July 27, 1996)

party dress. But the purchase of a glossy four-square-foot portrait raised the purchase price to 800 rmb, or $100. Despite advertising featuring boys and girls, the product appeared to be primarily targeted at parents and relatives of young girls, and in the stores and in people's homes it was girls not boys whom we saw transformed into "glamour kids."

Many meanings can be attached to or inferred from these extravagant expenditures, and just as it is speculation to say that unisex clothing demonstrates equal gender treatment, it is not justified to see parental spending on girls' photographs as a signal that spending on girls was tilted toward "display" rather than "investment." Rather, what emerged in interviews with primary-school teachers and in family visits was a powerful desire for parents to use purchases for children to develop their individuality. Thus when mothers talked about knitting a special sweater or buying an extra hair ornament, they articulated the hope that their daughters would stand out as individuals. Both working-class and upper-middle-income mothers expressed this desire to use consumer choices to permit greater individuation and distinction. However we only heard this desire made explicit by mothers about daughters. And we did not hear mothers or fathers speak about providing their sons with clothes for the same purpose. Thus for primary-school children the link between dress and individuation may be restricted to girls. However, what we did hear repeatedly for both sons and daughters was that purchases of clothing demonstrated a new consumer consciousness and affluence. All parents expected to purchase several sets of clothing for their school-age children, and few expected to use hand-me-downs, which had been a common practice in the past. Clothing purchases for children thus revealed that Shanghai families had achieved the "relative prosperity" of a *xiaokang* lifestyle (see Lu, Chapter 6), in which parents of all economic strata could afford to provide their children with alternatives to school uniforms for weekends and summer vacation.

TOYS

One of the most dramatic differences between the childhoods of today's parents and those of their children is the availability of high-quality toys at prices well within the budgets of all Shanghai families. In the mid-1990s, sets of Chinese-made Lego, Duplo, and Techno building blocks identical to those sold in the United States were available in stores throughout the city. The simplest starter collection of Lego sold for as little as 12 rmb; common purchases we observed in the stores were the beginner Duplo set and a 100-piece Lego vehicle, both of which sold for 147 rmb. Play-doh was also ubiquitous, and small jars sold for 5–7 rmb, while a more elaborate set containing several jars of clay and a variety of plastic molds sold for 67 rmb. The choice of stuffed animals was vast, as was the variety of metal die-cast trucks and electric train sets. For between 110 and 198 rmb, customers could choose from a wide selection of video games, and all large department stores had one or two monitors around which small groups of boys clustered throughout the day. Model ships, tanks, planes, and cars for 20 rmb were also widely displayed, and many stores provided a track that children (we saw only boys) could use to race cars they had bought or built. Dolls (almost all with long blond hair) were popular, and although elaborate Barbie sets were being sold at 128 to 178 rmb, a Chinese-made clone named Cindy was available for as little as 13 rmb. We saw girls between ten and thirteen years old playing with the doll in their homes, on the street, in restaurants, and in the stores. Less common, or at least not visible during this visit, were cloth baby dolls. Action figures, especially those in the Japanese Ultraman series (22–28 rmb), were very popular with both boys and girls, and in stores and homes we saw a wide range of transformers, Ninja turtles, and dinosaurs.

Another indicator of how Western- (and especially American-) style toys had penetrated the children's market of urban Shanghai was the similarity between toys sold in Shanghai stores and those featured in the 1995 Disney film *Toy Story*, which received wide publicity for its summer 1996 opening in Shanghai. After attending a morning performance July 25 in a movie theater on East Yan'an Road, the twelve-year-old son of a Shanghai colleague spoke at great length about the similarity between his collection of plastic soldiers and those in the movie. Thus, although the July 16 *Xinmin wanbao* ran an editorial criticizing *Toy Story* as excessively foreign, it appeared that Shanghai children already owned many of the American-style toys and could easily relate to the central moral dilemma of this Disney tale about the conflicts aroused when a new glossy purchase replaced an old favorite. Moreover, during the weeks before and after the opening, replicas of the movie's two heroes (cowboy Andy and spaceman Buzz) were sold throughout the city for as little as 13 rmb. Thus rather than tantalizing Shanghai children with a foreign world of unimagined affluence, *Toy Story* and its two plastic heroes appeared to speak as directly to audiences in Shanghai as they did to those in Des Moines and Detroit.

However, during interviews and in conversations overheard in stores, parents did make clear that they disapproved of primary-school children's heavy involvement with dolls, robots, and anything that was obviously not an educational aid. Many parents insisted that they did not buy toys for children older than seven or eight because they believed that after the first year of primary school a child should focus on school and that toys were frivolous or inappropriate. Frequently parents told us that buying toys for a child older than eight was "meaningless" (*mei you yise*).[17]

One conversation overheard in the No. 2 Department Store on Huaihai Road was typical. It was between a father of about 40 and his ten-year-old daughter. They were Mandarin speakers but seemed to be living in Shanghai. The father had taken the daughter to the top floor of the store, which sold primarily children's clothes, shoes, toys, and stationery. As they got off the escalator the daughter ran over to the collection of plastic Ultraman figures (which sold for 28 rmb):

FATHER: You want this? *(pointing at the Ultraman)*
(Daughter nods and picks up a boxed set of two smaller figures to compare with the larger single one hanging on a wall display.)

17. The types of toys bought by fathers and mothers may have differed, but our research did not systematically address this issue.

FATHER: What does it do? It is meaningless, and besides you are too old to buy toys. It is just a strange toy to play with. What do you need it for?

They then walked over to the display of 22 rmb watches featuring *Toy Story* heroes cowboy Andy and spaceman Buzz. After looking for a short while, the girl seemed eager to purchase one. But again her father expressed his disapproval (his exact words were not clear), and they walked back toward the stuffed animals. The father then saw the stationery section and led his daughter to the other side of the store, passing another man and his seven- or eight-year-old son who were looking at book bags. The father picked up pencil cases, which ranged in price from 18 to 55 rmb. Then the two of them looked over all those in the 18–22 rmb range. He selected one with the Taiwan Bon-Bon cat motif and asked: "Do you like this? This looks good? I'll buy you two. Here, take the money to the cashier and get these."[18] The daughter seemed reasonably satisfied and left with the money to buy the pencil boxes.

Interviews and observations in stores revealed that primary-school children were very involved with their toys and that they received toys throughout the year. The most important times were International Children's Day on June 1 and a child's birthday. Lunar New Year still seemed to be a time to emphasize gifts of clothes or money. Some children were also rewarded with toys for getting good grades or receiving other types of honors, such as winning a calligraphy competition.

In interviews parents and children also said that even when an adult purchased a toy the child was usually actively involved, either accompanying the parent or grandparent to the store or making a specific request. During our observations, children's participation in purchasing their toys was striking and appeared to begin at a very young age. For example, one Saturday afternoon in the Parkson Department Store on Huaihai Road we observed a boy no older than three being urged by his grandfather to choose a toy. They began with a large 247 rmb remote-controlled pink plastic convertible. After the sales clerk raced it around, crashing it into one pillar after another, to the boy's dismay and the mother's cries for caution, the little boy rode a succession of large cars with sound effects controlled by buttons on the steering wheel. After much deliberation he chose a large plastic police scooter that cost 187 rmb.

Earlier that week, in the No. 6 Department Store in Xujiahui, we saw another example of the child as consumer. A mother announced to a clerk that her son, who had just finished first grade, could choose a new toy as a reward for good grades. They had already bought new shorts and shoes, and now they had come to the toy section. He was immediately attracted to a toy in the Japanese "Hello Kitty" line that we had just been examining. In this

18. This observation was made by Davis on July 27, 1996.

toy, pushing a button created a jet of water that lifted a kitten out of the water and into a boat suspended in the "sky." Another slightly larger and more expensive (38 rmb) rectangular variation without the "Hello Kitty" logo required the child to manipulate the water stream to elevate rings onto the hook of a fisherman's pole. The boy wanted the smaller toy, but his mother and then the sales clerk tried to persuade him to get the larger version with the fisherman. But the little boy insisted on his choice, arguing that it cost 9 rmb less. His mother said the price made no difference to her and insisted he buy the large one because it was more grown up and because he would be teased if he took the "Hello Kitty" one to school. The clerk took up the mother's argument and emphasized that the bigger one was more boyish. They then drifted away and looked at a few more toys in the same price range. In a short while the boy returned, took the money to the cashier booth, and bought the smaller version with the kitten.[19]

In the large department stores, where the most expensive toys were sold, adults and children shopped together. By contrast, at street stalls and small neighborhood stores, children used their pocket money to buy toys in the company of their peers and, in some cases, in defiance of adult preferences. One popular pastime among children of all social backgrounds was playing games with the "free" tokens that came inside Cheeto snack packs. Parents and teachers complained that such toys had no educational merit and that often children made the purchases just to augment their token collection and never ate the snack.

As independent and informed consumers, Shanghai children in the 1990s were directly courted by advertisers. The advertisement of the Guomai beeper company played to the desires of the child, not the parent, and for as little as 10 rmb a preteen could cover the monthly service charge. As the advertisement proclaimed, what better way to plan gatherings with friends and smoothly arrange your study time. In the children's biweekly *Xiaonian bao*, whose primary advertiser was the Cheeto snack company, promoters for Brands Chicken Essence greeted their young readers/customers with the slogan, "You are my good friend" and concluded with a childishly handwritten exclamation: "Healthy, clever little friend, that is you" (April 9, 1996, p. 4). An advertisement in the same issue also urged children to send in labels from two boxes of the elixir in order to get a cap emblazoned with the logo of Brands Chicken Essence.

Unlike clothing, which was selected primarily by parents, the choice of toys was frequently made by the discriminating child. And in stark contrast to the

19. Of course, the boy may have found the smaller toy more desirable because we were foreigners and had been paying attention to it when he arrived. This conversation was observed by Davis and two members of the Yale-CUHK summer seminar on July 16, 1997.

parents' own childhood experiences, this generation of Shanghai primary-school students spent hours evaluating the merchandise and comparing prices, after which one member of the group usually made a small purchase. Although their options were tempered by a prevalent parental desire to provide educational toys that would help children learn while they were having fun, the explosive growth of a commercial toy market created a social and fantasy environment in which children operated autonomously from adults and such adult-controlled institutions as school and the workplace. In addition, the rapid commercialization of retail settings and the greater floor space devoted to children's products created new public realms for play.

PLAY IN PUBLIC PLACES

In spring 1996, the Japanese retail giant Yaohan opened "Nextage" in partnership with the renowned Shanghai No. 1 Department Store. Located in the Pudong development zone, just minutes from the site of the new Shanghai stock exchange, the store was open twelve hours a day, seven days a week. Huge twenty-foot glass portals at each entrance defined the dramatic threshold that separated the dusty, hot, everyday world of Shanghai from the climate-controlled elegance of the emporium. Yet while the store displayed tantalizing extravagance far beyond the means of the average consumer, it was accessible both for window shopping and for ordinary purchases. For example, in July 1996, adjoining the Adidas boutique to the left of the entryway, was an alcove dedicated to toys and clothes for swimming. For only 15 rmb, a parent could purchase a Mickey Mouse inner tube, for 138 rmb a large plastic raft in the shape of the feline hero of the Disney hit *The Lion King*. In a section set aside for promotional sales, customers were encouraged to buy any three high-quality Japanese plastic items for 45 rmb. Each floor of the store contained a similar mix of the extravagant and the affordable. Party dresses for 200 rmb were sold next to pinafores for 28 rmb. On the toy floor, parents confronted a similar range of choices: 7 rmb for a can of Play-doh, 68 rmb for a Lego set, 800 rmb for a new Sega video system, and 1300 rmb for Aprica (Japanese-made) strollers.

Yaohan, like most Japanese department stores, also provided "no-cost" entertainment for children. In the Pudong store adjacent to the toy section was a play area the size of the infield of a baseball diamond, where any child under 1.3 meters could romp free of charge. At the center of the play area on a surface of synthetic grass were slides and a running track, and along the periphery were alcoves dedicated to quieter activities such as reading picture books, playing with Lego, or listening to music. Designers had overlooked no details; at the entrance were benches where parents could rest and small lockers in which children placed their shoes. On a hot Tuesday morning in July when we visited, four young female store employees dressed in red aprons were monitoring 25 or 30 infants, toddlers, and primary-school-age boys and girls.

Because land is plentiful in the new development zone in east Shanghai, the Pudong Yaohan was more spacious than stores in the older, more densely settled city core, and the children's play area was especially large. However, stores in the city center, both Japanese- and Chinese-owned, offered a similar range of consumer goods for children as well as areas dedicated to children's play.[20] Even in the No. 12 Department Store on the outer reaches of Putuo district, one of the city's poorest and most remote, half of the top floor had been set aside as a play area for children, and during a visit on the morning of July 27, 20–30 children, most unaccompanied by an adult, were playing video games, racing cars, or buying toys.

A comparison of articles and advertisements published in Shanghai's main local newspaper (*Xinmin wanbao*) between 1983 and 1996 during the weeks leading up to International Children's Day further documents how completely stores have become public play spaces and how intensely children's leisure had been commercialized.[21] When advertising of children's products first appeared in the early 1980s, it endorsed such "near necessities" as books, food supplements, and medicines.[22] International Children's Day was celebrated primarily in official venues such as parks, schools, and city stadiums, where children performed for dignitaries and received such orthodox rewards as plaques emblazoned with the national flag. By 1996 the holiday had been dramatically privatized and commercialized. The singing contests, which during the 1980s had been held in auditoriums sponsored by such official educational enterprises as *Ertong shidai* (children's epoch) moved to department stores where children competed in singing promotional jingles. For example, the Orient Department Store published four promotional jingles lauding the child as "customer king" and promised prizes to all children under age nine who gave complete performances at the singing contests held in the store every Saturday and Sunday in June (*Xinmin wanbao* May 25, 1996, p. 12). The use of public commercial venues for children's singing contests, however, was not limited to up-scale department stores. On July 17, 1996, at Big World Amusement Center (*Da shijie*) on Nanjing Road (which was filled with thousands of non-Shanghai families) an entire wing of the center was devoted to talent shows, one of which featured an emcee who called on young

20. For example, the large department stores Orient and No. 6 in Xujiahui and in Yimin on Huaihai Road have tables set up for children to play with Lego and tracks for children to race cars that were brought from home.

21. David Fraser's chapter in this volume considers how advertising created status and demand for previously unknown commodities.

22. See for example, *Xinmin wanbao*, May 27, 1983, p. 6; May 29, 1983, p. 6; and June 1, 1983, p. 6.

children to compete by singing their favorite songs, albeit not jingles about being a loyal customer of the amusement center.

Fast-food restaurants also tapped into this marketing technique of targeting children. For example, the Ding Gua Gua Chicken franchise at the IMM shopping mall in the southwestern part of the city had set aside a portion of its space for a children's play facility. With a minimum 20 rmb food purchase, a child could romp for an hour (or half an hour on the weekend) in a combination climbing, sliding, and ball-pit play area, similar to the play areas found in some fast-food chains in the United States. While their children were having fun, parents either stayed nearby enjoying their meals or shopped in the mall. We observed that children often arrived in pairs, demonstrating that such an excursion for a meal and play was probably not routine but a special treat. In many cases, two mothers came together with their children, or one parent hosted her own child as well as a friend or cousin.

Fast-food restaurants also capitalized on the trend toward increasingly elaborate birthday celebrations. Before the reforms, children's birthdays passed with little fanfare, but by the mid-1990s special meals and gift-giving had become common, and families of all social classes were making efforts to celebrate children's birthdays. In Shanghai, Kentucky Fried Chicken heavily promoted birthday parties, and in July 1996 McDonald's was trying to cut into the KFC market by assigning a hostess to visit tables with a child in order to register the child's day of birth and telephone number. In exchange, the child immediately received a Ronald McDonald cutout and the promise of a card on his or her next birthday. Needless to say, McDonald's hoped that upon receipt of the birthday card parents would spend 100 rmb to treat the birthday child and four friends to Happy Meals (for more details on McDonald's as a social space, see Chapter 11). But parents also hosted dinners at hotels, purchased elaborate cakes, and even sought out radio recognition.[23] "Tenth birthdays" (the ninth birthday by Western calculation) received the greatest emphasis, but our interviewees made it clear that every birthday was the cause for some celebration and gift-giving by parents and grandparents, and often by aunts and uncles as well.[24]

23. Dedicating songs on the radio to honor birthdays was a popular fad, and this gift was considered particularly appropriate if the announcement could be timed to occur during a birthday party.

24. Before conducting our interviews in Shanghai, we reviewed the interview questions with a graduate student from Taiwan. In the section devoted to discussion of toys, we had planned to ask the parents what they would buy for their child's next birthday. The Taiwanese student suggested we reword the query, dropping any reference to birthday. She explained that in her experience Chinese parents did not celebrate a child's birthday. However, as soon as we began interviewing and visiting stores and restaurants it became clear that mainland families were indeed celebrating their children's birthdays with gifts, cakes, and even parties, and we reinserted

THE DECLINING INFLUENCE OF PARTY-STATE INSTITUTIONS

On International Children's Day 1996, the Song Qing-ling Foundation, a major state organization dedicated to the welfare of children, opened China's first children's museum. In line with current efforts to "socialize" welfare expenditures, which in China means to solicit private donations and bank loans, only three-fifths of the 50 million rmb construction costs were supplied by the government, and maintenance costs were to be covered largely by admission fees. In 1996 the museum was still not complete, and the installation of air conditioning had been postponed indefinitely. The museum consisted primarily of large exhibition halls, one filled with photos of China's missile program and a few small models of Chinese-made satellites and rockets, another dedicated to a photographic exhibit of shipbuilding in Shanghai. The museum provided few activities for children, and with admission fees of 10 rmb for children and 20 rmb for adults and its remote location, which required visitors to come by taxi, the total cost for a family outing approached 100 rmb. In contrast, for no cost, parents could drop their children off in the air-conditioned Yaohan department store recreation area, and for less than 50 rmb the entire family could spend the day at an amusement park.

The steady shift away from state dominance over much childhood activity was also evident in children's participation in extracurricular activities. Many children of professional parents we interviewed attended classes in calligraphy, brush painting, martial arts, or English. Others took private lessons in piano, violin, or accordion or received academic instruction (often in small groups) with private tutors. Parents noted that these classes taught discipline, and thus such lessons fit with the often-voiced idea of investing in a child's future.[25] They gave children a productive activity during the summer, pro-

---

the question about birthday celebrations. The focus on the tenth birthday also deserves more attention than we can give it in this essay. Advertising suggests that banquets were held at least as early as 1993, particularly to celebrate the tenth birthday. (See *Xinmin wanbao*, June 9, 1993, in which parents announced a tenth birthday party for their daughter to be held at the Park Hotel.) This emphasis probably stems from pre-1949 tradition, when wealthy families in urban China celebrated tenth birthdays. For example, in the 1951 version of Lao She's story *This Life of Mine*, directed by Shi Hui, one of the hero's early insights into the inequities of life occurs while he is standing guard outside the courtyard of a corrupt official who is celebrating the tenth birthday of his daughter with a lavish mahjong party. Even in the early imperial era, ten was a critical turning point, the year when one ceased being a child and boys began to seriously study and prepare for exams (Wu Hung 1995, pp. 79–99). In other studies of nineteenth-century childhood, six was usually the age that marked entry into the student role, however ten was a critical turning point because it was "only after ten [that] a child was thought to be out of danger" (Saari 1990, p. 81).

25. One mother even reported that her ten-year-old son's "household chore" (*jiawu*) for the summer was to practice his calligraphy each day, writing each assigned character ten times.

vided an appreciation of traditional Chinese culture, or helped develop important skills critical to their future success in school. In the past, the school curriculum offered introductions to some of these activities, and children who showed talent were channeled into specialized training at Children's Palaces or other officially sponsored programs. By the mid-1990s such classes, while still sponsored by Children's Palaces, were also routinely offered by private organizations (such as the numerous privately run English schools) and individuals, many of whom were moonlighting college students or elementary teachers. Even schools embraced commercialism by renting out empty classrooms on the weekend for instruction in calligraphy or painting by teachers who wanted to augment their incomes.

Commercializing extracurricular educational options significantly altered the experience of childhood by shifting a portion of the responsibility for managing a child's activities and self-improvement away from the schools to parents and private instructors. Previously the state organized and controlled these activities by limiting the number of positions and selecting only those who exhibited unusual talent and came from the proper political background. Such state-sponsored instruction created a group of skilled individuals who felt privileged and indebted to have had such opportunities. By the mid-1990s, state investments in these types of programs had declined dramatically, and most extracurricular enrichment activities were open to anyone whose family could pay the fees.[26]

Previously the parents' employers played a central role in supplying children's leisure activities by distributing tickets to movies, performances, and exhibitions as well as organizing outings or day trips. Families could make their own arrangements for such activities, but monetary and logistical constraints made them unlikely to do so. In the 1990s, although some work units continued to provide some of these services, families could tap into a wealth of other entertainment options. Especially among upper-income families, children expected family-planned summer excursions to swimming pools, amusement parks, and even special destinations such as aquariums.[27] The expense for these types of activities could be substantial, so, unlike expenditures on toys and clothes, leisure expenditures varied widely according to the parents' economic status. Most families considered visiting the zoo or the Jingjiang Amusement Park to be a special treat, but well-paid professionals

26. This shift of instruction from an officially organized function of state agents to the private sphere has made such lessons available to anyone with money to pay the fees, which ranged from 120 rmb for ten weeks of group lessons to 30 (or more) rmb an hour for an experienced private tutor.

27. Children seemed less interested in going to the Jingjiang Amusement Park, perhaps because many had been before, but a special Sea World–type show held during the summer at Heping Park attracted much attention, probably in part because it was highly advertised on television.

routinely spent 20–35 rmb to allow children to swim in less-crowded hotel pools, and many took week-long excursions to scenic spots in China.[28] We interviewed parents who reported that they had taken their children to their *jiaxiang* (hometown), to Beijing, on a Three Gorges boat trip, and to the seaside resort at Beidaihe. Often a cousin was invited along, or two (usually related) families traveled together with their children to provide companionship for each family's single child. Such activities emphasized the importance of the family (and extended family) unit for providing alternative summer leisure activities.

In 1996, children in Shanghai had access to a wide variety of leisure activities, most of which were "sold" by nonstate entrepreneurs and commercial enterprises. Although children relied on their parents or grandparents to make arrangements and pay for outings, they could explore many venues, such as the stores and amusement arcades on their own. Particularly in the summer, with both parents busy at work, primary-school children enjoyed significant amounts of freedom to shape their own leisure time. By the age of ten, both girls and boys were spending much free time socializing with their peers in the newly commercialized and privatized spaces of Shanghai. It is premature to speculate about the effect of these trends on children's values and subsequent behavior, but the substantial differences between their experiences and those of their parents strongly suggests pronounced generational distinctions.

Spending on children's leisure and enrichment activities also clearly defined emerging class distinctions. However, what was striking was how quickly consumer items that previously had defined the quintessential bourgeois childhood—parties, movies, new clothes, and fancy toys— had reached working-class children and that class differences as experienced through consumption and family habitus still remained quite fluid. In 1996 parents from a range of economic groups were willing and able to provide comparably comfortable lifestyles for their children and to invest heavily in their son's or daughter's future. In interviews, parents noted that wealth could shape the experience of childhood, but much more common were parental observations that demonstrated their still blurred awareness of class distinctions among primary-school children.

For example, one mother contended that her neighbor's purchase of a piano to provide lessons for her child was ultimately an attempt to demonstrate affluence, because the window was always open during lessons to let neighbors know they owned a piano. On the other hand, we also encountered working-class parents whose children studied piano because they

---

28. Parents, most of whom had never experienced travel for pleasure, were often even more eager than children to visit these sites.

wanted the children to develop a talent that they would keep throughout their lives. Another mother related that someone had stolen the bicycles of both her preteen daughter and her neighbor's son; although both families had been able to purchase bikes for their children (which would have been viewed as an extravagance in the 1970s or early 1980s), only the neighbor, a private entrepreneur, could immediately buy a new bike. Another mother reported that she gave educational toys her daughter had outgrown to a neighbor's son because his parents both worked for a low-paying, struggling state enterprise. She mused that although the boy wore hand-me-downs, the parents still managed to buy their son a Nintendo-type game and purchase ready-made breakfast snacks on the street each morning. These examples illustrate that parents noted contrasts in their ability to provide various experiences for their children, but the distinctions did not yet fall neatly into a hierarchy of social-class positions.

CONCLUSION:
DOMESTIC CONSUMPTION IN AN ERA OF COMMERCIALIZATION

During the late-Mao era, urban families had little disposable income and made few discretionary purchases. The focus of domestic saving was a bicycle to provide daily transportation to work for an adult, an electric fan for the household, or leather shoes for the father. For the majority of urban households with at least one state employee, the work unit rather than the market was the primary supplier of consumer items, either directly through the periodic distribution of goods or the allocation of coupons that allowed the bearer to purchase cotton goods, consumer durables, meat, and oil. Without a good work unit, life in Chinese cities was meager, because variation in the material standard of living reflected the resources of an enterprise as much as those of an individual.[29]

The central role of collective consumption and the absence of market alternatives also created a distinctive relationship between work and family lives. In most discussions of contemporary North American or European societies, work is a location of production and family is a location of consumption. Family is also assumed to be the institution where core identities, loyalties, and enduring obligations are centered. In this model, family represents a haven, or at least a social and cultural arena distinct from the workplace. By contrast, for urban residents in the Mao years, the workplace was the locus of production, consumption, identity, and often even residence. The domestic sphere was a residual location, and in all domains of social in-

29. Bian 1994.

teraction the regime privileged the public over the private, structuring resource flows so that—at least officially—loyalty to the collective was rewarded
and individual attachments were maligned as selfish.

Connections among friends and kin did affect consumption patterns,
and *guanxi wang* (networks of relationships) were cultivated to enable families to move higher up the queue for coupons or to be the first to hear
about the arrival of Guangdong-made electric fans at the local state department store. Ties to people in positions of authority could translate into more
material comfort. But overall, what was strikingly different from capitalist
societies was the absence of marked social-class differentiation in levels of
consumption.[30]

But egalitarian distribution of material resources did not produce an un-
stratified society. On the contrary, politically inscribed class labels created a
searingly clear social hierarchy of prestige and honor, and political stigma
handicapped both children and adults. Social discourse and interactions were
strongly influenced by inequalities of power, but it was a parent's political
purity rather than the ability to sustain conspicuous consumption that distinguished class boundaries in everyday life during the late-Mao era.

After 1978 the economic reforms of the Deng regime fundamentally altered the distribution of power and authority between the enterprise and
the family. As consumer markets multiplied and rationing disappeared, the
workplace lost its role as the primary supplier of consumer goods, and political purity became an issue of marginal concern. Income more than political connections determined who owned an imported refrigerator, learned
to drive a car, or took piano lessons. Families were important units of accumulation and for a small number of self-employed had even become the site
of production. When viewed from the perspective of how individuals spent
time and made financial, professional, and emotional investments, family
autonomy had increased and the domestic side of life had become more
clearly distinguished from nonfamily life. By contrast, the scope of the workplace had shrunk.

Patterns of parental expenditures on school-age children confirm these
realignments in Shanghai society. Parents perceived the consumer needs of
their child as the focus for much of a family's discretionary expenditures,
and in interviews several parents mentioned that a decision to change jobs
was based on costs associated with schooling of their son or daughter. Shanghai families of the 1990s lived their lives more completely within the discipline and vagaries of a cash nexus than at any other time since 1949. Parents of all occupational groups held high aspirations for their singleton and
considered purchase of home videos, leather shoes, and birthday parties to
be virtual necessities. For leisure activities they turned to commercial venues,

30. Whyte and Parish 1984, p. 95.

including stores, amusement parks, and first-run movies. Shopping became a major form of leisure, with stores serving as a recreational setting where children socialized with their peers.

By embracing consumerism, this generation of parents and children had, at least implicitly, rejected the egalitarian and collectivist ideals espoused by the party-state during their childhoods. With a new social structure based on success in the market place rather than political purity or party affiliation, Shanghai parents focused on investing in a superior education and social and extracurricular activities, which they believed would foster adult success at work. But in compensation for their own difficult childhoods they also wanted their children to be happy and enjoy the new material comforts and sources of entertainment, and therefore many also drew vicarious pleasure in consuming for their children.

The homes we visited were usually simple one- or two-room apartments with a kitchen in an alcove and a bathroom shared with another family. Telephones and VCRs, however, were the norm, and children were adept with video games and familiar with pagers and cellular phones. Thus, although their homes were small, their operative social world was large and expanding through their family's private purchase of the instruments of modern media and communication. When asked what they hoped for their child's future, parents answered, "Whatever he or she does best." When asked why they had made a fancy party dress or bought a piano for a tenth birthday celebration, they answered, "So she can be special." In short, this close look at how and why Shanghai parents used their new purchasing power to consume for their children revealed that the previous dependencies on and loyalties to the collective had greatly attenuated and that the language of acquisition and mastery was both intensely commercial and individualistic.

CHAPTER 4

What's in a Dress?

Brides in the Hui Quarter of Xi'an

Maris Gillette

In the 1990s, a new trend in wedding gowns and bridal appearance swept the People's Republic of China.[1] Dresses that imitated Western bridal gowns became the fashion as the PRC's urbanites followed trends that had begun a decade or more earlier in Hong Kong and Taiwan.[2] Residents of Xi'an's old Muslim district, or Hui quarter (*Huiminfang*), were no exception to this rule. There, young women, like their Han counterparts all over the city, chose elaborate long-skirted and tight-bodiced gowns in pink or coral to wear on their wedding day and for commemorative wedding photos.

These new Western-style wedding gowns meant different things to brides, their peers, their older female relatives, the community's religious specialists (*ahongs*) and municipal officials. An examination of wedding gown consumption provides insight into the meanings various people attached to the gowns. It also illuminates the nature of social relations in this urban neighborhood, shedding light on important transformations that have occurred there since China's economic reforms began in 1979. A young woman's economic capacity and the economy within which she functioned, her position and decision-making power within her family, her religiosity and relationship to the mosque, and her goals and self-image were all implicated in the goods and services she used to prepare for her wedding.

This study demonstrates that the young women who lived in the Muslim district during the mid-1990s had more control over their weddings than their mothers and grandmothers had had over their own. They had the power and the means to create a bridal image that disturbed both government

1. See Faison 1996; Agence France-Presse 1997.
2. As described in Yang, Ch'ing-ch'u 1981.

officials and religious specialists. Yet the bride's autonomy was not unlimited. Female peers and older female relatives, both blood relations and in-laws, influenced brides' fashion choices and encouraged young women to dress in a manner that adhered to their notions of proper wedding attire. In the Hui quarter, in Xi'an, and, evidence suggests, in many other urban sites in China, 1990s brides and the women surrounding them held each other to an aesthetic rooted in Western fashion and that signified a great deal about contemporary urban China.

Davis suggests in the introduction to this book that marketization and privatization have opened a new space for Chinese citizens to express their personal taste, ideals, and values. Anthropologists and others have argued that consumption is the primary arena in which consumers in urban industrialized societies actively construct their identities. Consumers manipulate commodities and the images and ideas that goods represent to create self-images and public personas.[3] In China, Western-style wedding gowns and the other consumer goods associated with weddings allowed young women and their families to define and present themselves publicly. The gowns evoked images of the West, cosmopolitanness, development, and to some extent wife-and motherhood. By choosing to wear these gowns, young women, and their family members and friends who encouraged and collaborated in such consumption, associated themselves with these ideas.[4]

Unlike more routine forms of consumption, consumption activities such as renting a wedding gown occurred only once in a lifetime for most Hui women. Nevertheless, the wedding preparations described here share with food- and clothes-shopping a degree of inevitability. Getting married is an integral part of the lives of most Chinese, a step men and women must take to achieve social adulthood.[5] While weddings were special events, or a "big deal" (*da shi*) as informants phrased it, they were neither unusual nor unexpected. Wedding preparations, like shopping for food and purchasing clothing, were seen as necessary and natural activities in life.

RESEARCH AND BACKGROUND

This chapter is based on fieldwork carried out in the Hui quarter of Xi'an between 1993 and 1997. I conducted the primary research during eighteen months of residence in Xi'an from January 1994 to August 1995. In 1994, Xi'an was a predominantly Han city with a population of about 2 million lo-

3. See, e.g., Miller 1992; Humphreys 1995; Kondo 1992; McCracken 1988; and Wilk 1994.
4. Wilk (1994) and Yan (in this volume) make similar arguments.
5. As argued by Rubie Watson in R. Watson 1986. See also Davis 1989.

cated in Shaanxi Province in northwestern China. The Hui quarter was located in the oldest part of the city within the city walls. According to residents and local officials, Hui have been living in the quarter for more than 1,000 years. In the mid-1990s the quarter contained about 30,000 Hui as well as a few Han Chinese residents.

The Hui are one of China's 55 officially recognized ethnic minorities or "nationalities" (*minzu*). Citizens of the PRC tend to regard the nation's ethnic minorities as distinctly different from the Han majority, attributing to them a non-Chinese pedigree and history. Such beliefs are more accurate for some minorities than others. Although the Hui nationality possesses minority status, its ethnic differences from the Han Chinese should not be overplayed. Hui are, as Dru Gladney has put it, "Muslim Chinese" whose ethnic differences from the Han all derive in some fashion from Islam.[6] To a large extent, Hui share a history, culture, and ethical system with their Han Chinese compatriots. Most aspects of Hui cuisine, architecture, and dress and significant portions of their intellectual heritage and religious practice derive from China's dominant (Confucian) tradition.

Without a doubt, many Hui, including a number of my informants, would take issue with the formulation that the Hui are Chinese. Residents of the quarter stressed they were distinctly different from the Han and possessed a separate history and heritage. This stance relates to the government privileges that, as Gladney reveals, undergird what it means to be non-Han in the contemporary PRC. The nationality policies of the Chinese government have played an enormous part in fostering rigidly defined ethnic identities and instilling in PRC citizens a belief in them as immutable. Despite this "politics of difference," however, residents of the quarter knew that an intimate relationship existed between the Hui and Han nationalities. They chose to describe this relationship in terms of descent, encapsulating their identity with an aphorism that stated they were "born of Muslim grandfathers and Chinese grandmothers." This choice of parentage is telling, for in the Chinese context descent is traced through the paternal line. Hui consider themselves primarily Muslims and deemphasize their Chinese roots.

Most residents of the quarter were small-scale private entrepreneurs operating family businesses out of their homes. The majority of these enterprises were food-related; one local official estimated that 50 percent of the quarter's households engaged in the production and sale of food. Few other parts of Xi'an had such a dense concentration of private businesses. Resi-

6. See Gladney 1991, in which Gladney examines how the Chinese government has defined the Hui as non-Han and, in some sense, non-Chinese, and the ways that the Hui as a group have appropriated and reified that distinction. See also Lipman 1987 and 1998. In his introduction to the latter work Lipman provides a critique of what he calls "the *minzu* [nationality] paradigm" in China.

dents of the quarter also had marriage patterns and educational backgrounds that differed from those of some other Xi'an urbanites. They preferred to marry other Hui, particularly Hui who lived in the quarter. Their levels of education were lower than the citywide average; most Hui ended their formal schooling after junior middle school (about age fourteen).[7]

The information on which this chapter is based comes from hundreds of discussions about weddings with dozens of women, participant observation at five Hui weddings and one Han wedding, and viewings of videos and photographs of three other Hui weddings. In the next section I provide a historical sketch of wedding fashions in Xi'an. The key informants for this discussion were four women who married before 1949, two who married in the 1950s, three in the 1960s, one in the 1970s, three in the 1980s, and seven in the 1990s. With the exception of one 1960s bride and one 1990s bride, all my informants were Hui. Nevertheless, popular articles and the experiences of other ethnographers in China, as well as my own observations in Beijing, Yinchuan, and Xining, suggest that few if any significant differences existed in Hui and Han bridal attire. The most significant variation in Xi'an was that Han adopted Western-style wedding gowns before Hui did.

WEDDING DRESS AND "WEDDING GOWNS" (*HUNSHA*)

The clothes that most Xi'an brides, whether Hui or Han, wore in 1994 and 1995 were known as *hunsha*, wedding gowns. This word referred specifically to Western-style wedding dresses, namely the dresses worn by brides in America and Europe that residents had seen in magazines and on television. "You Westerners wear *hunsha*" was a comment I heard repeatedly. What provoked this remark was the relative novelty of such bridal attire in Xi'an; women who had been married more than five years had not worn wedding gowns in their marriage ceremonies. They described their wedding clothes with other terms: *qipao*, which referred to the tight-fitting dress associated with prerevolutionary China; "traditional Chinese clothes" (*Zhongguo chuantong yifu*), which consisted of a tunic and trousers; Sun Yat-sen or "Mao" suits, as they are known in the West (*Zhongshan zhuang*); or Western suits (*xizhuang*).[8]

7. According to a publication of the Xi'an Statistical Bureau, in 1994, 67 percent of the city's middle-school children continued their education, and in 1995, 72 percent did (see *Xi'an tongji nianjian 1996*, p. 381). In the Hui Middle School's 1994 graduating class of 70 students, only eleven (15 percent) went on to school. Note that the citywide figures for Xi'an high-school entrants are lower than elsewhere in China. For example, in 1992 in Guangdong, 78 percent of middle-school students entered high school (Ikels 1996, p. 148); in Xi'an the 1992 figure was 59 percent.

8. See Finnane 1996 for a historical examination of women's attire in China that focuses specifically on the *qipao*.

The women of my acquaintance who had been married before 1949 stated that they wore either tight-fitting, skirted *qipao* or a tunic and trousers during their weddings. Women younger than 65 also described the marriage clothes their mothers and grandmothers wore in this way. Xi'an Hui and Han associated the *qipao* with imperial China and the wealth and power of the upper classes, although the *qipao* first appeared in China during the 1920s.[9] A bride who wore a *qipao* before 1949 showed her family's affluence and sophistication. By contrast, most women associated the tunic and pants with the countryside and poorer lifestyles. The women who married during the 1950s, and one who married in the countryside during the 1960s, wore tunics and trousers in their weddings. None of my informants characterized tunics and trousers as desirable bridal attire; rather, many contrasted the poverty and plainness of such clothing with the elegance and costliness of the wedding gowns popular in the 1990s. A common complaint was that tunics and trousers strongly resembled everyday wear. Their red color—red being the traditional color for bridal attire in China—was the main feature demarcating wedding clothes from ordinary clothes during this period.

As CCP policies grew increasingly leftist during the 1960s and the political climate grew more harsh, brides traded their red garb for suits in more restrained hues. Several women who had married during the 1960s wore Mao suits of gray or blue, as did their grooms. These changes reveal the impact of Maoist propaganda, which characterized traditional wedding attire and marriage practices as feudal.[10] The changes in clothing paralleled changes in ritual: the switch from traditional clothing to Mao suits was mirrored by a greatly simplified wedding ceremony that focused on the state rather than on the families of the couple.[11] Almost without exception, women who married during this period characterized their bridal attire as impoverished. Aifeng, married in 1967, recounted that she had had to borrow clothing for her wedding. After 1969, however, when the worst of Cultural Revolution radicalism had passed, brides exchanged their Mao suits for Western-style ones. During the 1970s and 1980s, Western jacket and trouser suits in cream, pink, and yellow became popular in the quarter.

According to my informants, wedding gowns debuted in the quarter around 1990. Several residents pointed out that Xi'an Han had begun wearing them even earlier. Xue, a young woman in her early twenties who helped her family operate a private business, described the appearance of Western-style wedding dresses like this: "Wedding gowns have only recently sprung

9. Ibid.

10. Examples of this propaganda are provided in Lu Yang 1969 and Zhang Zhigang 1966.

11. See Whyte 1993 for a brief description of wedding rituals during the 1950s and 1960s and the changes that have taken place since 1979.

up (*cai xing qi lai le*). We saw the gowns on the streets: there were stores selling them, they were displayed in shop windows. That is where we [Hui
women] saw them." She and the other women I asked said Hui started wearing the dresses because they were fashionable and pretty. Several explained
the switch by saying "a bride has to look like a bride." Such comments revealed that an important transformation in Chinese ideas about bridal appearance had taken place since the PRC's open-door policies were implemented in the early 1980s. A "proper bride" in the mid-1990s was largely
defined by Western fashion.[12]

In the following pages I describe the wedding gowns worn at the six weddings I attended and the three I saw on video and in photographs. There
are obvious differences in color and style between the wedding gowns worn
in the United States and Europe and those worn in the quarter, even though
Hui strongly identified the gowns they wore with the West. Many Hui brides
chose to wear white gowns for their formal wedding portraits (a relatively
new addition to the marriage ritual sequence), but at no wedding I attended
in 1994 and 1995 did Xi'an brides wear white. Whereas in the West white
symbolizes purity and virginity, in China white has traditionally been associated with mourning. The wedding portraits alluded directly to the West by
showing the bride dressed in white in a luxurious setting containing furniture and props vaguely reminiscent of elite European or American lifestyles
(see Figure 4.1). However, the actual wedding ritual did not parallel this fantasy depiction. All the Xi'an brides I observed wore either pink (*fenhongse*),
coral (*rouse*), or red (*hongse*) dresses during their wedding ceremonies, colors that accorded more closely with the long-standing Chinese association
between the color red and good fortune, happiness, and prosperity. In addition, the variety of wedding dresses available to purchase, rent, or model
for photographs in Xi'an was smaller than the selection in the United States
or Europe. Stylistically, the dresses adhered to a standard model: tight
bodice, sleeves, and floor-length skirts with petticoats.

WEDDING RITUALS

Weddings in the quarter showed significant differences from Xi'an Han weddings in duration and in the kinds of ritual events that took place. Some of
these differences can be attributed to Islam and its regulations about Muslim
food and the marriage sequence, while others derive from the propensity of
Hui to run private businesses rather than to work in work units. Hui weddings
do share key structural elements with Han weddings, however, particularly in

---

12. See Y. Yan 1997a and Yan, this volume, for another example of how Western goods have
affected China during the post-Mao period.

FIGURE 4.1. Wedding portrait of Xue, dressed in white in a vaguely European setting. (Photo by Golden Lady Beauty Salon)

terms of the relationship established between the bride's family and the groom's family and some of the ritual acts that manifest that relationship.

The Han wedding I attended in Xi'an lasted one day. The main events were the transfer of the bride and her dowry from her natal home to her marital home and a large banquet hosted in a restaurant. The dowry transfer and subsequent bride transfer differed from the Hui ritual only in the time of day these events took place (earlier in the day during the Han wedding) and the amount of time between them (shorter during the Han wedding). The restaurant banquet, attended by the families and guests of both the bride and the groom, was a ritual feature that Hui weddings did not share. At the Han wedding I attended, the leaders of the groom's work unit were specially acknowledged and honored; one read aloud the information written on the couple's official marriage license, which was procured several weeks before the ceremony. Other events included the bride and groom toasting each of the guests with alcohol (*baijiu*) and some teasing of the newlyweds by the groom's best man (*banlang*).[13]

13. What I saw in Xi'an seems quite similar to the Han weddings in Chengdu described briefly by Whyte (1993).

By contrast, Hui weddings spanned a four-day period. On the first and second days, ritual banquets were held at the bride's household and at the groom's household. According to Hui tradition, the bride's guests attended only the wedding banquets at her (natal) residence and the groom's guests attended only those at his. In each case, the banquets opened with a recitation of the entire Qur'an by *ahongs* (the term Hui use for Islamic ritual specialists) and the other men in the community who could recite in Arabic. After the recitation was finished, the banquet began. Guests ate in a prescribed hierarchical order: first the *ahongs* and men of religion, then the adult male guests, and finally the women and children. After the banquets was a series of food presentations between the bride's and groom's families, including the delivery of an entire meal (at least twelve dishes) to the bride's family.[14]

On the first day of the wedding, the other important event came in the afternoon when the groom and an *ahong* from the bride's family's mosque arrived at the bride's household. The *ahong* sat with the bride and groom in a public place, usually her family's courtyard, and asked them formally if they consented to the wedding. These vows were known as the *yizabu*, a term transliterated from Arabic that means "to make a contract." After this ceremony was completed, members of the bride's family and her friends transferred the bride's dowry from her natal home to her new residence (the "new house"), which was usually part of the groom's parents' household.

The second day of the marriage ritual was the day residents regarded as the "wedding day." In addition to a banquet, the second day included the transfer of the bride from her natal home to the groom's parents' residence (this was true even if the couple's "new house" was not part of the groom's parents' home). The groom's family sent a team of ten or more cars to the bride's home to transport her, members of her family, and her guests to the groom's home. After picking up the bride, the team of cars returned by a circuitous route, making sure to drive in a procession down some of the main streets of Xi'an and around the bell tower in the city's center. After a short stay of fifteen or twenty minutes at the groom's parents' home, the bride's guests adjourned. The remaining events of the second day included public teasing of the groom and an extended period during which the bride was displayed to the groom's family and guests.

At about five o'clock in the morning on the third day, before morning prayers, the groom's family presented the bride with gifts, and she returned to her natal household escorted by her brother (or, lacking a brother, any man who stood in the categorical position of brother to her, such as a male first cousin on her father's side). She remained at her natal home that night. On the fourth and final day of the ritual, several members of the bride's fam-

---

14. For a brief description of these food presentations, see Gillette 1997, chap. 5.

ily escorted her back to the "new house," where the bride presented gifts to her new in-laws and the groom's family served her guests dinner.

Wedding rituals in the quarter were shaped by local traditions, Islamic law, and modern consumerism. They were key occasions for conspicuous consumption, as the numerous banquets, the car processions, and the exchanges of food and goods indicate. Wedding consumption practices also included spending large sums on fashions inspired by those found in the West.

DRESSING FOR MARRIAGE: XUE'S STORY

At about 1:00 P.M. on the day of her wedding (the second day of the marriage ritual), Xue was extremely upset. Her sister and brother-in-law had just returned from picking up the wedding gown Xue had rented from a store that was twenty minutes away by car, and the gown was dirty. When she looked at the outfit they had brought, Xue found mud stains on the gown's hem and headpiece and spots on the skirt. After a few minutes of furious discussion with her maid of honor, the two women (both in their early twenties) determined to take the dress back to the store and exchange it.

It was after 3:00 P.M. by the time Xue returned, to the consternation of her aunts (her father's sisters) who were guests at her family's home. They worried aloud whether Xue could be ready by the time the cars arrived to take her to the groom's home. Xue was more sanguine, although she remarked that exchanging the gown had made her miss her 2:30 P.M. makeup and hair-styling appointment at "Golden Lady," the fanciest beauty salon in the city. More immediately important, however, was that she had successfully changed the dirty pale-pink gown for one in better condition. Although the new dress was coral in color, like the other gown it had a floor-length full skirt, large puffy short sleeves, and a tightly fitted bodice embroidered with an elaborate pearl and lace design. The gown's low-cut princess neckline was attached with transparent gauze to a pearl-and-lace collar.[15] With the gown came long gauze-and-lace gloves and a long gauze veil.

Xue left the dress in her room for her aunts and cousins to inspect and immediately set out for the "Golden Lady," which was on the other side of town. Her maid of honor, bridesmaid, the bridesmaid's three-and-a-half-year-old son, and I accompanied her.[16] Xue and her fiancé had previously visited the salon to be photographed for their formal wedding portraits, but none

15. What I describe here as "low cut" is not low by contemporary American fashion industry standards, but is much lower than the usual neckline worn by Hui women, including young women. The neckline of the wedding dresses is relevant to the following discussion of modesty.

16. "Maid of honor" and "bridesmaid" are terms I have applied to the two young women who played a significant role at Xue's wedding. They helped the bride dress, accompanied her on her journey to the groom's home, and stayed with her during the evening's public ritual activities.

of the rest of us had been there before. "Golden Lady" was the most opulent beauty salon and studio I had ever seen. It was packed with young women getting made up, having their hair done, and being photographed in a variety of fanciful bridal costumes supplied by the store. Fortunately for Xue, a stylist was available to tend to her face and hair immediately. Over the next hour, the bridesmaids and I watched the stylist apply makeup to Xue, gawked at the other women being beautified, paged through the books of wedding photographs the studio provided as samples, and chatted amongst ourselves in the crowded waiting room. The little boy fell asleep on one of the couches in the waiting area, causing the receptionist to complain.

When Xue emerged from the stylist's chair, her hair was swept on top of her head in a sophisticated style that left two long ringlets hanging down by her ears. Fresh pink carnations and baby's breath artfully decorated the top, with the coral-pink veil draped down the back. Liquid makeup and powder, meticulously applied, made her face look pale and polished. Deep brown eye shadow, black eyeliner, and mascara enhanced her eyes, and bright red lipstick drew attention to her lips.

By the time we left the salon it was already 5:00 P.M. No one knew exactly when the groom would send the cars to meet Xue (around 6:00 P.M. was typical of the weddings I attended), but all of us fretted that she would be late. Upon our return to her home, Xue dressed quickly, first donning the gold jewelry she had received as gifts from her husband's family, and then putting on her wedding gown. With her flowers, elaborate makeup, perfect hair, and flowing dress, she reminded me of a fairy-tale princess. When Xue emerged from her room, her female friends and relatives rushed to her side, clamoring to have their photographs taken with the bride. Xue carefully posed with all her female relatives according to their generation: one photograph with her grandmother, great-aunt, and grandfather's brother's wife, another with her five paternal aunts, others with her peer-age cousins, and one with all of her cousins' and brother's progeny.

Xue spent about five hours that day preparing for her appearance as bride. After the photographs, her formal performance began when the *ahong* arrived to recite the *qifa*, a prayer of leave-taking. All the guests crowded around her, the *ahong*, and her maid of honor in a tight circle in the family's courtyard to watch and hear Xue be blessed (see Figure 4.2). Later that evening, Xue spent seven hours on display in the groom's household. Like all Hui brides, she maintained a silent demeanor with eyes cast down while the groom's relatives and wedding guests came by the room where she was seated to look at and be photographed with her. Several of her new in-laws com-

---

At other weddings, only one woman attended the bride. On one occasion, I heard such women referred to as *ban niang*, but most Hui did not use a formal term for the women in this role.

FIGURE 4.2.   Xue on her wedding day being blessed by the *ahong*.
(Photo by Maris Gillette)

mented favorably on Xue's appearance to the other guests in her (and my)
hearing: "Look at what a beautiful new daughter-in-law we have."

UNPACKING BRIDAL ATTIRE: WOMEN, SHOPS, AND FAMILIES

Several features of Xue's wedding preparations were striking; among the most
notable was Xue's sense of consumer rights. Dissatisfied with the condition
of the gown she had originally rented, Xue hesitated only briefly before going to the store to demand a replacement. Her willingness to fight for a clean
gown stemmed in part from the cost of the rental: the 360 renminbi (rmb)
she paid was the equivalent of a month's salary for a clerical worker in one
of Xi'an's state enterprises. Even though Xue's family (which included eight
people at the time of her marriage), as owners of a small private restaurant
in the quarter, earned about 500 rmb a day in net income (making them
quite comfortable by Xi'an standards), neither she nor her family undertook
large expenditures lightly.

Just as important as the size of Xue's investment was the fact that she had
procured the dress from a private business. Since Xue helped her family sell
steamed stuffed buns (*baozi*) on Barley Market Street, she knew that the quality of the goods and services she provided largely determined how well her

restaurant would do. Xue and her family worked hard to ensure that the foods they sold were tasty and attractive. I frequently heard Xue's mother, Aifeng, criticize her children and the other employees for producing inferior *baozi*. Xue's experience as a private entrepreneur enabled her to recognize that market competition and the general availability of wedding gowns gave her power as a consumer. When I asked her how the rental exchange had gone, she replied that it had been easy. She pointed out that many stores rented bridal clothes in that part of town, so she could easily have taken her business elsewhere had that store refused to satisfy her demands.

More than two years after her wedding day, Xue and I were talking about her wedding and I asked her how she had managed to change the bridal gown. To my surprise, Xue told me she had not successfully persuaded the store to exchange the gown. She and her maid of honor had argued at length with the storekeeper about the gown's condition, but the storekeeper kept waffling about how to handle the problem. Ultimately the urgency of the situation caused Xue to abandon her efforts. Xue said she simply rented a different, cheaper gown from a nearby store.

This was not the story Xue had recounted to me, her other guests, or her relatives on her wedding day. Perhaps then Xue had represented her efforts to exchange the gown as successful in order to avoid criticism and prevent the incident from spoiling her marriage ceremony. Yet regardless of whether Xue successfully completed her mission, her story reveals an awareness of consumer rights that is new to the post-Mao era. Xue's attempts mark a significant transformation in the Chinese economy and the powers of Chinese citizens.

Stories Xi'an residents told me about the Maoist era painted a portrait of scarce goods and lack of choice.[17] Many people in their forties and older remembered eating a monotonous diet of sweet potatoes during the late 1960s and 1970s and shuddered at the prospect of ever eating another. The ration coupons urbanites received limited the kind and amount of food and other goods (such as cloth) they could procure. During this period China's citizens were recipients of the state's largesse—they were its clients, not consumers who chose the products they desired from an array of possible options. Xue's agency as a consumer shows that the Deng-era market reforms have taught potential customers they have the power to both select and reject commodities. Xue's later account indicates that this power relates directly to the rising standard of living—and is most easily exercised when the consumer becomes more affluent.

The second noteworthy feature of wedding gown consumption in Xi'an was the level of interaction between Hui and Han that it revealed. "Golden Lady" and the store where Xue rented her dress were both popular estab-

17. Yan's discussion of work-unit canteens and restaurants during the Maoist era in this volume confirms this image.

lishments among Xi'an brides. Like most of the city's bridal stores, photography studios, and expensive salons, they were located in the northeastern part of Xi'an within the city wall, a good distance away from the quarter. A few other wedding gown establishments and marriage portrait studios were located on the main east-west street that bisected the city's center. In 1994 and 1995 the quarter had no places to rent gowns or have formal photographs taken, but it did have a few beauty salons that styled brides' hair and made up their faces (see Figures 4.3 and 4.4).

Xi'an's marriage-related businesses were privately operated and for the most part run by Han entrepreneurs. Since Xi'an was predominantly a Han city, most of the patrons of these enterprises were Han. When young Hui women rented dresses from wedding gown stores, they wore clothing that had been worn by their Han peers. When they visited the beauty salons in the northeastern part of the city, they received beauty treatments from Han employees. Surprisingly, this did not disturb the Hui brides of my acquaintance, even though residents of the quarter tended to limit their contacts with Han and regarded themselves as very unlike their fellow urbanites. Western scholars of the Hui have frequently commented on the barriers to social relations that the Hui erect between themselves and the Han. The most obvious of these barriers is the Hui refusal to eat or drink in Han homes or restaurants or to use dishware, utensils, or cookware that had ever been used by a Han.[18] Despite the ways Hui asserted they were different from Han and rejected sociability with them, however, young Hui women were perfectly willing to don a gown previously worn by a Han woman.

That young Hui women shared clothing with Han and received intimate physical attentions from Han beauty salon employees shows how close Hui and Han dealings could be. The history of Western-style wedding gowns in China suggests that Han have mediated Hui contact with global fashion, first introducing the gowns to Xi'an and then exclusively retailing them. Residents of the quarter, however, obscured the essential role that Han Chinese have played in transforming wedding attire by the rhetoric they used to discuss and describe the gowns. Hui characterized wedding gowns as distinctively Western apparel, not as Han apparel. Discussions of bridal attire were couched exclusively in terms of which kinds of clothing were "Western," "modern," and "trendy" (*liuxing*) and which were "Chinese" or "traditional." The contrast Hui invoked was between China and the West, or between tradition and modernity—a mode of description that dismissed the Han role as the purveyors of modernity in this case.

18. See Gillette, forthcoming, chap. four, for a discussion of Hui eating practices and avoidance of Han. Gladney (1991) provides other examples of the limited nature of Hui-Han interactions, including ethnic endogamy. See Pillsbury 1975 and 1978 for a discussion of Hui-Han relations based on fieldwork in Taiwan.

FIGURE 4.3.   Yan
getting her hair done
at a salon in the quarter
on her wedding day.
(Photo by Maris Gillette)

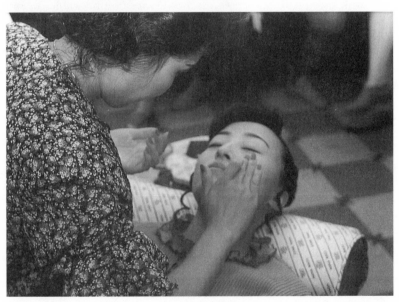

FIGURE 4.4.   Yan getting her face made up by a woman whose beauty credentials
(or at least her certificate) were from Hong Kong. (Photo by Maris Gillette)

Another illuminating aspect of Xue's wedding preparations was the participation of her friends and relatives in creating her appearance. Particularly remarkable were the ways in which her older female relatives collaborated to ensure that she "looked like a bride," for Xue's appearance on her
wedding day differed dramatically from the norms of female dress and ideas

about modesty characteristic of the quarter. Xue's story reveals that Hui bridal fashion was defined collectively by the female population, both young and old, and that it subverted some commonly held mores.

Xue's bridesmaids, two women in their twenties and another in her early thirties, participated in her beauty preparations at every step. Their presence signified their approbation of her appearance and also gave them the opportunity to critique Xue should she attempt to deviate from how they thought she should look. On the first day of Xue's wedding, for example, when she was preparing for the *yizabu* ceremony, I heard Xue's maid of honor shame Xue into wearing flowers in her hair. At such ceremonies, brides usually wore dressy versions of daily wear, such as a long-sleeved sweater with trousers. What demarcated the bride from her female guests at these events were the flowers she wore in her hair and the scarf with which she covered her head. Xue had been complaining about the flowers she had prepared and suddenly stated she would not wear them. Her maid of honor was shocked and insisted Xue put them on: "Otherwise no one will know you are the bride!" Similarly, Xue's aunts and cousins inspected her attire both before she dressed and afterward. They gave their opinions of the gown's color, the way it looked on Xue, the shoes they thought she should wear with it, and so forth. At these moments the older Hui women also helped create and maintain an image of the "proper bride."

By having their photographs taken with the bride, Xue's peers and relatives signified their approval of her appearance. Through this act the female wedding guests communicated not only that Xue as a bride was important but also that they valued the way she looked. Their comments and actions showed an element of possessiveness, as if the bride were a valuable commodity they owned and were showing off. When Xue was on display at the groom's home, her new in-laws behaved in a similar manner, reinforcing the appropriateness of her appearance with verbal commentary about her comeliness and taking turns being photographed with her (as with Yan in Figure 4.5). During Xue's beauty preparations, the photography sessions, the formal wedding photographs, and the other ritual events, Xue's peers and older women relatives colluded to produce a normative image of how a bride should look and disseminated this image to young unmarried women.

The proper bridal "look," though informed by Western aesthetics, was highly standardized. Xue's makeover was more expensive than those of the other six brides whose weddings I attended, but her preparations and appearance (as well as her ritual role) were remarkably similar. At seven of the nine weddings with which I am most familiar, the brides dressed in a manner virtually identical to Xue's. All wore long pink or coral gowns with tight bodices, low-cut necklines, fluffy skirts, gloves, and veils. They also wore high heels and flesh-toned nylons. Each had a formal hair-styling session on her "wedding day," during which the hair was elaborately coifed: piled on top of the head with two long ringlets left dangling by the ears, crowned with flowers, and sprayed with colorful sparkly confetti. A specialist carefully applied base and powder to whiten the face, eye shadow, eyeliner, and mascara to emphasize the eyes, and bright red lipstick to accentuate the lips. Matching scarlet nail polish was applied to their fingernails. All the brides adorned their ears, necks, arms, and hands with jewelry, much of it gold. Although two of the nine brides chose not to wear long pink gowns, their hairstyles, makeup, shoes, stockings, and jewelry matched those of the other women.[19]

The experiences of one young Hui bride who attempted to avoid wearing the standard wedding attire provides further evidence that women created and enforced an image of the "proper bride." Yue was a 24-year-old Hui intellectual, a Ph.D. candidate in computer science at the time I concluded my fieldwork in August 1995 (she has since completed her degree). During the eighteen months I lived in Xi'an, Yue set and reset the date for her wedding several times: it was first scheduled for April 1995, then moved to May, and then July. Yue finally married in September 1995, a month after I had left China.

The difficulty with fixing Yue's wedding date sprang from the fact that Yue did not want to have a typical wedding. She did not want to follow the customary four-day wedding ritual, and she was determined not to dress like the brides described above. However her fiancé's family, and as Yue told me, her future mother-in-law in particular, felt strongly that Yue and her fiancé should follow the marriage traditions of the quarter. Perhaps some of their insistence stemmed from their awareness of how exceptional a Hui woman Yue was, with her graduate education and work experience far removed from the petty entrepreneurial lifestyle common to most women in the quarter. Since Yue was unable to procure her in-laws' agreement that she marry in the style she wished—necessary because like most young Chinese she depended on her own and her husband's family to pay for the wedding—Yue repeatedly delayed the ceremony.[20] She had been engaged for a year when we first met in the spring of 1994; most Hui I knew felt that after a year it was time for an affianced couple to get married.

I first received photographs and a description of Yue's wedding from her

19. One of the two wore a deep-pink Western-style suit with a calf-length skirt. The other bride donned a red silk tunic and narrow floor-length skirt elaborately embroidered with a dragon and phoenix, an ensemble my fellow guests called "traditional." In each case the bride's accoutrements and the general effect produced closely resembled that of her bride peers. Three of the nine brides discussed here wore "dragon and phoenix" gowns for at least one of their formal wedding portraits (usually a bride has several portraits taken, mostly alone but a few accompanied by her groom). In my reading, "dragon and phoenix" bridal costumes are a modernized version of the *qipao*.

20. Whyte points out in his study of marriage in Chengdu that the percentage of young Chinese who pay for their own wedding expenses has declined dramatically in the post-Mao era (see Whyte 1993).

FIGURE 4.5. Yan at the "new house" being photographed with her new sisters-in-law. (Photo by Maris Gillette)

younger sister, who wrote a week after the marriage. The pictures showed Yue in a light-pink gown, veil, high heels, makeup, and jewelry, all typical in the quarter and in Xi'an. Shortly thereafter, Yue herself wrote and sent more photographs. In that letter and in a subsequent telephone conversation, Yue explained why she had acceded to her mother-in-law's wishes. Her own aunts and female cousins had added their voices to the pressure from her husband's family that Yue marry in the current style until finally she gave in. Her wedding had been "exactly like the ones" I witnessed, Yue told me. "Actually," she wrote in her letter, "it was a hard time for me."

The importance placed on being a bride who "looks like a bride" is also illustrated by the trend I observed among married women in early middle age to have themselves photographed in bridal attire even though they had been married for several years. Most of the women I knew who did this were Han. The influence Yue's female relatives and in-laws exerted over her appearance attests, however, to how taken older Hui women were with wedding gowns. At one wedding I attended, the bride's youngest aunt excitedly tried on her niece's wedding gown (see Figure 4.6). She then called her husband and two teenage children to join her and asked me to photograph them while she was wearing the dress.

Older women's willingness to countenance wedding gowns and their encouragement of their young relatives to wear them was surprising. Under normal circumstances, few Hui women wore skirts, and those who did were almost all younger than 30. Older women and men strongly disapproved of skirts and were extremely vocal in their criticisms of the Hui women who wore them. Most residents of the quarter said skirts violated the Islamic code of modesty—known locally as *xiuti* or "shamed body"—which dictates that women's bodies be covered from ankle to wrist.

In its rejection of skirts the Hui notion of *xiuti* differs from the modesty code practiced in the Middle East. There long skirts are the hallmark of a modest woman; when trousers were introduced in the Middle East during the early twentieth century they provoked public censure, personal attacks, and even riots. By contrast, in Xi'an observing modesty dictates meant wearing trousers and avoiding skirts. This notion of modesty derives from traditional Chinese costume for women. *Xiuti* must be understood as a profoundly Chinese expression of Islamic modesty.

Older women and *ahongs* were the two main sources of censure about clothing styles in the quarter. In the heat of June 1995 when Yan decided to wear a dress late in her pregnancy, her aunt disapproved. "Naked, revealed body!" (*chi shen luo ti*), she exclaimed. She then told Yan and me that the *ahong* of the mosque she attended had criticized a family in public because the women wore skirts. One elderly member of this family had successfully completed the pilgrimage to Mecca, so his family hosted a large celebration in his honor. When the *ahong*, a guest of honor at the party, saw that some of the pilgrim's female relatives wore skirts, he angrily scolded the man in front of the guests for not ensuring that his own family dressed modestly.

Yet while women like Yan's aunt strongly disapproved of skirts for everyday wear, they did not object to brides who wore Western-style wedding gowns. The calf-length, high-necked dress worn by an overheated and heavily pregnant Yan occasioned her aunt's reproaches, but this same aunt looked on approvingly during Yan's wedding when Yan wore a long pink gown with a low-cut neckline. Indeed, at her wedding, Yan's aunt was photographed with Yan and joined in the general admiration of her beauty. Comments like those recounted at Xue's wedding, where affinal relatives bragged about the beauty of the family's new daughter-in-law, were commonly made by older women, despite the conflict between the bride's attire and most of the older women's own standards of dress. With few exceptions, when I asked women ranging in age from 35 to 80 if they had worn such wedding gowns they laughed and told me they had never worn skirts in their lives.[21] Middle-aged and older women tended to dress extremely conservatively and cover their hair in observation of the dictates of Islamic modesty.

21. One exception to this rule was a Hui woman who was principal of the Hui middle school. She frequently wore skirts and dresses to school. However, her education at a military college in Harbin and extensive work experience made her exceptional in the quarter.

FIGURE 4.6.   Yan's aunt
tries on Yan's wedding gown.
Married in the early 1970s,
Yan's aunt had never worn
a wedding gown or even a
skirt. Moments after putting
on the dress, Yan's aunt
assembled her husband and
two adolescent daughters
and asked me to take a
family photograph of them.
(Photo by Maris Gillette)

One of the most notable features of Western-style wedding gowns was the emphasis the gowns placed on the body. In 1994 and 1995, Hui women rarely wore form-fitting clothes. I saw a few young women wearing relatively tight clothing at festive occasions like weddings, but most preferred to dress fashionably in a manner that did not emphasize the shape of their bodies (see the bride's in-laws in Figure 4.5). No Hui women I knew considered close-fitting attire suitable for daily wear. This preference contrasted with the outfits I saw a visible minority of young Han women wearing in Xi'an, who apparently favored short, tight miniskirts and close-fitting blouses for their daily dress. Young Hui women generally wore trousers and shirts (with extra layers in the winter); miniskirts were out of the question. Women in their thirties, forties, and fifties usually wore roomy blouses loose over unfitted trousers. Hui women in their sixties and older wore late imperial-style tunics with high collars over wide cotton trousers. Older women were likely simply to wear newly laundered versions of these clothes at weddings. Unlike young women, they did not dress up on festive occasions.

Contemporary bridal attire challenged Hui notions of modesty, but wedding gowns were acceptable because they conveyed an image that resonated with and supported certain ideals residents of the quarter held. One important set of ideals the gowns symbolized had to do with youth and reproductivity. Wedding gowns were seen as the domain of the young; neither of the two older women (both widows) I knew who got married during the early 1990s wore this type of bridal attire. One of the gown's undeniable effects was to emphasize the nubility and, through the enhancement of the bust and hips, the fertility of a young bride. Some of the popularity of Western-style wedding gowns may have derived from the role they played in establishing the bride's new identity as wife and mother.

In post-Mao China, as Chinese women attempt to define their identities outside of the government's reach, mothering seems to have taken on an increased importance. In her study of home interiors, Davis points to the large double beds in Shanghai workers' apartments as evidence that women are creating a private identity that focuses on reproduction and their sexual obligations in the spheres of life (such as home decor) left unregulated by the state. Davis argues that the CCP's population control and residential policies have, paradoxically, heightened the importance of wife- and motherhood by making children a limited good. Rofel writes that many young married silk workers in Hangzhou have rejected their worker identities in favor of mothering. She interprets this as an effort by women to assert control over their bodies and lives and resist the work-place discipline imposed by the state.[22]

Although no women in Xi'an discussed wedding gowns in relation to sex or mothering, the dresses are nevertheless connected to the roles of wife and mother. Most obviously, the gowns are worn during the ritual that marks a woman's transition into these roles. The way the gowns accentuate the body and the vast amounts of time and money spent on the bride's appearance indicate the importance placed on becoming a wife and a mother for young women and the community at large. The emphasis placed on the gown and the rite of passage suggests that family roles and domestic life were central concerns to the quarter's residents.

Even more clearly, Western-style wedding gowns represented certain ideals of modernity, sophistication, and affluence. Women who were married in the 1970s or earlier contrasted their bridal attire unfavorably with that of more recent brides. Likewise, young, marriage-age women described the wedding gowns and clothes their grandmothers wore as "traditional" and the 1990s wedding gowns as "elaborate" (*jiangjiu*), "fashionable" (*liuxing*), and "modern" (*xiandaihua*). A young Hui woman's choice of a Western-style wedding gown made a statement about her values and how she wanted to be perceived by her family and neighbors, relatives and friends, local religious specialists, casual passersby, and the other residents of Xi'an who saw

22. Davis 1989; Rofel 1994b.

the bride as she was driven down the main city streets and around the bell tower en route to the groom's household. The identity she established for herself imitated Western images on television and in magazines and was associated with cosmopolitanism and sophistication. Wedding gowns enabled young Hui women to see themselves as participating in the international fashion world and gave them the chance to display their cultural capital.

While wedding dresses conveyed an image of affluence (as embodied by the West) on a symbolic level, they also demonstrated wealth more literally. The young brides I knew in the mid-1990s possessed large amounts of money to spend on their appearance (see Table 4.1 for an expense record of Xue's wedding attire). Renting bridal attire in Xi'an cost between 200 and 400 rmb; this included the gown, gloves, and veil. Young women specially purchased the shoes and nylons they wore on their wedding day and paid for the services of the beauty parlor; Xue's makeover, hairstyle, and flowers cost 100 rmb. Brides also wore large amounts of gold jewelry, some of which they had purchased themselves, and some of which had been given as engagement gifts by the groom's family.

A great deal of the money women spent on their wedding clothes came from the marriage payments made by the groom's family. In 1994 a man who became engaged was expected to give the bride 10,000 rmb in cash and a plethora of gifts ranging from facial cleansing cream to a bicycle or motor scooter. The bride was expected to use the money to provide a dowry for herself at marriage, but since her family also gave her cash and household items towards this end, ultimately she had a large amount of money to spend.[23] The bride also had her own earnings, since most young Hui women worked after completing junior middle school but continued to live in their parents' homes. The opulence and extravagance of bridal attire demonstrates the large sums of money a young Hui woman had at her disposal.

Older women recognized and frequently remarked upon the economic resources a young bride possessed in the mid-1990s. Many women who had married in earlier periods complained bitterly about the poverty of their weddings. During the Cultural Revolution, I was told, a bride who brought a single pair of leather shoes as a dowry was considered exemplary; two pairs were exceptional (and occasioned teasing about how many feet the bride had). As Xue's mother, Aifeng, put it, "Back then we were poor. Today, they have everything" (*Nashihou, hen qiong. Jintian tamen shenme dou you*).

The lavishness or paucity of weddings influenced the social standing of the families involved. The new wedding gowns were highly visible emblems of affluence, given the centrality of the bride's role during the ritual. How the bride's appearance affected the status of her natal and marital families is especially apparent in Yue's case: what Yue wore for her wedding was too

---

23. The same traditions are practiced elsewhere in China. See Y. Yan 1996.

TABLE 4.1   Xue's Wedding Attire Expenses, May 1995

Wedding gown deposit	500 rmb
Wedding gown rental (includes gloves and veil)	250 rmb
Wedding shoes (imitation leather)	220 rmb
Nylons	6 rmb
Underwear and bra	20 rmb
Fresh flowers for hair	30 rmb
Makeover at "Golden Lady" salon	70 rmb
10.4 carat gold bracelet	1,019.20 rmb
6 carat gold ring	588 rmb
Total (including the deposit but not the cost of the first wedding gown):	2,703.20 rmb

NOTE: Xue also wore a great deal of jewelry on her wedding day that she had been given by the groom's family, most of it gold. It included a gold necklace, earrings, bracelet, and ring, and a sapphire ring set in gold. Xue did not know how much these had cost, or how many carats the gold was, but she knew that the price for a carat in 1995 was 98 rmb. Xue also carried a handkerchief that had been made for her by her father's sister's daughter. We did not discuss the monetary value of this.

important to be left to her own whims. The prospect that Yue might fail to conform to community standards mobilized her female relatives to pressure her and insist that she have a wedding that demonstrated their knowledge of contemporary fashions and their ability to afford them.

For a bride's in-laws, the attractiveness of the bride signified their success on the marriage market. The beauty and fashionableness of their new daughter-in-law (*xin xifu*) demonstrated that a family could entice a worthy bride. The bride spent six or more hours on display in the groom's household during the Hui wedding ceremony to show off her appearance (see Figure 4.7), a tradition that long predated the 1990s. Relatives' and guests' comments about the beauty of the new daughter-in-law, such as the remarks made at Xue's wedding, also show the power the bride had to make the groom's family look good. Though perhaps to a lesser extent than in pre-revolutionary China, the evidence suggests that the bride was still a valuable commodity to her husband's family.[24]

DON'T WEAR THAT! THE MOSQUE AND THE STATE

Whereas most residents of the Hui quarter approved of wedding gowns, tacitly or otherwise, *ahongs* censured them. Common complaints were that the

24. Siu, based on fieldwork conducted in the Pearl River Delta, found that women became more valuable to their families during the 1980s, largely for their economic contributions (Siu 1993).

FIGURE 4.7. Yan on display in the groom's household. The bride remains in this posture for six or seven hours. (Photo by Maris Gillette)

gowns were "against Islam" (*fan Yisilanjiao*) and "not like Hui" (*bu xiang Huimin*). Some *ahongs* also said that the gowns too closely resembled the bridal attire of Christians. Residents stated that a few *ahongs* had spoken out against wedding gowns during the exhortation at collective worship services on Fridays. One man in his forties explained the *ahongs*' disapproval by saying, "they are afraid the young people will run away (*pao*) [from Islam]."

Some members of the religious establishment saw wedding gowns as a threat to the future of Islamic practice in the quarter. For some *ahongs*, the censure of wedding gowns was tied to a wider distrust of Westernization; these men refused to use Western commodities (or commodities associated with the West, such as factory-produced packaged foods). The older *ahongs* in the quarter tended to interpret changes as movements away from Islam. They feared the popularity of Western goods among the young signaled a decline in Islamic morality and the rising influence of a non-Muslim lifestyle.

The Islamic core of Xi'an Hui identity was perhaps most visible on a daily basis in the scrupulousness with which residents of the quarter treated the Islamic dietary prescriptions. Other facets of community life, such as the celebrations of major Muslim holidays, the popularity of after-school and vacation classes in Qur'anic education, and the centrality of Qur'anic recitation to Hui life-cycle rituals like circumcisions, engagements, marriages, and funerals, made the importance of Islam obvious more sporadically.[25] The majority of Islamic traditions practiced in the quarter (with the exception of the dietary rules) primarily involved men. For example, males were required to attend collective worship services by Islamic law, but women were not; consequently, many more men than women visited the mosque regularly. More men, especially as adults, studied the Qur'an, in part because only men could serve as ritual specialists. The mosque's role in the lives of women, particularly young women, was comparatively limited. Indeed, when I spoke about various Islamic practices with some women in the quarter, they described such things as "men's business" (*nanren de shi*).

Young women's willingness to violate the dictates of modesty during Hui weddings, and the complicity of older women in helping them to do so, suggest that the *ahongs'* concerns about the decline of Islamic morality were not entirely misplaced. Rather than signifying a new Westernization process that caused youth to reject Islam, however, women's penchant for wedding gowns could equally well be related to pre-existing gender biases within the local practice of Islam. Certainly the young Hui woman of the mid-1990s spent far more time window-shopping than she did worshipping. Yet when women's bridal attire is placed in the general context of formal Islamic observance, historically and in the mid-1990s the prerogative of men, the gowns look like part of a widespread and long-standing gendered division of labor in the quarter. Superficially the wedding gowns may appear "not like Hui," but the underlying pattern of behavior, whereby women are less concerned than men with Islamic practice, seems far from new.

The mosque was not the only institution disturbed by contemporary marriage attire. Wedding gowns also exacerbated tensions between the state and the Hui community. Government officials, both Hui and Han, expressed discomfort with the conspicuous consumption that bridal fashions embodied. For example, 56-year-old Liangxun, the Hui vice-director of the Shaanxi Bureau for Religion and Nationality Affairs, criticized the Hui weddings of the 1980s and 1990s as excessively expensive. Liangxun stated that although he welcomed the public return of traditional marriage practices, which had been performed secretly or omitted during the 1960s and 1970s, he worried that the elaborate Hui marriage preparations put too much strain on a family's

25. All of these features of Xi'an Hui life are discussed in more detail in Gillette, forthcoming.

resources. Liangxun believed that families competed to host the most luxurious wedding. He worried that some families lacked the necessary income to spend large sums of money on bridal attire, marriage payments, and wedding banquets without going severely into debt.

Underlying Liangxun's remarks, which I heard echoed by other local officials who were Han, was a concern with the class differences and social inequalities that were emerging in 1990s China. Weddings and wedding gowns showcased consumerism and the increasing importance placed on personal wealth that characterized China in the years following Mao's death. They also required the expenditure of large sums of money on activities seen as ephemeral and "unproductive." Officials like Liangxun were perturbed by the enormous income differential between the rich and the poor in the PRC's socialist market economy. They also saw it as their job to encourage residents to invest in their own and the nation's economic betterment rather than frittering their money away on inessentials.

Xue's exercise of her consumer rights (although unsuccessful) demonstrates the government's much diminished role in regulating commerce. As Davis points out in her introduction, the privatization of businesses and general loosening of economic restrictions have diminished state power, even though such policies originated with the state. A powerful connection between commerce and politics exists if only because increased incomes and access to consumer goods give Chinese citizens the tools to create and maintain social relationships outside of the government's purview.

The significance of wedding gowns lies less in their power to generate spaces for conversations outside the state's hearing than in demonstrating that Chinese citizens desired things that existed beyond the state's capacity to provide. On one level, Western-style wedding gowns were literally outside the government's domain: as far as I know, state enterprises did not produce or sell wedding gowns and thus could not regulate their consumption. In Xi'an at least, official control over wedding gown distribution was limited to licensing or refusing to license marriages.[26]

Western-style bridal attire symbolized values and ideals that were not officially generated. As is true of all governments to some degree, the PRC state of the mid-1990s wanted to control the identity of the populace it governed. One way it did this was by establishing the terms with which people could construct their identities: providing the categories of identity such as "Hui nationality" (*Huizu*) and "private entrepreneur" (*getihu*) and educating people to use them. After the market reforms, however, the state was

26. Information on the production of wedding gowns is extremely scarce. Informants told one anthropologist working in Nanjing that the gowns available in China came from Taiwan and Hong Kong. When dress styles changed, the older gowns were shipped to the PRC (Lida Junghans, personal communication).

forced to compete with an outside world newly able to influence China through tourism, the media, and commerce. Economic privatization and the accompanying decline of the work-unit system further decreased government control by giving individuals the opportunity and incentive to work for themselves. Generally speaking, wedding gowns represent a decline in the state's power to determine Chinese citizens' perceptions and goals.

Wedding gowns denote the longing many Hui felt for an affluent, cosmopolitan, and modern lifestyle. Their ideological association with the West, wealth, sophistication, and modernity gave Hui a means to resist state categorization of them as "backward." As many researchers have pointed out, the Chinese government devalues minority cultures as evolutionarily primitive in relation to the Han majority.[27] At the same time, it romanticizes and fetishizes minority costumes and cultures; for example, official images of China in pictorials and tourism advertisements usually show minority women dressed in colorful attire. By wearing Western-style wedding attire, Hui brides in Xi'an rejected this government classification. In their emulation of the modernized, wealthy West, they placed themselves at the developed end of the primitive-modern spectrum and arguably removed themselves from the PRC's scale of nationality social evolution altogether.

WHAT'S IN A DRESS?

On one level, Xi'an bridal attire was about conformity, a conformity women enforced on other women. Yet paradoxically, on another level, wearing the long pink wedding gown and its accompanying apparel was about agency. This agency was primarily manifest with respect to two extremely important institutions in the quarter, the mosque and the state.

By the mid-1990s, Western-style wedding gowns were virtually indispensable to Hui (and Han) weddings. As Xue put it, "a bride has to look like a bride." A significant feature of this attire in the quarter was that it created an opportunity for young Hui brides to wear "immodest" clothes. Most young women eagerly seized this chance and were strongly supported by their older female relatives in doing so, despite the reproach of the religious establishment. That young Hui women wore wedding gowns testifies to their autonomy from the mosque. Male and female religious observance in the quarter has characteristically been separate, but it is likely that wedding gowns mark a more public and visible expression of the differences in men's and women's religiosity than was seen in earlier periods.

Although local wedding attire was extremely standardized, women in the

27. See, e.g., McGranahan 1996; Harrell 1995b; Gladney 1991; and Swain 1990. See also Gillette 1997, chap. 2.

1990s had a wide selection of clothes and fashions available to them. The mothers of the brides could not have purchased or rented Western-style clothes when they were married: there were none to be found, and the mother of a 1994 bride had married at a time when the state closely regulated the appearance of Chinese citizens.[28] During the post-Mao era, however, women, including young Hui women, could wear makeup, high heels, and feminine clothing if they wished. Many Western fashions were available in the stores, and those who had the economic resources could purchase them. Young Hui women and a great many other members of the urban Chinese populace increasingly had both the money and the will to follow such trends.

Also significant is the symbolic load wedding gowns carried: they enabled young women to express their desire for, and to a limited extent attain, a lifestyle outside the confines of the Chinese state. Wedding gowns moved women into a domestic and familial realm, an arena of life over which the state exercised comparatively little control. They attested to a degree of knowledge about the European and American-dominated world of fashion and Western lifestyles. By donning such bridal attire, Hui women created images of themselves that contravened the parochial, backward, and "primitive" stereotypes the state perpetuated on China's ethnic minorities. They carved out for themselves, their families, and their community identities that appeared prosperous, cosmopolitan, and modern.

The consumption practices surrounding Hui weddings speak to a hotly debated issue in contemporary Chinese studies: the extent to which China possesses a public sphere.[29] State-society relations in the PRC have been significantly reconfigured in the post-Mao era. Although China clearly lacks an autonomous realm in which critical opinion and political dissent can be freely expressed, this study suggests that consumption provides Chinese citizens with a means of rejecting, resisting, or simply ignoring the state and its ideals. During the mid-1990s the market was a "zone of indifference" that the PRC government tolerated to further its goals of economic development.[30] When young brides bought their bridal accoutrements, rented wedding gowns, and prepared for their wedding days, they functioned within this zone. The agency displayed by wedding gown consumers—in particular their ability to define and present their own identities without government intervention, and in the case of the Hui, against the government's own perception—suggests that with the urban consumer revolution China has taken a critical step toward the creation of a public sphere.

28. See Finnane 1996, pp. 120–23.

29. See Kraus, Chapter 13 in this volume; see also Madsen 1993; Rankin 1993; Wakeman 1993; Wasserstrom and Liu Xinyong 1995.

30. Thomas Gold says that the same was true in the 1980s; see Gold 1993.

CHAPTER 5

The Revitalization of the Marketplace

Food Markets of Nanjing

Ann Veeck

Among the more visible and colorful outcomes of the reforms of the 1980s and 1990s in urban China are the lively food markets. Though some scholars have implied that the term "socialist market economy" is an oxymoron, skeptics need look no further than these markets to see miniature socialist market economies functioning in full, vibrant health. A complex blend of state management and entrepreneurship, the markets are a vivid contrast to the prereform state food stores. People still recall standing in line to buy produce of low quality and limited variety and being treated in a surly manner to boot. Privatization of the agriculture sector, improved distribution systems, technological innovations, the liberalization of trade regulations, and competition among food retailers has resulted in active commercial areas, where wholesalers, retailers, farmers, consumers, and the state mix to engage in economic activity.

Beyond being some of the more visually conspicuous centers of commercial pursuit, food markets also provide a public forum in which to explore how the reform era has transformed the private lives of individuals in urban China. Food has long been recognized as a central vehicle for analyzing identities, roles, relationships, rituals, ceremonies—in short, all that is important in human lives. Through activities relating to the acquisition, preparation, and distribution of food, individuals communicate the nature of their relationships with others.[1] During the Mao era of food rationing and communal agriculture, choices related to food consumption were quite limited, stifling this fundamental form of communication. In urban China in the 1990s, the new abundance of food choice reaffirmed a leading role for food consumption behavior in the establishment and maintenance of relationships.

---

1. Douglas 1984 and 1975.

The high profile of food markets, not only as economic centers but also as hubs of socially significant activities, makes them useful places to investigate the societal implications of changing consumption patterns. The focus of this study is the food markets of Nanjing, the capital and largest city in Jiangsu Province. The research is part of a larger study of changing food consumption patterns carried out during the 1995–96 academic year in Nanjing in collaboration with the School of International Business of Nanjing University. Standard ethnographic field methods were used to place food shopping patterns in their full environmental context. This study draws from extensive interviews with 70 informants, which were audiotaped and then transcribed, as well as from interviews with retailers and structured observations of food shopping trips and focus groups. In addition to these qualitative methods, a random household survey of 320 Nanjing primary food shoppers was conducted in order to quantify the incidence of food shopping activities among Nanjing residents. Taken together, these research methods allow the examination of food consumption activities in Nanjing from a number of perspectives.

Specifically, the purpose of the study was to investigate the formation of newly emerging or re-emerging values and relationships in China, with the urban food markets serving as the sites of investigation. The chapter first describes the rather recent transformation of the food retail industry in China and the amount of time and money that is spent by the primary food shoppers of households engaged in food consumption activities. Next, it examines the role of the state in the management of food markets and the effect of state-imposed regulations on the expression of choice by the consumer. The following section addresses the potential for food markets to become centers of social activity among consumers and explains why this promise has not been realized in Nanjing. The chapter then explores how food markets contribute to the maintenance of valued relationships by reinforcing shoppers' ties to family members. The final section of the chapter discusses the future of Nanjing food markets, including the role the state is likely to assume in their management, and discusses how future changes will ultimately affect the expression of choice by the consumer. It is hoped that the findings from this investigation will enrich our understanding of the formation of relationships and values in urban China's changing consumption landscape.

THE TRANSFORMATION OF FOOD MARKETS

Any study related to food in China would be negligent not to acknowledge the central position that food has traditionally occupied in the Chinese culture. The celebrated position of food in Chinese society is shown in the language (the Chinese word for population, *renkou*, is literally translated as "people's mouths), the arts, religious ceremonies, rites of passages, and business exchanges. The reverence of the Chinese to practices surrounding food consumption can be traced back at least 3,000 years.[2]

In the decades between 1949 and 1979, food could not occupy its traditional elevated position in people's lives. The state exercised complete control over the food system of China, from the farms to the systems of distribution to the retail outlets. The state even dictated consumer choices to a large extent, by controlling agricultural activity and rationing most staple products, including oil, rice, meat, and bread.[3] During these decades of austerity and rationing, agricultural activity concentrated on grain production and an extremely limited number of vegetables. Although a small number of diverse varieties of vegetables grown in household plots adjacent to urban areas sometimes trickled into the cities, produce choice was by and large restricted by season and variety. During the winter season, the vegetable selection of northern residents often consisted only of potatoes, cabbage, and turnips. Reports from this period include claims that consumers would leave their baskets in front of a food counter the night before to hold their place in line to buy a poor selection of vegetables.

In a remarkably speedy turnaround, Chinese citizens today enjoy a bountiful variety of foods from which to choose as well as a transformed food retail infrastructure. It would be hard to understate the depth of these changes. As Zha writes, "This is probably the most savored aspect of the current Chinese economic prosperity: suddenly there is so much to eat!"[4] The variety and number of food retail outlets exploded during the reforms of the 1980s and 1990s. The changes include greatly expanded food markets, as well as a proliferation of small private grocery stores, supermarkets, bakeries, poultry stands, and other specialty food outlets.

As the retail infrastructure changes in China, so has the service that is provided. In the past, few food retail outlets featured self-service. Instead consumers had to point to the desired products and wait for a clerk to retrieve the items. Today the newly built supermarkets and bakeries are self-service, and customers are free to roam the stores and examine the products. A vestige of the past, however, is that very few retailers offer credit, and consumers generally must pay for their purchases with cash. Still, automatic-teller machines (ATMs) have appeared in major cities, and these cash machines, along with the pubescent credit card industry, are indicators of changes to come.

2. A number of books have described various facets of the food culture of China, including the rituals of historical dynasties, the portrayal of food in the arts, and the etiquette of food. Among the most comprehensive are E. Anderson 1988; Chang 1977; and Simoons 1991.

3. Tang and Jenkins 1990.

4. Zha 1995, p. 122.

The greater choices in food for Chinese consumers include both fresh food and processed food. Improvements in the distribution and transportation infrastructure allow food to be distributed throughout the country and imported from other countries. Farmers and vendors are becoming more aware of consumers' desires and have begun to respond to demands. For example, according to seasonal preferences, vendors offer cut and prepared food items for use in *huo guo* in the winter and wild vegetables in spring.[5] Altogether, there is a greater congruence between consumer needs and product offerings.

Once limited in supply, packaged food of many types is now readily available in China. International packaged food corporations such as Procter & Gamble, Philip Morris, and Quaker Oats have steadily increased their presence in China, competing alongside Chinese food companies with brand names such as Maling, Lion Brand, and Pagoda. Independent importers, wholesalers, and retailers increasingly represent a major force in the food distribution industry of China.[6] Production of Chinese frozen foods, reported at 2.2 million tons in 1996, is projected by the Ministry of Agriculture to increase fourfold to 8 million tons by 2000.[7]

The expansion of choice for Chinese consumers is readily apparent in the newly transformed markets of Nanjing. Nanjing has 61 major food markets scattered throughout the residential areas in the city. Results of the household survey show that most households are within 500 meters of a market, and almost all families live within 1,000 meters of a food market (see Table 5.1). As in other urban areas of China, the alternative food retail options, both state and privately managed, that have emerged in Nanjing in recent years include supermarkets, bakeries, cooked poultry and meat stands, and *xiao mai bu* (kiosks). Still, the food market remains the primary outlet for the daily food needs of Nanjing households. The use of food markets for household food shopping is a matter of choice, rather than convenience, since by 1996 virtually all food markets had a supermarket nearby. Owing both to historical lines of distribution and to the attitudes of consumers, only the rare supermarket attempts to sell fresh produce. Instead, supermarkets concentrate on packaged goods, including staple condiments, soft drinks, snack foods, canned goods, and lavishly packaged gift items. Many supermarkets are part of state-owned chains and often occupy the spaces formerly held by the state-owned grain and oil stores of the days of food rationing and coupons.

Food markets are located in a variety of places. Some are housed in large warehouses or semicovered pavilions, some occupy a crisscross of alleys, and others take over entire streets. At present, even the smaller Nanjing markets

5. Zhou Yiling 1996; Li Dingqiang 1996.
6. McNiel and Nilsson 1994.
7. *Clear Thinking Agriculture Newsletter* 1997, p. 1.

TABLE 5.1   Distance of Nanjing Residences
from Nearest Food Market, 1996

Distance (in meters)	Percent
100 or less	26
101–250	26
251–500	30
501–1,000	15
>1,000	3

SOURCE: Author's survey.

feature a wide variety of vegetables, pork, and fish year round. The bigger
Nanjing food markets can easily rival large Western gourmet supermarkets
in variety and breadth. Increasingly, semiprocessed convenience items are
appearing in many of these food markets. *Jiaozi pi* (dumpling wrappers),
ground pork, and fish balls are common. In distinct departure from the past,
some Nanjing food markets are known for their specialties, such as exotic
seafood or gourmet tofu, and for special occasions shoppers will go considerable distance to procure these treats. The food markets also often feature
food that has been cooked and prepared, most frequently *baozi, mantou,
youtiao,* and *shaobing.*[8] Many food markets incorporate (or at least tolerate)
vendors selling complementary items such as sewing notions, housewares,
and clothing. The food markets tend to attract other businesses in proximity, particularly restaurants, pharmacies, and general stores.

Most food markets open at about 6:00 in the morning and remain open
until about 6:30 in the evening, or until the final food shoppers have returned
home to prepare their meals. The vendors usually procure their produce
from wholesale markets the preceding evening in preparation for the following day or very early in the morning before the market opens. The peak
times for shopping are at 7:00 A.M. before the workday begins, at 11:00 A.M.
before lunch, and starting about 4:30 P.M. when people begin to leave work.
Still, except for a slow period from about 12:30 to 2:00 P.M. when many vendors and consumers nap, the markets remain active all day long. Retirees
shop at all times of day, factory workers have diverse work schedules, and
some state workers take breaks from their jobs to do their daily shopping.

Except for the ceiling prices for specific types of produce that are set by
the state, few venues of economic activity anywhere in the world come as close
to a model of perfect competition as these food markets. All major food items
are offered by multiple vendors within each market, so consumers have a

8. *Baozi* are steamed stuffed buns; *mantou* is steamed bread; *youtiao* is deep-fried dough;
shaobing is baked bread.

TABLE 5.2 Food Expenditures as a Proportion
of Household Income, Nanjing, 1996

Number in sample (total = 330)	Household income (monthly in rmb)*	Mean household food expenditures (monthly in rmb)*	Percentage of household income spent on food
34	750 or below	501	77
48	751–1,000	566	65
102	1,001–1,500	611	50
65	1,501–2,000	690	39
54	2,001–3,000	811	32
13	3,001 or above	912	18

* At the time of the survey 1 rmb = U.S.$0.125.
SOURCE: Author's survey.

chance to compare quality and price. Prices are established through negotiation by each vendor with each consumer. Paying the "proper price" for food items requires some skill on the part of the consumer, since the price depends on a wide range of factors. These factors can include the season of the year, the time of day, the freshness of the food item, the place of origin of the food item, the weather condition at the time of purchase, the market in which it is sold, and the price set by the competition in the immediate vicinity.

But the most notable characteristic of Nanjing food markets is the amount of time and money that Nanjing consumers spend at these sites. My survey of Nanjing households in 1996 found that the mean amount of time spent food shopping by primary food shoppers was almost six hours a week. In addition, although this proportion is expected to decrease in the future with growing incomes and increased spending on housing and medical care, in the mid 1990s, a full half of household spending in Nanjing was allocated to food, a figure consistent with the national average.[9] A closer look at these statistics, however, shows that while 52 percent is the average proportion of household budget allocated to food, the percentage spent by individual households varies greatly. Table 5.2 shows how food budgets change with income level. As expected, as incomes rise, food expenditures also increase. Even more dramatic, however, is the inverse relationship between income level and proportion of income spent on food. The lowest-income households spend 77 percent of their budget on food, and the highest-income households only 18 percent. This disparity shows that higher-income individuals tend to use their extra income to supplement expenditures other than the family meal.

9. World Resources Institute 1994.

THE STATE AND THE MARKETPLACE

The food markets in Nanjing provide a vehicle for studying the complex, simultaneously cooperative and competitive relationships that developed between the state and private enterprises throughout China in the 1990s. Each food market is a collection of hundreds of individual entrepreneurs. They are regulated by a commercial administrative office that is a branch of the government, which in each market is responsible for licensing vendors, protecting legal transactions, protecting the rights of consumers, mediating disputes between vendors, and maintaining the cleanliness of the market. Although the state no longer issues food coupons to consumers, the influence of the state in the food purchases of consumers is still visible and profound.

When the "free" markets for food first appeared in Nanjing in the early 1980s, the vendors were farmers who brought their own wares to the markets, selling the produce that they had grown in excess of their commitment to the state at whatever price the market would bear. By the mid 1990s, owing to the monthly fee of several hundred renminbi to rent a space in the market, the farmers had been largely replaced by middlemen who buy produce at Nanjing's wholesale markets. Although many of these middlemen are from farm families, often from northern Jiangsu or nearby Anhui Province, they sell other families' crops that they acquire daily from Nanjing's wholesale market.[10]

Some food markets in Nanjing provided a special area where farmers could vend their own wares for a daily rate. Consumers often preferred to buy directly from the farmers, believing that farmers are more trustworthy than vendors. Yet it seems clear that in the future consumers will have fewer opportunities to buy directly from farmers as commercially organized middlemen take over the vendor spaces. In 1996, when the then biggest indoor food market opened in Nanjing, the first of eight planned for that year, businesspeople from Shanghai, Suzhou, and Guangdong had ordered counter space.[11]

The state also played the leading role in deciding where new markets were to be located and which markets were allowed to operate. In older neighborhoods, markets were usually conveniently located and within bicycling or even walking distance from people's homes. In the newer residential areas, food markets were distributed much more sparsely. The location of food markets has a fundamental effect on the food shopping patterns of con-

10. Qu Huahan and Yuanshen Wu 1996. In the 1990s farmers could be seen arriving at the Nanjing food markets, sometimes carrying hundreds of kilograms of vegetables on their shoulders. Because they risked being fined by the market administrators for selling wares illegally, these farmers often were forced instead to sell their wares to the market vendors for low prices to avoid paying a fine and having their goods confiscated.

11. Wang Yong and Zhi Long 1996.

sumers; logically, consumers who must go greater distances to shop make fewer trips.

A dramatic example of the state's role in the management of food markets was the decision of the Nanjing government to shut down the Gulou (Drum Tower) Market in 1997 to create space for a new Sino-American resort hotel. The Gulou Market, established in the early 1980s, was Nanjing's first free market. Offering housewares and clothes as well as food, the market had functioned as an inexpensive alternative to the upscale stores in the commercially developed Gulou district. The market was well-patronized by the lower-income residents in the area and the students of nearby universities. When asked if this change was in the best interest of the consumers, the manager of the administrative office of the Gulou Market responded: "This kind of market is truly not suited for the growing market economy. It's bound to disappear. But anyway, residents are not very happy about a hotel being built here, because many will have to change their living residences to make room for the hotel."

The composition and even the layout of the markets is also determined by the local government. In 1996 the Nanjing Trade and Business Bureau decreed that all 61 of the outdoor food markets within the city limits must be enclosed within the next few years.[12] The purpose of this decree was to improve the sanitation and cleanliness of the markets. It would also provide a safe place for vendors to leave their wares overnight. The change was also certain to affect the atmosphere of the market in fundamental ways, since enclosing a retail area can affect frequency of purchase, purchasing behavior, product offerings, and prices.[13] For example, it is highly likely that the extra entry and exit barriers created by enclosing the markets will cause many customers to make fewer food shopping trips. It is a certainty, though, that moving the food markets indoors will affect experiential aspects of the food shopping trip for Nanjing shoppers.

The state also played the leading role in regulating the sanitation of the food sold at markets. The government developed the rules of sanitation to which food manufacturers and retailers must adhere and then decided how and when to enforce them according to its resources, motivations, and whims. Food manufacturers and retailers that were found to be engaged in unhygienic practices might receive a warning, be fined, or be shut down, temporarily or permanently. These infractions were then frequently reported in the state-controlled media, sometimes in frighteningly colorful detail. For example, one 1996 newspaper article reported that some bakeries were illegally reusing icing from cakes that had reached their expiration dates, making the cakes on filthy counters, and working in rooms with spider webs on

12. Zhu Gongbing 1996.
13. See, for example, Sherry 1990.

the walls.[14] Another article reported that in a routine inspection of cooked meat products 60 percent of packaged cooked meat, 80 percent of unpacked cooked meat products in stores, and 87 percent of unpacked cooked meat products on street stands did not meet the government's standards for hygiene. "The majority of unqualified products were contaminated by bacteria," the article explained.[15] In the first half of 1996, the widely read *Yangzi wanbao* (Yangzte evening news) reported several times a week on retailers or manufacturers that had been found to be engaged in unsanitary practices in the Nanjing area. Not surprisingly, these media reports affected the purchasing choices of Nanjing residents. One 24-year-old female avoided pork for a time after reading that much of the pork sold was not sanitary. Several other informants remarked that they tried to avoid buying processed foods because they doubted the quality of factory-made products.

An interesting twist in the relationship between the state and the vendors at food markets was that the government sometimes operated its own booths, which competed directly with the independent food vendors. Consumers' comparisons of state and privately run booths mirrored their ambivalent attitudes, in general, toward the privatization of the economy. Although consumers expressed an appreciation of the new choices offered as a direct result of privatization, they still preferred to buy from state-run booths. Consumers believed they were less likely to be cheated at state-run booths, where the vendors had no incentive to overcharge consumers.

Finally, to control inflation and growth, the government established the maximum prices that vendors could charge for most fresh produce. These ceiling prices were printed regularly in newspapers and posted on large signs at the market entrances. Vendors were free to set the prices of their wares as low as they wished, but they could not legally exceed the price ceilings. In 1996 in Nanjing, during the Spring Festival the government even lowered the maximum prices for food, meat, eggs, vegetables, and fish.[16]

ALLIANCES IN THE MARKETPLACE

Researchers who study open-air markets in areas of the world outside Asia have described the informal communities that can develop among the vendors and the customers.[17] Studies of food shopping in developing countries emphasize the social value to consumers of making daily excursions to the market. Public food markets have been found to be centers of social activ-

14. See, for example, Hirschman 1984.
15. Hua Li and Xiao Ding 1996.
16. Yi Qiang and Wang Yi 1996.
17. See, for example, Sherry 1990, pp. 13–15; Richardson 1982.

ity, providing a daily opportunity for consumers to mingle with their neighbors and form new friendships. Long-term, trusting relationships can develop between the food retailers and their customers, with both partners gaining economically and socially from the alliances.[18]

Since most Nanjing food shoppers made frequent shopping trips, usually at the same time to the same food market (the one closest to their homes), one might expect the shoppers and vendors to have developed social networks similar to the ones that have been observed at other nations' open-air markets. The food markets of Nanjing would seem to have the potential to become a public sphere that supports relationships beyond those of the family and the state. Yet in 1995 and 1996, little social activity could be observed in Nanjing food markets between customers and vendors.

Extended alliances can provide benefits for both partners in exchange relationships. As transactions move from discreet exchanges to relational exchanges, buyers and sellers alike experience less risk and more satisfaction in the exchanges.[19] But the main ingredient necessary for relational transactions to develop is trust. Without trust, transactions are necessarily extremely restricted.[20] In the food markets of Nanjing that I observed, there was a distinct paucity of trust. Almost all of the food shoppers expressed their distrust of the men and women who managed the booths from which they bought their fruits, vegetables, meats, and other staples. A 52-year-old shopper explained her choice of a particular vendor by saying, "I like to buy pork from this man, because, compared to other vendors, he's fair. Of course, he also cheats, but he cheats a little less than the others."

A few shoppers had established relationships with particular vendors and accrued benefits from those relationships, such as the ability to order special products in advance, but most consumers were cynical about their relationships with vendors. The shoppers claimed that vendors cheated them in a number of ways: by selling unsanitary or counterfeit products, charging unreasonable prices, and using scales that inflated the weight of products. This last practice seemed the most prevalent. To defend themselves against these dishonest vendors, many consumers brought their own scales with them to the market and reweighed products themselves, particularly more costly items. Many claimed that they weighed everything with their own scales before paying for their produce. One consumer felt that it was enough just to show vendors that she carried her own scale to be confident that she would be charged fairly.

Some food markets placed a public scale prominently in the middle of

18. See Goldman 1974; Kaynak 1985; Kaynak and Tamer 1982; Yavas, Kaynak, and Borak 1981.

19. Dwyer, Schurr, and Oh 1987; see also MacNeil 1980.

20. Schurr and Ozanne 1985; Douglas 1989.

the market to allow consumers to check the weight of their produce before they paid the vendor. One market manager said that he routinely performed surprise checks of vendors' scales. If he found a vendor's scale to be faulty, the scale was destroyed. Any vendor found to persistently use faulty scales was expelled from the market.

The phenomenon of food shoppers routinely arming themselves with their own scales and unapologetically reweighing their selections demonstrates their open distrust of the men and women who sell produce. It represents a deep-seated opinion that, by nature, vendors are dishonest and that smart shoppers must simply cope with that fact. The attitude is comparable to many Americans' opinion of used-car salespeople. A 54-year-old female matter-of-factly explained: "Of course, vendors try to make as big a profit as they can off of us. They have to make a living, don't they? But you can protect yourself. To keep from being cheated by their scales, you can bring your own scale with you. If the price is unfair, you can bargain and compare the prices of other vendors. And we have the freedom to decide what to buy and what not to buy." To be fair, it should also be pointed out that most consumers would agree with one woman who said, "Some vendors aren't too bad."

Clearly, the distrust of vendors can discourage the formation of long-term buyer-seller relationships. The distrust has it origins in the long period of time that capitalist activities were illegal. When the reforms were first initiated, only the few and the daring were willing to risk going into business for themselves for fear that the reforms would be only temporary. Many of the first entrepreneurs were said to be ex-criminals whose reputations were already ruined. In addition, as in all urban areas of China, Nanjing has a "floating" population of men and women from rural farming households, many in search of employment. A significant proportion of vendors in Nanjing markets are part of this rural floating population, and the traditional rural-urban friction exists between them and their customers. At the turn of the twenty-first century, however, a diverse group of people has new incentives to become self-employed businesspeople. With the recent decline in work security, many state employees, particularly middle-aged female factory workers, lost what they thought were lifetime jobs, and new high-school graduates became responsible for finding their own employment. Thus, a much more diverse group of people have elected to try their hand at selling food. These changes in the composition of the vendors could alter the dynamics of buyer-seller relationships.

Another factor affecting buyer-seller relationships in Nanjing food markets was the transient nature of the food vendor. Such positions only became available after the mid-1980s, and food vendors often considered their jobs temporary. Many of the vendors come from Anhui Province with plans to stay just a few months, earn a bit of money, and then return to their families. Certainly this situation deters relational exchanges. Several consumers remarked that they knew none of the vendors because they seemed to change so often. By contrast, many vendors in Latin American markets are literally born in the market to vendor families.[21]

Another factor that affected the nature of buyer-seller relationships in food markets was that, in contrast to markets in other developing economies,[22] credit exchange was not common in Nanjing. As credit is introduced into an exchange relationship, the alliance by nature lasts longer.[23] When vendors offer credit, they must go beyond the market relationship with their customers to learn whether they are trustworthy.[24] A credit relationship can reduce risk for both parties and create dependencies and loyalties.[25] In Nanjing's food markets, no money, no deal. The lack of a tradition of credit exchange in Nanjing markets reduced the opportunities for a private buyer-seller community to develop.

When consumers are reluctant to form enduring relationships with retailers, each exchange becomes a discrete transaction, and consumers must then rely on the state or their own ingenuity to protect themselves from fraud. Since the concept of forming a relationship with retailers outside of state control is new, the dynamics of these relationships could change quickly.

PERSONAL CHOICE AND THE MARKETPLACE

As described in the previous section, food markets in Nanjing were not the hub of social activities among consumers and vendors that I anticipated before undertaking my study. Nevertheless, I found that food markets provided a valuable setting in which to investigate the social ties of urban shoppers. The most visible signs of important relationships in the marketplace turned out to be the shopping activities on behalf of family members.

The proportion of people's time and income spent in the food markets of Nanjing provided some insight into who and what consumers value in their lives. Greater competition in the workplace and increased pursuit of leisure activities led to a faster pace of life for Nanjing residents. More retail food establishments, including small grocery stores, supermarkets, and restaurants of all sizes and variety offered competition to the food markets. More processed food choices, including instant noodles, frozen *jiaozi* (dumplings), and instant cereals, allowed consumers to prepare meals quickly at home. Finally, appliances with the potential of transforming food consumption pat-

---

21. Swetman 1990.
22. Goldman 1974, p. 10.
23. Dwyer, Schurr, and Oh 1987.
24. Swetman 1990, pp. 265–68.
25. Clark 1991.

terns appeared in Nanjing households, including rice cookers, microwaves, food processors, and most significant, refrigerators.

While these dramatic technological changes in the food retail environment undoubtedly restructured the shopping patterns of the Chinese, it is important not to overlook the equally vital role of consumer choice in the shaping of consumption habits.[26] The trends listed above would seem to suggest that Nanjing consumers could make fewer food shopping trips. And in fact, some consumers said they shop less than they used to. Nevertheless, daily trips to the food market continued to be the norm for most households.

My survey found that in about three-fourths of Nanjing households at least one family member bought food for the family at least six days a week. There were several reasons for the persistence of the daily food shopping habit. For example, although 95 percent of Nanjing households in 1996 had refrigerators, many Nanjing residents believed that once food was placed in the refrigerator it was no longer fresh. A 51-year-old female explained: "We don't put vegetables in the refrigerator because we like them fresh. If they are stored out of the refrigerator they will be more fresh, more tasty, and have better nutrition. If you put them in the refrigerator, when you cook them it will change their taste. Putting vegetables in the cold outside is different than putting them in the refrigerator—it doesn't change the taste."

Inventories of refrigerators revealed that most refrigerators were sparsely filled and not meant to prevent daily trips to the market. Refrigerators did provide convenience, but using them to store vegetables for several days conflicted sharply with the values and attitudes of many consumers.

Likewise, the increase in availability of processed foods did not obviate the need for frequent shopping trips. The survey of Nanjing households showed that some types of packaged and prepared foods were important staples for Nanjing families. For example, within 30 days of the survey, 80 percent of Nanjing households had purchased cooked duck, 70 percent had purchased instant ramen noodles, and 56 percent had purchased packaged tofu. (see Table 5.3 for other frequently purchased processed items).[27] Still, the processed food was usually served alongside the home-cooked main dish rather than as a main course. Certainly, at the time of this research there was no sign that the purchase of processed food was contributing to, or an outcome of, a trend toward consuming food alone, as some studies have found has happened in the West.[28]

The emphasis on serving fresh foods, and, even more important the en-

26. Mukerji 1983; and Sack 1992.

27. It should be noted that the survey was taken within 30 days of Spring Festival, the most important holiday in China. As such, the purchase incidence of some food items, such as duck and beef, may have been inflated from the incidence over a normal 30-day period.

28. Fischler 1980.

TABLE 5.3   Proportion of Nanjing Households
That Purchased Selected Packaged or Prepared
Food Items within One 30-Day Period, 1996

Item	Percent
Roasted/salted duck	80
Instant ramen noodles	70
Salty snacks	58
Packaged tofu	56
Cooked *baozi* (steamed stuffed buns)	54
Cooked *youtiao* (deep-fried dough)	54
Roasted beef	52
Ground pork	41
Julienned pork	40
Cooked *mantou* (steamed bread)	40

SOURCE: Author's survey.

during mind-set that defined food as "fresh" only when it had been bought that day and not refrigerated, can be viewed as part of a larger set of values that emphasized the centrality of the family unit and the family members' responsibility to look after their own. When food consumption is interpreted as more than an economic activity and properly examined as a fundamental part of the identities, roles, and rituals of the people who buy the food, it does not seem illogical for busy consumers to habitually conduct daily shopping trips.[29] Indeed, food shoppers in Nanjing again and again framed their food purchase choices in terms of the benefits the food items would bring their family members, particularly children.[30] The duty to please and nourish their children dictated the need to conduct daily shopping trips. Further, this attitude seem to be shared equally by male and female primary shoppers.

The importance of the children's needs in making food choices was represented poignantly by a 57-year-old female retiree who was left with an empty nest:

> I am often puzzled when I have to decide what to eat every day. At our age, we have neither old parents nor young children living with us. Since before we always cared about them more than we cared about ourselves, it is only in recent years that we've been able to think of ourselves. One should not save money

29. See Douglas 1984; Farb and Armelagos 1980; and Heisley and Levy 1991.
30. See Davis and Sensenbrenner's chapter in this volume for information related to the role of the child in household expenditures.

by eating poor-quality food. I think it's true that you look after your children by looking after yourselves. So I pay a lot of attention to nutrition. I will not buy fashionable food.

Note that the woman has solved her dilemma by continuing to frame her food choices in terms of taking care of her children, even in their absence.

In most Nanjing households with children, the needs of the children were given first priority, which included satisfying their preferences and giving them the highest-quality food. This pattern was evident even in multiple-generation households, whether a parent or a grandparent served as the primary food shopper. This is a distinct departure from studies of Western families, in which researchers have found a hierarchy of food distribution that places men first, women second, and children third.[31]

Although the role of food shopper was often shared, the household survey revealed that women conducted the majority of the shopping for approximately two-thirds of Nanjing households. When asked why the person who assumed the role of food shopper for the family had that particular chore, many families claimed to assign the duty on the basis of who had the most time. In one Nanjing household in which a tailor had recently started a moderately successful business out of her home, her factory-worker husband had assumed most of the food shopping and cooking duties in the face of her ten-hour days, seven days a week.

Predictably, in other households the food shoppers assumed their role simple because it was expected of them, and sometimes they were not entirely happy with this responsibility. One 45-year-old male explained the routine in his own household as follows: "I do almost all of the shopping and the cooking. My wife hardly every shops for food, so she doesn't know how to do it well. It started when my wife was pregnant. I wanted her to rest, so I did all of the shopping and cooking. But then, even after she was no longer pregnant, the pattern continued, and I still did all the shopping and cooking. Some days I don't mind, but some days, it is a real bore."

Whether the shopping role was assumed by preference or default, many consumers expressed an opinion that food shopping was a creative job, requiring skill and experience, and seemed to take pride in their ability to perform the chore well. This pride spanned a number of functions, including choosing the freshest food, bargaining for the lowest prices, selecting nutritious food, and again, taking care of their families. In short, personal choice was manifested in the marketplace most prominently by the large number of primary food shoppers in Nanjing who conducted daily shopping trips to provide their families with fresh, nutritious foods.

31. Charles and Kerr 1988; and DeVault 1991.

THE FUTURE OF FOOD MARKETS

Using the first-person experience of consumers in food markets, this chapter has explored the formation of new networks and values in Nanjing in the 1990s. Although environmental trends suggest that Nanjing shoppers will visit their food markets less frequently in the future, personal choice and habits suggest that most food shoppers will continue to conduct daily shopping trips for fresh food for some years to come. Frequent food shopping trips seem to be an important way for food shoppers to demonstrate the importance of their families and their responsibility for nurturing and pleasing their family members.

Nanjing adults' frequent use of these vital and highly visible markets offers them an opportunity to develop new alliances, yet in Nanjing in the mid-1990s there was little evidence of the sense of community that has been documented in the markets of other nations. Despite the fact that most Nanjing shoppers patronized the same markets almost daily, the shoppers generally did not develop loyalties to any one vendor. The single most important reason shoppers gave for this lack of loyalty was lack of trust in the vendors. They appreciated the new choices available as a direct result of privatization, but they lacked trust in the entrepreneurs who made it possible for them to enjoy more options.

The role of the state in the management of the market can have a great effect on the formation of seller-buyer relationships. The larger the state's presence in the market, the less the opportunity for alliances to develop between the private sellers and the buyers. Yet consumers seemed to welcome the state's oversight of vendors, who did not police themselves. In the future, it is likely that vendors will form horizontal alliances, formal or informal, among themselves. Alliances among vendors would create a unified body to negotiate with the state, as well as allow some much-needed self-policing.

As for the future evolution of Nanjing food markets, there are at least three possible scenarios. First, food markets may remain more or less on their present course, in which case there will be little opportunity for social relationships to develop in the marketplace for quite some time. Second, it is possible that that as avenues of employment become more stable the job of food vendor will become a more permanent position. Individuals will sell produce in the same locations for years, developing specializations and differentiating themselves from other vendors through some combination of price, quality, and service. As loyalties develop among patrons, the vendor will have a stable customer base and the consumer a stable source of supply. To ensure loyalty, vendors will police themselves, and the state will retreat quietly, with no need to exercise a strong presence. The economic relationships among buyers and shoppers will begin to expand to social relationships. A sense of community will develop in the market, with buyers and sellers looking after

each other in a number of ways. The establishment of this community will begin to have far-reaching effects, sapping strength from traditional sources of power.

The third and most likely scenario is that the commercialization of food retailing and wholesaling will continue at an even greater pace. Although the enclosing of all Nanjing food markets will offer important benefits to both retailers and consumers, this simple change is likely to have dramatic effects on the structure of the food markets. At the very least, the new structures are bound to lead to higher rental fees and greater entry barriers for individual entrepreneurs. Increasingly, the selling spaces will be rented by commercial organizations rather than by individuals. These organizations will be based both in Nanjing and throughout the country, and probably even outside the country. Some of the food markets will be completely privatized and employ workers from a single corporation, rather than being loose organizations of individual entrepreneurs. Rather than developing into minicommunities of buyers and sellers, the Nanjing food markets will likely develop the impersonal culture of large supermarkets in the West.

In summary, unlike in other areas of the world where open-air food markets are common, the privatization of food markets in Nanjing did not foster the development of a public sphere in which shoppers meet to engage in social activities. Nevertheless, the food markets of contemporary Nanjing were vital with respect to the maintenance and enhancement of family relationships. The expanded food choices available in the 1990s allowed food shoppers to nurture, please, and, sometimes spoil their family members within their means. As the dynamics of the retail food industry evolve and the rhythm of people's lives shifts to accommodate China's changing social environment, relationships between food markets and shoppers will probably change as well. For the first one or two decades of the twenty-first century, however, frequent shopping trips to buy the freshest possible food to provide tasty and nutritious meals for family members will remain the norm.

CHAPTER 6

To Be Relatively Comfortable
in an Egalitarian Society

Hanlong Lu

In 1979, when Deng Xiaoping made his general plan for economic reform, he proposed that a minimal goal of China's modernization was to allow the Chinese people to achieve a *"xiaokang"* or relatively comfortable life by the end of the century. In 1984 he concretized this objective by defining a *xiaokang* lifestyle as one with a per capita GNP of U.S.$800 by the year 2000.[1]

The concept of *xiaokang* first appeared in the classical *Record of Rites* (*Li Ji*) from the Warring States period (475 B.C.–221 B.C.),[2] where it identified the society that followed the era of "great equality" (*datong*). In the age of "great equality," heaven and man were in harmony, people cared for one another as if they were kin, and there was neither hoarding nor theft.[3] But when the Great Way was lost, "the world was (divided into) families. Everyone loved

---

This chapter was translated by Ken K. Liu and edited by Deborah Davis. Translator's note: The Chinese title of the paper is " '*Datong*' *shehui li de* '*xiaokang*' *fazhan mubiao*." It means, literally, " 'Small well-being' development in a 'great equality' society." As will become clear in the chapter, Lu intends the juxtaposition of two key Chinese terms, 'small well-being' and 'great sameness' to convey a sense of tension similar to that contained in the phrase "socialist market economy." In the body of the paper, however, I have chosen to gloss the term *xiaokang* (literally, "small well-being") as "relative comfort" to highlight the sense of comparison implied in contemporary usage.

1. *Deng Xiaoping wenxuan* 1983, vol. 2, p. 237. According to the exchange rate at the time, a per capita GNP of U.S.$800 would place China within the ranks of lower-middle-income nations.

2. Translator's note: See *The Li Ki* 1885, (henceforth *LK*) vols. 27–28. See also Derk Bodde's translation of the passages on "great equality" and "relative comfort" cited by Lu in his translation of Fung Yu-lan 1952, p. 377–78. I have modified their translations substantially.

3. In the chapter "Evolutions of Rites" (*Liyun*) in the *Record of Rites*: "When the Great Way was practiced, the world was common to all. People chose the virtuous and talented (to govern), and they spoke truthfully and cultivated harmony. Thus they did not love only their own

only his family and his own children, and each accumulated wealth and exerted himself for his own benefit."[4] This society of "relative comfort," where people pursued private interests and gave priority to advancing family interests, was therefore considered morally inferior to the society of "great equality." Nevertheless, the concept of "relative comfort" or *xiaokang* came to represent an accepted middling sort of society where family interests were paramount, inequality persisted, and government imposed laws to regulate people's behavior.

Within this society of relative well-being there was also the folk notion of the "relatively comfortable family" (*xiaokangzhijia*), which referred to a family of modest wealth living securely above subsistence worries. In the 1990s, the National Bureau of Statistics and the Chinese Academy of Social Sciences estimated that when China's per capita GNP reached $800–1,000, residents of China would have met this standard. The consumption pattern would shift from one focused on meeting survival needs to one that could consider needs of pleasure and personal development. People would spend less than less than half of their incomes on food and increase spending on discretionary items.[5] Home ownership would become the norm, and people would be able to afford to travel domestically at least once a year. The income gap between urban and rural areas would shrink, and average life expectancy would reach 72 years. Both the health of the population and the

---

parents and raise only their own children, and they made sure that the aged were supported till their death, the able-bodied were fruitfully employed, and the young were educated. They also made sure that widows, widowers, orphans, and the disabled and diseased were provided for. Men had their occupations, and women had their homes. People disliked throwing away goods, but they didn't want to hoard them for themselves. They disliked not contributing their labor, but they didn't want to labor only for themselves. In this way, there were no secret schemings nor robbers, filchers, or rebellious traitors. Hence the outer doors were not shut, and this was the period of 'great equality.'" [Cf. *LK*, pp. 364–66, and Bodde, pp. 377–78. Tr.]

The idea of "great equality" and its principle that "the world is common to all" have been important throughout modern Chinese history. The late Qing thinker and reformer Kang Youwei wrote *The Book of Great Equality* (translated by Laurence G. Thompson as *Ta T'ung Shu: The One-World Philosophy of K'ang Yu-wei*) in which he advocated a world where there would be "no national boundaries, no kings and emperors, no differences between rich and poor, and all people would be equal and the world would be common to all" (K'ang Yu-wei 1958). The influence of the social philosophy of "great equality" also appeared in the work of the republican revolutionary Sun Yat-sen. Later, Mao Zedong would combine this egalitarian ideal with Marxism and communism to build socialism under the leadership of the Communist Party.

4. Translator's Note: Cf. *LK*, pp. 366–67. Here, however, I have followed Bodde in rendering "*tianxiaweijia*" as "all the world is (divided into) families." Fung Yu-lan 1952, p. 378.

5. Translator's Note: The original text reads: "When Engel's index would be below 0.5. . . ." Ernst Engel (1821–1896), a German statistician, formulated "Engel's Law," which states that expenditure on food drops as a proportion of income when income rises. Thus "Engel's index" refers to the percentage of income spent on food. Here, the Chinese government uses it to define one aspect of its goal of a "relatively comfortable" living standard.

quality of life would have essentially matched that of the average level of middle-income nations.[6]

After the economic growth of the 1980s and 1990s, study after study has reaffirmed that residents of China's coastal cities have reached the *xiaokang* standard. However few have dealt with the complexity of the historical legacies of four decades of socialist redistribution and CCP reeducation. Instead, previous research has simply compared the growth in discretionary expenditures and rising per capita income and ignored how 30 years of striving toward communism shaped both people's understanding of their current prosperity and the institutional complexity of the contemporary era. During the fervent communization drive initiated by Mao Zedong in 1958 and during the Cultural Revolution in the second half of the 1960s, Chinese leadership under Mao blended the traditional ideal of "great equality" with the ideal "communist society" described by Marx. Under the banner of this somewhat heterodox ideology, Chinese leaders of the 1950s built the new China. However, by 1979, faced with a social, economic, and ideological impasse, Deng explicitly reached back into the Chinese classics and endorsed a marriage of *xiaokang* and market socialism. Thus, in the popular consciousness, Deng's political slogan relegitimized the pursuit of personal and family comforts. It also suggested that new social stratification would be unavoidable and that there would be new rules to regulate economic and social life. However, how Deng's hybrid market socialism would evolve was unclear to both the leaders and the citizenry. On one hand it was clear that the egalitarian ideals and socialist institutions embedded within the "socialist" component of market socialism would not disappear overnight, but the ways in which the past would persist were unknown. To explore these tensions between old and new, this chapter analyzes changes in household consumption in Shanghai, one of the first cities where residents achieved per capita incomes of $800. By exploring the determinants of variation in consumption levels, I explain how the emergence of a relatively comfortable standard of living must be understood in the context of the persistence of the redistributive economic and social practices of a residual egalitarian societal framework.

Three premises guide my observations and analysis. First, the Chinese pursuit of relative comfort began from the basis of a low level of consumption and a high degree of egalitarianism. Second, the government has reformed its Communist central planning economy by boldly adopting a market economy to allocate resources and by acknowledging that it is permissible for some to get rich first; but at the same time it has continued to affirm the superiority of socialism. Third, the juxtaposition of the terms "socialism" and "market economy" can be read as articulating "public" and "private" value-orientation, and therefore an investigation of the degree to which personal

6. Zu Qingfang 1992, p. 89.

consumption occurs more in a socialist than a market context reflects the relative positions of the public and the private spheres in Chinese society.

The numerical data on consumption used here come from published government statistics and my own quality-of-life surveys of urban residents conducted between 1987 and 1995. The subjects of the surveys were more than one thousand Shanghai residents randomly drawn from the city's urban population. Shanghai is the most populous as well as the largest industrial and commercial city in China. During the 1990s the city's main social and economic development indices had reached the "relatively comfortable" level. Therefore consumption trends in Shanghai can provide insights into the near future of other cities on the brink of achieving a relatively comfortable standard of living.

"KEEP THE WEALTH WITH THE PEOPLE":[7] THE MARKETIZATION OF RESOURCE ALLOCATION

The first decade of economic reform in China created new wealth and altered the norms by which profits and resources were distributed to individuals and among different enterprises. Under the previous framework of central planning and collective ownership, the state controlled almost all means of production, appropriated most of the income from production, and allocated social wealth through redistributive mechanisms. In this system, where redistributive power dominated, many goods had been decommodified or demonetized. In rural villages, the communes maintained a relatively self-sufficient collective economy where cash changed hands only infrequently. Even in cities, many goods and services were obtained without money. For example, because of shortages, certain essential goods were rationed through government coupons, and virtually all luxuries were available only to foreigners or high-ranking cadres. The whole society lived at a level of low income and low consumption, egalitarianism was dominant, and the consumer goods economy was underdeveloped.

At the same time, there were no scientific criteria to indicate whether redistribution under central planning was to be directed toward consumption or accumulation. Owing to the rejection of the market, the ratio of accumulation to consumption was largely decided subjectively. For a long time, while the national income increased, the relative share devoted to consumption declined and the people's living standard stagnated. According to statistics provided by the Shanghai Labor Bureau, the highest real average wage between 1950 and 1980 was in 1952 (adjusted for price fluctuations). Table 6.1 gives the figures for total wages (*zhigong gongzi zonge*) and total in-

7. Translator's Note: "*cangfuyumin.*"

TABLE 6.1   Income and Workers' Wages in Shanghai, 1952–1990
(in 100,000,000 rmb)

Year	Total income	Total wages	Index of real average wage (1952 = 100)
1952	33.45	9.93	100
1957	63.50	14.79	99.2
1962	74.10	15.00	90.4
1965	103.28	—	—
1978	245.51	28.12	81.8
1980	282.42	38.10	99.5
1983	303.49	42.91	100.4
1985	409.70	68.99	134.7
1987	473.61	94.78	156.6
1990	617.22	146.78	162.8

SOURCE: Shanghai Labor Bureau.
NOTE: There are no wage data for 1965 and no income or wage data for 1965 to 1975.

TABLE 6.2   Distribution of National Product, 1978–1994
(percent)

Year	State income	Enterprise incomes	Individual incomes	Urban	Rural
1978	31.6	17.9	50.5	20.1	30.4
1979	27.2	19.2	53.6	20.5	33.1
1980	23.7	19.6	56.7	22.0	34.7
1981	21.7	17.9	60.4	21.8	38.6
1982	20.5	19.9	59.6	21.7	37.9
1983	20.6	19.2	60.2	21.3	38.9
1984	20.9	18.2	60.9	21.9	39.0
1985	20.9	17.7	61.4	23.4	38.0
1986	19.3	17.9	62.8	25.7	37.1
1987	16.9	19.4	63.7	26.8	36.9
1988	14.5	20.9	64.6	27.3	37.3
1989	14.4	21.5	64.1	27.9	36.2
1990	14.5	21.5	64.0	29.1	34.9
1991	13.7	21.9	64.4	30.6	33.8
1992	11.6	20.1	68.3	34.6	33.7
1993	11.5	20.7	67.8	36.7	31.1
1994	10.9	19.5	69.6	38.0	31.6

SOURCE: China Planning Commission, cited in Wang Chunzhen 1995, p. 59.
NOTE: "State income" includes state tax revenues and local extra-fiscal budgetary income, but excludes debt income, social welfare, and pensions. "Individual incomes" include all remuneration for labor, incomes from property, and financial transfers such as welfare and government scholarships. "Enterprise incomes" include the after-tax incomes of enterprises (including rural collectives) and administrative and financial units of the government, excluding benefits and bonuses paid to individuals.

come (*guomin shouru*) in Shanghai. Here we clearly see the steady decline in the worker's share of total income before the Deng reforms. In the early 1950s, wages equaled almost 30 percent of total income; by 1978 they had fallen to 11.5 percent. Only in 1990 did they regain their 1957 level.

The above figures indicate that during the first 30 years after 1949, Shanghai urban households had limited consumption power and that consumption levels failed to grow even as the economy developed. However, growth in public consumption, especially in expenditures on workers' welfare benefits and insurance, did produce significant transfers of the total income to the urban residents and raised residents' standard of living. In state-owned work units, labor insurance premiums equaled 12.3 percent of total wages in 1952, 39.8 percent in 1986, and 45.11 percent in 1994. Thus labor insurance premiums as a type of transfer payment reduced income inequality and effectively increased the general level of consumption. At the same time, however, reliance on transfer payments retarded the development of consumption power and created significant inequalities among employees of different enterprises.

By increasing the role of market transactions in resource allocation, the Deng reforms directly reduced the state's dominant role in the economy and radically altered the distribution of the national product and national income. According to the calculations of the National Planning Committee (see Table 6.2), after 1978 the distribution of total national income was characterized by two trends: (1) a steady decline in the state's share of total national income and (2) a steady increase in personal incomes.

FROM PLANNED DISTRIBUTION
TO OPEN SUPPLY OF CONSUMER GOODS

In the years of central planning, urban families relied heavily on direct allocation of goods and services from their employers or from the agents of the municipal government. From milk and cakes for the newborn baby to funerary items for the deceased, everything fell within the range of government-planned supply. Housing was assigned according to criteria of hardship, and rents took less than 3 percent of monthly income. Consumer goods were distributed along two parallel tracks. Staple foodstuffs and daily necessities such as cotton cloth and fuel coal were distributed on a per capita basis; "special" items such as furniture, bicycles, and watches were bought with coupons issued to households on special occasions (such as when a couple got married). It has been calculated that the Shanghai city government at one time issued as many as 32 kinds of coupons. And after the establishment of the National Planning Commission in 1953, the categories of industrial products directly distributed through the commission increased from 110 to more than 300 between 1953 and 1957; those supplied through central allocation increased from 227 to 532.[8]

Planning and supply by coupons distorted the relationship between production and demand and hindered the development of monetized consumer goods markets. At the same time, there existed an "underground" market for the exchange and trading of coupons. This illegal market really never disappeared in all the years of central planning. It was a feeble sign of the private sphere under the collective economy. It began in the exchange of coupons for cooking oil and nonstaple foods and later developed into the exchange of industrial product coupons and priced trading of all kinds of coupons. In the mid-1970s, the price of a coupon for a black-and-white television was just about equivalent to the actual money price. The black market in coupons for industrial goods also profited officials in departments responsible for dispensing coupons and overseeing product circulation. The exchange of power for material gains in consumer products eventually developed into a series of corruption scandals involving the distribution and purchase of production materials and industrial goods, when two-track price reform began in the 1980s.

Such distortions of supply and demand due to planned distribution and insufficient supply actually persisted for a considerable time after reform began. Thus before grain coupons were finally abolished across the country in 1993, peasants often went to the city to trade agricultural products for grain coupons. In major cities like Beijing and Shanghai, they usually exchanged eggs for grain coupons. "Egg women" (*maidannü*) (most of them were young women) carried baskets of eggs through the cities' streets and alleys, ostensibly selling eggs but actually exchanging eggs for grain coupons. At its height, Shanghai had an estimated 20,000 "egg women." Later they also sold used light industrial products to trade for grain coupons. The reason this type of barter existed was that a kilo of grain purchased with coupons cost less than the procurement price the government paid villagers for their harvest. Hence the "egg women" got coupons not to buy food but to buy grain in bulk in the cities. They then transported it back to their villages to sell to the government! There thus arose the peculiar situation in which the city "produced" food, the countryside "bought" food, and "egg women" dealt in industrial products.

Planned distribution and the low level of private consumption led to a consumption egalitarianism parallel to income egalitarianism. Under the planning system, the vast majority of people wore the same kinds of clothes and ate the same kinds of food. They all took the bus or rode a bicycle to work and on Sundays they stayed home to do laundry or visited relatives. They had the same special dishes and drinks on holidays. To a certain extent, this pattern of "massified" (*dazhonghua*) consumption explains the rapid

---

8. Liu Guoguan 1988, p. 238.

spread of refrigerators, televisions, and washing machines into every house-hold within a few years after the start of reform; if one family purchased an item, all families in the neighborhood followed suit. Also, massified consumption was manifest at the ideological level. Because the individual was not allowed to own productive materials under the system of planned distribution, ownership of consumer goods became the major form of personal wealth. Hence, in the mid-1980s when reform began in the cities, "make money, spend hard" (*nengzheng huihua*) became a fashionable new lifestyle widely reported in the media. And the several instances of panic buying by ordinary people as a reaction to price rises were clearly also influenced by the idea that personal ownership of consumer goods was the best way to protect family assets.

Central planning suppressed the normal processes of personal consumption by rejecting normal market mechanisms. In the total consumption structure of the society, public consumption enjoyed a commanding position. It became the most direct expression of economic growth, while household and personal consumption were ignored or even suppressed. Low income and low consumption, planned distribution, and shortage formed a vicious cycle in the lives of the Chinese people, transforming the ideal of "great equality" into shackles. Personal consumption was constrained. Moreover, consumer goods were of very low quality, and there was little choice or diversity. Economic reform simultaneously opened the two floodgates of demand and supply. Two torrents converged and opened up the space for private economic activities in China, enriching the content of people's material and cultural consumption and raising their quality of life.

CHANGING CONSUMPTION PATTERNS
AND THE INTERACTION BETWEEN PUBLIC AND PRIVATE

By the late 1990s, after more than ten years of reform, rising personal incomes, and a growing abundance of material goods and commercial services, Shanghai households had radically improved their standard of living and quality of life.[9] On the one hand, these gains simply document a transformation of material conditions. On the other hand, they reflect the changing relationship between the individual and the state as well as new boundaries between the private and public spheres. First let me briefly summarize the material gains by describing broad shifts in the consumption of food, clothing, housing, transportation, and household goods and services.

9. In 1987 the per capita income for China's urban population was 316 yuan. It was 3,179 yuan in 1994. With 1978 as the base, the per capita income index was 237.7 in 1994. *ZGTJNJ 1995*, p. 257.

Food and Drink

Traditionally, Shanghainese have spent a lower percentage of total income on food than residents of other Chinese cities. During the 1990s the percentage spent on food consumed at home dropped even lower as the dietary pattern of the Shanghainese underwent enormous changes. The increase in people's consumption power and the growing abundance of foodstuffs led people to buy better-quality foods and more nonstaple foods. The proportion of grain in food purchases has steadily declined while consumption of high-protein food and other healthy food has clearly risen.[10] Meanwhile, as the tempo of urban life accelerated and the work-unit cafeteria system changed, fast-food and takeout industries enjoyed robust growth. America's Kentucky Fried Chicken alone had 27 franchises in the city, and restaurants of all price levels were common. According to some estimates, in 1994 the Shanghainese already spent 11 percent of their total food expenditures on eating out.[11]

Changes in food consumption also altered the meaning of private and public consumption and spending. For example, work-unit-operated dining halls have gradually disappeared, and many employee cafeterias have been commercialized by subcontracting out the lunch service to former managers. Work units have also largely stopped distributing nonstaple foods. However, another kind of "group consumption" (*jituan xiaofei*) has intensified—namely, feasting on public accounts. Before reform, the state had strict regulations on banquets for guests and business clients. Now such regulations exist in name only. Restaurants of all types cater to a sizable clientele who charge their bills to public accounts, and in this way many "private" restaurants have functionally become public arenas for socializing and conducting business.

Clothing

Shanghai has always led China in clothing fashions. Even during the Cultural Revolution, when the consumption level was low and efforts to be fashionable were viewed as signs of reactionary values or bourgeois taste, the Shanghainese still modified their state-issued work uniforms in various ways to make them more fashionable. In the 1980s, when clothing from Taiwan, Hong Kong, and Macau arrived in Shanghai's clothing markets, imitating and retailing their styles became trendy. Since then, there has been a clear

---

10. According to sample studies by the Shanghai Statistical Bureau, the per capita grain consumption in Shanghai was 148.56 kg in 1980 and 79.2 kg in 1994. See *Shanghai tongji nianjian 1995* (henceforth *SHTJNJ 1995*), p. 66.

11. Ibid., p. 66.

tendency toward greater individuation in Shanghainese dress, as well as a deliberate effort by people to develop a distinctive "Shanghai style" (*haipai*). The Shanghainese choose their clothes carefully but are restrained in their purchases of brand-name wear. Although 10,000 renminbi (rmb) leather jackets and 1,000 rmb shirts are displayed in high-class stores, the average Shanghainese maintains a level of clothing expenditure at around 10 to 15 percent of total spending.[12] Meanwhile, our surveys on quality of life in Shanghai have found that Shanghainese put clothing expenditures in the same category as spending on socializing and culture and leisure.[13] Thus it seems that clothing purchases both enhance an individual's wardrobe and appearance and imply participation in the public sphere.

Housing

As in all other Chinese cities, there was no housing market in Shanghai before reform started. Rather, the state or the work unit distributed residential units according to the needs of applicants and the resources of the enterprise. In February 1991 the city government passed the "Plan for the Implementation of Housing System Reform in Shanghai," which proclaimed the twin goals of raising rents to be closer to market values and popularizing home ownership.[14] The initial consequences of these efforts to recommodify residential real estate, however, reveal that strongly nonmonetized economic practices of the prereform era continued to pattern urban consumption.

Since 1994 the government and various work units have systematically sold existing housing stock to their occupants at an average price of one year's household income. Within two years, 50 percent of public housing had been sold and 45 percent of Shanghai households had become home owners.[15] In this way, enterprises commodified real estate by turning collective property into fixed private assets.

Water and electricity sales have also been recommodified. Fees for these public utilities have gone up, and as modern amenities such as flush toilets, hot-water heaters, and gas stoves have become widespread, cash expenditures have rapidly increased. In addition, 40 percent of Shanghai homes have installed telephones and two-thirds subscribe to cable television (see Table 6.3). Nevertheless, because subsidies for housing costs continued through 1994

12. *ZGTJNJ 1995*, p. 270. Even in absolute terms, Shanghainese spent less than urban residents of nearby Zhejiang Province.

13. This conclusion is based on a factor analysis of various categories of personal consumption. See Lu Hanlong 1990.

14. *Shanghai zhuzhai 1993*, pp. 136–41.

15. This figure was supplied by the Shanghai Municipal Real Estate Bureau.

TABLE 6.3   Ownership of Consumer Items
in Survey Households, 1995
(percent)

Consumer durables	Own	Domestic	Imported	Domestic and imported
Color TV	93.6	47.9	41.2	4.5
Black and white TV	30.7	27.3	3.5	0
Refrigerator*	94.4	72.0	21.7	0.8
Electric fan	95.3	92.5	2.0	0.8
Camera*	58.2	32.0	24.9	1.3
Stereo*	68.0	49.2	17.3	1.5
Air conditioner*	26.1	16.0	9.5	0.6
Washing machine	83.3	75.0	8.1	0.2
Water heater*	32.5	29.1	3.4	0.1
Motorcycle	3.0	1.9	1.1	0
Bicycle	84.6	81.4	1.6	1.6
Sewing machine	67.5	66.4	1.1	0
Watch (over Y200)*	68.5	28.4	27.9	12.2
Piano	3.6	2.9	0.8	0
Video	53.6	9.2	44.0	0.5
Video camera	2.3	1.0	1.3	0
Stereo set	14.9	6.4	7.8	0.7
Personal computer	4.3	1.3	1.7	0.1

SOURCE: Results from "Urban Residents' Quality of Life" research conducted by the Institute of Sociology, Shanghai Academy of Social Sciences, 1995. The sample included 1,042 households.

* Consumer items that have a high correlation with the degree of life satisfaction.

Shanghai families on average devoted only 4.1 percent of their total household budgets to rent and utilities.[16]

Shanghai families have also improved the quality and quantity of their living space. "All-in-one" housing units— that is, self-contained apartments with their own entrance, private bath, and kitchen— have become the norm in new buildings and the standard in most renovations. By 1996, 60 percent of Shanghai families were living in such units, more than double the number just four years earlier.[17] As a result, urban residents have more space and comfort in their homes and also enjoy greater privacy.

Despite the rapid increase in the number of families who "own" their homes, residential real estate is only partially commodified. Most people still obtain their housing through work units or government allocation, and thus

16. *SHTJNJ 1995*, p. 66.
17. This figure was supplied by the Shanghai Municipal Real Estate Bureau.

the work unit and certain prereform redistributive norms continue to play a major role in determining a family's standard of living.[18] In the late 1990s, the state announced plans to accelerate the pace of housing commercialization. It is hoped that by the end of the twentieth century people will spend about 15 percent of their household incomes on housing. But because most families still spend more than 50 percent of their income on food, any increase in the percentage spent on housing will reduce the living standard. Therefore, for the foreseeable future, it seems likely that personal and collective consumption will continue to coexist and that commercialization of housing will indicate the degree to which the market economy in China is expanding.

Transportation

Our 1995 study of quality of life in Shanghai showed that only 30.1 percent of workers took public buses or the subway to work, 5.9 percent took work-unit buses, 50.6 percent still rode bicycles (including motorized ones), and 8.2 percent walked. Before reform, 50 percent of workers commuted by public bus or subway.[19] Thus in the reform era public services have ceded their leading role in commuter transportation to private and group suppliers. Yet another manifestation of the rise of private consumption is the popularization of the taxi. In the late 1990s there were 34,000 taxis in Shanghai that carried about 1.5 million rides every year.[20]

New forms of transportation have also caused new problems. The Old City district has narrow roads that are often congested. In addition, motorized bicycles have joined regular bicycles in the streets in ever increasing numbers.[21] Motorized bicycles produce a large amount of exhaust, and the problems of air pollution and environmental safety they cause are attracting more attention. If the market for privately owned automobiles expands as some predict, the contradiction between the private and the public will become even more acute as a result of the expansion of private enjoyment in a consumer society.

Household Equipment, Goods, and Services

In the mid-1990s, Shanghai urban residents spent about 10 percent of their total household budgets on household equipment, goods, and services.[22]

18. Bian Yanjie et al. 1996, p. 22.

19. The figures on 1995 are from the 1995 report of Sociology Institute of the Shanghai Academy of Social Sciences. The prereform figure was supplied by the Shanghai Municipal Public Services Bureau.

20. *SHTJNJ 1995, 1996, 1997*, and the Shanghai Municipal Public Services Bureau.

21. According to the Public Security Bureau, in 1996 Shanghai had 400,000 registered motorized bicycles.

22. In 1994, Shanghai residents spent an average of 460.08 rmb on household equipment, goods, and services, or 9.9 percent of their total expenditures, out of which 300.24 rmb were

Their spending on durable goods, bedclothes, and household sundries has always led the nation. Nevertheless, perhaps as a result of the intense crowding, only 20.8 percent of households owned a full set of furniture, and Shanghai families had the lowest percentage of desk ownership in the country; more than half did not own a desk.[23] At the same time, Shanghai spent the most on home services. Shanghai households employed many women from rural Jiangsu, Zhejiang, and Anhui (including some former "egg women") as nannies. Most earned an hourly wage and worked in several homes every day.

The purchase of household durable goods is an important component of consumption by families seeking a relatively comfortable lifestyle. There are two reasons for this. First, durable goods such as color televisions and refrigerators directly improve living conditions and raise the quality of life. Second, in times of inflation, durable goods maintain their value and signify wealth. Thus as incomes rose and new products entered the market, Shanghai households steadily redefined which household purchases were considered "major items" (*dajian*). Table 6.4 lists the ownership rate of major consumer durable goods in three decades. During the 1970s, bicycles, sewing machines, and watches were considered substantial household purchases. In the 1980s, color televisions, refrigerators, and washing machines were the new status objects and quickly entered most homes. In the 1990s, stereo sets, air conditioners, and microwaves began to enter homes, and sales of personal computers were just taking off. The rapid proliferation of new consumer items indicates that Shanghai living standards have moved beyond subsistence levels to relative comfort.

The declining percentage of annual savings needed to make substantial purchases is a second indicator of improvements since 1980. In the 1970s a family needed to save for several years to buy a 100 rmb sewing machine. In the 1990s, a microwave cost less than a single person's savings for half a year. The significant increase in household income and the abundance of consumer goods have strongly stimulated the desire to consume. People are not satisfied just to follow trends and fashions. They have begun to compete for prestige and style. Table 6.3 lists the consumer durables owned by the 1,042 households surveyed for our 1995 quality-of-life study. The range and quantity give a glimpse into how the material life of Shanghai families has been transformed.

---

spent on daily durable goods. If we add spending on culture and entertainment (95.52 rmb), then each household spends about 12 percent of its total budget on household equipment, goods, and services. See *SHTJNJ 1995*, p. 66.

23. *ZGTJNJ 1995*, p. 274.

TABLE 6.4   Ownership of Household Consumer Durables in Shanghai,
1981–1996
(per 100 households)

Consumer durables	1981	Ownership in 1986	1990	1996
1970s				
Bicycle	65.0	85	114	—
Sewing machine	80.0	96	87	—
Watch	225.0	381	380	—
1980s				
Color TV	1	36.4	77	109
Refrigerator	<1.0	46.8	88	100
Washing machine	1.4	39.0	72	80
Video recorder	—	<1.0	14	49
1990s				
Stereo set	—	—	3.4*	14
Air conditioner	—	—	0.4*	37
Microwave	—	—	<1.0	40
Personal computer	—	—	—	3.4

SOURCES: *Shanghai tongji nianjian 1986, 1987*, and *1992*. The figures for the first half of 1996 were provided by Shanghai Statistical Bureau.
    * 1991 data.

SOCIAL INEQUALITY IN URBAN CONSUMPTION

Even in the prereform society of collective ownership and egalitarianism, the "society of great equality" was only an ideal, and some individuals and households enjoyed a higher standard of living than others. The major mechanism for the production of inequality was the work unit's control and power over resource allocation. As Deng's reform enlarged the role of markets and reduced the redistributive powers of bureaucratic institutions, the influence of work units in determining inequality shifted. However, in this period of transition, redistributive power persists, and even when transformed by new market practices it continues to shape consumption in decisive ways.

One of the most telling examples is how members of an enterprise use their access to enterprise power to convert collective goods into items for private or individual consumption. In the years of central planning, collective consumption was the norm, and when a new product appeared the work units were usually the first customers. This phenomenon persists at the turn of the twenty-first century, though to a different degree and with different consequences. Previously, group consumption mainly met the business needs of state agencies and enterprises or existed in the form of goods distributed to employees as benefits. It was thus similar to public welfare spending. In recent years, however, sentiment has turned toward the slogan "eat the old public" (*chi laogong*)— that is, "eat the state, eat the collective, and eat everybody (except oneself)" (*chi guojia, chi jiti, chi dajia*).[24] To many, this seems like a return to the pre-Communist practice of "helping oneself in the guise of performing a public duty" (*jiagongjisi*). In other words, whatever can be claimed as business expense will be claimed. As a widely accepted way of life, group-consumption-turned-private-consumption has resulted in the privatization of virtually all kinds of property, from cars, housing, and luxury furniture to soap, toilet paper, and toothpicks. People complain that some cadres "depend on gifts for their cigarettes and liquors, depend on invitations for their meals, and save their salaries." "Having the means to claim expenses" (*huibaoxiao*) has become a claim to prestige for some people. Such perverse consumption behaviors are holdovers from the time when all the world was a public realm, and they have significant effects on life in the new society of relative comfort.

Overall, however, marketization and privatization have raised consumption levels of most Shanghai families, and higher standards of living are associated with higher levels of satisfaction. In support of this conclusion, I briefly review here a study I did of life satisfaction. As before, the data come from the 1995 quality-of-life survey conducted by the Institute of Sociology, Shanghai Academy of Social Sciences. First we analyzed the correlation between respondents' degree of satisfaction about urban life and 24 durable goods. We selected twelve goods that correlated highly with satisfaction about living in the city. Then, taking into consideration that consumption and household composition and the number of employed persons are closely related, we selected 480 two-income households of nuclear families from the total sample. Table 6.5 shows the characteristics of those 480 households.

We then conducted a multiple regression analysis with the number of consumer durables as the dependent variable and seven household characteristics as independent variables: (1) average total household income; (2) age of the interviewee (husband or wife); (3) housing condition (quality of residence); (4) number of Communist Party members in the household (index of power); (5) number of persons in new economic units (that is, all nonstate or collective-owned enterprises); (6) average number of years of education (of the husband and the wife); (7) the shared occupational status of the husband and the wife. There were 479 effective cases, and the variation explained is 24.95 percent (see Table 6.6).

The results of the regression analysis show that, of the seven variables, five have a high level of significance for the quantity of durables owned. Among

24. Pan Yunkang et al. 1995, p. 191.

TABLE 6.5   Characteristics of Sample Households in Shanghai, 1995
(two-income nuclear households; N = 480)

		Standard deviation
Average age (years)[a]	42.13	7.03
Average education of husband and wife (years)	11.37	2.27
Average total income (rmb)	1,510.79	621.27
Household members employed in new economic units[b] (%)	16.46	
Household members who were party members (%)	15.63	
Housing quality[c]	2.36	1.60
Average number of durable goods owned[d]	7.13	3.43
Number of imported durable goods owned	2.83	1.27
Households without imported durable goods (%)	23.2	

SOURCE: Results from "Urban Residents' Quality of Life" research conducted by the Institute of Sociology, Shanghai Academy of Social Sciences, 1995.

[a] "Average age" refers to the age of the interviewee, which was either the husband or the wife.

[b] "New economic units" refers to work units that were neither state-owned nor collective-owned.

[c] "Housing quality" was measured by scoring one point for having each of the following: own tap water, own kitchen, own bathtub/shower, own bathroom. The highest score was four, and the lowest was zero.

[d] Twelve "durable goods" were included in the survey: refrigerator, camera, stereo, air conditioner, water heater, bicycle, watch (over 200 rmb), telephone, fax machine, satellite TV, cellular phone, pager.

those, total household income, quality of residence, and combined occupational status have the closest correlation with the number of durables owned. Educational level and number of party members have a smaller amount of influence. Age and whether family members work in new economic units have no influence. This result shows that household consumption has indeed established a certain relationship to its members' socioeconomic status and circumstances.[25] It also shows that inequality in consumption is affected to different degrees by different mechanisms such as the market and power.

Housing, education, and occupational prestige are thought of as the three

25. See Lu Hanlong 1997, pp. 114–66. There I analyze the three kinds of wealthy households in prereform China: (1) households that received remittances from overseas relatives; (2) households of rehabilitated former capitalists, intellectuals, and senior cadres; (3) households where both the elderly spouses worked and had one or no children. These three kinds of household did not owe their economic wealth to the state of the economy or their own economic activities.

TABLE 6.6   Regression Analysis of Household Ownership
of Durable Goods in Shanghai, 1995
(two-income nuclear families)

Variable	Beta	T
Total household income	0.2313	5.207****
Age of interviewee	0.0114	0.273
Housing quality[a]	0.1873	4.555****
Number of party members in the household	0.0781	1.811*
Number of in the household employed by new economic units[b]	0.0049	0.117
Average education of husband and wife (years)	0.1196	2.387**
Combined occupational status[c]	0.1677	3.298****
R^2		24.95%

[a] "Housing quality" was measured by scoring one point for having each of the following: own tap water, own kitchen, own bathtub/shower, own bathroom. The highest score was four, and the lowest was zero.

[b] "New economic units" refers to work units that were neither state-owned nor collective-owned.

[c] "Occupational status" is based on the chart of "occupational status in China" provided by Prof. Yanjie Bian of the University of Minnesota.

* $p < 0.10$ ** $p<0.05$ *** $p<0.01$ **** $p<0.01$

main determinants of social status in a market economy. These factors, especially housing quality, have been shown to be related to the consumption power of Shanghai residents. Positions within the power structure and the economic structure (work-unit ownership, administrative rank of the unit and of the individual, party membership) are considered the main stratification indices in the centrally planned economy of a Communist society. Party membership still retains a certain influence, while the influence of work-unit ownership has all but disappeared. It is worth pointing out the intimate connection between living conditions and durable goods. Because housing in urban China is allocated mainly by employers, it usually has no direct relation to household income but rather is related to people's work unit or their sociopolitical status. Therefore the contribution of housing to ownership of durable goods in essence reflects the result of the redistributive mechanism. Furthermore, we know that some items are not completely marketized. For example, the installation of satellite television reception is restricted by the government, and in the spirit of "helping oneself in the guise of the public duty" it is still common for people to use public money or workplace accounts to subscribe to cellular phone services and install fax machines or pagers for private purposes. In these ways persisting redistributive mechanisms influence contemporary consumption patterns.

CONCLUSION

Reform in China has made the achievement of a relatively comfortable living standard its primary objective. However, in calling on the people to strive toward this goal, the leadership has also invoked a renewed identification with traditional Chinese culture. In particular, the call to pursue a life of relative comfort endorses cultural principles fundamental to the society of private interests described in *The Book of Rites:* the autonomy of the individual and the family, the inevitability of social inequality and social stratification, and the importance of establishing rules and laws to regulate social and economic life.

To realize the goal of relative comfort, the Chinese government has adopted policies that have increased individual wealth, revitalized the economy, rejuvenated the market, and raised popular living standards. A relatively comfortable society with the household as the basic social unit is being carved out of the egalitarian society. Money has become generally accepted as the primary medium of exchange, and new desires for material acquisition combined with the inherent pragmatism of traditional Chinese culture are transforming both the economy and the society. In a "relatively comfortable" society based on the principles of "all for their families" and "accumulate and work for oneself," the capacity and space of family consumption have greatly expanded. But while their material living standards have risen, the Chinese people's improved quality of life is tempered by the ceaseless pursuit of material gains in the market. The private use of public goods persists, as do inequalities rooted in the bureaucracy of the workplace. The long slumbering genie of the market cannot be recalled once let out of the bottle, but for consumers in Shanghai in the mid-1990s the government's effort to create a "socialist market economy" meant that the new relative comforts were still deeply entwined with an ideological and institutional legacy of Maoist commitment to a social structure of "great equality."

PART 2

—

SOCIABILITY IN A MORE COMMODIFIED SOCIETY

CHAPTER 7

Heart-to-Heart, Phone-to-Phone

Family Values, Sexuality, and the Politics of Shanghai's Advice Hotlines

Kathleen Erwin

One striking change in the style of social interaction among China's urbanites in the 1990s was precipitated by rapid growth in telecommunications. Until the late 1980s, few families had private telephone lines. In 1985, when I lived as a foreign student in Shanghai, making a phone call was an inconvenience second only to finding a heated room and hot water in the blistering winter cold. Usually made from noisy public phones on street corners, at the end of a lane, or at the workplace, telephone calls rarely allowed enough privacy for more than perfunctory conversations to set up a meeting time or place. Often, Chinese friends, colleagues, and teachers told me to "just stop by" (*suibian lai*) when I was in the neighborhood, since communication and transportation were both inconvenient and unreliable. When I returned for brief visits to Shanghai in 1988 and 1989, there had been some improvements in the phone system—particularly in international calling—but the changes were not enough to affect the general pace of life or style of communication I had experienced in the mid-1980s.

By 1994, though, the changes were dramatic. Instead of the casual invitations to "stop by," my old and new friends, most of whom had acquired private lines at home, would say (just as casually) "call any time" (*you kong jiu*

The research and writing of this essay were made possible through financial support from the National Science Foundation Graduate Fellowship, the U.C. Berkeley Vice-Chancellor's Research Fund, a Department of Anthropology Lowie Travel Grant, and a U.C. Berkeley Chancellor's Dissertation Award. I am also grateful to the many people who provided assistance and guidance. They include Gail Hershatter, Wang Zheng, Julia Sensenbrenner, Yanlei Wu, Aihwa Ong, Nancy Scheper-Hughes, Thomas Gold, Elizabeth Perry, Deborah Davis, Joshua Gamson, Jean-Christophe Agnew, Mary Erbaugh, Sandra Cate, Arthur Kleinman, and Karen Franklin. I am especially indebted to the hotline staffs for welcoming my visits. Any errors in interpretation or fact are my own.

lai dianhua). Not only were many of my associates now reachable by telephone at home, but many more also carried either pagers (*bibiji*) or cellular phones (*da ge da*): they could be contacted anytime, anywhere. Though the waiting list for phone installation could be up to several years in some parts of the city, a *bibiji* or *da ge da* could be purchased instantly at any of the hundreds of electronics stores throughout Shanghai. These gadgets facilitated social communication as well as business and market relations. To wit: the most popular pagers had message screens that also provided constant updates on Shanghai's stock market prices, news headlines, and the weather forecast!

Telecommunications technology has played a crucial role in the transformation of personal and market relationships in urban China's increasingly fast-paced, mobile, and commodified lifestyle. Telephones in particular allow more direct communication even among people who may never meet, bridging the social gap between personalized face-to-face relations and long-distance relations previously mediated by written forms of communication. This essay examines how the infiltration of telephones into the homes, pocketbooks, and briefcases of ordinary citizens has transformed the nature and means of personal disclosures regarding marriage, family, and sexuality in China. This transformation is most evident in the proliferation of telephone "hotlines" (*rexian dianhua*)—a phenomenon that reveals the reconfiguration of public and private discourse and practices in the shaping of Chinese modernity at the turn of the twenty-first century.

COMMUNICATIONS TECHNOLOGY AND THE CHINESE PUBLIC: THE ROLE OF ADVICE HOTLINES

Recent analyses in anthropology and cultural studies on the impact of telecommunications and mass media in the construction of modernity have emphasized their role in the formation of new publics that transcend previous time-space boundaries. Much of this work has focused on how visual media utilize images to construct shared imaginaries of modernity and community within and across national boundaries even among people who may be spatially and socially distant.[1] Telephones, like other forms of telecommunications and the mass media, allow people to transcend their embodied localizations to establish connections across expanses of geographic and social space.[2] However, unlike visual media, telephones allow—indeed *require*—a kind of interpersonal verbal intimacy, even in the absence of other bodily

1. On time-space compression as a feature of postmodernity, see Harvey 1989. On mass media and the formation of alternate publics see Lee 1993; Abu-Lughod 1993; M. Yang 1997 and 1999; Erwin 1999; and Deleuze and Guattari 1983. See Anderson 1991 for a discussion of "imagined communities of nationalism."

2. See Nonini 1997; Erwin 1997.

cues.[3] The conjoining of intimacy and anonymity via telephones is manifest perhaps most clearly in the context of hotline counseling.[4]

Advice hotlines sprang up all over urban China in the 1990s, providing an outlet for the disclosure of personal ordeals that Chinese call "heart talk" (*xinli hua*). Despite improving material conditions and greater personal freedoms in the contemporary period, the rapid and often unsettling social changes are fraught with uncertainties and trade-offs for many. In a society where saving face is a paramount concern, hotlines allow Chinese citizens to voice their uncertainties, heartaches, and hopes to sympathetic but socially distant ears. Because they provide relative anonymity, hotlines represent an escape, or freedom, from direct party-state and family constraints on individual expression and personal relationships. Moreover, the rapid expansion of urban China's phone system has made hotline calling a relatively democratic practice in China: many more people are directly engaged in producing the "scripts" of suffering and desire that constitute hotline calls than in, say, the production of soap opera scripts that enter their living rooms via television.[5] In this context, the disclosure of private ordeals via hotlines can be seen as a means by which disparate individuals connect across space to explore and redefine the boundaries of newfound private freedoms.

And these connections are not merely didactic. Despite the privacy they imply, hotlines have contributed to a vibrant public discussion of family and sexual matters in urban China. Hotline centers publish popular and specialized books and articles for distribution to wider audiences. And since 1992 advice hotlines have expanded into the realm of listener-participation talk radio, allowing hundreds of thousands of listeners to "eavesdrop" on the ordeals of others. Hotlines thus provide a vehicle by which personal and highly individualized disclosures are made into quantifiable and qualifiable speech acts that are both consumed and transformed by their circulation among the Chinese public. This dissemination of sexual knowledge and advice in turn generates even greater public interest and discussion of the private ordeals of others and fosters a sense of connectedness among otherwise disconnected individuals.[6]

The nature of the callers' concerns and the advice and commentary generated by the calls have thus produced a new shared vocabulary and set of practices that define new possibilities for modern Chinese subjectivities. Among these is the affirmation that social and sexual "openness" (*kaifang*)

3. On the social impact of the telephone, see Aronson 1979; Gumpert and Cathcart 1979; and Pool 1977.

4. See Lester 1977.

5. On the role of Chinese television serials in public culture in China and the Chinese diaspora, see, for example, Rofel 1994a; Shih 1997; and Zha 1995.

6. On how mass media and spectatorship produce shared subjectivities and desires in a populace, see Deleuze and Guattari 1983; Lee 1993; and Nonini 1997.

is an essential characteristic of China's continuing and rapid modernization. In marked contrast to both the repression associated with the Maoist era and China's feudal legacy, the disclosures of marital, family, and sexual problems via hotlines seem an obvious manifestation of this modern openness. Certainly this representation of hotlines dominates their coverage in both the American and the Chinese press.[7]

Although advice hotlines indeed offer a means to discuss marriage and sexuality more openly and publicly than was possible in the past, their social effects are nevertheless complex. That the advice is dispensed by party cadres and credentialed experts points to the official sanction hotlines enjoy and to the disinterested interest that the state maintains in monitoring the populace. That is, following Foucault's elaboration of the operations of modern discursive power, I suggest that more open discussion of sexuality fostered by hotlines does not necessarily imply greater individual freedom.[8] Instead, it may point to the construction of new subjectivities and notions of modernity that themselves implicate new forms of power. Thus, hotlines and the calls they generate reveal how citizens negotiate the new possibilities and constraints of their rapidly transforming social environment and might best be approached as a means of examining the articulations and contestations over gender roles, cultural values, and even the forms and meanings of Chinese modernity.

OPENING LINES: PRIVATE PHONES, SOCIAL CHANGE,
AND THE PROLIFERATION OF HOTLINES IN URBAN CHINA

The hotline phenomenon vividly illustrates urban China's rapid transformation in material conditions and lifestyle in the 1990s. Beginning in 1989, the Chinese government made the expansion of telecommunications, especially in urban areas, a high priority in its modernization efforts. That year, only 5 percent of China's urban households had private telephones (rural areas had far fewer). By 1995, 25–30 percent of households in the nation's largest cities had phones. As late as 1991, only 5 percent of households (250,500) in Shanghai had private telephones, although some central neighborhoods could boast telephones in 60–74 percent of homes.[9] And subse-

7. See Kristoff 1993; Ding Lu 1995. This perspective was also widely shared among the Shanghainese populace.

8. Foucault 1978. Foucault debunks the notion that sexual liberation in the West replaced Victorian repression and argues that more talk about sexuality reveals new modes of modern power.

9. See two separate reports in *China News Daily*, May 11 and September 14, 1995; see also *Shanghai Star*, May 19, 1995, p. 7, and *Shanghai jingji nianjian 1992*, p. 307.

quent expansion of phone service was rapid: an additional 100,000 urban households were connected to private phone lines from 1991 to 1992, and by the end of 1995, approximately 1 million Shanghai households had a telephone.[10] Moreover, since the mid-1980s the cost of phone installation has soared. Whereas in 1986 it cost 300 renminbi (rmb) to have a private phone line connected (where available), by 1995 the cost had increased tenfold to 3,000 rmb.[11]

Despite the increase in availability and cost, demand for telephones outstripped the pace of construction of telephone infrastructure, and throughout the 1990s the wait for a telephone was as long as several years in some parts of the city. Illustrating both the affluence of the urban population and its impatience with the lengthy wait for phone installations, mobile phone use grew even more rapidly. The number of cellular phone users (generally synonymous with urban dwellers) jumped nationally from 20,000 in 1990 to 1.57 million in 1994,[12] then more than doubled in 1995 to 3.4 million.[13] This phenomenal leap occurred despite the high cost of cellular phones: At 10,000 rmb, not including monthly service fees or phone charges, cellular phones cost two to ten times the monthly income of urban professionals.[14] Not surprisingly, Shanghai and Guangzhou boast the largest growth and numbers of mobile phone customers in China. This rapid expansion of tele-

10. Because statistics for household telephones in Shanghai were incomplete and inconsistent, my estimates are derived from several sources, and in some cases they are based on my own calculations. For example, the estimate of 100,000 new households from 1991–92 is my own. According to the *Shanghai Economic Yearbook* of 1993, by the end of 1992, Shanghai had connected 780,000 residential phone lines, of which more than 50 percent (at least 390,000) were private family lines. Using these figures, I calculate that approximately 139,500 private family lines were added (390,000 in 1992; 250,500 in 1991). *Shanghai jingji nianjian 1993*, p. 287. I also consulted *Shanghai jingji nianjian*, p, 307; *Shanghai tongji nianjian 1996*, p. 278; *Shanghai Star,* May 15, 1995, p. 4. Chapter 6 in this volume states that by 1995, 42.3 percent of Shanghai households had a telephone. This finding is based on a survey sample size of 1,042.

11. *China News Daily,* September 22, 1995 (based on figures from the Postal and Telegraph Research Office). This cost 5,000 rmb in Beijing and as much as 6,000 rmb in other cities.

12. *China News Daily,* December 25, 1995 (citing *China Daily*'s *Business Weekly,* December 10, 1995).

13. *China News Daily,* January 3, 1996; The *Xinhua Evening News* said in a report from Shanghai that mainland China had become the fourth largest mobile phone market. *China News Daily,* November 4, 1995.

14. These prices are based on information derived from personal interviews during my fieldwork in 1995. Ten thousand rmb was equivalent to approximately U.S.$1,200 in 1995, which is ten times the average monthly income of most residents and twice the monthly income of the upwardly mobile elites who were earning approximately 5,000 rmb per month. Most mobile phone users, however, did not purchase mobile phones out of their own incomes. The phones were provided by their employers or charged as a business expense.

communications in a five-year period—especially phone access among private citizens and consumers—dramatically transformed phone calling from an inconvenient and very "public" undertaking to both a symbolic and a real manifestation of China's increasingly privatized and highly mobile urban lifestyle.[15] Certainly, the proliferation of advice hotlines is predicated in part on this new ability of ordinary citizens to make "private" calls at their convenience.

The nation's first hotlines were directed at suicide prevention and crisis intervention for the general (nonpsychiatric) population. Tianjin is credited with opening the first such hotline, followed in July 1989 by Beijing's Hotline of Hope, operated by the Beijing Fitness and Beauty Research Center.[16] By March 1990, the Hotline of Hope had received 3,124 calls from all over China. Shanghai's first hotline, the Psychological Health Hotline (discussed below), opened in November 1990, and Nanjing opened its first crisis hotline in 1991.[17] In its first four years, the Nanjing hotline answered more than 4,000 calls. The number and scope of telephone hotlines expanded dramatically in a very short time. By 1992, Shanghai alone had at least a dozen hotlines in place, and by 1995 the nation's largest city boasted more than twenty counseling hotlines—the largest number of any city in the nation—including ones for AIDS, women and children, youth, and students, among others.[18] Moreover, the perceived purpose of the hotlines has shifted in recent years, from primarily crisis intervention to providing advice on love, marriage, family, and sexuality.

The emergence and growth of hotline services stems not only from rapid improvement in the telecommunications infrastructure but also from a shift in both private and official attitudes toward love, marriage, and sexuality. During most of the Maoist decades, and especially during the Cultural Revolution, such personal aspirations were disparaged as bourgeois distractions from revolutionary fervor, and public discussion of them came under close party scrutiny.[19] More open discussion of sexuality is now seen as both a re-

15. See Lu (this volume) on the importance of having a household telephone in determining satisfaction with one's material conditions.

16. Tianjin opened the first crisis hotline in China in 1987, according to Hu Jin and Zhao Pinghe 1995; see also Ding Lu 1995. Li credits Beijing with opening the first crisis hotline (X. Li 1990), but Xie, Weinstein, and Meredith (1996) say Nanjing had the first in 1991. For a discussion of the Beijing Women's Hotline, see Cornue 1999.

17. Personal communication from Ji Jianlin, August 1995; see also Ding Lu 1995; Ji Jianlin et al. 1995; and Xie, Weinstein, and Meredith 1996.

18. Ding Lu 1995, p. 8, lists the women and children's hotline (described herein), middle-school students' hotline; elderly folks' hotline, youth hotline, and others. Ji Jianlin et al. 1995 reported that Shanghai had fifteen hotlines in 1993 and 26 in 1995 but that only about ten of them were "active" (*renao*). *Renmin ribao*, March 6, 1993, reported that Shanghai had the largest number of hotlines in the nation.

19. See Honig and Hershatter 1988.

jection of the repression and isolation of that era and a means of achieving family stability and personal fulfillment outside the realm of politics. In addition, the Cultural Revolution itself and the changing requirements for a market-driven economy together have spawned a number of new and different social problems in China—among them, divorce, layoffs, dislocation, inadequate education, and mental distress. Psychological counseling represents a modern means of dealing with people's distress that is "scientific" rather than overtly political. As such, it too has been gaining public and official acceptance as a means of addressing what are now seen as personal problems.

Thus, both the content of the phone calls and the emphasis on psychological counseling carve out a space outside politics in which hotlines are seen to operate. The focus on family and sexual matters that keeps the hotlines buzzing is widely viewed as revealing an authentic dimension of Chinese experience that is otherwise obscured by either face-saving reticence or by official efforts to orchestrate "speaking bitterness" in formal political ritual in previous historical eras and political climates. As an American anthropologist studying marriage and family in contemporary Shanghai, I was frequently urged to glean as much as I could from the hotlines: listening to the calls would be invaluable in my understanding of contemporary Chinese life.

COUNSELING HOTLINES IN SHANGHAI: OVERVIEW OF TWO CENTERS

During my fieldwork in 1995, I observed the operations of two psychological hotlines (*xinli rexian*) in Shanghai, both of which operated in the evenings. One, the women and children's psychological hotline (hereafter "women's hotline"), was run by the Women's Cadre School and funded by a private Singapore joint-venture company that marketed products for women in China. The other was the psychological health hotline (hereafter "PHH"), which operated in and was sponsored by the Shanghai psychiatric hospital. As already mentioned, this hotline was Shanghai's first and was the most widely utilized in the city.

During my visits to both centers and in the log books and published materials I reviewed, it was clear that the hotlines were kept busy receiving anywhere from two to six calls per night, which ranged in length from five minutes to one hour.[20] The hotlines operated only in the evenings because people were more likely to call from home (more than two-thirds of calls in 1995 were made

20. Both hotlines had a time limit of one hour per call so that the line would not be tied up indefinitely. Most calls that I observed lasted 15–20 minutes and usually not more that 30 minutes.

from home phones);[21] less frequently, people phoned from their workplace after hours. Each counseling center had one phone line and one person on duty to answer the calls. I did not take any calls myself. I listened to the counselor's end of the conversation and took notes, then discussed the calls with the counselor afterward.[22] These conversations gave me additional information about the calls and provided insights into the counselors' interpretations.

Both hotlines were staffed by counselors who had received at least rudimentary training in psychology and hotline counseling techniques. At the PHH, most of the staff were psychologists or psychiatrists, but they too received additional training in hotline counseling. In both settings, the counselors were married party members, male and female, and were solicited as volunteers. Being married was a requirement, I was told, because otherwise the counselors would not have the experience to address the marital and sexual concerns so many of the callers raised. And despite their volunteer status, counselors were paid for their time. For instance, at the women's hotline, counselors received 35 rmb per two-to-three-hour shift.[23] Their party membership reflected both their status in their respective institutions and consideration of the sensitive (*mingan*) nature of the calls.[24] Though they did not give uniform advice, their advice and commentary did fall within the range of acceptable, even mainstream, discourse circulating in China's public sphere.

The requirements for the counselors points to the interest the state maintained in the operations of the hotlines. Advice hotlines were viewed as opportunities for providing education as well as advice. Both hotlines published popular and scientific books and articles for wider circulation. The women's hotline published a book of 100 examples of hotline calls and advice, supposedly based on actual calls to the center,[25] and the PHH published a popu-

21. Personal communication from Ji Jianlin, August 1995.

22. The majority of calls were conducted in Mandarin, the official dialect of China, and not in the local Shanghai dialect. This was because many of the callers were not native Shanghainese, some of the counselors were not native Shanghainese, and some callers preferred to express themselves in Mandarin to the counselor, regardless of where they were from. When a caller did speak the Shanghai dialect, the native Shanghainese counselors responded in kind. However, callers to the radio hotlines were more actively encouraged to speak in Mandarin. Even when a caller spoke Shanghainese, the host virtually always responded in Mandarin.

23. Personal interviews. Each evening consisted of two shifts, from 4:30 to 7 P.M. and 7—10 P.M. Thirty-five rmb = approximately U.S.$4 in 1995.

24. Communist Party membership is often conferred on the basis of one's status in an organization or profession. Party cadres (*ganbu*) are party members (*dangyuan*) who work for a state organization like the Women's Federation. All party cadres are party members, but not all party members are cadres. I interviewed two radio hosts and six counselors at two different hotlines. All were party members. Especially by the 1990s, their party membership was not necessarily an indication of their political views.

25. Hun Jin and Zhao Pinghe 1995. Whether the published advice was the actual advice given and how much the problems may have been altered is difficult to ascertain. Nevertheless,

lar book on techniques and advice for hotline counseling, as well as scholarly articles analyzing the calls.[26] And although some outsiders might find it surprising that Chinese citizens would confide in party members, this practice is well established in the history of the People's Republic. The Communist Party has always used its extensive personnel and the infrastructure of neighborhood committees to help people resolve interpersonal and familial problems. In fact, to some the value of the advice might even be greater because it came from people who had the expertise and official sanction to dispense it.

Despite their emphasis on resolving family and sexual problems, even counseling center hotlines had to adjust to China's increasingly market-driven, commodified economy. As state support for social services dwindled, corporations became more important in financing them. For example, the Shanghai women's hotline was sponsored by a Singapore feminine products company. Similarly, the Beijing Sexual Health Hotline, which opened in 1995, saw its primary purpose as providing sex education, but it also wanted to "introduce callers to goods produced by the firm that established the hotline."[27] Thus the dual but joined hands of the state and of the market could be found in the operation and structure of hotlines, pointing to the complicity of state and capitalist interests in the promotion of hotline counseling.

The Women and Children's Hotline

The Women and Children's Hotline opened in April 1992 and laid claim as the nation's first hotline aimed primarily at resolving women's problems (*funü wenti*). It operated three evenings a week, from 4:30 to 10:00 P.M., and I visited regularly from January to March 1995 to listen to calls and interview the counselors, whose specializations included women's education, psychology, sexology, and medicine.

Although the hotline received calls from both sexes, more of the callers were women than men. In its first two and a half years of operation, the hotline reported receiving more than 1,600 calls; after almost three and a half years, the total number had risen to more than 2,000 calls.[28] The women's hotline did not provide me with comprehensive statistics, but a pamphlet compiled by the hotline supervisors noted that shifts in the type and number of calls received reflected changing conditions:

> Looking at the hotline statistics from the first half of 1993, 62 percent of callers asked for advice about children's problems, 35 percent about women's prob-

---

the publications show that these private ordeals and personal stories circulated beyond the narrow context of the hotline call.

26. Deng Zhanpei 1993.

27. *China News Daily*, November 15, 1995.

28. "Wei'er'fu rexian xinxi" (Wei'er'fu hotline news), pamphlet dated August 1995.

lems, and 3 percent other. In the second half of the year, following the deep-
ening of reforms, as women experienced greater change in their daily lives and
were confronted with more daily complications, calls seeking advice for
women's problems increased to 72 percent, children's problems 26 percent,
and other 2 percent. The content of calls is increasingly rich.[29]

Women's problems were defined as marriage and family problems (*hunyin
jiating wenti*). The most common types of marital problem concerned infidelity
(*disanzhe*; literally, third-party relations) and divorce.[30] Other common problems included postdivorce child-rearing, children's developmental health,
mental health, study difficulties, personal relationship problems, work-related
problems,[31] women's employment rights, sexual harassment by factory bosses,
and questions about homosexuality; some calls came from Shanghai's high
number of laid-off women workers, who wanted help dealing with being unemployed.[32] Almost all calls about sex were made by men, who sometimes
claimed to be calling on behalf of their girlfriends or wives. Less frequently,
men called to discuss child-rearing problems and marital and family problems.[33]

The Psychological Health Hotline

I made three visits to the psychological health hotline in the spring and summer of 1995 and conducted two interviews with its director. The PHH answered calls nightly from 6:00 to 9:00 P.M. and received 20,000 calls in the
four and a half years from November 1990 through April 1995. Half of the
calls were made in the first year, and the annual numbers declined steadily
as more hotlines opened throughout the city, giving people a greater variety of places to seek advice.[34]

The PHH provided much more comprehensive statistics on the callers
and types of calls than the women's hotline. In the six months between February and August 1994, the PHH received 917 calls, of which 29 percent
were from depressed callers; more than one-third (309 calls or 34 percent)
were recorded as dealing directly with courtship, marriage, or family problems (see Table 7.1).[35] Interestingly, over 60 percent of courtship and marriage calls were made by (or ascribed to) women, while 81 percent of calls

29. Ibid. Author's translation.
30. Ibid.
31. From an informational pamphlet entitled "4046765 Wei'er'fu funü ertong xinli rexian
jianjie" (4046765 short introduction to the *Wei'er'fu* women's and children's psychological hotline), published by the Shanghai Training Center for Women and Children and the Wei'er'fu
Company. The pamphlet was given to me in December 1994 and provided statistics through
the year ending 1993.
32. "Wei'er'fu rexian xinxi" pamphlet dated August 1995.
33. Ibid.
34. Ding Lu 1995.
35. Ji Jianlin et al. 1995.

TABLE 7.1   Calls to the Psychological Health Hotline by Sex, 1995

Topic of call	Number of calls (women/men)		% of total
Mild depression	265	(128/136 = 264)[a]	28.9
Courtship problems	196	(119/77)	21.4[b]
Marriage and family problems	113	(65/43 = 108)[c]	12.3
Personal relations problems	100	(42/58)	10.9
Health/illness problems	79	(38/41)	8.6
Sexual questions/problems	62	(12/50)	6.8
Other problems (work, study, spiritual illness, child-rearing, insomnia, suicidal crisis)	102		11.1
Total	917		100.0

SOURCE: Ji Jianlin et al. 1995.

[a] The sex breakdown equals 264 people, one fewer than in the essay cited.

[b] The article published by Ji Jianlin et al. mistakenly gives this percentage as 21.73.

[c] Marriage problems: 42 women/23 men (65 total); family problems: 23 women/20 men (43 total). The combined total is 108 callers, a difference of 5 in this category from the total number of calls in this category provided in a separate table in Ji Jianlin et al. 1995.

related to sex were made by (or ascribed to) men—a finding that will be analyzed more critically later in this essay.

There was a wide age range among the callers to the PHH, and the age breakdown indicated that young people were more likely to call. In fact, 25 percent of all callers in 1994 were 21–25 years old, and among the 907 callers who gave their age to the counselor during the same six-month period cited previously (February–August 1994), 76 percent (690 callers) were between ages 16 and 35 (see Table 7.2). The high number of calls in the 16–35 year-old range was to be expected since courtship, marriage, and family problems are the most common topics brought to the hotline, and this is the age range in which most of these problems arise.[36] For example, in 1994 the hotline received 400 calls categorized as courtship problems. Of those, 291 of the callers (73 percent) were 16–25 years old, and 109 callers were 26–35 years old. Of the 152 calls in 1994 categorized under marriage and family problems, only 20 callers (13 percent) were 16–25, whereas 81 callers (53 percent) were 26–35, and 51 (34 percent) were 36–45 years old.[37]

Young people, the hotline director explained to me, were more "open" (*kaifang*) than the older generation and therefore more likely to use a hotline

36. Similarly, Beijing's Hotline of Hope (*Xiwang rexian*) reported that 88.7 percent of callers were under age 35. Li Xingjian 1990. Nanjing's crisis intervention center reported that over half of it callers were between 20 and 30 years old.

37. Interview, June 22, 1995.

TABLE 7.2   Calls to the Psychological Health Hotline
by Age, 1995

Age of caller	Number of callers	% of total
Under age 16	35	3.8
16–25	436	48.1
26–35	254	28.0
36–45	130	14.3
46–55	35	3.9
56 and over	17	1.9
Total	907	100.0

SOURCE: Ji Jianlin et al. 1995.

to resolve their problems. They have been more socialized into a telephone-oriented culture of communication, just as they are most directly immersed in the kinds of problems that were brought to the hotlines. Clearly, despite their comparative material comfort (relative to previous generations), the majority of callers did not believe that modern conveniences necessarily alleviated the bitter circumstances of their lives—indeed they might even bring into sharper focus their unfulfilled desires of the heart, as the following analysis of several calls explains.

RADIO HOTLINES:
ADVICE, EDUCATION, AND ENTERTAINMENT FOR THE MASSES

Despite the relatively high use of both hotline counseling centers, neither one received the volume of calls that came into the widely known and extremely popular advice hotlines broadcast over the radio. In Shanghai, these hotline programs are the hallmark of Dongfang (Orient) Radio, which began broadcasting in 1992 in direct competition with Shanghai Radio. Orient Radio established its niche by making call-in shows the basis of most of its programming.[38] Although Orient airs many different types of call-in shows, those dealing with questions of love, marriage, and sexuality, broadcast late into the night, are their most popular. Their presence on the airwaves and seemingly limited censorship were seen as evidence that party controls on the media were loosening and that public discussion of sexuality was no longer taboo.[39] According to the *New York Times*, Orient Radio's four phone

38. Kristoff 1993; see also M. Yang 1997.
39. Ibid. See also Lawrence 1993.

lines were constantly busy, receiving up to 4,800 calls per minute at peak times.[40] One of the most popular of these shows, which aired around midnight, was called "Your Partner til Dawn" (*Xiangban dao liming*). Like calls to the counseling center hotlines, calls to "Your Partner til Dawn" (and to other similar call-in shows such as Beijing's popular "Life Hotline"),[41] primarily concerned unrequited love, extramarital affairs, and other romantic or familial difficulties.

Radio call-in hotlines thrust telephone counseling into the limelight of popular culture and public discourse.[42] People listened to the call-in advice programs in taxis, at work, and late at night after turning off the television. Their popularity in Shanghai was obvious, and the shows often entered into people's daily discussions. A 24-year-old female host of "Your Partner til Dawn" told me: "Shanghainese people like gossip, so they like to listen to these kinds of programs. . . . They listen for fun [rather than serious social commentary]. For so long people couldn't talk publicly about such things [extramarital affairs, bad marriages, courtship, etc.] so now that China is more open they want to talk endlessly about them. . . . Some people joke that calling the show is like going to the temple: you say what's in your heart and feel better for a while. You know you have options, even if you don't follow the advice."[43]

Of course, calling a radio talk program is not just like going to a temple or like calling a hotline counseling center. Personal disclosures on the radio reach many more ears and enter much more directly into the realm of public discourse. Neither, however, are these disclosures on the radio the antithesis of private communication. In Shanghai's cramped living conditions where many extended families share only two or three rooms, the anonymity of public space often offers more privacy than one's own home.[44] Likewise, the anonymity of phone calling, especially in the wee hours after midnight, offers a kind of intimacy for discussing private ordeals, even in as seemingly "public" a venue as a radio broadcast.

According to the program hosts I interviewed, the professed aim of radio hotlines was to help callers solve their problems and to provide an outlet for pent-up feelings that could not be expressed openly in the family. Equally important, they acknowledged, was utilizing these scintillating topics to draw listeners to the program for its entertainment value. With wan-

---

40. Kristoff 1993.
41. Lawrence 1993.
42. See Kristoff 1993; Lawrence 1993; M. Yang 1997.
43. Interview, May 9, 1995.
44. On the cramped living quarters typical of Shanghainese homes, see Pellow 1993. See also Yan 1997a.

ing state financial support, broadcasting has become an increasingly competitive endeavor, even as censorship persists. In this context, broadcasting companies must appeal to popular tastes while remaining politically palatable. That official permission exists for hotline programs to air suggests that they are *not* viewed as politically threatening. And indeed, the inherent structure of phone counseling explains this situation: unlike the specter of the Tiananmen and other mass demonstrations in modern Chinese history, telephone hotlines allow people's discontent to remain individualized and relatively anonymous, not only for the caller but also for the dispersed and disparate listeners.

Moreover, radio hotlines retain a dimension that serves the state's interests: they provide inexpensive, widely available education to the masses. Radio hotlines have the potential to reach vast numbers of listeners and potential callers, and like counselors at the psychological hotlines, program hosts were all party members who had official sanction to discuss personal matters and dispense advice. The 60+-year-old host of a show dedicated to responding to sexual concerns told me that such programs were important to provide people with scientific information that they lacked in the past.[45] She observed that many of her listeners were migrants living in Shanghai who were lonely, had no one to confide in, and were unfamiliar with other kinds of services or information in the city.

Given the hotly debated topic of the emergence of "civil society" in contemporary China that has suffused Western academic discourse in recent years,[46] what is strikingly absent from the observations of program hosts is any suggestion of the hotlines' potentially politically transformative role as a means of voicing political discontent in China. Certainly some censorship was involved in selecting which calls made it onto the air,[47] but the two hosts I interviewed assured me that censorship was rarely needed. People who called *wanted* to discuss their personal problems: "Shanghainese people don't care about politics," I was told. "Nobody believes anything will change, especially after June 4 [1989—the date of the violent suppression of demonstrations in Tiananmen Square]. They just want to improve their own personal lives and stay out of politics"—that is, state politics. But disinterest in official politics thrusts callers (and listeners) squarely into the realm of family and sexual politics, as an examination of the hotline calls reveals.

45. I heard this explanation many times, from counselors at hotline centers and from sex educators I met in other aspects of my fieldwork. This explanation was also cited in Lawrence 1993 and Xie, Weinstein, and Meredith 1996.

46. See Huang 1993; also Davis, Kraus, Naughton, and Perry 1994.

47. See Lawrence 1993.

HOTLINE CALLS: NEGOTIATING GENDER, SEXUALITY, AND MODERN FAMILY VALUES IN CHINA

From the perspective of examining the role hotlines played in producing a shared vocabulary and set of practices in the Chinese public, listener-participation radio clearly has the broader and more direct effect. Nevertheless, both counseling hotlines and radio call-in programs shared important characteristics that point to similar social effects. As already noted, in both settings the calls were answered by counselors and hosts who had official sanction to advise in personal matters. And both types of hotlines represented China's new social openness, with all its possibilities and problems. Both radio and counseling hotlines generated calls that dealt primarily with family and sexuality and contributed to the vibrant public discourse on modern values and lifestyles. Thus, although the radio programs had substantially larger audiences, both might be seen as producing more discussion and more knowledge among China's public about the private ordeals faced by ordinary citizens.

Indeed, a common thread throughout these calls was the problem of striking a balance between newfound pleasures, freedoms, and material comforts and responsibility for family relations and marital stability. Family obligations, mate choice, sexuality, and divorce were viewed as common predicaments of modern life that posed a challenge to cultural wisdom and traditional values. That is, what was being negotiated in these calls were the gender roles and sexual expectations of modern men and women whose lives were structured not only by new economic and political realities but also by cultural constraints imposed by notions of Chinese tradition. It is not possible to recount all the types of calls and their variations here. However, a few examples of specific calls will illustrate the negotiations of gender, sexuality, and Chinese family values, as well as the meanings and boundaries of new freedoms and opportunities that were at the heart of the majority of calls to all advice hotlines.

Sex Talk, Gendered Talk

As already noted, callers sought information and advice on matters they felt unable to discuss with family or close friends. Common among these were problems related to sex and sexual fulfillment, whether inside or outside of marriage. For example, during one of my visits to the women's hotline, a 26-year-old man called to discuss sexual problems in his marriage: he had been married more than a year, and his 25-year-old wife, he said, had no interest in sex. The caller said he had urged his wife to phone the hotline, but she refused to do so. Neither did she know her husband was calling. He wanted to know what might be causing his wife's problem. The counselor, a woman in her thirties, urged him to have his wife call if she had specific questions about sex. She said that it is easier for women to talk between themselves about these problems, and then maybe she could help the wife. But the husband reiterated that his wife had refused to call.

The counselor told him that his wife's feelings might be based on lack of affection in the marriage, on her being too tired after work, or a fear of getting pregnant. The husband said that she had had one miscarriage, so he did not think she feared pregnancy, unless it was due to psychological problems related to the miscarriage. Their marriage was based on mutual affection, he said, and there was no outside lover. He wanted to know what he should say or do to change his wife's feelings about sex.

The counselor told the caller to wait for his wife to show some interest and not force her to have sex. Since his wife would not call, the counselor could only guess at the reasons for her lack of interest. She asked if they had had premarital sexual relations, and the man said no. Perhaps, she suggested, his wife had never experienced an orgasm, and what he needed to do was use better methods to raise the quality of their intercourse. They could buy books that described different methods, and if that did not work, there were also medications that might help.

The call lasted half an hour. Afterward, the counselor told me that it was common for Chinese women to be indifferent to sex and that they were unlikely to call about sexual problems. That was part of the reason, she said, that so many more men called about sex. Indeed, one of the most notable similarities among the hotlines was that men and women raised different types of concerns.[48] But the distinction between calls related to sex (attributed more to men) and calls related to marital problems (attributed more to women) was often hard to define, begging the issue of whether the categorization of calls by the hotline's staff was in part influenced by the sex of the caller.

Another call to the women's hotline on a different evening illustrates the relationship of gender to the negotiation of sexuality and marriage that occurred in hotline counseling. The second call bore some striking resemblances to the one just described, except in this case a wife called to discuss her repulsion to her husband's sexual advances. The caller was 26 years old and had been married three years. She said she was dissatisfied with her marriage because she did not love her husband. They had met and courted in college. Although her feelings for her boyfriend had already begun to change, the woman felt compelled to marry him for the sake of his parents: at the time, her husband's father had been very sick and had wanted to see his son married before he passed away. She said her husband was not a bad person, just distant (*mosheng*). She felt she did not really know him or feel

48. Although this finding is substantiated only in the PHH statistics, this same observation was made by counselors and program hosts I interviewed and by other written materials produced by the various hotlines.

close to him. After marriage, they had lived apart for one year. When her husband returned, she could not bear his touch. It gave her gooseflesh. Although they had resumed sexual relations, she was very disappointed in them and felt distant from her husband. When this counselor, a 36-year-old veteran of the hotline, asked how her husband felt, the caller said they had not discussed the problem but that it seemed his affection for her was very strong. Although she had raised the question of divorce with him several times, he had dismissed it and refused to take her seriously.

The counselor told the woman she had two choices. First, she could wait to see if love would grow in their marriage in accordance with the Chinese saying, "First marry, then fall in love" (*xian jiehun, hou lian'ai*). This kind of slow-growing love is thought by many to be the basis for a more satisfying and stable marriage. The caller seemed unhappy with this option and reiterated that she was strongly considering divorce, especially since there were no children who would be affected by it. But she feared she would not do better in a second marriage. The counselor said if the woman really felt the marriage was hopeless, then her second choice was indeed to divorce. She told the woman to consider carefully whether divorce was what she really wanted and to feel welcome to call again if she needed.

Both of these calls involved relatively newly married couples in their twenties in which the wife did not enjoy sex. And in both cases, the wife was reluctant to discuss the problem with her husband. But the first call, made by the husband, was described as dealing with a sexual (*xing*) problem, while the second, made by a different wife, was described as a marriage (*hunyin*) problem. And in the first case, the husband was encouraged to await his wife's interest and try to kindle it with more sexual knowledge and better technique. That is, the advice retained the sexual emphasis of the call, and he was not encouraged to examine the feelings in the relationship, except his own patience with his wife.

In the latter call, the counselor did not discuss sexual technique or knowledge with the wife—either her own or her husband's. Rather, the problem and the advice were discussed in terms of the kinds of affection needed to foster marital stability. That is, the wife's agency was viewed not in terms of whether she could transform their sexual relationship, but whether she could develop deeper affection for her husband as the basis of marriage. Of course, the calls were made by different people and handled by two different counselors, which may account somewhat for these differences. But the gender effect of the two types of advice is still significant: in both cases, the husband is seen as the sexual agent responsible for successful intercourse and the wife as the emotional agent who determines marital stability.[49] More

49. Harriet Evans describes similar gender distinctions in discourses of sexuality throughout post-Liberation China. See Evans 1997.

sex education—a thoroughly modern concept—is held up as the answer for the man, while reliance on traditional notions of stable affection that grows after marriage is suggested for the woman.

Although the gender distinction in marital and sexual obligations shows both the internalization and reinscription of what might be seen as patriarchal norms, these phone calls also reveal transformations in both social conditions and traditional gender roles. The first caller made frank reference to the possibility of an outside lover (though only to deny it). Moreover, the calls demonstrate that women as well as men feel that their own sexual pleasure is a legitimate desire that they are justified in pursuing, at least within the sanctity of marriage. In both cases, a satisfying sexual relationship is viewed as a constituent (indeed expected) aspect of modern, monogamous marriage, rather than a duty to ensure reproduction. These expectations about sexuality and marriage are taken as givens; it is the specific gender and sexual roles *in relation to marriage and family* that were negotiated in each case.

Gender, Family Relations, and Chinese Family Values

The gendered construction of women's role in the Chinese family and household was especially evident in the discussion of the wife's predicament in the second call. Her primary obligation, as expressed by her own articulation of her situation, is to the maintenance of family relations. She marries in the first place to fulfill her sick (future) father-in-law's wishes, making her an obedient daughter-in-law. She engages in unpleasant sexual relations with her husband, thereby making her a dutiful wife. And she considers divorce after taking into account that there are no children to suffer the consequences, making her a good (potential) mother. Although this woman's call was motivated by a sexual concern, in the course of the conversation her situatedness in a web of family relations both explains her actions and offers a potential escape from those bonds: that is, not yet having borne a child, she feels freer to leave an unhappy marriage to pursue a better one. After articulating the conditions that demonstrate her fulfillment of the requirements of a Chinese woman in traditional terms, she nevertheless considers, and is given license by the counselor to consider, a modern solution for her unhappy marriage: divorce.

This call demonstrated the simultaneous interweaving and contestation between what might be seen as the remnants of entrenched "feudal" family values and new expectations for sexual and marital satisfaction predicated on changing social and material conditions. This negotiation of modern family values "with Chinese characteristics" presented potential challenges to other family relationships as well. Among these was the volatile realm of mother- and daughter-in-law relations (*po-xi guanxi*). *Po-xi guanxi* is considered one of the greatest determinants of marital happiness, and thus marital stability, in Shanghai's cramped living quarters where married couples often still live with the husband's parents.[50] It is also the site of the restructuring of power and social relations in the Chinese family.

One call to the women's hotline came from a woman who was angry about living with her parents-in-law. She had such severe conflicts with her mother-in-law that she did not even want to share meals with her. According to the caller, the other family members felt she was in the right but that she was wrong to refuse to eat with her mother-in-law. The woman recently had been given a second, smaller apartment by her work unit. She felt the in-laws should move to the new apartment and leave the bigger one to her and her husband. The father-in-law was willing to move, but the mother-in-law refused. Likewise, the wife's husband was willing to move to the smaller apartment, but the wife felt that if she agreed it would signal her mother-in-law's victory. Thus, both women refused to move, and now they were not even on speaking terms. Wasn't she right, the caller wanted to know, to expect her mother-in-law to move in order to allow the younger generation a more comfortable home?

The counselor, a woman in her mid-thirties, was less certain. The most important thing, she suggested, was maintaining cordial and stable family relations. Perhaps, if the wife was so unhappy, *she* should move with her husband. At least she should resume speaking to her mother-in-law. Otherwise everyone in the family would suffer, and a good daughter-in-law should think about the older generation and try to get along. The caller seemed unconvinced: by refusing to move, her mother-in-law just wanted to make her unhappy.

Daughters-in-law have long held claim to suffering in China, and in this case the wife used her culturally legitimate claim to this bitter status to justify a perhaps less culturally legitimate expectation that her mother-in-law should move. In refusing to fully endorse her expectations, the counselor invoked another "traditional" expectation of daughters-in-law: that they acquiesce to their position in the patriarchal family hierarchy. Thus, the caller was claiming a moral position based on being a lowly daughter-in-law—but used that claim to seek a less bitter, more materially comfortable "modern" life living in a nuclear family unit, where she could potentially exert more influence. The same moral claim, though, was used to counter her demands

50. In Shanghai, less than 50 percent of newly married couples have a separate home from their parents. Liu Ying and Xue Suzhen 1987, p. 122. In 1987 in Shanghai, between 50 and 70 percent of households were nuclear family households, depending on the district (p. 114), and the trend was toward an increasing number of nuclear family households in the 1990s. However, these percentages are still lower than for other major Chinese cities, and sociologist Xu Anqi noted a slight increase in multigenerational households in Shanghai from the early 1980s to the early 1990s. Xu Anqi 1995, p. 9. See also D. Davis in Davis and Harrell 1993.

and admonish her to fulfill her role as a good daughter-in-law. Again, living as a modern nuclear family was acceptable, but the caller's insistence on having a higher-status home than her in-laws became the bone of contention.

The family, as the primary social unit in Confucian ideology, is a fundamental structural unit shaping people's subjectivities within Chinese culture. That is, while one's class position is a politically (state-) or economically (capitalist-) imposed category, the family constitutes what is seen as the most natural and enduring social unit. Throughout the twentieth century, feudal family relations, which oppress women in particular, were seen as a primary impediment to China's modernization.[51] In the contemporary era, the family (rather than one's class or party status) has reemerged as the fundamental structure of Chinese social relations. But the form and structure of *modern* family relations remains a contested domain, and one that symbolizes both the endurance of Chinese cultural values and the bitterness those values can engender.

Negotiating family obligations and a new family order often brought forth the contradictory demands of men and women in those domains—even within a single generation. These contradictions were especially evident in a hotline call to the popular late-night radio hotline, "Your Partner til Dawn." After five years of trying with his wife to conceive a child, the male caller had just learned that his wife was finally pregnant. But the pregnancy was a result of her having slept with his brother. The caller described the terrible fight that ensued with his brother and said that he could no longer even look at his wife without feeling angry. She told him she was justified because she wanted to have a child; this way, she would still carry on his family lineage. She told her husband she still loved him and did not have feelings for his brother. She only slept with her brother-in-law to get pregnant. The caller said he wanted to believe his wife, but he couldn't get it out of his mind that she and his brother had slept together. The radio host was sympathetic to the caller, but she said it was only natural for a woman to want a child. He should be more understanding of her desire to be a mother. Now that she was already pregnant, the host advised, the husband should not divorce her, because divorce would have a terrible effect on the child.

The morning after this call, I discussed this program with Mrs. Zhao (a pseudonym), a 65-year-old regular listener who commented: "I try not to miss [the program], because it shows how Chinese people's lives really are. It's very realistic. That kind of thing happens in China all the time. In feudal times, a man could sleep with his son's wife, and the son had to accept it. That's the way it is in Chinese families. Chinese people eat so much bitterness. That man was very troubled, but of course his wife would want to have a child. In China, a married woman without a child gets looked at. It's natural for her to want a child; you can't blame her. It's because family is so im-

---

51. See Barlow 1994; Yuning Li 1992; Honig and Hershatter 1988.

portant, so people have to eat bitterness for the sake of their families. It's always been this way in China. It's better now, but anyone who listens to these stories can relate to them because of their own situation."

Here again the woman's subjectivity was constructed in relation to motherhood and to her family obligation to continue the male line. Even the husband was urged to think of the effect on the progeny of this lineage, rather than the affront to his own sexual prowess. By claiming that this kind of thing happens all the time in China, Mrs. Zhao conveyed the sense of connectedness that listeners experienced when hearing personal and even highly individualized revelations over the radio hotline. It was not so much the details of the story to which she and other listeners related (although in some cases it might be), but rather the importance of family relations, hierarchies, and gender roles in determining one's lot in life.

Thus this rather sensational call evoked a discourse on the bitterness of Chinese lives based on the complex hierarchy of family relations and "Confucian" demands to maintain the male family line. At a time when improving material life should have implied the reduction of hardship, this discourse of bitterness imposed by family obligation nevertheless emerged in many of the calls. The shared language and assumptions of family obligation legitimized the callers' complaints and connected listeners and callers to people they had never seen or met and even to generations of Chinese before them. Thus, despite the inherent modernity of advice hotlines, and even the modernity of many of the people's problems, callers (and listeners) often justified their claims by relying on the language of the "traditional" bitterness of Chinese lives.

EATING AND SPEAKING BITTERNESS: HISTORICAL LEGACY AND THE LANGUAGE OF LEGITIMIZATION

Derived from a Buddhist poem, the Chinese expression "to eat bitterness" (*chi ku*) evokes life's hardships through a bodily metaphor. The expression is linked to notions found in Chinese medicine, in which the eating of bitter herbs is often considered necessary for good health. In the culinary domain, Chinese culture divides foods into five flavors that are associated with five viscera. Bitterness corresponds to fire and to the heart (*xin*).[52] "To eat bitterness" implies enduring the hardships that usually result from one's gendered and class position—that is, hardships that are one's fate within a stringent Confucian social hierarchy. For instance, peasants and daughters-in-law were two categories of social identity widely acknowledged to have eaten the most bitterness in pre-Liberation China.

In contrast, "to speak bitterness," at least in Communist China, implies chal-

52. See Chang 1977.

lenging the fate imposed by one's social status. After Liberation (1949), speaking bitterness at public meetings was a party-state ideological effort not only to transform the consciousness of the people but also to root out the "five bad classes" that socialism would eradicate.[53] The historical antecedents of the "speak bitterness" campaigns have not been thoroughly explored. However, Vera Schwarcz has argued that advocacy for more public speech about one's hardships can be traced back at least to the May 4 Movement of 1919.[54]

And perhaps ironically, although it was Mao who exhorted the populace to speak bitterness against feudal and capitalist oppressors, the chaos and excesses of the Cultural Revolution have made that era its own source of bitterness to speak out against.[55] For example, many callers blamed their marital woes on politically driven matches made during the Cultural Revolution; laid-off workers noted that they did not have the skills needed for the new job market because they had missed being educated during the Cultural Revolution; and even spoiled and unruly children were said to be the product of parents who had not learned good child-rearing skills because their own mothers had been busy making revolution instead of stable homes. This last example again points to the reinvigoration of family values and traditional gender roles that have replaced the socialist values and revolutionary fervor of the Maoist decades.

These examples highlight the fact that, despite the creature comforts associated with an expanding consumer culture and improved standard of living, many Chinese people share the perception that they continue to eat bitterness in their everyday lives. In affluent Shanghai, this bitterness is less the hardship of poverty than an expression of their unmet desires presented by the possibilities of the new economic and social conditions in urban China. By utilizing the cultural idiom of bitterness to evoke one's suffering, the speaker also gains a legitimacy to voice his or her desire to capitalize on the opportunities and openness of the new era. For example, both men and women would like to lead sexually fulfilling lives that reject the revolution-

53. See Kleinman and Kleinman 1996. Tu 1996; Butterfield 1982; and Mihalca 1992.

54. Ann Anagnost argues that the historical antecedents of the speak-bitterness campaigns in Communist China have not been adequately explored (Anagnost 1992). But challenging the commonly held view that public speech about personal grief was a product of Maoism, Vera Schwarcz (1996) argues that by the Cultural Revolution (1966–76), "China's traditional reticence about personal sorrow had been under assault for almost one hundred years" (p. 123). The erosion of the imperial system, the introduction of social Darwinism, and a climate of disillusionment following the Opium Wars all contributed to China's first "Cultural Revolution" in the early twentieth century in which the expression of "individual suffering was seen as useful because it had a distinctive social purpose: it could improve the lives of future individuals" (p. 123). This view provided the foundation for viewing the expression of *ku* (sorrow or bitterness) as moral practice, despite Confucian dictates that "sought to mute, or at least to moderate, the public expression of personal sorrow" (p. 122).

55. See Tu 1996.

ary puritanism of the Cultural Revolution, and young couples would like to have their own apartments and live at least partially outside the power structures of the multigenerational family. That is, invoking bitterness in the contemporary era expresses both a critique of the Maoist excesses and dissatisfaction with persistent "feudal" family values; it also reveals the desire for greater individual agency—not only in relation to the state but also in relation to the family.

Thus, invoking bitterness is a legitimate way to *voice* complaints and perhaps even implies people's ability to transform constraining cultural and economic circumstances. But the bitterness of contemporary family and sexual politics is often exacerbated, rather than mitigated, by the flourishing consumer lifestyles of affluent urban Chinese. Thus "consumerism" does not ease the bitterness of Chinese lives; rather it highlights the extent to which Chinese cultural identity is validated through the moral practice of enduring hardship, even as material conditions improve. This process of cultural validation highlights the ways in which "traditional" ideologies about eating bitterness persist alongside of, and perhaps because of, new technologies and practices of everyday life. And although "heart talk" (*xinli hua*)—as personal revelations are often called—is perceived to be outside the political realm, it is in fact a direct product of new and reconstituted political-economic relations in late-twentieth-century China.

The language of bitterness draws on the long shared history of injustice that the Communist Party is dedicated to alleviating. But utilizing a quintessentially modern medium like the advice hotlines confers the gloss of modernity and openness upon those who provide and use the services. Despite the anonymity of hotlines, the expressions of bitterness and injustice rooted in their social circumstances make the callers feel justified and foster a sense of historical and cultural connectedness. Moreover, the hotlines provide a medium for more open discussion of sexuality, in some cases even condoning the more open pursuit of sexual and marital satisfaction: even the wife who slept with her brother-in-law receives sympathy for her desire to bear a child. In a word, people's use of hotlines to voice complaints about their modern predicaments immediately implicates them in the practices of modernity and thereby poses a challenge to both the traditional values and the Maoist legacy that nevertheless have provided the vocabulary and context for their complaints.

PRIVILEGED TALK, SILENCED TALK:
ADVICE HOTLINES, FAMILY VALUES, AND THE STATE

As an examination of Shanghai's advice hotlines demonstrates, love, sexual pleasure, and material comforts were pursuits that engaged the minds, bodies, and hearts of the populace in the 1990s. Over the course of the decade, urban residents experienced increasing latitude in personal and familial decision-making, due in part to their growing affluence and in part to the retreat of the state from direct intervention in the "private" lives of its citizens. For most urbanites, this increasing latitude represented a modernity that eschewed their collective memory of China's repressive past. Talking more openly (and often publicly) about sexuality was the hallmark of that modernity.[56]

But I have tried to show that more talk about sexuality in the Chinese public does not necessarily imply greater individual freedom. Nor is it necessarily the case that the state allows more open discussion of sexuality and family problems in order to distract the citizenry from politics, although that may be one aspect.[57] Rather, the flourishing public discussions of sexuality via hotlines may point to new insertions of discursive and disciplinary power. Hotlines provide a means for the state to "overhear" (and thus monitor) the discursive negotiation of personal fulfillment and reconfigured family relations. They also allow the state to influence citizens' actions and identities by promoting "scientific" interventions like psychological counseling and sex education (*indirect*, discursive forms of power that Foucault called "biopower").[58]

Specifically, the advice and commentary generated by the hotlines draws on and promotes three ideologies that shape the constitution of modern Chinese citizens: (1) the importance of psychological health; (2) the importance of pleasure and leisure in daily life, and (3) the renewed emphasis on family values and stability in family relations as the basis for Chinese society. Each of these ideologies is constructed against what are seen as the crucial impediments of China's modernization: the feudal Confucian legacy and the excesses of the Cultural Revolution.

Moreover, hotline talk engenders discourses that rework "traditional" notions of bitterness and Chinese family values to allow people to negotiate modern predicaments of the late twentieth century. In the context of the state's diminishing capacity to provide social services through the party and the work unit, there is an increasing reliance on the Chinese family as the safety net. The state is acquiescent therefore in the reprivatization of social relations and social responsibilities into the family domain. And indeed, hotlines participate in rendering "family values" (including sexuality, marriage,

56. See also Hershatter 1996 and 1997.
57. See Gold 1993
58. Foucault 1979. Anagnost 1994 discusses the relevance of Foucault's notions of modern power to China. Of course, as I discussed earlier in this essay, the state also retains direct forms of control through media censorship, distribution of telephone infrastructure, and the like. My point here is to emphasize that even where the state seems to be retreating it continues to exercise indirect forms of state power.

and family relations) a privileged topic whose prevalence in fact masks a re-configuration of power relations in the Chinese public.

That is, the promotion of family values bolsters the disciplinary regime of the Chinese family, to which the socialist state had historically constructed itself in opposition.[59] In the 1990s, the Chinese party-state no longer positioned itself as uniformly antagonistic to either capitalist enterprises or the privatized family realm.[60] Rather, it became aligned with both in the constitution of a productive, socially stable, and consuming citizenry to drive the engines of economic growth and modernization. The fostering of extensive public discussion of sexuality should therefore be understood as a means by which the subjectivities of Chinese urbanites are redefined in relation to family, sexuality, and privatized consumption, rather than the outmoded ideals of the Maoist era. This redefinition poses not just new freedoms in sexual and familial domains, but as I have shown, also new constraints structured by familial relations and obligations.

Thus, it is perhaps too facile to view advice hotlines solely as providing opportunities for free and unencumbered speech in urban China's expanding public sphere. The discursive negotiation of Chinese family values should not be seen as a space *outside* power.[61] Rather, these speech acts, and the domain of family and sexual relations more generally, are themselves constitutive of power relations in the Chinese public. Their analysis reveals a language and set of practices utilized to negotiate (as well as challenge) the parameters of modernity, personal fulfillment, and family values as China embarks on the new millennium.

CONCLUSIONS

Hotlines and the discourses they promote can be seen as prototypically modern "technologies" (both technological and institutional) of biopower that allow Chinese citizens to express their narratives of suffering as well as their modern desires.[62] Though products of China's "opening," hotlines should not be viewed solely as providing opportunities for free and unencumbered speech in urban China's expanding public sphere. The calls and the advice, like the very technology that fosters them, are after-effects of both consumer capitalism (like the corporate sponsorship of hotlines to promote goods and

59. See Nonini and Ong 1997 for discussion of the Chinese family as a disciplinary regime (also Erwin 1998). Barlow (1991 and 1994) illustrates how the terms for "woman" in Chinese reflect shifting subjectivities in relation to the Chinese family and the state.

60. See also Honig and Hershatter 1988 and Dirlik 1994 for discussion of the resurgence of Confucian values in the post-Mao era.

61. See also Ong 1993 and 1997.

62. See Kleinman 1988 for discussion of "narratives" of illness and suffering.

services) and state agendas to promote modernization and social stability as a basis for prosperity and continuing political legitimacy. Even hotline calls broadcast on the radio are not free from censorship. And given the role of party cadres in providing advice and education, the state's intervening hand in the process must also be taken into account.

Nevertheless, the overwhelming focus of the calls on sexuality and family points to an important transformation in the *types* of speech the hotlines promote. Personal matters and private concerns are more public than ever before, and the extensive discussion of personal well-being seems to reject official state power and influence in daily life. But disinterest in official politics thrusts callers (and listeners) squarely into the realm of family politics—an arena that shapes their subjectivities and opportunities perhaps as much as direct state control did in earlier decades. Thus, rather than providing a means of escaping disciplinary power, hotlines contribute to a reconfiguration of power relations in the Chinese public. What they offer, therefore, is not as much an opportunity to articulate heartfelt problems outside regimes of power as a space of both anonymity and publicity in which to maneuver *among* structures of power in the pursuit of greater personal fulfillment and other modern desires.

CHAPTER 8

Greeting Cards in China

Mixed Language of Connections and Affections

Mary S. Erbaugh

THE GREETING CARD DELUGE

The Chinese invented paper. And in the 1990s, China was suddenly awash with hundreds of millions of foreign-looking Christmas cards festooning the offices of staunchly atheist bureaucrats, and birthday cards for young women whose birthdays went unmarked under patriarchy. As city dwellers develop wider social networks, cards trace a reworking of social relationships both inside and outside the family. Almost no cards existed in 1970s China or Taiwan, when my friends found the suggestion of Chinese New Year's or birthday cards odd and unattractive. They already enjoyed New Year's customs, they said, from making calls to pasting lucky couplets over their doors. Birthdays, they said, were for old men to celebrate on reaching 70 or 80. On their own birthdays, they were "sad, thinking of my mother's pain," at most celebrating with a bowl of long-life noodles. Still, they enjoyed Christmas and birthday parties with foreign friends.

Chinese cards emerged in the late 1980s, ballooning in popularity parallel to a commercialization of relationships that took 150 years in Europe and the Americas. Even in the 1990s, "greeting card" was not yet a dictionary entry. "Greeting card," *heka*, combines the second syllable of "express good wishes, to congratulate" (*zhuhe*) with the first syllable for a plain paper "card" (*kapian*), itself a loan from English "card." "Greeting card" seems coined by analogy with "greeting telegram" (*hedian*), long used for celebrating the births, weddings, and funerals that have required paper inscriptions for millennia.[1] But the new picture cards celebrate nonritualized

---

1. Dynastic China had a variety of predecessors to cards. Scholarly sorts, including the girl cousins in *Dream of the Red Chamber*, exchanged illustrated letters, as well as calligraphy, paint-

festivities outside this cycle, supplementing rather than threatening existing celebrations. In 1997, cards still celebrated only happy personal events. Get-well cards had barely emerged, and sympathy cards had yet to appear. In a stunning reversal of the Maoist iconography of selflessness, the cards pictured a consumer paradise of flowers, cars, jewels, and phones, an intriguing overlap with the paper models of luxuries that have long been burned after funerals to send them across to loved ones in the afterlife.

A YEAR'S CYCLE OF CARDS IN NANJING

Cards, like valentines in the West, represent a "modern reshaping of popular ritual in terms of vast markets, private exchanges, and standardized commodities."[2] A year's cycle of Chinese cards appears in a collection of 109 cards I bought and received in China between November 1995 and February 1997. Students and associates in China sent 49 cards to me or my spouse as regular greetings. I also bought 60 cards celebrating every type of event found in Nanjing, a city of 2 million, 200 miles inland from Shanghai. I did not attempt to buy every available card, since birthday cards alone come in dozens of styles. But cards for every popular occasion are for sale.[3] Cards for Christmas and the Lunar New Year, usually celebrated in February, are a bit over-represented in my collection because I collected during two Decembers. I talked about cards with numerous mainland and Hong Kong intellectuals and interviewed the owner of an upscale U.S. card shop and the director of North Asia marketing for Hallmark cards. A three-hour interview with three Chinese graduate students in Nanjing, two female and one male, was particularly helpful.[4]

All but one of the 109 cards mark happy personal events. (The get-well

---

ings, and poems tailored to all occasions. The less literate turned to model letter books. And the illiterate hired professional letter writers in the markets to write their letters for them and to read the responses. Both the letter books and professional scribes still abound. Name cards also had precedents that overlapped with greeting cards in size and color as far back as the Zhou dynasty (1066–771 B.C.). Old China also had New Year's cards (*he nian pian*) inscribed with the sender's name and address, as well as New Year's greetings as far back as the Song dynasty (960–1279 A.D.). By the seventeenth century, red New Year's cards had become popular and were often sent with a gift. Liu Guiqiu 1986. Yu Wenxue and Zhang Lehe 1988.

2. Schmidt 1995, p. 40.

3. The collection also includes a dozen cards that Ming historian Cynthia Brokaw bought for me in western Fujian. I also include the three cards Deborah Davis bought in Shanghai in February 1997, which include the only baby card and get-well card any of us spotted.

4. I thank especially Nanjing students Huang Xiaofang (of Jiangxi), Huang Xiuping (of Putian, Fujian), and Sun Qixiang (of Zhejiang). Kim Rexius, the owner of Jabberwocky Cards and Gifts of Eugene, Oregon, contributed two helpful hour-long interviews (August 19 and 21, 1996). Clive Smith, Hallmark marketing director for North Asia, provided a useful phone

card is the exception.) Classifying the cards by their main Chinese caption, I assembled 35 New Year's cards, 26 Christmas cards, 24 birthday cards, and 15 friendship cards. Much less common are cards for congratulations (3), weddings (2), a teacher (1), a mother (1), a new baby (1), and with get-well wishes (1) (see Table 8.1). The cards are strikingly apolitical. The sole exception is a 1997 New Year's card celebrating the reunification with Hong Kong. I found no cards for national holidays or party relationships, and none to mark an event in the workplace, such as an employee's transfer or promotion. Instead, foreign themes and English captions predominate, especially on the birthday cards, which are sent disproportionately by young people.

Crossover Captions and Collage Images.

Mixed images abound in the fast-changing world of celebrations. A crossover caption presents two conflicting main headings, such as "Season's Greetings" in English above the Chinese for "Happy Birthday." Crossover captions appear on 38 percent of the cards collected before December 1996. Better editing eliminated crossover in main captions in the later subset, bringing the overall percentage down to 24 percent. However, crossover subheads and imagery remained abundant. Some cards are literal collages, including two with pasted-on cork and twine. Collage-like images are more common still, for designers literally mix images from different cards by cutting, pasting, and using scanners. Santa joins a baby elephant in diapers and other Japanese cartoon characters on one card. On another, Santa floats over illustrated instructions on "how to grow artichokes" lifted from an English gardening book. A third pictures a Volkswagen beetle, a fountain pen, a wristwatch, and a football jacket in drawings lifted from U.S.-made gift wrap. Collage images are so common that Beijing artists produced parodies to sell at an art exhibit at McDonald's. One showed "a bizarre creature—with the body of a dragon, the head of Donald Duck, a foot in a Nike sneaker, and claws clutching a stack of dollar bills—against a Ming vase pattern."[5] Christmas cards have especially high crossover with birthdays; a card with a sleigh full of gifts may be recycled by stamping "Happy Birthday" on it in gold. Other collages are more harmonious: a friendship card adds a Chinese fortune-telling wheel to a desktop full of roses, lace, and a handwritten English letter.

---

interview (March 11, 1998). I also thank Dick Kraus, Cynthia Brokaw, and Deborah Davis for help collecting and discussing the cards. Thanks also to colleagues at the City University of Hong Kong, especially Jenny Wang, as well as students Florence Wan-ping Kwok and Ada Shuk-lan Chan.

5. Unfortunately, the exhibit planned for 1993 never took place because the artists forgot to get a police permit. Zha 1995, pp. 111–12.

TABLE 8.1 Types of Greeting Cards and Motifs
(percent)

Type of card (N = 109)	Foreign words	Flowers	Cartoon	Luxury	Cross-over	Chinese symbol	Food	Human figure	Humor	Music	Music chip
New Year (35 cards)	42	42	31	17	11	34	14	20	14	3	—
Christmas (26)	96	68	50	19	15	12	8	8	15	12	—
Birthday (24)	79	71	37	42	37	8	13	8	8	13	33
Friendship (15)	53	73	20	40	27	7	27	13	13	13	7
Congratulations (3)	100	66	33	33	33	33	33	—	—	66	—
Wedding (2)	50	100	—	—	50	—	—	50	—	—	—
Teacher (1)	100	100	—	100	100	—	100	—	—	—	—
Mother (1)	—	100	—	—	—	—	—	—	—	—	—
Baby (1)	100	—	—	—	—	—	—	100	100	—	—
Get well (1)	100	—	—	—	—	—	—	—	100	—	—

CARDS THAT DON'T EXIST (YET)

Customs for birth, illness, and death are relatively intact, and people seem to feel little need to replace or add to them. So get-well cards and baby cards are rare, and sympathy cards, a major Western genre, do not exist. The Nanjing students shuddered an emphatic, "No!" when asked if they had seen one in 1996. Sympathy telegrams are standard, they said, having sent a few themselves. Get-well cards did not appeal to this young and healthy group either. No one had seen one, though someone heard that something like it was available in Shanghai. (It was.) Illness and death may seem too dangerous to be treated with a mere card, requiring more substantial shows of support such as visits and gifts of food and medicine. Such views are less distant from U.S. norms than one might think. Even Hallmark is "still not comfortable with the word 'death' in sympathy cards." And some card sections omit get-well cards, including the bookstore at a Christian Science college in Illinois.[6] U.S.-style cards for divorcing men and women, alcoholics, dieters, and people whose pets have just died seem more distant still. Although birth is a happy event, it retains some taboos in China. Baby cards did not yet exist in Nanjing either. But the students were intrigued: "What's a baby card? What does it look like? Who gets it, the baby?" Young adults do celebrate a birth by sending gifts of food, clothing, and silver baby bracelets. For weddings, also, they telegraph greetings, attend banquets, and give cash gifts, but sending cards is rare.

Asked about sending cards for Chinese festivals other than the Lunar New Year, these students laughed at the idea of a card for the Grave-Sweeping Festival (*Qing ming jie*), or for the Dragon Boat Festival (*Duan wu jie*). The Grave-Sweeping Festival is a happy family event, which generally includes a trip to the cemetery and a picnic. But both the intimate family focus and a death taboo may preclude a need for cards. The Dragon Boat Festival is celebrated with exciting races in dragon-shaped boats and includes ritual activities to ward off drowning, plague, and the "five pestilences." At the Mid-Autumn Festival, families gather to eat moon-shaped cakes and watch the full moon. A family dinner also marks the winter solstice. Outside relationships are not emphasized at these times. One celebrates by staying in with the family, not by sending a card. No one had thought of sending a National Day card on October 1. (One Hong Kong leftist told me she plans to design such a card.) Other national holidays also lacked cards, including Labor Day (May 1), Children's Day (June 1), and Teacher's Day (September 10). The Nanjing students had not sent cards when they were children but mused that prosperous children of the 1990s might well do so, although they had not seen cards designed for children. None had sent a Mother's Day card, though they thought it a nice idea. They scoffed at the idea of Father's Day cards, though

6. Hirshey 1995, p. 23. I thank Carol Rupprecht for the anecdote about Principia College.

they knew the date. They were familiar with the idea of valentines but had never seen one. Hearing that Japan had transformed Valentine's Day into an occasion requiring young women workers to send cards and chocolates to their male bosses, they hoped these customs would not reach China.

MIXED THEMES IN THE CARDS: FLOWERS, CHRISTMAS, WEALTH, AND WARMTH

Cards in my collection are overwhelmingly sentimental: flowers appear on two out of three (68 percent). A typical card shows a cuddly pink cartoon rabbit delivering a huge basket of flowers (see Card 1 in Figure 8.1). This birthday card includes more of the card motifs listed in Table 8.2 than any other card: complex Chinese characters, an English caption, flowers, a cartoon character, a crossover caption, and a music chip playing "Happy Birthday." The outside of the bunny card prints "Seasons Greetings" in English above the Chinese for "Happy Birthday." Inside, the bunny's large plastic headband reads, "Happy to you" [sic] in English, and "Wishing you [honorific] happiness" in Chinese (*zhu nin kuaile*); battery-powered, it lights up red and plays "Happy Birthday." The caption in small black characters says simply, "A bunch of flowers, a heartfelt wish / That every moment, every day, will bring you [honorific] joy" (*yi shu xian hua, yi ge xin yuan / mei shi mei ri nin yong heng tong zai*). Other motifs listed in Table 8.2 do not appear on the bunny card, including: luxury goods, Chinese symbols such as dragons, food, human figures, and musical instruments. But this same bunny appears also on Christmas and friendship cards. The envelopes show press runs of 100,000. Such flowery cards resemble Western cards of early industrialization, which were also full of flowers, lace, glitter, and effusively literal good wishes. The most popular Hallmark card of all time, which has sold 28 million copies since 1939, pictures a basket of pansies with the tag, "Thinking of you," a sentiment that blends well with current Chinese taste.[7]

Raw humor is rare on the Chinese cards, and rarely is an image presented without a caption or explicit greeting. Compare the bunny birthday card with a best-selling U.S. birthday card, a satirical cartoon. A fat, middle-aged woman posts a "lost puppy" flier, oblivious that she has sat on her tiny dog, smashing it into her huge behind. The inside caption reads, "Another birthday behind you! Happy Birthday!"[8] Humor depends on knowing the idiom "to put

---

7. Ibid., pp. 22–23. Americans buy 7.5 million cards a year. Only the British buy more. The pansies silently invoke English folk flower symbols. As Ophelia says in *Hamlet*, "Pansies, they're for thoughts."

8. The caption for this 1996 Noble Works card is used with the permission of artist Eric Decetis.

FIGURE 8.1 (Card 1).
A crossover birthday card:
"Season's Greetings—Wishing
you [honorific] happiness /
Happy to You / A bunch of
flowers, a heartfelt wish /
That every day will bring you
[honorific] joy."

[something unpleasant] behind you," as well as the faintly off-color idiom
for an unpleasant surprise, "[something] just bit you on the butt." Heavily
allusive comic cards probably require a print-saturated society, sodden with
too-readily expressed emotions. Humorous cards make up 25 percent of the
Hallmark inventory and much more for smaller companies. But only 15 of
the 109 Chinese cards (14 percent) are funny by any stretch of the imagination. In one, a famous historical figure, the righteous Judge Bao, charges
a ghostly defendant with losing touch with his friends (Card 2, Figure 8.2).
Humor is riskier in China, restricted to closer relationships. Raw jokes like
the smashed puppy risk giving offense. Birthdays are no laughing matter in
a subsistence society. A deep sense of entitlement to long life is required before a whole society turns rueful about the sufferings of middle age. However, the Nanjing students said they wished more funny cards were available.

Secular Christmas Cards

Christmas cards, the most popular card category after the New Year's cards,
often look entirely Western. In fact, like the distinctively Chinese uses of Mc-
Donald's described by Yunxiang Yan in Chapter 9, Christmas cards adapt
also to Chinese social use. Cards convey not religious messages, but over-

FIGURE 8.2 (Card 2).
A friendship card: "Judge
Bao's Strange Judgments /
'Unjust!' / Divination dish."

whelmingly secular winter greetings. Indeed, only one of the 26 cards collected includes a religious image, toddler angels around a manger.[9] Religion is still tightly controlled in China, and the state firms that publish cards are particularly cautious. The Nanjing students had never heard that some non-religious Westerners do not send Christmas cards or say "Merry Christmas" on the grounds that Christmas is a religious celebration. Instead, the Chinese students, like the rest of China and much of Asia, increasingly celebrate Christmas as a secular festival, both as a marketing tool and to extend winter festivities for more than a month before the Lunar New Year. The Singapore government sponsors enormous secular Christmas street decorations as a cross-ethnic bridge for festivals beginning with Hindu Deepavali in November through the Lunar New Year. One McDonald's won a government Christmas prize for its five-meter Ronald McDonald's dancing under eight-meter orange conga drums. In Japan and Thailand, Christmas celebrations and cards are also popular. One Thai card pictures the Emerald Buddha;

9. Two additional cards had tiny angels stamped on the rear. And Davis spotted a card in Shanghai offering "prayers for your birthday."

TABLE 8.2   Greeting Card Motifs
(percent)

Complex characters	89
Foreign caption	68
Flowers	61
Cartoon character	34
Luxury goods	27
Crossover heading	
(e.g., "Happy Birthday" on a wedding card)	24
Food	15
Chinese symbol	17
Picture of a human being	15
Humor	14
Music	9
Music chip	8

another shows the cigar-smoking Buddhist monk celebrity who works miracles, including winning at the race track. Even Khmer Rouge guerrillas once used a Christmas card to get in touch with a U.S. contact.[10]

Wishing You Wealth

Chinese good wishes often wish the recipient wealth. The time-honored equivalent to "Happy New Year" is literally, "Congratulations! Get rich!" (*gongxi facai*). New Year's symbols include gold ingots and fish (*yu*), a pun on "abundance" (also *yu*); carp (*li*), a pun on "advantage" (also *li*); and oranges, the word for which is the same as that for gold and good luck. Flowers, the most common card motif, symbolize the words "flowers open" (*hua kai*), a near pun on "prosperity." The most elegant cards feature classical-style flower paintings of fastidiously rendered peonies, which symbolize wealth, and plum blossoms for enduring winter hardship. Cheaper cards sometimes paint unfamiliar Western flowers jumbled together out of season, holly bunched with tulips in the snow. Other historical symbols include eagles, menacing to Western eyes but appropriate as symbols of bravery for someone facing a challenge in a new year or a new job (see Card 3, Figure 8.3). Food appears on about one in six cards (15 percent) as a link with subsistence society. Fish and fruit and cream cakes abound under captions such as, "sending you a beautiful cake and an abundance of gifts." One New Year's card shows oranges set on a newspaper with the distracting English headline, "Passover

10. Singapore visit November 1996; Thai cards from Chiang Mai visit January 1996; Fitzgerald 1997.

FIGURE 8.3 (Card 3).
A New Year's card:
"Season's Greetings /
Merry Christmas /
and a / Happy New
Year. / May even the
mountains seem small.
/ 1995, Autumn.
Su Ren paints this."

Prices." Another (Card 4, Figure 8.4) shows a collage of Garfield the comic-strip cat gobbling up sausage, catsup, grapes, pineapple, and canned fruit next to a different Garfield served up on a platter like a suckling pig.

Consumer society is marked by a self-indulgent sense of entitlement, one Agnew describes as dependent on fantasy and postponing fulfillment by window-shopping, imagining the objects wrapped in plastic, then patiently unwrapping them at last.[11] Most Chinese cards come in cellophane folders that the sender leaves on; the cellophane keeps the dust off and adds to the recipient's excitement about what is inside. Many cards release perfume on opening. Luxury items are pictured on 42 percent of the birthday cards (and 27 percent of all cards): cell phones and tennis rackets; skis, cars, and fountain pens; electric lamps and irons; sauce pans, warm jackets, and white lace gloves and strings of pearls that match the elaborate Western-style wedding dresses Gillette describes in Chapter 4. The word "luxurious" appears printed above a crown on one card. Travel fantasies are also popular: the teacher's card pictures a Paris sidewalk cafe. Cards with music chips feature

11. Agnew 1993, p. 25.

FIGURE 8.4 (Card 4).   A friendship card: "A beautiful dream / Like a beautiful poem / Both appear by chance, but not on request, / Ever present and / Sometimes the unexpected happens in an instant. / Fantastic scenery / Stubborn beliefs."

Western music; eleven cards play the first few bars of "Happy Birthday," "Jingle Bells," or "Santa Claus Is Coming"—or all three in succession.[12] One Nanjing student wished for less tinny music, as well as Chinese tunes. Other cards portray music with a picture of a guitar or an angel choir. Hong Kong and Taiwan pop stars appear in photo collages on four cards, including Card 5 (see Figure 8.5). Stealing celebrity photos is common: one pictured a star whose face had been spliced onto the body of the lead actress in a Hong Kong pornographic film.

Pictures of spacious, warm, and sturdy houses echo the urge for oasis that Fraser sees reflected in Shanghai real estate ads (Chapter 2 in this volume). A large U.S. tract house with Santa's sleigh on the lawn appears to have been lifted from a homemade U.S. card (Card 6, see Figure 8.6). Other cards show brick houses nestled under snowy roofs and a Disney-style castle on a hill. Institutions also show off their newest buildings. One professor says she prefers photos of campus buildings to cards featuring happy students because, "I like my friends to see where I'm working." But the biggest real estate fantasy of all pictures Hong Kong's glittering highrises and governor's mansion under the Chinese flag.

12. Music chips disappeared by December 1996, perhaps because students in Malaysia sent a letter bomb that adapted a musical card as a fuse.

FIGURE 8.5 (Card 5).
A birthday card: "Happy
Birthday."

Wishing You Warmth

Many Chinese cards strike Westerners as sentimental. Less expressive than
people of many other cultures, the Chinese may use cards to convey affec-
tions that they are uncomfortable expressing aloud. The repressiveness of
Chinese government and adult norms render playfulness, sentimentality, and
fantasy the more enticing.[13] One card prints English "Romanticism" above
a cartoon kitty and teddy bears. Cuddly cartoon figures appear on 34 percent of all cards and on 50 percent of the Christmas cards, more than twice
as often as realistic drawings of humans (15 percent). Garfield and Mickey
Mouse appear, unlicensed, along with the cuter Japanese cartoon characters; but generic figures are more common still. Schematic cartoon faces may
be more perceptually accessible than realistically rendered faces. Experiments with babies show this preference even among newborns. Cartoon bun-
nies, frogs, and pigs, called "neuters" in the card trade, bypass gender, race,
age, and class divisions. Evoking the simple indulgences of Chinese early
childhood, they offer nonsexualized affection to friends of both sexes that

13. See Agnew 1993, pp. 25–26, for a discussion of asceticism and sentimentality.

聖 陣陣無聲的祝福自心底發出 ♥ 愿你每日都在心中留下芬芳 誕

快 樂

MERRY CHRISTMAS.

FIGURE 8.6 (Card 6). A Christmas card: "[Four corners] Mer-ry Christ-mas; Wishing you Good Fortune Silently from the Bottom of my Heart. Hoping you Find Some Sweet Pleasures in Your Life Every Day. Merry Christmas."

makes no demands for commitment. Unlike advertising images, cartoon animals do not impose impossible ideals of female beauty. Instead, they walk about mostly naked, often carrying high-tech luxuries like cell phones.

LANGUAGE AS MIXED AS THE PICTURES

The language in the cards is as mixed, flexible, and colloquial as the pictures. Chinese is by far the dominant language; all but one card carries a Chinese caption. Yet 68 percent include some foreign words. Code-mixing is the term linguists use for the mixing of languages or styles. Nouns such as "love" and *amour* and formulaic greetings such as "Happy Birthday" are especially likely to be mixed. Code-mixing does not indicate language weakness, but rather growing sophistication in circles where many people are at least marginally familiar with another language or style. Code-mixing typically shows order beneath a surface chaos in its selective insertion of words that are unavailable or have different connotations in the dominant language. The Chinese cards take foreign formula phrases such as "Happy Birthday" and translate, adapt, and mix them into highly colloquial spoken-style Chinese. I had expected the Chinese captions to resemble existing rhymes, poems, couplets, and greetings used to mark major life events. But the card captions almost never rhymed and never even made a poem. The language, like the occasions celebrated, complements rather than replaces existing celebrations. Multiple styles compete almost everywhere in modern written Chinese, but the cards are eclectic in the extreme. One card humorously mixes a terse written Chinese bureaucratic warning: "*Jinji* [an urgent message]: Merry Christmas." Literary Chinese captions do not appear, not even a quoted couplet. Most Chinese cannot read extended classical texts, which require years of elite instruction. The cards do lift the occasional well-known literary phrase, much as an English valentine might ask "How do I love thee? Let me count the ways." The inside of Figure 8.2 shows Judge Bao issuing a semiclassical command to a neglectful friend, "Immediately book a ticket home, round trip from Harbor to Tai" (*Mashang dinggou Gang-Tai laihui jipiao yi fen*). And then in recognition that few will understand the classical phrase, the card adds an explanation: "from the Southern Harbor to [Sacred] Mount Tai [in the Chinese heartland]" (*Zhuming: Nangang dao Taishan*).[14] Archaic and colloquial language mix in the additional tag, "Alack—hope you can pull it off!" (*Xi—xiwang ni keyi bandao!*).

Mixed styles are scarcely new. A Yunnan cloth merchant's son outraged 1940s sensibilities by issuing a wedding invitation in his own name rather than his father's and by using a wild mixture of classical and modern styles.[15] Most current cards, however, use spoken styles that range from using lush phrases for wedding speeches to the ordinary playful banter of teenage girls, such as "Have you gone pee-pee yet?" (*Ni you mei you niaoniao?*) (Gan Wang, reports). Surprisingly, neither slang nor dialect appears in the collection. Both remain stigmatized in written Chinese and also would pose barriers to nationwide marketing.

Formulaic Greetings

Almost every card includes formulaic greetings such as "Happy Birthday" in English, Chinese, or both. Most formula phrases are conspicuous European imports. The most frequent rendition of "Happy New Year" (*xinnian kuaile*), a literal translation, adapts to both the Western and the Lunar New Year. The socialists promoted this greeting in a sustained but unsuccessful effort to move festivities to January 1 (as Japan has done) and to wipe out superstition and the love of money voiced in the venerable greeting, "Congratulations, get rich!" (*gongxi facai*). This old greeting, common on cards found in Hong Kong and Taiwan, is back in spoken mainland greetings. However, it appears in print on only two mainland cards, including inside the Judge Bao card (Figure 8.2). And the socialist-approved phrase "Happy Spring Festival" (*chun jie kuaile*) does not appear at all. Yet only two cards consist entirely of traditional lucky phrases, one of them the "Passover" card. Quite a

---

14. The text, however, simultaneously sends another message: the usual understanding of *gang-tai* would be Hong Kong–Taiwan.

15. Hsu 1948, p. 96.

送你一片真诚的心意，
送你一朵美丽的鲜花。
我要把千言万语和纯洁的爱，
变成一张美妙的贺卡，
为你的生日增添欢快的光彩。

FIGURE 8.7
(Card 7).   A birthday
card: "Happy Birthday."

few do append such phrases as "Wishing you happiness and good fortune" (*zhu ni yukuai xingfu*); "May all your wishes come true each and every year" (*niannian ruyi*); or "Peace in our time and every year" (*niannian ping'an*). But these mix with more colloquial sayings and imported formula phrases. The most-used phrase for "Happy New Year" (*xinnian kuaile*) parallels the Chinese for "Merry Christmas," (literally "Christmas happy," *shengdan kuaile*). Many cards print both, a stylistic bridge as strong as the picture of Santa embracing a cow for the upcoming Year of the Ox. "Season's Greetings" appears frequently, equidistant from socialist and religious ideology. "Happy New Year to You" also pops up, modeled on the familiar birthday song. Even "Happy to you" [sic], the all-purpose coinage, is considered warmer than the icily correct, "Wishing you much happiness." Some cards are already self-referential. A birthday card pictures a white angora cat, a white china violin, a red rose, and a string of pearls under the caption, "I want to take 10,000 words and the purest of love / And transform them into a beautiful card" (*Wo yao ba qian yan wan yu he chunjie de ai/ biancheng yizhang meimiao de heka*) (Card 7, see Figure 8.7). One card takes ritual greetings farther still: "Sincerest congratulations on greeings [sic]."

In a static, hierarchical society, formulas offer security to those who know how to use them. As Bourdieu points out, "In social formalism, as in magical formalism, there is only one formula in each case which 'works.' And the whole labor of politeness strives to get as close as possible to the perfect formula."[16] Hierarchical politeness in old China was fraught with anxiety, spawning thousands of courtesy guides from *The Book of Rites* on. Still, conventional sayings offer a basic script, and many argue that the wide repertoire of ritual sayings in many societies offers comfort in stressful situations. And one can always add a few personal words to the card in one's own handwriting. The United States differs from most other cultures in its passion to say something "new" or "not cliched." Even at funerals, Americans often gasp an embarrassed, "I just don't know what to say," itself a cliche. Turks and Greeks, Chinese and Japanese, less likely to view formulas negatively, may often behave with more poise under stress.[17]

But during rapid social change, people adopt new formulaic phrases, from "Vive la revolution!" to "Have a nice day!" They also manipulate them humorously or for special effect; a sarcastic "Have a nice life!" might be hurled at someone set on an action the speaker thinks is disastrous. Humorous greeting cards, Matisoff argues, form a relatively new genre designed to fill the needs of people who are unhappy with the "canned sentiments" of conventional sentimental cards.[18] Conveying wishes can even take a special grammar. Many languages, from Latin to Pawnee to Maasai, also express wishes with an optative verb, expressed by, for example, "May all your wishes come true!" The optative mood is also used for the provocatively overlapping purposes of putting a curse on someone ("May his name be erased!"); granting permission ("You may go now"); and making indirect commands ("You may go now"). Optatives often appear in advertising and slogans. In English, optative is archaic, and Chinese has no optative grammar, though it does have many slogans, ads—and greetings. The Chinese verb *zhu*, meaning "to offer wishes; to congratulate," has long been used to close letters. A New Year's card with happy snakes in hats and bubble baths adds the lone English phrase, "Wish you," probably to translate the *zhu* used alone (Card 8, see Figure 8.8). The verb also appears in combinations tailored to the situation, as in "With wishes for health and long life" (*zhu jiankang changshou*).

Formula phrases are short and thus especially easy to borrow; often they contain the only foreign words someone knows. Sometimes a familiar imported phrase appears beside a native phrase for special effect, as in the English folk song, "Say *au revoir*, but not goodbye!" [which sounds final]. Formula

---

16. Bourdieu 1991, pp. 80–81.
17. Tannen and Oztek 1977. One of the few comprehensive linguistic discussions of formulaic expressions is Matisoff 1979. As an American, I despised model letter-writing books until I moved into Chinese society, where I was happy to find models of conventional written style.
18. Matisoff 1996.

FIGURE 8.8 (Card 8).
A New Year's card:
"Wish You."

phrases are culture-specific, so we translate them at our peril, even within a single language. "Good on you!" is an Australian phrase of approval for doing something courageous, from taking a difficult job to deciding to accept chemotherapy. It cannot be rendered as "congratulations," as Wierzbicka discusses, just as "aloha" cannot mean "hello" or "I love you," however much the Hawaiian tourist board tries to make it so.[19] Sending an "I hate you" card with black roses is conventional in India after a romantic breakup. Although the phrase "Take your medicine!" is an ordinary English imperative, it is not appropriate on a Chinese get-well card picturing a huge black attack dog looming above a tiny white kitten because it functions also as an idiom reserved for jocular but real criticism when one deserves punishment: "You missed that meeting with the boss? Well, I guess you should just take your medicine!" [and be reprimanded]. The idiomatic "take your medicine!" sounds cruel when addressed to an innocent sick person. But the literal meaning blends well with conventional Chinese expressions of sympathy by denial, as in telling an unhappy person, "Don't cry! Don't be upset!" (*Bie ku! Mei shi!*)—the implication being: There's nothing you can do! It's fate. He's dead / gone off with

19. Wierzbicka 1992, pp. 152–55, 388–91.

another woman / absconded with the cash—so forget it! English-dominant ears hear these Chinese formula expressions as unfeeling because they understand them literally rather than idiomatically. The literal reading of "Take your medicine!" also harmonizes with Chinese positive politeness, ritualized exhortations to take care of your health, wear warmer clothes, stay out of drafts, and—take more medicine! (These often sound intrusive to Westerners.) However, the get-well card does not translate "Take your medicine!" into Chinese. Instead, it lifts a sentimental English verse from a much different card: "This brings you get-well wishes / And comes to cheer you, too. / Hope it won't be long until / You're feeling good as new." A Chinese translation appears in terse, accurate, but nonrhyming phrases.

Humor, of course, is particularly culture-bound. Several amusing cards parody specialized written genres from scientific writing to fortune telling. The inside message on the snake card skewers both astrology and survey research (see Figure 8.8):

According to research
The majority of people born in the Year of the Snake are:

Glamourous	100%
Talented	99%
Loving	100%
Wise	99%

Even terrifying, archaic legal style is fair game for Judge Bao inside Card 2:

Crimes: Staying aloof from old friends
Being stingy. When you have something nice to eat, you gobble it all
   yourself. . . .
Punishment: Get in touch immediately. . . .
Mitigation of Sentence: The concern and good wishes of your friends. . . .

Mixed Typography

Chinese typography evokes rich symbolism. The house on Card 5 stands protected at all four corners by the four Chinese characters for "Merry Christmas." Chinese characters exist in two main styles. Old-fashioned, complex characters continue to be standard in Taiwan and Hong Kong. But since 1956 the People's Republic has officially promoted literacy by using simplified characters, which eliminate an average of eight brush strokes per character. So it is striking that the unofficial, complex characters appear on all but one of the cards collected before December 1996.[20] Complex characters reveal both the strength of elite tradition and the allure of prosperous Taiwan and

20. Singapore prescribes simplified characters but accepts the complex forms as a status symbol. A few cards mix the odd simplified character with a majority of complex ones. How-

Hong Kong. Calligraphy, however, is surprisingly rare. It appears on only two cards: the eagle painting (Card 3) and inside the Judge Bao card (Card 2), where it also includes the English symbols "P.S.": "P.S. Don't forget to take my good wishes along with you too, wherever you go!" (*P.S. Bie wang le ye ba wo de zhu fu sui she xiedai*). Typefaces are overwhelmingly square and standard (*kai shu*), though the proliferation of fonts in advertising augurs more variety soon.

English

English functions largely as an alphabetic symbol of modernity in the 68 percent of the cards that include a foreign word. (One birthday card has an Italian caption, and four print Christmas greetings in Dutch.) The alphabet fonts are extremely limited, though they include pleasing styles reminiscent of the 1930s. Lingering hostility to Japan means that no Japanese captions appear; the many Japanese cartoon characters are probably perceived as American. English not only legitimizes the fluid foreign holidays; it may also allow senders to be more romantic. A giant wedding card, for example, prints "I love you" above a dewy red foil rose. The Chinese words for "I love you" (*wo ai ni*) still sound foreign, blunt, and improper, so the Chinese caption reads, "A hundred years of harmony / Hearts forever as one" (*bai nian hao he/ yong jie tong xin*). Many Chinese captions mention more idiomatic "warm feelings" (*wenqing*) or "human feelings" (*ganqing*), which range from romantic love to concern for a colleague. Not every language uses an exact equivalent to English "love." People from every culture feel a range of warm and passionate feelings, but their words are both subtly nonequivalent and revealing. The card for a teacher says, "To Sir, with love" in English; the Chinese caption is literary and restrained, "a memorable teacher" (*shi en nan wang*).[21]

Mixed Terms of Address

Terms of address such as "you" and "friend" are rapidly changing. Expanded use of the honorific "you" (*nin*) is striking. Long associated with formal speech toward elite Beijing males, the honorific spread first to Taiwan and Hong Kong in advertising directed at women, especially ads for feminine-hygiene products, then to ads for makeup, clothes, and furniture. Now *nin* has spread to general advertising and to all sorts of greeting cards, from the

---

ever, horizontal rather than vertical Taiwan-style printing appears almost everywhere except when inscribed on paintings (e.g., Card 3).

21. Wierzbicka 1992;see especially pp.153–54 for cultural variations among words that roughly overlap with English "love." "To Sir, with love" is itself mixed code from Caribbean English, and the gently ironic title of a film about a teacher starring Sidney Poitier.

bunny birthday (Card 1) to the mother's card discussed below. In the past, Chinese used the word for "friend" (*pengyou*) much less than Europeans. Warm relationships with nonkin were once more typically labeled by the type of connection: a classmate (*tongxue*), a colleague (*tongshi*), someone from the same native place (*tongxiang*), and so on. Now "friend" stretches to wider connections, from business contacts to sex partners, as Wang and Wank discuss in Chapters 11 and 12 in this volume. Advertising, a genre that seeks to create instant closeness between advertisers and masses of strangers, uses "friend" freely. Ads for chicken bouillon address child customers and their parents with the Chinese for "You are my good friend." Greeting cards to a "friend" also salute an all-purpose addressee with at least an illusion of warmth. Even so, the English phrase "To my best friend" appears jarringly often, on seven cards, and is occasionally sent to near-strangers (Suzanne Wong Scollon, reports). The Chinese for "best friend" sounds both snobbish and unnatural in a society that values group relations, and the cards do not translate it. Relationships other than friendship remain unnamed, despite the Chinese emphasis on naming every relationship properly, and in marked contrast to the U.S. trend toward cards tailored to every relationship from "best boss" to "new kitty." However, Chinese senders handwrite a salutation on cards that includes the addressee's name and his or her relationship to the sender or professional title.

Spoken Style

Spoken style predominates. A New Year's card depicting lilies and brandy snifters reads, "Old friends share warm feelings. / I hope you can eat your fill / Sleep well/ And always, always find good luck" (*Pengyou lao ganqing hao / Zhu ni chi de bao / Shui de hao / Xingfu yongyuan, yongyuan /Xiangzhi de suiyue*). Strict classical style omits many grammatical features that are common both in modern speech and on the cards: reduplications, diminutives, a possessive marker (*de*), a passive marker (*ba*), and verbs marked for progressive or completed actions (aspect). Noun classifiers, such as "bud" (*duo*) for flowers, clouds, and drifts of snow, are especially abundant. Classifiers appear most often at the first mention of a new topic in extended conversation or text. Opening a card is an archetypical new topic context. Many usages add an emotional, even feminine, tone. Repeating a classifier or adjective in large type or italics adds intensity roughly comparable to that achieved by varying intonation in English intonation: "Drifts and drifts of snow" (*duo duo de xue*), "teeny-tiny" (*xixiao*). In spoken Chinese, as on the cards, warm positive politeness often "intensifies interest to the hearer" by using expressive style also associated with speech to small children, girlish flirtation, and lovers' private talk.[22]

22. Zhan 1992, pp. 24–28.

Literal baby talk and childish hand-scrawled characters do not appear, though they are popular on cards for young Hong Kong women. But emphatic or sentimental adjectives such as "sweet and beautiful' (*tianmei*) and "warm and lovely sounding" (*wen xiang*) appear frequently. A friendship card sends "good wishes flowing from the tip of a pen. . . . with a heart full of memories. . . . " (*bi duan liuchu de zhu fu . . . . / xin zhong manhuai de xiangnian . . .*). Since cards also spare the sender the embarrassment of speaking aloud, many cards invoke the value of silence, which the Chinese heritage praises over foolish speech. Several romantic cards send "silent good wishes" (*momo de zhufu*). And one New Year's card, illustrated by cartoon mice catching carp in a lotus pond, says, "Let us silently agree to the happiest of relationships, to an eternal friendship" (*Rang women gongtong de moqi xingxin xingxin de jiaoliu / zu ge yongyuan de zhiji*).

Boilerplate Stifling of Communications?

Even U.S. card manufacturers deplore "prefab passions" and blame the popularity of cards on baby boomers who don't know how to write letters.[23] But greeting cards literally expand the places to write good wishes. Chinese customers prefer more white space for writing than Western card buyers. Since more Chinese are now literate than at any time in history, they undoubtedly send more original greetings than ever before. Commercial products themselves are not entirely rigid. I did not see computer-generated cards for sale, but card design kits are available on cheap pirated CD-ROMs. One includes Chinese instructions for printing Japanese designs of Santa, cartoon warriors, snowmen, and Mt. Fuji; another offers 1,300 designs for all occasions. Affluent Chinese are undoubtedly designing cards as eclectic as the Hong Kong wedding invitation that includes a photo of the happy couple, their new address, phone, fax, and beeper numbers, a picture of the church, and a map of tram routes to get there.

Eclecticism and code-mixing reveal a lack of convention, not insincerity. One friendship card pictures roses atop a book of French poetry. Its message mixes the English "Merry Christmas" with a Chinese rendering of "hi" (*hai*), formerly taboo because it is pronounced exactly like the Chinese word for "catastrophe" (*hai*). The Chinese word for "friend" and the impersonal "translatese," "Hello, how are you" (*ni hao ma?*), were formerly reserved for strangers. Yet these merely preface a colloquial Chinese message:

Hi! Old friend, hello, how are you?	*Hai! Lao you ni hao ma?*
The years pass by, neither well	*Zhe xie nian lai, wo guo*
nor badly for me,	*de bu hao, bu huai*
Amidst the bustle of daily life,	*Zai manglu de rizi li*

23. Hirshey 1995, p. 20.

You are still, always,	*Ni yiran shi wo bu bian*
endlessly on my mind	*de guanhuai.*

Even the family is a site of newly honed relationships, honored by formal greetings once reserved for outsiders. The mother's card conveys modern-style respect by using the both the honorific "you" (*nin*) and the very formal word for "mother, maternal parent" (*muqin*), which is not spoken in direct address. Yet these come embedded in more effusive language than that used on any other card:

Mother, you [honorific] are. . . .	*Muqin nin shi . . .*
A stove of warmth on a dark,	*Bao feng yu ye zhong*
stormy night	*wennuan de luhuo*
A cradle of softness and tenderness,	*Shi rouhe de yaolan,*
a dazzling candle of light	*huihuang de hu guang*
I respect and love you [honorific], Mama!	*Wo jing ai nin, mama!*
Respectfully wishing you	*Jing zhu*
Happiness, Mother	*Muqin kuaile*

Patriarchy once denied women even their own names on ancestor tablets. Yet women gained protection, as well as affection, by nourishing their own emotionally powerful "uterine family" bonds with their children.[24] Many Chinese now value daughters especially for their loyalty to their mothers. The wording of the mother's card resembles many sentimental popular song lyrics about mothers. This card is also the only card collected before December 1996 that prints its message entirely in simplified characters. Since many older women were educated when simplified characters were at their peak, the card accommodates their reading habits even as it implicitly celebrates women's rising literacy.

WHO SENDS CARDS?

Many card senders appear to be administrators of white-collar offices and young women living in the city. Offices from factories to universities now display elaborate arrangements of Christmas and New Year's cards for months at a time. And virtually the only customers I observed buying cards were young women. Though no published surveys of card-sending exist, proprietary research indicates that some 85 percent of Chinese card senders are women, about the same as in the United States, the United Kingdom, and Australia. Both Chinese tradition and socialist central planning reinforced vertical hierarchical relationships at the expense of lateral ties. And administrators and young women benefit particularly from lateral relationships in rapidly changing and competitive urban societies. As relationships, patron-

24. Wolf 1972, p. 41.

age, and subsidies loosen or disappear, people seek out alternative sources for everything from machine tools to overseas scholarships. Marketing needs and greater freedom of movement have greatly enriched networking. The sending of cards overlaps with advertising and other publicity. Even scholarly associations send out cards: one sent a card depicting a pop-up model of a circular fortress-like roundhouse distinctive to the Chinese Hakka subgroup. Cards also facilitate wider contacts, much like Chinese name cards, which contain more information and circulate more widely than comparable U.S. business cards. Each of the Nanjing students sends 20–30 Christmas and New Year's cards to classmates and teachers, as well as a few birthday cards to friends. The expense is significant, around 100 renminbi (rmb) ($12.00), including postage, to send even a cheap 3 rmb (36 cent) card to 25 people. They also described making their own cards, often with pictures and humorous poems. Cards, they said, have the advantage of replacing time-consuming New Year's calls and are cheaper and easier to select than gifts, which entail greater obligations. Cards also allow one to inscribe the recipient's name and title on the outside and to include a handwritten salutation, signature, and date. (Even a gift book or offprint must include an inscription.) Intellectuals can use cards to display their calligraphy, while those uneasy about their handwriting can rely on cards with preprinted messages.

Foreignness and modernity are central to the appeal of cards. The old society required strict hierarchical etiquette at New Year's and other celebrations. But Christmas and birthdays may be acknowledged by anyone, even strangers and women. The first cards to be sent in China appear to have been Christmas cards. In the late 1980s bureaucrats with overseas ties, such as the external affairs officers at universities, began sending cards to overseas acquaintances and then to domestic peers. Many early cards simply pirated messages from cards received from abroad. The fad spread to other city people and other festivities. Shanghai writer Wang Weiming emphasizes the exotic freedom of "festivities [that] no longer express government political forms or old traditional styles, but rather a transformation into a joyous sensual celebration . . . as Christmas cards, pieces of paper with excellent and elegant sentiments, serve to express the feelings of the city people."[25]

Politeness among the Chinese elite emphasized distance and deference, what Brown and Levinson's cross-cultural survey of politeness describes as "negative politeness." But close Chinese personal relations also strongly encourage the "positive politeness" that enhances closeness by claiming common background, kinship, and other connections.[26] Greeting cards convey

25. Wang Weiming 1996, p. 179.
26. Brown and Levinson 1987. For a discussion of Chinese politeness, especially positive politeness, see Zhan 1992. For a discussion of rapidly changing relationships and exchanges of favors in reform China, see M. Yang 1994.

wishes for stronger positive politeness, and displaying the cards received advertises the richness of one's connections. One can send a card to almost any connection. Professors, bosses, and possible patrons receive dozens, even hundreds, of calendars and cards. Card-sending, of course, is not used strictly for business purposes; affection, respect, and sentiment are also central. Most previous research has viewed Chinese networks instrumentally, neglecting to consider the affection in Chinese relationships, which is also expressed by sending gifts.[27] Even illiterate people have long exchanged small gifts such as embroidered bags and paper cutouts on which symbols and good wishes convey messages similar to those in cards.

Women and Cards

Traditional courtesies often excluded women completely or cast them as bystanders in clan and village rituals. Changing roles for women make cards especially attractive, even as they trace a reworking of gender boundaries and increasing participation in previously male-dominated written discourse. Cards offer commercialized validation of women's broader and more complex relationships outside the home. Woman-friendly printed messages reinforce affiliation with an imagined community; they let women know that they are not the only ones who feels particular emotions or sentiments, the same benefit offered by the telephone hotlines discussed by Erwin in Chapter 7. Because modern Chinese families are small, friendships are increasingly important; women cultivate many stable and respected relationships outside the family. They are many times more likely to attend school than their grandmothers and to study long enough to write fluently. At the end of the 1990s, women married approximately four years later than in 1949, at age 22.67 on average, and age 24.5 in Shanghai. Women now also hold paying jobs nearly their whole lives. They need to develop relationships among coworkers as well as supervisors, who may be flattered to receive a card. Cards are flat, cheap, and easily concealed even in the most crowded factory dormitory. Like the tiny painted bookmarks sold beside them, a card can be enjoyed for months or years. Cards, like calendars, can also brighten ugly desktops, paper over gray walls, or be pasted over windows for privacy, like the cut paper designs that preceded them.

Cards are trinkets of conspicuous consumption that also offer pictures of affluence. The goal of consumption is not to be different, but to be the same with delightful variation. Teenage girls in Shenzhen can be heard phoning one another to say, "I'm sending you a card that cost X" to prompt a comparable card in return. Many boast of receiving 45–50 cards (Gan Wang, re-

---

27. Yan 1996, pp. 220–22.

ports). Modern women also much more likely than their grandmothers to travel, study, or work far from home. Cards are simpler to write than letters, with fewer stylistic constraints. Women in Japan buy millions of cards, probably for similar reasons. And women of all ages in the United States, who buy most of the cards, send most of them to other women.[28] Older Chinese women appear less likely to send cards than young women, though not necessarily because they are less interested in doing so but because they have heavier financial responsibilities at home. In Japan and the United States, women send out most family Christmas and birthday cards, doing what Di Leonardo calls the crucial but unpaid "kin work" of maintaining family ties.[29] In China, where most people live with or very close to their birth families, a greater percentage of cards may go to nonkin. This is likely to change.

Cards also offer anonymity for testing the romantic waters. Marriage negotiations, of course, have long called for careful exchanges of letters, which are elaborately described in courtesy books.[30] Love letters, the nexus of so many stories and opera plots, are other precursors. The patriarchs feared love letters for their potential to disrupt arranged marriages. One old viceroy snorted, "I don't believe that Chinese women should be educated. . . . For if a woman learns how to read and write, the first thing she thinks of is to write poetry about love, or to write letters to, and receive letters from, *men!*"[31] Letter writing, of course, is one of the main reasons people learned to write. Some women even adapted their own script, such as the Japanese women who popularized the simpler and more phonetic *katakana* writing. Women in extreme southwestern Hunan modified standard Chinese characters into "women's characters" (*nu shu*) to write letters of support to their sworn sisters after their marriages.[32] A century ago, when the United States was at a similar stage of industrialization, young American women who also gave most of their salaries to their families indulged their fantasies by exchanging valentines and colorful flower-printed name cards.[33] Western greeting cards developed along with valentines and individual choice in marriage. Chinese friendship cards show every sign of being adapted to courtship, just as valentines and Valentine's Day have started to enter Chinese cities.

28. Hirshey 1995.

29. Americans send about fifteen cards per capita each year, a staggering 7.5 billion. Only the British send more. The observation on kin work is from Di Leonardo 1987.

30. Yu Wenxue and Zhang Lehe 1988.

31. Princess Der Ling. 1929. *Kowtow.* New York: Dodd Mead. 1929. 90.

32. Silber 1994.

33. Selecting, exchanging, and collecting cards occupies a whole chapter of Laura Ingalls Wilder's *Little Town on the Prairie* (Wilder [1941] 1971, pp. 185–200). The heroine exchanges cards at her first meeting with the man she later marries.

MAKING AND SELLING CARDS

Hundreds of millions of cards are made largely as a sideline by state firms and are sold largely by entrepreneurs. Christmas card sales flourish far from the metropolis, in market stalls along the Vietnam and Lao borders and in "more or less iconographically accurate form" in the wild mountains of western Fujian.[34] One Shanghai department store sold 100,000 cards in 1990; by 1995, single street stalls in Beijing sold 80,000 cards *per day*. Post offices put out extra mailboxes before Christmas.[35] Although I have found no national figures for card sales, the number of letters sent rose 30 percent between 1985 and 1992.[36] Many card envelopes come stamped with press runs to comply with new post office regulations. Runs of between 100,000 and 1 million are routine. Although one envelope can fit many card designs, manufacturers have no incentive to inflate the numbers and expose themselves to higher taxes. Cards have not reached the national, sanitized mass production of commodity culture that Agnew describes as characterizing the United States and Europe since the 1930s.[37] Production is still regional, scattered from Guangxi to Tianjin. Most cards are printed as a sideline by state publishing houses, propaganda units, and paper factories, all scrambling to replace state subsidies with profits from advertising, calendars, and cards. Amateur designs are common. Every card from the Hai Tian paper factory of Luoyang, for example, includes a flier asking customers to submit designs. Everyone who submits a design receives three free cards in return, and each design actually published receives up to 520 rmb ($65), the equivalent of nearly a month's wage. Artists are to send in original art and captions "not taken from existing Hai Tian cards." Designs are to be "interesting, humorous or novel, clever and marketable. Original art is best. Grade school–level work is not welcome."

Commercial card producers now sell more cards than the post office, which has long supplied preprinted postcards and telegrams for births, graduations, funerals, the New Year, and other occasions. Telegrams are read out at televised funerals of national leaders, at the opening of national meetings, and at wedding parties. Some telegram forms also provide for wiring a cash gift. In 1997 the post office introduced a very popular combination New Year's

34. Yunnan visit, December 1994. Quotation from Cynthia Brokaw, letter from Changting, Fujian, January 14, 1996.

35. Wang Weiming 1996, p. 178; Xu 1995–96; Yan Li 1996. Some Chinese rationalize the fad by saying that "the foreigners must be very happy" to see Christmas displays.

36. *China: A Directory and Source Book* 1994, p. 222. The percentage of households owning desks rose to 87 percent in the cities and 64 percent in the villages (pp. 229–30). However, only 56 percent of villages have daily mail delivery, a drop of 6 percent over the same period.

37. Agnew 1993, p. 27.

postcard and lottery ticket for only 1.8 rmb (22 cents) postpaid. But the best, cheapest, and most varied cards come from the street markets, especially before the New Year, when huge hanging displays festoon the pushcarts. Some cards appear in twelve variants, one for each animal in the Chinese zodiac, like the happy snakes in Card 8. State-run stores lagged behind in selling cards, despite their profitability. Nanjing's huge main Xinhua bookstore had just one bin of mixed cards shoved into a corner in 1995. You had to ask the clerk for cards at the Commercial Press bookstore in June 1996, when the dozen birthday cards on sale were stacked together invisibly, like books on a shelf. Yet in December of that year the store displayed 120 upscale New Year's cards. Virtually all the designs were Chinese: no Santas, elves, or trees. Store-bought cards in Nanjing cost between 3 rmb (36 cents for a simple card to 6 rmb (72 cents) for a musical one. The most expensive Nanjing card sold for 27 rmb ($3.25) in 1996, when the most expensive Beijing card went for 45 rmb ($5.47).[38] Street stalls sold identical cards at half the marked price and offered further discounts for multiple purchases. The card market grew so lucrative that both Hallmark and American Greetings began to market cards under local brand names in Shanghai, Beijing, and Guangzhou.[39]

COULD THE HOUSE OF CARDS COLLAPSE?

Will shoppers stop buying as suddenly as Shenzhen entrepreneurs quit bowling (see Chapter 11)? Will paper greetings crumple as phone calls grow easy and cheap? Or could environmental forces bring them down? The environmental group Friends of the Earth formed a pact with the hotel and airline associations in Hong Kong to send 200,000 fewer cards in 1995, donating the money saved to plant trees in China. (Companies, of course, saved much more on labor costs.) Some mainland work units have already tried to curb card-sending as an unnecessary expense. And the post office in one city criticized an unnamed government agency for sending too many cards. Yet collapse seems unlikely. Designs can be changed easily to meet changing fashions, while printing houses already rely on diversified product lines. Most important, consumers are increasingly mobile, anomic, and hungry for affiliation. Western research indicates that phones do not cut into card sales; sociable people who make lots of calls also send lots of cards.

Consumption represents more than spending. Cards, like wedding banquets and gifts of cigarettes, also represent an investment in relationships. Cards will likely proliferate, become professionalized, conventionalized,

38. Xu Binglan 1995–96.

39. Interview with Clive Smith, director of North Asia marketing for Hallmark Cards, March 11, 1998.

and obligatory as an expression of courtesy in enterprises and nonelite families. The family rituals and satisfactions of kin work seem already increasingly feminized. Juvenilization, or spread of an adult habit to teenagers and children, also signals that once-elite behaviors have spread throughout society, as Norbert Elias documents in his monumental history of European courtesy.[40] Similar processes are well under way for Chinese card-sending. McDonald's and Kentucky Fried Chicken provided the model by sending cards just before children's birthdays. And six-year-old girls perform modern rites of filial piety by making New Year's cards for faraway grandparents and other kin.[41] Schools may add card-making projects, including cards for classmates. Children are also likely to demand store-bought cards over homemade ones, another commercialization of childhood, which Davis and Sensenbrenner describe in Chapter 3.

Women comment that they already send cards to ever-more-distant and long-lived kin. Just as the card boom was beginning in 1987, advice on kin work in a women's handbook revealed the foundation for a commercial house of cards: If a classmate won an honor, the handbook suggested inscribing greetings on "a postcard of a scene he or she would particularly enjoy." When a child had a birthday, it said, throw a party. It explained how the New Year is celebrated overseas and suggested phrases to include in letters sent abroad.[42] The mother's card described in the handbook shows that cards for kin are entering the market. Hallmark now markets Mother's Day and Father's Day cards in Shanghai and Beijing. Cards for every relative, real or fictive, as well as for graduation and Children's Day, are likely to appear. Both Hallmark and American Greetings have already begun selling cards associated with family-oriented celebrations like the Mid-Autumn Festival. The winter solstice and the twelve minor intervals of the year such as "first frost" are other potential card-giving opportunities. More foreign holidays may be adapted to the Chinese culture. Valentines are becoming popular, and even Japanese holidays such as Girl's Day and Boy's Day might catch on. Novelty may stretch even to inauspicious events such as Halloween; cards that defy Chinese repugnance at skeletons and ghosts already find buyers in ordinary Hong Kong supermarkets. Religious cards, including perhaps Daoist and Buddhist cards, may emerge. Cards may also appear to mark difficult life events, including illness, funerals, and perhaps even the abortions and sterilizations that northern Chinese villagers mark with gifts of food and cash, as they would a birth.[43]

40. Elias 1978.
41. Wendy Ren, daughter of Nanjing University professor Ren Donglai, December 30, 1996.
42. Wang Jinhai et al. 1987, p. 113.
43. Yan 1996, pp. 54–55.

A street vendor cannot carry thousands of cards. But commodified and centralized card stores can, especially if manufacturers develop a Hallmark-style distribution and return policy for cards that do not sell. Since the cards in my collection almost never name a relationship other than "friend," the market seems ripe for specialized cards. Hallmark now sells a teacher's card; cards for bosses and coworkers may follow in a nod to the Chinese genius for making connections. Card-sending to near strangers may increase. One Chinese student sent an Internet Easter bunny card to a professor he saw at a convention (Ron Scollon, reports). Intimate communications between lovers will be increasingly documented on cards, and valentines are likely to become popular. Humorous, ironic cards may proliferate to make the messages more palatable, and possibly even critical.

Could cards become political? Any writing can be bent to any purpose; even criticizing calligraphy is a time-honored pretext for bringing down national leaders.[44] Current cards seem relentlessly nonsubversive and are encrusted with the literal glitter of consumerism. Like advertising, picture cards full of luxuries divert attention from a broader critique. As an ideology of consumption, cards tacitly reinforce state power, as long as the economy expands. Or, rights may silently be redefined as individual entitlement to a certain standard of living, as Agnew argues.[45] Politicization of cards might also come from the state. Presses and even laser printers are still overwhelmingly state-owned, as are expensive paper, inks, and professional skills, which are tightly controlled. Scenarios of neo–Cultural Revolution–style requirements to demonstrate political loyalty by sending cards on national holidays, inscribing them with closely monitored statements, and displaying a patriotic minimum of cards received appear unlikely.Bureaucrats will more likely demand cards stuffed with cash on national holidays.

Commercialization, juvenilization, and politicization are all part of the growing greeting card market in China. In 1997 a chocolate Easter egg company, Kinder Surprise, sponsored a card-coloring contest in which Hong Kong children created 28,000 cards to send to their mainland peers. The children drew on cardboard hearts printed with the logos of both UNICEF and the candy company, and the effort raised nearly $13,000 for UNICEF in China. When thousands of the nicest cards went on public display in a private shopping mall, it was clear that the prizewinners were explicitly political; they in-

44. See Kraus 1991, pp. 123–27.
45. Agnew 1993, p. 23; see also Hart 1990.

cluded, for example, a card showing China and Hong Kong colored red like a Chinese flag, with children dancing in the air above.[46] In December 1995, cards carried serious messages of protest when supporters of dissident Wei Jingsheng mailed 20,000 signed cards from Hong Kong to his Beijing prison cell.[47] In 1998 the deposed Communist Party chief Zhao Ziyang lobbied for rehabilitation by sending Christmas cards to former associates, and the People's Liberation Army sent out cards as well.[48] Cards have become thoroughly integrated into Chinese political and personal life.

46. Luk 1997.

47. TVB Pearl Evening News Report, December 22, 1995. Organizers referred to the cards as "winter solstice greetings," adding that "families should be together at this time." Wei probably did not receive them, since they were mailed in cartons printed with his photo on the side.

48. Lam 1998; Tabakoff 1998.

CHAPTER 9

———

Of Hamburger and Social Space

Consuming McDonald's in Beijing

Yunxiang Yan

In a 1996 news report on dietary changes in the cities of Beijing, Tianjin, and Shanghai, fast-food consumption was called the most salient development in the national capital: "The development of a fast-food industry with Chinese characteristics has become a hot topic in Beijing's dietary sector. This is underscored by the slogan 'challenge the Western fast food!'"[1] Indeed, with the instant success of Kentucky Fried Chicken after its grand opening in 1987, followed by the sweeping dominance of McDonald's and the introduction of other fast-food chains in the early 1990s, Western-style fast food has played a leading role in the restaurant boom and in the rapid change in the culinary culture of Beijing. A "war of fried chicken" broke out when local businesses tried to recapture the Beijing market from the Western fast-food chains by introducing Chinese-style fast foods. The "fast-food fever" in Beijing, as it is called by local observers, has given restaurant frequenters a stronger consumer consciousness and has created a Chinese notion of fast food and an associated culture.

From an anthropological perspective, this chapter aims to unpack the rich meanings of fast-food consumption in Beijing by focusing on the fast-food restaurants as a social space. Food and eating have long been a central con-

This chapter is based on fieldwork in Beijing, August to October 1994, supported by a grant from the Henry Luce Foundation to the Fairbank Center for East Asian Research, Harvard University, and on further documentary research supported by the 1996 Senate Grant, University of California, Los Angeles. I am grateful to Deborah Davis, Thomas Gold, Jun Jing, Joseph Soares, and other participants at the American Council of Learned Societies conference at Yale University for their valuable comments on earlier drafts of this chapter. I also owe special thanks to Nancy Hearst for editorial assistance.
    1. Liu Fen and Long Zaizu 1996.

cern in anthropological studies.[2] While nutritional anthropologists emphasize the practical functions of foods and food ways in cultural settings,[3] social and cultural anthropologists try to explore the links between food (and
eating) and other dimensions of a given culture. From Lévi-Strauss's attempt
to establish a universal system of meanings in the language of foods to Mary
Douglas's effort to decipher the social codes of meals and Marshal Sahlins's
analysis of the inner/outer, human/inhuman metaphors of food, there is a
tradition of symbolic analysis of dietary cultures, whereby foods are treated
as messages and eating as a way of social communication.[4] The great variety
of food habits can be understood as human responses to material conditions,
or as a way to draw boundaries between "us" and "them" in order to construct group identity and thus to engage in "gastro-politics."[5] According to
Pierre Bourdieu, the different attitudes toward foods, different ways of eating, and food taste itself all express and define the structure of class relations in French society.[6] Although in Chinese society ceremonial banqueting is frequently used to display and reinforce the existing social structure,
James Watson's analysis of the *sihk puhn* among Hong Kong villagers—a special type of ritualized banquet that requires participants to share foods from
the same pot—demonstrates that foods can also be used as a leveling device
to blur class boundaries.[7]

As Joseph Gusfield notes, the context of food consumption (the participants and the social settings of eating) is as important as the text (the foods
that are to be consumed).[8] Restaurants thus should be regarded as part of a
system of social codes; as institutionalized and commercialized venues, restaurants also provide a valuable window through which to explore the social meanings of food consumption. In her recent study of dining out and social manners, Joanne Finkelstein classifies restaurants into three grand categories: (1)
"formal spectacular" restaurants, where "dining has been elevated to an event
of extraordinary stature"; (2) "amusement" restaurants, which add entertainment to dining; and (3) convenience restaurants such as cafes and fast-
food outlets.[9] Although Finkelstein recognizes the importance of restaurants
as a public space for socialization, she also emphasizes the antisocial aspect
of dining out. She argues that, because interactions in restaurants are condi-
tioned by existing manners and customs, "dining out allows us to act in imi-

2. For a general review, see Messer 1984.
3. See, e.g., Jerome 1980.
4. See Douglas 1975; Lévi-Strauss 1983; and Sahlins 1976.
5. See Harris 1985; Murphy 1986; and Appadurai 1981.
6. Bourdieu 1984, pp. 175–200.
7. Watson 1987. For more systematic studies of food in China, see Chang 1977 and E. Anderson 1988.
8. See Gusfield 1992, p. 80.
9. Finkelstein 1989, pp. 68–71.

tation of others, in accord with images, in responses to fashions, out of habit, without need for thought or self-scrutiny." The result is that the styles of interaction that are encouraged in restaurants produce sociality without much individuality, which is an "uncivilized sociality."[10] Concurring with Finkelstein's classification of restaurants, Allen Shelton proceeds further to analyze how restaurants as a theater can shape customers' thoughts and actions. Shelton argues that the cultural codes of restaurants are just as important as the food codes analyzed by Mary Douglas, Lévi-Strauss, and many others. He concludes that the "restaurant is an organized experience using and transforming the raw objects of space, words, and tastes into a coded experience of social structures."[11] Rick Fantasia's analysis of the fast-food industry in France is also illuminating in this respect. He points out that because McDonald's represents an exotic "Other" its outlets attract many young French customers who want to explore a different kind of social space—an "American place."[12]

In light of the studies of both the text and context of food consumption, I first review the development of Western fast food and the local responses in Beijing during the period 1987 to 1996. Next I examine the cultural symbolism of American fast food, the meanings of objects and physical place in fast-food restaurants, the consumer groups, and the use of public space in fast-food outlets. I then discuss the creation of a new social space in fast-food restaurants. In my opinion, the transformation of fast-food establishments from eating place to social space is the key to understanding the popularity of fast-food consumption in Beijing, and it is the major reason why local competitors have yet to successfully challenge the American fast-food chains. This study is based on both ethnographic evidence collected during my fieldwork in 1994 (August to October) and documentary data published in Chinese newspapers, popular magazines, and academic journals during the 1987–96 period. Since McDonald's is the ultimate icon of American fast food abroad and the most successful competitor in Beijing's fast-food market, McDonald's restaurants were the primary place and object for my research, although I also consider other fast-food outlets and compare them with McDonald's in certain respects.[13]

FAST-FOOD FEVER IN BEIJING, 1987 TO 1996

Fast food is not indigenous to Chinese society. It first appeared as an exotic phenomenon in novels and movies imported from abroad and then entered

10. Ibid. p. 5.

11. Shelton 1990, p. 525.

12. See Fantasia 1995, pp. 213–15.

13. For an anthropological study of sociocultural encounters at McDonald's in Hong Kong, Taipei, Beijing, Seoul, and Tokyo, see chapters in Watson, ed., 1997.

the everyday life of ordinary consumers when Western fast-food chains opened restaurants in the Beijing market. *Kuaican*, the Chinese translation for fast food, which literally means "fast meal" or "fast eating," contradicts the ancient principle in Chinese culinary culture that regards slow eating as healthy and elegant. There are a great variety of traditional snack foods called *xiaochi* (small eats), but the term "small eats" implies that they cannot be taken as meals. During the late 1970s, *hefan* (boxed rice) was introduced to solve the serious "dining problems" created by the lack of public dining facilities and the record number of visitors to Beijing. The inexpensive and convenient *hefan*—rice with a small quantity of vegetables or meat in a styrofoam box— quickly became popular in train stations, in commercial areas, and at tourist attractions. However, thus far boxed rice remains a special category of convenience food—it does not fall into the category of *kuaican* (fast food), even though it is consumed much faster than any of the fast foods discussed in the following pages. The intriguing point here is that in Beijing the notion of fast food refers only to Western-style fast food and the new Chinese imitations. More important, as a new cultural construct, the notion of fast food includes nonfood elements such as eating manners, environment, and patterns of social interaction. The popularity of fast food among Beijing consumers has little to do with either the food itself or the speed with which it is consumed.

American fast-food chains began to display interest in the huge market in China in the early 1980s. As early as 1983, McDonald's used apples from China to supply its restaurants in Japan; thereafter it began to build up distribution and processing facilities in northern China.[14] However, Kentucky Fried Chicken took the lead in the Beijing market. On October 6, 1987, KFC opened its first outlet at a commercial center just one block from Tiananmen Square. The three-story building, which seats more than 500 customers, at the time was the largest KFC restaurant. On the day of the grand opening, hundreds of customers stood in line outside the restaurant, waiting to taste the world-famous American food. Although few were really impressed with the food itself, they were all thrilled by the eating experience: the encounter with friendly employees, quick service, spotless floors, climate-controlled and brightly-lit dining areas, and of course, smiling Colonel Sanders standing in front of the main gate. From 1987 to 1991, KFC restaurants in Beijing enjoyed celebrity status, and the flagship outlet scored first for both single-day and annual sales in 1988 among the more than 9,000 KFC outlets throughout the world.

In the restaurant business in Beijing during the early 1980s, architecture and internal decoration had to match the rank of a restaurant in an officially prescribed hierarchy, ranging from star-rated hotel restaurants for foreigners to formal restaurants, mass eateries, and simple street stalls. There were strict codes regarding what a restaurant should provide, at what price, and

---

14. See Love 1986, p. 448.

what kind of customers it should serve in accordance with its position in this hierarchy. Therefore, some authorities in the local dietary sector deemed that the KFC decision to sell only fried chicken in such an elegant environment was absurd.[15] Beijing consumers, however, soon learned that a clean, bright, and comfortable environment was a common feature of all Western-style fast-food restaurants that opened in the Beijing market after KFC. Among them, McDonald's has been the most popular and the most successful.

The first McDonald's restaurant in Beijing was built at the southern end of Wangfujing Street, Beijing's Fifth Avenue. With 700 seats and 29 cash registers, the restaurant served more than 40,000 customers on its grand opening day of April 23, 1992.[16] The Wangfujing McDonald's quickly became an important landmark in Beijing, and its image appeared frequently on national television programs. It also became an attraction for domestic tourists, a place where ordinary people could literally taste a piece of American culture. Although not the first to introduce American fast food to Beijing consumers, the McDonald's chain has been the most aggressive in expanding its business and the most influential in developing the fast-food market. Additional McDonald's restaurants appeared in Beijing one after another: two were opened in 1993, four in 1994, and ten more in 1995. There were 35 by August 1997, and according to the general manager the Beijing market is big enough to support more than a hundred McDonald's restaurants.[17] At the same time, Pizza Hut, Bony Fried Chicken (of Canada), and Dunkin' Donuts all made their way into the Beijing market. The most interesting newcomer is a noodle shop chain called Californian Beef Noodle King. Although the restaurant sells Chinese noodle soup, it has managed to portray itself as an American fast-food eatery and competes with McDonald's and KFC with lower prices and its appeal to Chinese tastes.

The instant success of Western fast-food chains surprised those in the local restaurant industry. Soon thereafter, many articles in newspapers and journals called for the invention of Chinese-style fast food and the development of a local fast-food industry. April 1992 was a particularly difficult month for those involved in this sector: two weeks after the largest McDonald's restaurant opened at the southern end of Wangfujing Street, Wu Fang Zhai, an old, prestigious restaurant at the northern end of Wangfujing Street, went out of business; in its stead opened International Fast Food City, which sold Japanese fast food, American hamburgers, fried chicken, and ice cream. This was seen as an alarming threat to both the local food industry and the national pride of Chinese culinary culture.[18]

15. See Zhang Yubin 1992.
16. See *New York Times*, April 24, 1992. For a detailed account, see Yan 1997a.
17. See *China Daily*, September 12, 1994; and *Service Bridge*, August 12, 1994.
18. See Liu Ming 1992; Mian Zhi 1993.

Actually, the local response to the "invasion" of Western fast food began in the late 1980s, right after the initial success of KFC. It quickly developed into what some reporters called a "war of fried chickens" in Beijing. Following the model of KFC, nearly a hundred local fast-food shops featuring more than a dozen kinds of fried chicken appeared between 1989 and 1990. One of the earliest such establishments was Lingzhi Roast Chicken, which began business in 1989; this was followed by Chinese Garden Chicken, Huaxiang Chicken, and Xiangfei Chicken in 1990. The chicken war reached its peak when the Ronghua Fried Chicken company of Shanghai opened its first chain store directly opposite one of the KFC restaurants in Beijing. The manager of Ronghua Chicken proudly announced a challenge to KFC: "Wherever KFC opens a store, we will open another Ronghua Fried Chicken next door."

All of the local fried chicken variations were no more than simple imitations of the KFC food. Their only localizing strategy was to emphasize special Chinese species and sacred recipes that supposedly added an extra medicinal value to their dishes. Thus, consumers were told that the Chinese Garden Chicken might prevent cancer and that Huaxiang Chicken could strengthen the yin-yang balance inside one's body.[19] This strategy did not work well; KFC and McDonald's won out in that first wave of competition. Only a small proportion of the local fried chicken shops managed to survive, while KFC and McDonald's became more and more popular.

Realizing that simply imitating Western fast food was a dead end, the emerging local fast-food industry turned to exploring resources within Chinese cuisine. Among the pioneers, Jinghua Shaomai Restaurant in 1991 tried to transform some traditional Beijing foods into fast foods. This was followed by the entry of a large number of local fast-food restaurants, such as the Beijing Beef Noodle King (not to be confused with the California Beef Noodle King). The Jinghe Kuaican company made the first domestic attempt to develop a fast-food business on a large scale. With the support of the Beijing municipal government, this company built its own farms and processing facilities, but it chose to sell boxed fast foods in mobile vans parked on streets and in residential areas.[20] Thus it fell into the pre-existing category of *hefan* (boxed rice) purveyors. Although the price of boxed fast foods was much lower than that of imported fast food, the boxed fast foods did not meet consumers' expectations of fast food. The Jinghe Kuaican Company disappeared as quickly as it had emerged. In October 1992, nearly a thousand state-owned restaurants united under the flag of the Jingshi Fast Food Company, offering five sets of value meals and more than 50 fast-foods items, all of which were derived from traditional Chinese cuisines. This company was also the first fast-food enterprise to be run by the Beijing municipal government, thus indicating the im-

19. Duan Gang 1991.
20. Zhang Zhaonan 1992a.

portance of this growing sector to the government.[21] The Henan Province Red Sorghum Restaurant opened on Wangfujing Street in March 1996, immediately across the street from the McDonald's flagship restaurant. Specializing in country-style lamb noodles, the manager of Red Sorghum announced that twelve more restaurants were to be opened in Beijing by the end of 1996, all of which would be next to a McDonald's outlet. "We want to fight McDonald's," the manager claimed, "we want to take back the fast-food market."[22]

By 1996 the fast-food sector in Beijing consisted of three groups: The main group was made up of McDonald's, KFC, and other Western fast-food chains. Although they no longer attracted the keen attention of the news media, their numbers were still growing. The second group consisted of the local KFC imitations, which managed to survive the 1991 "chicken war." The most successful in this group is the Ronghua Chicken restaurant chain, which in 1995 had eleven stores in several cities and more than 500 employees.[23] The third group included restaurants selling newly created Chinese fast foods, from simple noodle soups to Beijing roast duck meals. Many believe that the long tradition of a national cuisine will win out over the consumers' temporary curiosity about Western-style fast food.

Thus far, however, Chinese fast food has not been able to compete with Western fast food, even though it is cheaper and more appealing to the tastes of ordinary citizens in Beijing. Red Sorghum was the third business to announce in public the ambitious goal of beating McDonald's and KFC (after the Shanghai Ronghua Chicken and Beijing Xiangfei Chicken), but so far none have come close. By August 1996 it was clear that Red Sorghum's lamb noodle soup could not compete in the hot summer with Big Mac, which was popular year-round.[24]

The lack of competitiveness of Chinese fast food has drawn official attention at high levels, and in 1996 efforts were made to support the development of a local fast-food sector.[25] Concerned experts in the restaurant industry and commentators in the media attribute the bad showing of the Chinese fast-food restaurants to several things. In the mid-1990s, at least: (1) the quality, nutritional values, and preparation of Western fast foods were highly standardized, while Chinese fast foods were still prepared in traditional ways; (2) Chinese fast-food establishments did not offer the friendly, quick service of Western fast-food restaurants; (3) the local establishments were not as clean and comfortable as the Western fast-food restaurants; and (4) most important, unlike McDonald's or KFC, Chinese restaurants did not em-

21. See Zhang Zhaonan 1992b; You Zi 1994; and Zhang Guoyun 1995.
22. Yu Bin 1996; "Honggaoliang yuyan zhongshi kuaican da qushi" 1996.
23. Yu Weize 1995.
24. See Liu Fen and Long Zaizu 1996.
25. The development of Chinese fast food is incorporated into the eighth national five-year plan for scientific research. See Bi Yuhua 1994; see also Ling Dawei 1996.

ploy advanced technologies or modern management methods.[26] From a
Marxist perspective, Ling Dawei has concluded that the race between imported and local fast foods in Beijing is a race between advanced and backward forces of production; hence the development of the local fast-food industry will rest ultimately on modernization.[27]

There is no doubt that these views have a basis in everyday practice; yet
they all regard food consumption as purely economic behavior and fast-food
restaurants as mere eating places. A more complete understanding of the
fast-food fever in Beijing also requires close scrutiny of the social context of
consumption—the participants and social settings, because "The specific nature of the consumed substances surely matters; but it cannot, by itself, explain why such substances may seem irresistible."[28]

THE SPATIAL CONTEXT OF FAST-FOOD CONSUMPTION

As Giddens points out, most social life occurs in the context of the "fading
away" of time and the "shading off" of space.[29] This is certainly true for fast-
food consumption. Fast-food restaurants, therefore, need to be examined
both as eating places and as social spaces where social interactions occur. A
physical place accommodates objects and human agents and provides an
arena for social interactions, and it follows that the use of space cannot be
separated from the objects and the physical environment.[30] However, space
functions only as a context, not a determinant, of social interactions, and
the space itself in some way is also socially constructed.[31] In the following
pages I consider, on the one hand, how spatial context shapes consumers'
behavior and social relations, and how, on the other hand, consumers appropriate fast-food restaurants into their own space. Such an inquiry must
begin with a brief review of Beijing's restaurant sector in the late 1970s in
order to assess the extent to which Western fast-food outlets differ from existing local restaurants.

Socialist Canteens and Restaurants in the 1970s

Eating out used to be a difficult venture for ordinary people in Beijing because few restaurants were designed for mass consumption. As mentioned

---

26. For representative views on this issue, see Guo Jianying 1995; Huang Shengbing 1995;
Jian Feng 1992; Xiao Hua 1993; Ye Xianning 1993; Yan Zhenguo and Liu Yinsheng 1992a;
and Zhong Zhe 1993.
27. Ling Dawei 1995.
28. Mintz 1993, p. 271.
29. Giddens 1984, p. 132.
30. See Sayer 1985, pp. 30–31.
31. See Lechner 1991; Urry 1985.

earlier, the restaurants in Beijing were hierarchically ranked by architecture, function, and the type and quality of foods provided. More important, before the economic reforms almost all restaurants and eateries were state-owned businesses, which meant that a restaurant was first and foremost a work unit, just like any factory, shop, or government agency.[32] Thus a restaurant's position and function were also determined by its administrative status as a work unit.

Generally speaking, the restaurant hierarchy consisted of three layers. At the top were luxury and exclusive restaurants in star-rated hotels, such as the Beijing Hotel, which served only foreigners and privileged domestic guests. At the next level were well-established formal restaurants, many of which specialized in a particular style of cuisine and had been in business for many years, even before the 1949 revolution. Unlike the exclusive hotel restaurants, the formal restaurants were open to the public and served two major functions: (1) as public spaces in which small groups of elites could socialize and hold meetings; and (2) as places for ordinary citizens to hold family banquets on special, ritualized occasions such as weddings. At the bottom of the hierarchy were small eateries that provided common family-style foods; these were hardly restaurants (they were actually called *shitang*, meaning canteens). The small eateries were frequented primarily by visitors from outlying provinces and some Beijing residents who had to eat outside their homes because of special job requirements. The majority of Beijing residents rarely ate out—they normally had their meals at home or in their work-unit canteens.

In the 1950s the development of internal canteens (*neibu shitang*) not only constituted an alternative to conventional restaurants but also had a great impact on the latter. Most work units had (and still have) their own canteens, in order to provide employees with relatively inexpensive food and, more important, to control the time allotted for meals. Because canteens were subsidized by the work units and were considered part of employees' benefits, they were run in a manner similar to a family kitchen, only on an enlarged scale. The central message delivered through the canteen facilities was that the work unit, as the representative of the party-state, provided food to its employees, just as a mother feeds her children (without the affectionate component of real parental care). The relationship between the canteen workers and those who ate at the canteens was thus a patronized relationship between the feeder and the fed, rather than a relationship of service provider and customers. The tasteless foods, unfriendly service, and uncomfortable environment were therefore natural components at such public canteens, which prevailed for more than three decades and still exist in many work units today.

The work-unit mentality of "feeding" instead of "serving" people also made

32. For a comprehensive study of the work-unit system, see Walder 1986.

its way into restaurants in Beijing because, after all, the restaurants were also work units and thus had the same core features as all other work units—that is, the dominating influence of the state bureaucracy and the planned economy. Commercial restaurants also shared with the work-unit canteens the poor maintenance of internal space, a limited choice of foods, the requirement that the diner pay in advance, fixed times for meals (most restaurants were open only during the short prescribed lunch and dinner times), and of course, ill-tempered workers who acted as if they were distributing food to hungry beggars instead of paying customers.[33] It is true that the higher one moved up the ladder of the restaurant hierarchy the better dining environment and service one could find. But in the famous traditional restaurants and the star-rated hotel restaurants, formality and ritual were most likely the dominating themes. Still, until the late 1980s it was not easy for ordinary people to enjoy dining out in restaurants.

In contrast, Western fast-food restaurants offered local consumers a new cultural experience symbolized by foreign fast food, enjoyable spatial arrangements of objects and people, and American-style service and social interactions.

The Cultural Symbolism of Fast Food

It is perhaps a truism to note that food is not only good to eat but also good for the mind. The (Western) fast-food fever in Beijing provides another example of how in certain circumstances customers may care less about the food and more about the cultural messages it delivers. During my fieldwork in 1994 I discovered that although children were great fans of the Big Mac and french fries, most adult customers did not particularly like those fast foods. Many people commented that the taste was not good and that the flavor of cheese was strange. The most common complaint from adult customers was *chi bu bao*, meaning that McDonald's hamburgers and fries did not make one feel full: they were more like snacks than like meals.[34] It is also interesting to note that both McDonald's and KFC emphasized the freshness, purity, and nutritional value of their foods (instead of their appealing tastes). According to a high-level manager of Beijing McDonald's, the recipes for McDonald's foods were designed to meet modern scientific specifications and thus differed from the recipes for Chinese foods, which were based on cultural expectations.[35] Through advertisements and news media reports, this idea that fast foods use nutritious ingredients and are prepared using scientific cooking meth-

33. In prereform Beijing even the hotel restaurants and guesthouse canteens were open only during "proper" meal times. So if a visitor missed the meal time, the only alternative was to buy bread and soft drinks from a grocery store.

34. For more details on the results of the survey, see Yan 1997a.

35. See discussions in Xu Chengbei 1994.

ods has been accepted by the public. This may help to explain that why few customers compared the taste of fast foods to that of traditional Chinese cuisine; instead customers focused on something other than the food.

If people do not like the imported fast food, why are they still keen on going to Western fast-food restaurants? Most informants said that they liked the atmosphere, the style of eating, and the experience of being there. According to an early report on KFC, customers did not go to KFC to eat the chicken but to enjoy "eating" (consuming) the culture associated with KFC. Most customers spent hours talking to each other and gazing out the huge glass windows onto busy commercial streets—and feeling more sophisticated than the people who passed by.[36] Some local observers argued that the appeal of Chinese cuisine was the taste of the food itself and that, in contrast, Western food relied on the manner of presentation. Thus consumers would seem to be interested in the spectacle created by this new form of eating.[37] In other words, what Beijing customers find satisfying about Western fast-food restaurants is not the food but the experience.

The cultural symbolism that McDonald's, KFC, and other fast-food chains carry with them certainly plays an important role in constructing this nonedible yet fulfilling experience. Fast food, particularly McDonald's fast food, is considered quintessentially American in many parts of the contemporary world. In France, the most commonly agreed "American thing" among teenagers is McDonald's, followed by Coca-Cola and "military and space technologies."[38] In Moscow, a local journalist described the opening of the first McDonald's restaurant as the arrival of the "ultimate icon of Americana."[39] The same is true in Beijing, although the official news media have emphasized the element of modernity instead of Americana. The high efficiency of the service and management, fresh ingredients, friendly service, and spotless dining environment in Western fast-food restaurants have been repeatedly reported by the Beijing media as concrete examples of modernity.[40]

Ordinary consumers are interested in the stories told in news reports, popular magazines, and movies that the Big Mac and fried chicken are what make Americans American. According to a well-known commentator on popular culture in Beijing, because of the modernity inherent in the McDonald's fast-food chain, many American youths prefer to work first at McDonald's before finding other jobs on the market. The experience of working at Mc-

36. *Zhongguo shipinbao* (Chinese food newspaper), November 6, 1991.

37. *Jingji ribao*, September 15, 1991.

38. Fantasia 1995, p. 219.

39. Ritzer 1993, pp. 4–5.

40. Every time McDonald's opened a new restaurant in the early 1990s, it was featured in the Chinese media. See e.g., *Tianjin qingnianbao* (Tianjin youth news), June 8, 1994; *Shanghai jingji ribao* (Shanghai economic news), July 22, 1994; *Wenhui bao* (Wenhui daily), July 22, 1994. See also Han Shu 1994; Xu Chengbei 1993, p. 3.

Donald's, he argues, prepares American youth for any kind of job in a modern society.[41] To many Beijing residents, "American" also means "modern," and thus to eat at McDonald's is to experience modernity. During my fieldwork I talked with many parents who appreciated their children's fondness for imported fast food because they believed it was in good taste to be modern. A mother told me that she had made great efforts to adapt to the strange flavor of McDonald's food so that she could take her daughter to McDonald's twice a week. She explained: "I want my daughter to learn more about American culture. She is taking an English typing class now, and I will buy her a computer next year." Apparently, eating a Big Mac and fries, like learning typing and computer skills, is part of the mother's plan to prepare her daughter for a modern society.

Inspired by the success of the cultural symbolism of McDonald's and KFC, many Chinese fast-food restaurants have tried to use traditional Chinese culture to lure customers. As I mentioned in the preceding section, almost all local fried-chicken outlets during 1990–91 emphasized the use of traditional medicinal ingredients and the idea of health-enhancing food.[42] Others used ethnic and local flavors to stress the Chineseness of their fast foods, such as the Red Sorghum's promotion of its lamb noodle soup.[43] And some directly invoked the nationalist feelings of the customers. For instance, Happy Chopsticks, a new fast-food chain in Shenzhen, adopted "Chinese people eat Chinese food" as the leading slogan in its market promotion.[44] The power of cultural symbolism in the fast-food sector also has made an impact on the restaurant industry in general: the cultural position of the restaurant business is regarded as an important issue, and the debate about the differences between Western and Chinese cuisine continues in professional journals.[45]

A Place of Entertainment for Equals

According to older residents, in addition to different cuisine styles, traditional restaurants in pre-1949 Beijing also differed in their interior decorations, seating arrangements, and interactions between restaurant employees and customers. During the Maoist era, such features were considered inappropriate to the needs of working-class people and thus gradually disappeared.

41. Xu Chengbei 1992. In fact, I applied to work in a McDonald's outlet in Beijing but was turned down. The manager told me that the recruitment of employees in McDonald's involves a long and strict review process, in order to make sure that the applicants' qualifications are competitive.

42. The relationship between medicine and food has long been an important concern in Chinese culinary culture. See E. Anderson 1988, pp. 53–56.

43. See Yu Bin 1996; and "Honggaoliang yuyan" 1996.

44. Liu Guoyue 1996.

45. See Zhao Huanyan 1995; Xu Wangsheng 1995; Xie Dingyuan 1996; and Tao Wentai 1996.

Under the brutal attack on traditional culture during the Cultural Revolution period, some famous restaurants even replaced their old names with new, revolutionary names, such as Workers and Peasants Canteen (*Gongnong shitang*). As a result, by the late 1970s most restaurants looked similar both inside and out, which, combined with the canteen mentality in restaurant management and poor service, turned Beijing restaurants into unpleasant eating places.

When KFC and McDonald's opened their outlets in Beijing, what most impressed Beijing consumers was their beautiful appearance. As mentioned earlier, both the first KFC and first McDonald's are located near Tiananmen Square in the heart of Beijing, and both boast that they are the largest outlets of their kind in the world, one with a three-floor, 500-seat building and the other with a two-floor, 700-seat building. The statues of Colonel Sanders and Ronald McDonald in front of the two establishments immediately became national tourist attractions.

Once inside the restaurants, Beijing customers found other surprises. First, both McDonald's and the KFC restaurants were brightly lit and climate-controlled. The seats, tables, and walls were painted in light colors, which, together with the shiny counters, stainless-steel kitchenware, and soft music in the background, created an open and cheerful physical environment—a sharp contrast to traditional Chinese restaurants. Moreover, social interaction at McDonald's or KFC was highly ritualized and dramatized,[46] representing a radical departure from the canteen-like restaurants in Beijing. Employees wore neat, brightly colored uniforms, and they smiled at customers while working conscientiously and efficiently. As one observant informant remarked, even the employee responsible for cleaning the toilets worked in a disciplined manner. In his study of restaurants in Athens, Georgia, Allen Shelton commented: "The spectacle of McDonald's is work: the chutes filling up with hamburgers; the restaurant and the other diners are secondary views."[47] In contrast, both the work and the restaurant itself constituted the spectacle at McDonald's and KFC in Beijing.

One of the things that most impressed new customers of the fast-food outlets was the menu, which is displayed above and behind the counter, with soft backlighting and photographic images of the food. The menu delivers a clear message about the public, affordable eating experience that the establishment offers. This was particularly important for first-timers, who did not know anything about the exotic food. Another feature is the open, clean, kitchen area, which clearly shows the customers how the hamburgers and fried chickens are prepared. To emphasize this feature, Beijing's McDonald's also provides a five-minute tour of the kitchen area on customer request.

46. For an excellent account, see Kottak 1978.
47. Shelton 1990, p. 520.

The Western fast-food restaurants also gave customers a sense of equality. Both employees and customers remain standing during the ordering process, creating an equal relationship between the two parties. More important, the friendly service and the smiling employees give customers the impression that no matter who you are you will be treated with equal warmth and friendliness. Accordingly, many people patronize McDonald's to experience a moment of equality.[48] The restaurants also seem to convey gender equality and have attracted a large number of female customers (I will return to this point later).

All these details in internal space are important in understanding the success of McDonald's and KFC in Beijing: objects have a voice that originates in those who use them, just as the scenery on a stage shape the movements of an actor.[49] The impact of spatial context on people's behavior in McDonald's restaurants is well addressed by Peter Stephenson. He observed that some Dutch customers lost their cultural "self" in such a culturally decontextualized place because "there is a kind of instant emigration that occurs the moment one walks through the doors, where Dutch rules rather obviously don't apply."[50] Rick Fantasia observed that French customers undergo similar changes or adjustments in behavior in McDonald's outlets in Paris.[51] Given the sharper and deeper cultural differences between American and Chinese societies, it is natural to expect the cultural decontextualization to be even stronger in Beijing's McDonald's and KFC restaurants.

The interesting point is that, owing to the powerful appeal of modernity and Americana projected by McDonald's and KFC, when experiencing the same "instant emigration," Beijing customers seem to be more willing to observe the rules of American fast-food restaurants than their counterparts in Leiden or Paris. For instance, in 1992 and 1993 customers in Beijing (as in Hong Kong and Taiwan) usually left their rubbish on the table for the restaurant employees to clean up: people regarded McDonald's as a formal establishment at which they had paid for full service. However, during the summer of 1994 I observed that about one-fifth of the customers, many of them fashionably dressed youth, carried their own trays to the waste bins. From subsequent interviews I discovered that most of these people were regular customers, and they had learned to clean up their tables by observing the foreigners' behavior. Several informants told me that when they disposed of their own rubbish they felt more "civilized" (*wenming*) than the other customers because they knew the proper behavior. My random check of customer behavior in McDonald's and in comparably priced and more expensive Chinese restau-

48. *Gaige Daobao* (Reform herald), no. 1 (1994), p. 34.
49. See Douglas and Isherwood 1979.
50. Stephenson 1989, p. 237.
51. Fantasia 1995, pp. 221–22.

rants shows that people in McDonald's were, on the whole, more self-restrained and polite toward one another, spoke in lower tones, and were more careful not to throw their trash on the ground. Unfortunately, when they returned to a Chinese context, many also returned to their previous patterns of behavior. As a result, the overall atmosphere in a Western fast-food outlet is always nicer than that in Chinese restaurants of the same or even higher quality.[52]

A Multidimensional Social Space

In part because of the cultural symbolism of Americana and modernity and in part because of the exotic, cheerful, and comfortable physical environment, McDonald's, KFC, and other foreign fast-food restaurants attract customers from all walks of life in Beijing. Unlike in the United States, where the frequenters of fast-food restaurants are generally associated with low income and simple tastes, most frequenters of fast-food restaurants in Beijing are middle-class professionals, trendy yuppies, and well-educated youths. Unfortunately, there has yet to be a systematic social survey of Chinese fast-food consumers. Nevertheless, according to my field observations in 1994, a clear distinction can be drawn between those who occasionally partake of the imported fast foods and those who regularly frequent fast-food restaurants.

Occasional adventurers include both Beijing residents and visitors from outlying provinces and cities. It should be noted that a standard one-person meal at McDonald's (including a hamburger, a soft drink, and an order of French fries, which is the equivalent of a value-meal at McDonald's in the United States) cost 17 renminbi (rmb) ($2.10) in 1994 and 21 rmb ($2.60) in 1996.[53] This may not be expensive by American standards, but it is not an insignificant amount of money for ordinary workers in Beijing, who typically made less than 500 rmb ($60) per month in 1994. Thus, many people, especially those with moderate incomes, visited McDonald's restaurants only once or twice, primarily to satisfy their curiosity about American food and culinary culture. A considerable proportion of the customers were tourists from other provinces who had only heard of McDonald's or seen its Golden

52. For an interesting study of eating etiquette in southern China, see Cooper 1986, pp. 179–84. As mentioned near the beginning of this chapter, Finkelstein offers an interesting and radically different view of existing manners and custom in restaurants. Since manners and behavior patterns are socially constructed and imposed on customers, they make the "restaurant a diorama that emphasizes the aspects of sociality assumed to be the most valued and attractive"(Finkelstein 1989, p. 52). Accordingly, customers give up their individuality and spontaneity and thus cannot explore their real inner world in this kind of socially constructed spatial context (ibid., pp. 4–17).

53. The 1994 figure comes from my fieldwork; the 1996 figure is taken from Beijing Dashiye Jingji Diaocha Gongsi (Beijing big perspective economic survey company), quoted in "Kuaican zoujin gongxin jieceng" (Fast food is coming closer to salaried groups), *Zhongguo jingyingbao*, June 21, 1996.

Arches in the movies. The tasting of American food has recently become an important part of the tourist beat in Beijing; and those who partake of the experience are able to boast about it to their relatives and friends back home.

There are also local customers who frequent foreign fast-food outlets on a regular basis. A survey conducted by Beijing McDonald's management in one of its stores showed that 10.2 percent of the customers frequented the restaurant four times per month in 1992, in 1993 the figure was 38.3 percent.[54] The majority of customers fell into three categories: professionals and white-collar workers; young couples and teenagers; and children accompanied by their parents. Moreover, women of all age groups tended to frequent McDonald's restaurants more than men.

For younger Beijing residents who worked in joint-venture enterprises or foreign firms and had higher incomes, eating at McDonald's, Kentucky Fried Chicken, and Pizza Hut had become an integral part of their new lifestyle, a way for them to be connected to the outside world. As one informant commented: "The Big Mac doesn't taste great; but the experience of eating in this place makes me feel good. Sometimes I even imagine that I am sitting in a restaurant in New York or Paris." Although some emphasized that they only went to save time, none finished their meals within twenty minutes. Like other customers, these young professionals arrived in small groups or accompanied by girl/boy friends to enjoy the restaurant for an hour or more. Eating foreign food, and consuming other foreign goods, had become an important way for Chinese yuppies to define themselves as middle-class professionals. By 1996, however, this group had found other types of activities (such as nightclubs or bars), and gradually they were beginning to visit foreign fast-food restaurants for convenience rather than for status.

Young couples and teenagers from all social strata were also regular frequenters of McDonald's and KFC outlets because the dining environment is considered to be romantic and comfortable. The restaurants are brightly-lit, clean, and feature light Western music; and except during busy periods they are relatively quiet, making them ideal for courtship. In 1994, McDonald's seven Beijing restaurants had all created relatively isolated and private service areas with tables for two. In some, these areas were nicknamed "lovers' corners." Many teenagers also considered that, with only the minimum consumption of a soft drink or an ice cream, fast-food establishments were good places simply to hang out.

As in many other parts of the world, children in Beijing had become loyal fans of Western fast food. They were so fond of it that some parents even suspected that Big Mac or fried chicken contained a special, hidden ingredient. The fast-food restaurants also made special efforts to attract children by

54. Interview with General Manager Tim Lai, September 28, 1994.

offering birthday parties, dispensing souvenirs, and holding essay contests, because young customers usually did not come alone: they were brought to McDonald's and KFC by their parents or grandparents. Once a middle-aged woman told me that she did not like the taste of hamburgers and that her husband simply hated them. But their daughter loved hamburgers and milk-shakes so much that their entire family had to visit McDonald's three to five times a month. It is common among Beijing families for children to choose the restaurant in which the whole family dines out. Fast-food outlets were frequently the first choice of children.

A gender aspect of fast-food consumption is highlighted in He Yupeng's 1996 study of McDonald's popularity among female customers. In con-ducting a small-scale survey at four restaurants in Beijing—a formal Chinese restaurant, a local fast-food outlet, and two McDonald's outlets—He found that women were more likely than men to enjoy dining at fast-food restau-rants. According to his survey, while 66 percent of the customers (N=68) at the formal Chinese restaurant were men, 64 percent of the customers (N=423) at the local fast-food outlet were women. Similar patterns were ob-served in the two McDonald's restaurants, where women constituted 57 per-cent of a total of 784 adult customers.[55] The most intriguing finding of this survey was that women chose McDonald's because they enjoyed ordering their own food and participating in the conversation while dining. Many fe-male customers pointed out that in formal Chinese restaurants men usually order the food for their female companions and control the conversation. In contrast, they said, at a McDonald's everyone can make his or her own choices and, because smoking and alcohol are prohibited, men dominate less of the conversation.[56]

Furthermore, the imported fast-food restaurants provide a venue where women feel comfortable alone or with female friends. Formal Chinese restaurants are customarily used by elite groups as places to socialize and by middle-class people as places to hold ritual family events such as wedding banquets. In both circumstances, women must subordinate themselves to rules and manners that are androcentric, either explicitly or implicitly (the men order the dishes; the women do not partake of the liquor). These cus-toms reflect the traditional view that women's place is in the household and that men should take charge of all public events. There is a clear division between the private (inside) and the public (outside) along gender lines.

A woman who eats alone in a formal Chinese restaurant is considered ab-normal; such behavior often leads to public suspicion about her morality and her occupation. For instance, a young woman I interviewed in a Mc-Donald's outlet in 1994 recalled having lunch alone in a well-known Chi-

55. He Yupeng 1996.
56. Ibid. p. 8.

nese restaurant frequented mostly by successful businessmen. "Several men gazed at me with lascivious eyes," she said, "and some others exchanged a few words secretly and laughed among themselves. They must have thought I was a prostitute or at least a loose woman. Knowing their evil thoughts, I felt extremely uncomfortable and left the place as quickly as I could." She also commented that even going to a formal Chinese restaurant with female friends would make her feel somewhat improper about herself, because the "normal" customers were men or men with women. But she said that she felt comfortable visiting a McDonald's alone or with her female friends, because "many people do the same." This young woman's experience is by no means unique, and a number of female customers in McDonald's offered similar explanations for liking the foreign fast-food restaurants. Several elderly women also noted the impropriety of women dining in formal Chinese restaurants, although they were less worried about accusations about their morals.[57]

In his survey, He Yupeng asked his respondents where they would choose to eat if there were only a formal Chinese restaurant and a McDonald's outlet. Almost all the male respondents chose the former, and all the female respondents chose the latter. One of the main reasons for such a sharp gender difference, He argues, is the concern of contemporary women for gender equality.[58] The new table manners allowed in fast-food restaurants, and more important, the newly appropriate gender roles in those public places, seem to have enhanced the image of foreign fast-food restaurants as an open place for equals, thus attracting female customers.

The Appropriation of Social Space

Finally, I would point out that Beijing customers do not passively accept everything offered by the American fast-food chains. The American fast-food restaurants have been localized in many aspects, and what Beijing customers enjoy is actually a Chinese version of American culture and fast foods.[59] One aspect of this localization process is the consumers' appropriation of the social space.

My research confirms the impression that most customers in Beijing claim their tables for longer periods of time than Americans do. The average dining time in Beijing (in autumn 1994) was 25 minutes during busy hours and 51 minutes during slack hours. In Beijing, "fastness" does not seem to be particularly important. The cheerful, comfortable, and climate-controlled environment inside McDonald's and KFC restaurants encourages many customers to linger, a practice that seems to contradict the original purpose of

57. See Yan 1997a.
58. He Yupeng 1996, pp. 8–9.
59. See Yan 1997a.

the American fast-food business. During off-peak hours it is common for people to walk into McDonald's for a leisurely drink or snack. Sitting with a milkshake or an order of fries, such customers often spend 30 minutes to an hour, and sometimes longer, chatting, reading newspapers, or holding business meetings. As indicated earlier, young couples and teenagers are particularly fond of frequenting foreign fast-food outlets because they consider the environment to be romantic. Women in all age groups tend to spend the longest time in these establishments, whether they are alone or with friends. In contrast, unaccompanied men rarely linger after finishing their meals. The main reason for this gender difference, according to my informants, is the absence of alcoholic beverages. An interesting footnote in this connection is that 32 percent of my informants in a survey among college students (N=97) regarded McDonald's as a symbol of leisure and emphasized that they went there to relax.

Beijing consumers have appropriated the restaurants not only as places of leisure but also as public arenas for personal and family ritual events. The most popular such event is of course the child's birthday party, which has been institutionalized in Beijing McDonald's restaurants. Arriving with five or more guests, a child can expect an elaborate ritual performed in a special enclosure called "Children's paradise," free of extra charge. The ritual begins with an announcement over the restaurant's loudspeakers—in both Chinese and English—giving the child's name and age, together with congratulations from Ronald McDonald (who is called Uncle McDonald in Beijing). This is followed by the recorded song "Happy Birthday," again in two languages. A female employee in the role of Aunt McDonald then entertains the children with games and presents each child with a small gift from Uncle McDonald. Although less formalized (and without the restaurant's active promotion), private ceremonies are also held in the restaurants for adult customers, particularly for young women in peer groups (the absence of alcohol makes the site attractive to them). Of the 97 college students in my survey, 33 (including nine men) had attended personal celebrations at McDonald's: birthday parties, farewell parties, celebrations for receiving scholarships to American universities, and end-of-term parties.

The multifunctional use of McDonald's space is due in part to the lack of cafes, tea houses, and ice-cream shops in Beijing; it is also a consequence of the management's efforts to attract as many customers as possible by engendering an inviting environment. Although most McDonald's outlets in the United States are designed specifically to prevent socializing (with less-comfortable seats than formal restaurants, for instance) it is clear that the managers of Beijing's McDonald's have accepted their customers' perceptions of McDonald's as a special place that does not fit into pre-existing categories of public eateries. They have not tried to educate Beijing consumers to accept the American view that "fast food" means that one must eat fast and leave quickly.[60] When I wondered how the management accommodated everyone during busy periods, I was told that the problem often resolved itself. A crowd of customers naturally created pressures on those who had finished their meals, and more important, during busy hours the environment was no longer appropriate for relaxation.

In contrast, managers in Chinese fast-food outlets tend to be less tolerant of customers who linger. During my fieldwork in 1994 I conducted several experimental tests by going to Chinese fast-food outlets and ordering only a soft drink but staying for more than an hour. Three out of four times I was indirectly urged to leave by the restaurant employees; they either took away my empty cup or asked if I needed anything else. Given the fact that I was in a fast-food outlet and did all the service for myself, the disturbing "service" in the middle of my stay was clearly a message to urge lingering customers to leave. I once discussed this issue with the manager of a Chinese fast-food restaurant. He openly admitted that he did not like customers claiming a table for long periods of time and certainly did not encourage attempts to turn the fast-food outlet into a coffee shop. As he explained: "If you want to enjoy nice coffee and music then you should go to a fancy hotel cafe, not here."

CONCLUDING REMARKS:
DINING PLACE, SOCIAL SPACE, AND MASS CONSUMPTION

In the United States, fast-food outlets are regarded as "fuel stations" for hungry yet busy people and as family restaurants for low-income groups. Therefore, efficiency (speed) and economic value (low prices) are the two most important reasons why fast foods emerged as a kind of "industrial food" and remain successful in American society today. These features, however, do not apply in Beijing. A Beijing worker who loads the whole family into a taxi to go to McDonald's may spend one-sixth of his monthly income; efficiency and economy are perhaps the least of his concerns. When consumers stay in McDonald's or KFC restaurants for hours, relaxing, chatting, reading, enjoying the music, or celebrating birthdays, they take the "fastness" out of fast food. In Beijing, the fastness of American fast food is reflected mainly in the service provided; for consumers, the dining experience is too meaningful to be

---

60. According to John Love, when Den Fujita, the founder and owner of McDonald's chain stores in Japan, began introducing McDonald's foods to Japanese customers, particularly the youngsters, he bent the rules by allowing his McDonald's outlets to be a hangout place for teenagers. He decorated one of the early stores with poster-sized pictures of leather-jacketed members of a motorcycle gang "one shade removed" from Hell's Angels. Fujita's experiment horrified the McDonald's chairman when he visited the company's new branches in Japan. See Love 1986, p. 429.

shortened. As a result, the American fast-food outlets in China are fashionable, middle-class establishments—a new kind of social space where people can enjoy their leisure time and experience a Chinese version of American culture.

As I emphasize repeatedly throughout this chapter, eating at a foreign fast-food restaurant is an important social event, although it means different things to different people. McDonald's, KFC, and other fast-food restaurants in Beijing carry the symbolism of Americana and modernity, which makes them unsurpassable by existing standards of the social hierarchy in Chinese culture. They represent an emerging tradition where new values, behavior patterns, and social relationships are still being created. People from different social backgrounds may enter the same eating place/social space without worrying about losing face; on the contrary, they may find new ways to better define their positions. For instance, white-collar professionals may display their new class status, youngsters may show their special taste for leisure, and parents may want to "modernize" their children. Women of all ages are able to enjoy their independence when they choose to eat alone; and when they eat with male companions, they enjoy a sexual equality that is absent in formal Chinese restaurants. The fast-food restaurants, therefore, constitute a multivocal, multidimensional, and open social space. This kind of all-inclusive social space met a particular need in the 1990s, when Beijing residents had to work harder than ever to define their positions in a rapidly changing society.[61]

By contrast, almost all local competitors in the fast-food sector tend to regard fast-food restaurants merely as eating places, and accordingly, they try to compete with the foreign fast-food restaurants by offering lower prices and local flavors or by appealing to nationalist sentiments. Although they also realize the importance of hygiene, food quality, friendly service, and a pleasant physical environment, they regard these features as isolated technical factors. A local observer pointed out that it is easy to build the "hardware" of a fast-food industry (the restaurants) but that the "software" (service and management) cannot be adopted overnight.[62] To borrow from this metaphor, I would argue that an understanding of fast-food outlets not only as eating places but also as social space is one of the "software problems" waiting to be resolved by the local competitors in the fast-food business.

61. Elsewhere I have argued that Chinese society in the 1990s underwent a process of restructuring. The entire Chinese population—not only the peasants—was on the move: some physically, some socially, and some in both ways. An interesting indicator of the increased social mobility and changing patterns of social stratification was the booming business of name-card printing, because so many people changed jobs and titles frequently and quickly. Thus consumption and lifestyle decisions became more important than ever as ways for individuals to define their positions. For more details, see Yan 1994.

62. Yan Zhenguo and Liu Yinshing 1992b.

Why is the issue of social space so important for fast-food development in Beijing? It would take another essay to answer this question completely; here I want to highlight three major factors that contribute to fast-food fever and are closely related to consumers' demands for a new kind of social space.

First, the trend of mass consumption that arose in the second half of the 1980s created new demands for dining out as well as new expectations of the restaurant industry. According to 1994 statistics released by the China Consumer Society, the average expenditure per capita has increased 4.1 times since 1984. The ratio of "hard consumption" (on food, clothes, and other necessities of daily life) to "soft consumption" (entertainment, tourism, fashion, and socializing) went from 3:1 in 1984 to 1:1.2 in 1994.[63] In 1990, consumers began spending money as never before on such goods and services as interior decoration, private telephones and pagers, air conditioners, body-building machines, and tourism.[64] As part of this trend toward consumerism, dining out has become a popular form of entertainment among virtually all social groups, and people are particularly interested in experimenting with different cuisines.[65] In response to a survey conducted by the Beijing Statistics Bureau in early 1993, nearly half of the respondents said they had eaten at Western-style restaurants (including fast-food outlets) at least once.[66] A central feature of this development in culinary culture is that people want to dine out as active consumers, and they want the dining experience to be relaxed, fun, and healthful.

In response to increasing consumer demands, thousands of restaurants and eateries have appeared in recent years. By early 1993 there were more than 19,000 eating establishments in Beijing, ranging from elegant five-star hotel restaurants to simple street eateries. Of these, about 5,000 were state-owned, 55 were joint ventures or foreign-owned, and the remaining 14,000 or so were owned by private entrepreneurs or independent vendors (*getihu*).[67]

These figures show that the private sector has played an increasingly important role in the restaurant business. Unlike the state-owned restaurants, some private restaurants have used creativity to meet consumers' demands for a new kind of dining experience. The best example is the emergence of country-style, nostalgic restaurants set up by and for the former sent-down urban youths. In these places customers retaste their experience of youth in the countryside: customers choose from country-style foods in rooms and among objects that remind them of the past. Like customers in McDonald's or KFC, they are also consuming part of the subculture and redefining them-

63. See Xiao Yan 1994.
64. See, e.g., Gao Changli 1992, p. 6; Dong Fang 1994, p. 22.
65. Gu Bingshu 1994.
66. *Beijing wanbao,* January 27, 1993.
67. *Beijing qingnianbao* (Beijing youth daily), December 18, 1993.

selves in a purchased social space. The difference is that the nostalgic restaurants appeal only to a particular social group, while the American fast-food outlets are multivocal and multidimensional and thus attract people from many different social strata.

The rise of new consumer groups is the second major factor that has made the issue of social space so important to understanding fast-food fever in Beijing. Urban youth, children, and women of all ages constitute the majority of the regular frequenters of American fast-food restaurants. It is not by accident that these people are all newcomers as restaurant customers—there was no proper place for them in the pre-existing restaurant system, and the only social role that women, youth, and children could play in a formal Chinese restaurant was as the dependents of men. Women's effort to gain an equal place in restaurant subculture was discussed earlier, so here I briefly examine the place of youth and children.

Young professionals emerged along with the development of the market economy, especially with the expansion of joint-venture and foreign-owned business in Beijing in the 1990s. To prove and further secure their newly obtained social status and prestige, the young elite have taken the construction of a different lifestyle seriously, and they often lead the trend of contemporary consumerism in Chinese cities. Urban youth may be less well off than young professionals, but they are equally eager to embrace a new way of personal life. According to a 1994 survey, the purchasing power of Beijing youth increased dramatically over the previous decade, and nearly half of the 1,000 respondents in the survey had more than 500 rmb per month to spend on discretionary items.[68] With more freedom to determine their lifestyles and more economic independence, these youngsters were eager to establish their own social space in many aspects of life, including dining out.[69] A good example in this connection is the astonishing popularity among young people in mainland China of pop music, films, and romance novels from Hong Kong and Taiwan.[70]

The importance of teenagers and children in effecting social change also emerged in the late twentieth century, along with the growth of the national economy, the increase in family wealth, and the decline of the birth rate. The single-child policy—which is most strictly implemented in the big cities—has created a generation of little emperors and empresses, each demanding the attention and economic support of his or her parents and grandparents. Parental indulgence of children has become a national obsession, making children and teenagers one of the most active groups of

68. Pian Ming 1994.

69. For a review of changes in consumption and lifestyles among Chinese youth, see Huang Zhijian 1994.

70. See Gold 1993.

consumers. Beijing is by no means exceptional in this respect. According to Deborah Davis and Julia Sensenbrenner (see Chapter 3 in this volume), ordinary working-class parents in Shanghai normally spend one-third of their monthly wages to provide their children with a lifestyle that is distinctly upper middle class in its patterns of consumption. For many parents, toys, trips, fashionable clothes, music lessons, and restaurant meals have become necessities in raising their children. This suggests a significant change in patterns of household expenditure, and accordingly there is an urgent need to meet the market demands and special tastes of this important group of consumers.

The emerging importance of women, youth, and children as consumers results from a significant transformation of the family institution in contemporary Chinese society, which is characterized by the nuclearization of the household, the centrality of conjugality in family relations, the rising awareness of independence and sexual equality among women, the waning of the patriarchy, and the rediscovery of the value of children.[71] As far as fast-food consumption is concerned, the link between new groups of independent consumers and shifts in family values is found in other East Asian societies as well. After analyzing the relationship between the McDonald's "takeoff" in five cities (Tokyo, Hong Kong, Taipei, Seoul, and Beijing) and the changes in family values (especially the rising status of teenagers and children), Watson concluded: "More than any other factor . . . McDonald's success is attributable to the revolution in family values that has transformed East Asia."[72]

A third important factor in the success of Western fast-food enterprises is the new form of sociality that has been developing in market-controlled public places such as restaurants. A significant change in public life during the post-Mao era has been the disappearance of frequent mass rallies, voluntary work, collective parties, and other forms of "organized sociality" in which the state (through its agents) played the central role. In its place are new forms of private gatherings in public venues. Whereas "organized sociality" emphasized the centrality of the state, the official ideology, and the submission of individuals to an officially endorsed collectivity, the new sociality celebrates individuality and private desires in unofficial social and spatial contexts. The center of public life and socializing, accordingly, has shifted from large state-controlled public spaces (such as city squares, auditoriums, and workers' clubs) to smaller, commercialized arenas such as dancing halls, bowling alleys, and even imaginary spaces provided by radio call-in shows (e.g., see chapters in this volume by Kathleen Erwin, James Farrer, and Gan Wang).

71. On changing family values and household structure, see chapters in Davis and Harrell 1993. For a detailed study of the rising importance of conjugality in rural family life, see Yan 1997b.

72. Watson 1997, p. 19.

The new sociality has even emerged in conventionally state-controlled public spaces, such as parks, and has thus transformed them into multidimensional spaces in which the state, the public, and the private may coexist (see Richard Kraus's chapter in this volume).

Restaurants similarly meet the demand for a new kind of sociality outside state control—that is, the public celebration of individual desires, life aspirations, and personal communications in a social context. As indicated above, in earlier decades the socialist state did not encourage the use of restaurants as a social space in which to celebrate private desires or perform family rituals. Rather, by institutionalizing public canteens in the workplace, the state tried to control meal time and also change the meaning of social dining itself. This is particularly true in Beijing, which has been the center of national politics and socialist transformation since 1949. Any new form of social dining was unlikely to develop from the previous restaurant sector in Beijing, which consisted primarily of socialist canteens. It is thus not accidental that by 1993 nearly three quarters of the more than 19,000 eating establishments in Beijing were owned by private entrepreneurs (local and foreign) or were operating as joint ventures.[73] McDonald's and other foreign fast-food restaurants have been appropriated by Beijing consumers as especially attractive social spaces for a new kind of socializing and for the celebration of individuality in public. Moreover, consuming at McDonald's and other foreign fast-food outlets is also a way of embracing modernity and foreign culture in public.

To sum up, there is a close link between the development of fast-food consumption and changes in social structure, especially the emergence of new social groups).[74] The new groups of agents demand the creation of new space for socialization in every aspect of public life, including dining out. Fast-food restaurants provide just such a space for a number of social groups. The new kind of sociality facilitated by fast-food restaurants in turn further stimulates consumers' demands for both the food and the space. Hence the fast-food fever in Beijing during the 1990s.

73. See *Beijing qingnianbao,* December 18, 1993.
74. See especially Mintz 1994; see also sources cited in notes 2 to 13.

CHAPTER 10

Dancing through the Market Transition

Disco and Dance Hall Sociability in Shanghai

James Farrer

This chapter contrasts two types of commercial dance venues in Shanghai and describes how they are used differently by their different participants. I begin with some simple observations made between 1993 and 1996 in discotheques and social dance clubs in Shanghai and some other Chinese towns and cities, where I participated in dance hall activities, observed interactions, and interviewed customers and staff. In small discotheques in Shanghai and nearby towns I observed the same scene several times: as soon as the disco music began, young dancers rushed forward to the mirror that covered one entire wall. There they danced, watching and studying themselves in the flashing colored disco lights. In larger discos, daring city youth mounted stages to position themselves to be seen by the crowd. In both kinds of places, the logic of participation seemed to be display: the gaze was self-centered, and being watched and appearing desirable were the reasons for being there. The more self-confident patrons of the larger metropolitan discos seemed less in need of mirrors, able in their own minds to imagine how they appeared in the anonymous gaze of the crowd surrounding them.

In social (or ballroom) dances, on the other hand, I observed a different sense of urgency. Middle-aged patrons shifted about nervously at the beginning of each number, positioning themselves to find a desirable partner. Afterward, they danced in the embrace of strangers, their motions in confluence with the music. Patrons watched other dancers, but the dynamics of the dance were structured by the pragmatics of the "partnered" dance form. Put simply, in disco, the rush at the beginning of a number was to find an advantageous spot for self-display and self-viewing, while in social dance the rush was to find someone to dance with.

The questions that arise are also simple. Why did young people from a

Shanghai neighborhood or a small town, going to the disco for a taste of modern entertainment, want to dance in front of a mirror or show themselves off on a stage? Why did mostly middle-aged and married factory workers take time in the afternoon to dance romantically in a dimly lit warehouse with other married people?

I suggest that the use of the mirror was the most straightforward example of a culture of desirability in the disco, a culture in which Chinese youth worked on their self-image and emotional control in the mirror, in playful interactions with strangers and in view of the anonymous gaze of the crowd. The dark warehouse ballroom, in contrast, represented a culture of desire, a place to steal small pleasures from the routines of everyday work-unit and family life, not a place to be glamorous but a place to be embraced.

The sociological interpretations I give of these cultural forms are not exhaustive. The reasons, for instance, that young people in Shanghai preferred disco while middle-aged state enterprise employees preferred social dancing were overdetermined by local and global processes (e.g., the size of a local dance market and images of the global youth culture on television). There are also many similarities between the two cultural forms. However, it still seems useful to ask what youth found appealing in disco that differed from what somewhat older people found appealing in social dance; the answer may provide insight into how different sectors of the Chinese population differently experience the consumer revolution in China in concrete social contexts.

Both disco and dance hall patrons described commercial dance venues as places walled off from serious relationships. The adjective most frequently used to describe the commercial dance venue was "chaotic." The adjective most frequently used to describe the people one met there was "unreliable." The verb used to describe the activities there was "fooling around" or "play." Neither type of dance venue was typically seen as a place to engage in serious long-term social interactions, to make friends or meet a mate. These were defined as "chaotic" spaces to which people went to "fool around" with "unreliable" people. They were play spaces, and the goal of this chapter is to explain why different sets of participants found these particular forms of play rewarding and meaningful.

Dance halls have been largely ignored by sociologists. Dance fits poorly into the traditional sociological action paradigms constructed around goal-oriented or pragmatic activity.[1] Even in such accounts as do exist, "mainstream" commercial dance halls have been generally dismissed through comparisons of these mass cultural forms with more authentic activities.[2] So-

---

1. See Ward 1993.
2. See Cressey 1932; Rust 1969; Mungham 1976; Hebdige 1979; Willis 1984; Thornton 1996; and Redhead, Wynne, and O'Connor 1997.

ciologists have taken participants' definitions of commercial dance halls as "trivial" spaces purely for "play" or "fun" too much at face value and not investigated these definitions as social constructs. I find the interactions in commercial dance halls sociologically interesting precisely because they are defined as inauthentic "play." They involve distinct forms of sociability that interact with social life outside the dance hall but are deemed inconsequential and are thus allowed greater freedom of expression than activities in the "real world."[3]

In the most complete sociological study of social dance, Rust argues that changing genres of dance reflect larger changes in social organization. Describing the transition from paired, partnered dances like the waltz to partnerless dances such as the twist in 1960s Britain, Rust writes: "Partnerless dances such as the twist and the shake and their successors have such a strong appeal for the confident teenagers of today who, possibly, prefer to use the dance to express their individuality and even to show off rather than as an excuse for an embrace."[4] Despite her dated functionalist argument, Rust's work is relevant to Shanghai at the turn of the twenty-first century, where partnered and partnerless genres of dance coexist in a market, much as they did in Rust's 1960s Britain. Below we look at how different genres of dance allow for different styles of sexual play for different age groups with different experiences of the market economy emerging in Shanghai.

The distinction between discos and social dance halls goes beyond the dance steps and includes the engineering of the space itself. In contrast with modestly decorated social dance halls, large and technologically sophisticated city discotheques are designed as sites for experiencing a glamorous metropolitan modernity. Walsh asks of the new popularity of discotheques in Britain:

> What then is different about the discotheque and why has it replaced the Palais du Danse as the new venue for gathering through social dancing? Largely it is a matter of the ambience which the discotheque deliberately sets out to create, which is one of sophistication and glamour. It extends an invitation to young people to become participants in the "high life" which the wealth of Western societies has made available to the affluent sections of its population . . . bringing it down to an egalitarian level so that more people can share in it. So everything about the discotheque is geared to this self-presentation of glamorous sophistication. To go to one, one needs to dress up. The very names which discotheques call themselves are redolent of glamour.[5]

Sexuality is a dominant theme in dance. In sociological studies, dance is commonly described as a courtship activity, as a means of getting sex, or as

---

3. For an explication of how forms of sociability work as "play forms" of earnest interactions and as quasi-artistic commentaries on social life, see Simmel 1971 and Simmel 1984.
4. Rust 1969, p. 121.
5. Walsh 1993, p. 113.

a male predatory activity.[6] "What is missing in views of this kind is the realization that dance is not just a means to sex (although of course it may well be such) but that it is or can be a form of sexual expression in itself."[7] The discotheque and social dance hall also represent two different sexual cultures and very different styles of eroticism.[8] This chapter ties different forms of eroticism and sociability observed in dance venues to different generational experiences of the Chinese transition to a market society.

I base my analysis on ethnographic observations and open-ended interviews in Shanghai, where from 1993 to 1996 I conducted case studies of Chinese sexual culture—in media, everyday conversation, leisure, courtship and extramarital affairs.[9] I was a regular patron of several dance venues, but I visited many other places on a less regular basis. Dance halls were difficult places to study. They were noisy, confusing, and sometimes unfriendly, but the patrons were often willing to engage the ethnographer in their verbal games. Being a foreigner was an advantage in this respect. As a participant observer, I was the "measuring instrument," but I frequently checked my observations and interpretations with those of other patrons.

HISTORY AND MARKET SEGMENTATION

Shanghai has long been famous for its dance halls, and dance hall stars had their own fan magazines in the 1930s.[10] Western-style ballroom dancing spread out from Shanghai across the country by 1949. Communist-controlled work units and labor unions still organized dance parties during the 1950s in towns and cities including Shanghai, and according to older Chinese, dancing was a popular activity of high-level cadres including Mao. Nevertheless, social dancing was banned in Shanghai as a "bourgeois" tendency during the antirightist campaigns of the late 1950s.[11]

Western-style ballroom dancing reappeared in Shanghai in 1979 after a

6. On sexuality in dance, see Hanna 1988. On dance as courtship, see Rust 1969. On dance as a means of getting sex, see Cressey 1932 and Meckel 1995. On dance as a predatory activity, see Mungham 1976.

7. Ward 1993, p. 22.

8. See Frith and McRobbie 1990; McRobbie 1984; Polhemus 1993; Dyer 1990.

9. This research was made possible by an international predissertation research fellowship from the Social Science Research Council funded by the Ford Foundation and the American Council of Learned Societies, and by a Fulbright-Hays dissertation research fellowship from the U.S. Department of Education.

10. Andrew Field, personal communication.

11. Factory dance parties were described as "indecent rallies for propagating the bourgeois way of life" in a 1956 newspaper article and condemned for adversely affecting factory production. Indiscriminate black-market selling of tickets and sexual promiscuity were cited as problems at these events. *Shanghai wenhuibao*, November 28, 1956. Thanks to Maris Gillette for bringing this article to my attention.

hiatus of only a bit more than twenty years. During the initial phases of dancing's political rehabilitation, many older people were able to teach younger
people how to dance at home. Home dance parties were popular in the early
1980s, including infamous "lights out" dance parties where couples report-
edly groped each other in the darkness.

By 1979 labor unions and youth leagues were again organizing dance parties, attendance at which required a letter of introduction from a work unit
proving one was of age. Monitors kept men and women from dancing too
close together, but such puritanism quickly ended in rougher working-class
communities, where overzealous monitors were scolded and even attacked
by local toughs. This was the clearest example of how working-class youth
vigorously rejected the intrusion of the state into private lives after 1980.
"When they came up to monitor someone, we would pop them on the back
of the head. They wouldn't know what hit them," a 35-year-old shop owner
told me of his young dancing days.

In 1984 the first commercial social dance halls opened in Shanghai. Disco
dancing arrived in Shanghai in the mid-1980s, made popular by American
films like *Break Dance* and *Flash Dance* and the dance parties of foreign students
at Chinese universities (mostly Africans who introduced the still-popular reg-
gae music to Shanghai). Specialized discotheques did not open until the late
1980s and were first located in hotels restricted to foreigners. Therefore until the 1990s disco dancing remained a largely marginal though fashionable
addition to the social dance routine. A 31-year-old woman office worker described disco dancing in the mid-1980s:

> They already had disco then, but they only played a few minutes every night.
> Then only a few people could dance it. Maybe out of a hundred or two hundred
> people, only 25 or 30 would be out there dancing, twisting and turning, really
> ugly, not like people today. Everybody else would just stand around and watch
> them. These were really the most fashionable people, and back then people would
> brag that they could dance disco. The most popular music then was the Bee-Gee's.

In 1992 a mammoth disco called "JJ" opened in the center of the city and
was open to all local visitors. It drew between 1,000 and 2,000 customers a
day, despite ticket prices ranging from 48 to 68 renminbi (rmb). Although
JJ was later closed for violating the fire code (and because it had a reputation for "disorder"), it set a precedent for taking in massive profits, and by
1996 Shanghai boasted of at least ten multilevel "disco plazas," which legally
accommodated about 600 customers each. There were also 80 to 100
smaller discos scattered throughout the city. Including discos and social
dance halls, the number of commercial dance venues in Shanghai rose from
52 in 1985 to 310 in 1990, 1,022 in 1994, and 1,336 in 1996.[12]

12. Figures for numbers of dance halls were provided by the Shanghai Culture Bureau
(*Shanghai wenhuaju*).

Dancing in the early 1980s was an activity far less differentiated by age, dancing style, and income level than it was by the mid-1990s. People of all ages danced the same dance steps at the same public dance halls. With commercialization, the market began responding to the interests and styles of different age groups and to the increasingly wide distribution of income in the city. The cultural implications of this market differentiation are the focus of this chapter. Next, I briefly describe the two major types of commercial dancing venues in Shanghai. While city parks, labor union halls, and colleges were also popular dance sites, space does not permit discussion of these noncommercial venues here.

Social Dance Halls

Social dance halls were the most popular dancing venues in Shanghai, and probably the most popular form of commercial entertainment in the city (if eating out is excepted). At the time of my study, Shanghai had about a thousand commercial social dance halls. Social dance halls usually sold tickets for several two- or three-hour sessions a day, beginning in the morning. Admission prices ranged from 1 rmb for morning dance sessions to 40 rmb for an evening session at a top-end dance hall. A typical evening admission price was about 15 rmb and included a cup of tea. Customers rarely ordered other beverages or alcohol. Popular social dance halls were busy from nine in the morning to midnight every day of the week.

Social dance halls in and around Shanghai shared a format of an hour of social dance, half an hour of disco music, and a final hour of social dance. A common addition was a quarter-hour of slow dancing ("cheek-to-cheek" dancing) before the disco music began. Larger dance halls had live bands and singers in the evening who took their break during the disco period. The most popular dances were the waltz, four-step, and jitterbug, which were danced mostly to contemporary Hong Kong and Chinese pop tunes but also to some "revolutionary" songs and some songs dating from before 1949.

Most customers at these establishments were between the ages of 25 and 45. The typical customer was married, about 35, and a worker at a state-owned enterprise. Men usually slightly outnumbered women. The price of admission to social dance halls did not vary as much as it did for discos. Nor were there expensive and famous social dance halls that dominated the market financially and symbolically. Rather, the dance hall market was primarily local, and participants seldom bragged about visiting expensive dance halls.

Discos

In the mid-1990s there were about one-tenth as many discos as social dance halls. The smaller market was due to the narrower age range of customers (usually 17 to 25) and shorter business times (usually evenings).

Disco regulars—much more than social dance regulars—ranked discos on different "levels," roughly according to admission price. When asked where they like to go for fun, most young people in the small local discos would list several discos they considered much better than where they were sitting. Often the list began with the "JJ," the legendary mammoth discotheque, which was long closed by the time of my interviews. They then named "Time," "Touch," "Kiss," "New York," "L.A.," "Casablanca," and "Galaxy," the elite metropolitan nightspots in Shanghai where entrance prices ranged from 50 rmb to 100 rmb.

First-rate metropolitan clubs competed for taxi-riding, cocktail-drinking customers from all over the city and out of town in order to make a return on their substantial capital investments in imported lighting and sound equipment (5 to 10 million rmb for a first-rate setup). These metropolitan discos aspired to a cosmopolitan style. A foreign disk jockey (who was often overseas Chinese or from Hong Kong) was de rigueur. Foreign students were often let in free to provide a cosmopolitan atmosphere. All successful metropolitan discos were in fashionable "high-town" locations (Nanjing Road and Huaihai Road) or out toward the airport in the special development zone of Hongqiao; none were across the Suzhou River in the vast expanse of "low-town."[13] Despite their high price of admission, metropolitan discos attracted a cross-section of the city's youth. Most of the young people had regular jobs, so they were able to afford the admission price, but many poor youth occasionally bought tickets or received free tickets from friends. A few years older on average than the customers at the local discos, the crowds usually included a few visiting businessmen over age 30.

As in U.S. big-city nightclubs, Shanghai's metropolitan discos strove to capture the pleasures and dangers of city life. The decor was glass, special lighting, and Hollywood-style urban-industrial decay with day-glow English graffiti. (Shanghai-style urban decay would have been too familiar for youth who had to go home to it every night.) Prostitutes and "fishing girls" (*diaomazi,* who accompany male guests for tips) combed the floors for rich men colloquially described as "big monies." DJs called out "Hello, Shanghai"—in English and Chinese—emphasizing the identification of the dancers with the cosmopolitan city represented through the disco. Crowded at midnight, the megadisco portrayed itself through the exhortations of the DJ as the thumping heart of the big city. Being in the big city meant being cool, not minding—and even imitating in dress and style—the sexy "fishing girls" and

---

13. Low-town (*xiazhijiao*) and high-town (*shangzhijiao*) are terms Shanghainese use to refer to two large areas of the city: the former working-class slums of northern Shanghai (low-town) and the wealthier foreign concession areas (high-town). These terms are still used, and high-town is still considered much more fashionable than low-town, which is still associated with its working-class migrant labor origins.

grim-faced gangsteresque bouncers who patrolled the cast-iron catwalks and stairways.

Many of the small local discos were dingy and poorly equipped, but they imitated the larger clubs in design, music, and style. Local neighborhood youths, as young as 14 or 15 and seldom over 25, formed the bulk of the customers at the cheap local discos, which charged from 10 to 30 rmb for an evening admission. Some afternoon disco sessions cost as little as 4 rmb and were frequented by teenagers. The most regular customers were the least studious and academically successful of the local youths. They often quit school at an early age, started working at menial jobs, or just stayed at home; "waiting for work" was the formal expression, but many talked of just "messing around" (*hunhun*), meaning asking for money from parents, working odd jobs, or asking men for tips in clubs. On the weekends more young people with regular jobs showed up.

FORMS OF SOCIABILITY IN DISCOS AND SOCIAL DANCE HALLS

In the following, I contrast the forms of sociability cultivated in discos and dance halls. Discos shared with social dance halls the reputation that they were not good places to meet a mate or even to take a date. Shanghai patrons often said of both discos and dance halls that people there were "not reliable": "friends you make there are only play friends," "the people there are too complicated," "you can't trust people you meet in dance halls." Unlike karaoke rooms and banquets, the commercial dance venue was not usually a place for doing business and creating solidarities. Nor was it seen as a good place to find a mate. It was too "chaotic." One young woman said this about meeting men in discos: "I don't like to meet guys in these places. We play together inside, but other than this we don't ever have anything to do with them." Her friend continued, "Dance halls are from the start very complicated places. You can only play there, but you can't make friends there." Dance halls were seen by both men and women as a space in which they could avoid the restrictions imposed by permanent social relations: parents, neighbors, and also boyfriends. One young woman described why discos were not attractive places to go on a date with a boyfriend: "In dancing disco a girl would like to let herself go and show off her personality. On a first date especially, she would be more shy and wouldn't want to let a boy see her in that way, but if you *can't* let yourself go at a disco it's no fun. So I wouldn't usually go on a date to a disco." Similarly, at the social dance hall, married couples seldom came together. One taxi driver explained: "No they don't usually go out together. A woman doesn't want her husband along. She will feel restricted by him, uncomfortable. There's no freedom" (he laughed).

In sum, rather than spaces for constructing permanent erotic relations, discos and social dance halls were usually seen as spaces for avoiding them. Given this shared definition, the question becomes, what kinds of sociability are cultivated in these spaces and what kinds of transient eroticism are pursued there?

Forms of Eroticism

The disco supports what I call a *culture of desirability*—a highly visual eroticism of self-display, an emotional style of "coolness," and a style of interaction emphasizing social one-upmanship. In contrast, social dance halls support a *culture of desire* —a reserved but physical eroticism achieved through close dancing and a layered sociability of "fooling around" hidden under a reserved surface of collegiality.

Any form of sociability is to some extent an effect of the engineering of social space. The classic Shanghai dance hall of the 1920s was engineered for the star. The star stood on the stage, and prominent customers sat at tables directly in front of her. She was a star and their personal patronage made her a star—the relationship between star and customers was clearly articulated in the spatial layout. In the disco, everyone is a star. The disco dance floor is engineered for democracy. The rhythmic pulse of the strobe lights makes everyone a good dancer. The visual confusion makes everyone exotic and alluring while hiding any obvious flaws.

In contrast, contemporary social dance halls are darker, smaller, and more intimate than discos. By its very nature social dance is directed toward a partner. Closed booths with high backs line the walls, allowing for privacy. The social dance hall is an easier place than the disco to engage in physical contact and indulge in small intimacies with a casual dance partner, despite the fact that many of the patrons are married. The common wisdom of the social dance halls in Shanghai is that most dancers are married, but they never come with their spouses. The eroticism of the social dance hall is less showy and more tactile than that of the disco. It is a place where married men and women can engage in quiet intimacy under the pretext of dance, including holding hands and embracing in the darkness after the dance ends.

The disco is much more a cult of display. Disco dancing is formally "partnerless," opening the full body to the gaze of others. Many people in the discotheques simply watch others, but the real glory is in being watched. I interviewed one young woman who frequently danced on the stage at various downtown Shanghai discos. On the stage, dressed in a short skirt with a black bra visible under her unbuttoned jeans jacket, she liked to dance a gyrating samba. She said, "I like to dance. I think I have some natural talent at these movements . . . I learned from watching MTV." I asked her why she liked to dance such a sexy dance. She laughed and said, "I don't know. I just dance like that. . . . I like to see people watch me. I have a desire to show off myself. . . . " She added dismissively, "People can think what they want when I dance."

Disco dress was an important element of its visual culture. Almost everyone put on special clothing for their trips to the disco, including metallic miniskirts and stomach-revealing halter tops that first appeared in discos in the 1990s before they became acceptable on the streets. Some young men's clothing was intentionally "weird," as one trendy boy described it, including colorful shirts and stomach-revealing tops. Most young men, however, resembled the "teddy boys" of earlier decades in the West, their sober dress expressing emotional cool and an attempt at monied sophistication. Local disco girls and young women avoided traditional Shanghai standards of prettiness and wore black lipstick, leather, and metallic fabrics, showing a new style of urban cool. Young men and young women had different strategies of display, but participating in the commercial leisure world of the discotheque was about showing self-confidence and poise in the anonymous self-reflecting gaze of the mirror and the crowd.

Their dance styles reflected the emphasis on display and its highly gendered styles. Boys competed in "break dance" (*zhanwu*, literally "cut dance") contests in which they hurled themselves onto the floor and spun and flipped about in a style they picked up from U.S. videos and films in the 1980s. These exercises seemed as much tests of social daring as of dancing skill. In the smaller local discos boys and girls gathered in a circle in the middle of the floor and watched these dancing exhibitions, prodding reluctant boys into the center of the ring. Girls watched but seldom participated, unwilling to engage in the ungainly spectacle of twirling about spread-legged on the dirty floor.

Some dancers disparaged this "floor-rolling tribe" of break dancers and advocated a form of dance they called "voluptuous dancing" (*saowu*), which was becoming especially popular with young women and was sometimes described as a "girls' dance" (though boys also did it). Frequently, standing on stages above the dance floor, dancers gyrated their hips and torsos in moves likely copied from the backup dancers on music videos. This was also a display of social daring, a disingenuous sexual provocation aimed at an anonymous crowd but producing self-affirmation.

Contrary to our usual instincts about visual objectification, for participants in the disco becoming the object of the gaze was more empowering than merely looking on. Both men and women performed for the audience—though in their own gendered styles. In sum, the disco supports an eroticism of desirability in which the display of a desirable self contributes to the reflexive construction of a desirable self-image. Furthermore, the disco is deliberately engineered as a stage for successful self-display through lighting and sounds that make everyone's moves appear fluid and glamorous.

In contrast, social dance supports a much more tactile eroticism of desire, in which the motion and intimacy of the dance are an experience shared with a concrete other, a way of stealing small pleasures outside the usual routines of the work day. The decor of most social dance halls was spartan and the lighting subdued. Though some dancers were eager to impress others with their skill, even this display of dancing skill was organized differently from the narcissistic self-exposure of disco. The display depended on a partner, and the pleasure of dance was mediated through the concrete presence of the body of another dancer. There was much less emphasis on visual display. The dancers' clothing was much more conventional: lower-level office workers and factory workers wore the same suits, V-neck sweaters, ties and jackets, wool slacks, and polyester dresses that they wore on outings to the park with their families.

Emotional Styles

The culture of desirability in the disco also supported a new emotional style of "coolness"; a "feeling rule" determines what kinds of emotions are socially acceptable in a particular situation.[14] In the discos, young Shanghai women wore a cool, distant expression to accompany their equally "cool" grooming and dress. Young men I met in the disco frequently feigned disinterest in the young women around them, while bragging about the ease with which they could attract them—a playful show of desirability without desire. A handsome Shanghai DJ who called himself "Tiger" displayed this bravado of urban cool in his telling of a story about meeting a girl at the disco: "She wanted to go home with me that night. I could tell she just wanted sex. I said to her, 'Are you a virgin?' She said, 'yes.' She thought I would want a virgin. I told her, "Oh well then forget it, I don't want a virgin. That is too much trouble. When you are no longer a virgin then come find me.' She got really angry. Women hate being refused."

Both Tiger and the disco femme fatale wanted to convey the impression that they were sexually desirable but sexually indifferent. In the discotheque one could never be too desirable (in dress, dance, looks, charisma), but showing desire was simply uncool. This rule also applied in other contexts. For instance, urban Shanghai students made fun of rural students' tendency to fall head over heels in love. For Shanghainese youth, being sophisticated meant being capable of emotional detachment in an increasingly free sexual marketplace.[15]

The social dance hall interactions were less emotionally contrived. People's interactions were collegial, at least ideally, though women often criti-

14. See Hochschild 1979; Stearns 1994.

15. Similar descriptions of a change in emotional style in the United States have been made by historian Peter Stearns (1994). I suggest that "coolness" and a culture of "desirability" arise simultaneously in competitive markets where market savvy is a key to success in both marriage and labor. The simple logic is, "I am desirable as a product, but I am cool as a buyer."

cized men for the rude ways in which they asked women to dance, and men criticized women for refusing them rudely. In comparison with the youth in discos, middle-aged social dance patrons showed less concern for the impressions they made on strangers. They interacted warmly with the people they got to know there and very little with those they did not know well. Their expectations were for a collegial and "honest" or "straight" (*laoshi*) self-presentation. Too much enthusiasm or braggadocio seemed out of place. The emotional norm both men and women aspired to was a reserved and collegial self-presentation, more similar to the emotional norms in the state enterprises where most of them worked than to the showy, self-promotional styles of the youth in the discotheques.

Styles of Play

Youth described what they did with other people in the disco as "fooling around" or "play." This playful sociability of the disco involved a great deal of role playing. At its most crude level it was simply pretending to be someone else, like the English working-class girls described by Angela McRobbie who went to the disco pretending to be French vacationers.[16] For instance, I knew young women technical-school students who regularly pretended to be students at famous universities and a young man from Tianjin who regularly described himself as a foreign exchange student. More typically, such play involved games of one-upmanship in which identities and motives were manipulated for social advantage, a kind of flirtatious sociability in which sexuality might or might not be a theme. For example, I once met a group of five women and one man out together in the disco after a day's work selling real estate. Seeing me there as a lone foreigner, they called me over to their table for a laugh. Each woman in turn pretended to be the sister or the girlfriend of the lone man, making me guess which was his true girlfriend. After I picked one, she draped her arms around me. My face went red, and her friends laughed and said, "Are you sure she is his girlfriend now?" Their play consisted of mild flirtations and deceptions. Such play is a form of social one-upmanship, a display of humor, affability, and poise. To show too much emotion would be uncouth. Not to play along would be rude. Throwing your partner off balance is a win. Revealing your true identity is a loss.

Social dance hall participation is also described as "play" or "fooling around," but the forms this play takes and the discourses that surround it are quite different. The interactions of social dancers were both more reserved and more rigid. Too much humor and deception were generally not appreciated. Social dancers did not engage in guessing games or appreciate many questions. Most dancers earnestly described what they were doing as

16. See McRobbie 1984.

a form of "physical exercise"—even those who were clearly engaging in affairs. The playful aspect of the social dance hall was largely submerged in the private eroticism and conversations of dancing couples. Social dancers seldom used strangers like myself to demonstrate their poise and social skills. Their dancing was businesslike, and eroticism was articulated more through unseen actions than through words.

Sexual Cultures

Young Shanghainese used the disco to escape from both work and family. Girlfriends and boyfriends were often left at home. "I couldn't relax with my girlfriend (or boyfriend) here," was a typical excuse. The eroticism of the disco was overwhelmingly visual, but it sometimes extended to physical contact beyond the show and display described above. One 21-year-old woman described kissing a man she barely knew after dancing with him. Days after the event, she told me, "I don't know what happens to me. I just get dizzy and excited when I dance. I guess I have to control myself." Her statement reflects her embarrassment at her losing her cool; it also reflects the way the disco serves as a space for casual flirtations and intimacies.

I met many young people who had recently broken up with boy- or girl-friends or were bored in their current relationships. For them, the disco was a chance to reestablish desirability without the consequences of a long-term relationship. An article in a popular Shanghai magazine, *Youth Generation*, illustrated this shared definition of the disco. In this supposedly nonfiction story, Lizi is a successful young career woman working in a foreign advertising company, so busy that she does not even have time to spend with her boyfriend. After she misses his birthday, he calls her up and tells her he wants to break up. "Feeling like a speck of dust not knowing where she will land" but also sure that she "is not willing to be a little woman" and "that she loves her career and must control her own destiny," Lizi has no easy choice. The article concludes, "The night is darker and darker, she calms her heart. In front of her she sees a discotheque and marches toward it. After all, she thinks to herself, tonight there will be no dreams."[17]

Although narrated from the perspective of an older and wiser outsider, the article reflects the view that the disco can be seen by youth as a place to reestablish desirability in the face of confusing life choices about career and marriage. After the disillusion of her romantic "dreams" in real life, Lizi opts for the contrived dreams of the disco.

The disco, as I have said, was not usually seen as a marriage market. It is partly because of the inflexibility of the real marriage market that the disco became an important space for working on one's self-image and sense of de-

17. "No Dream Tonight," *Youth Generation (Qingnianyidai)*, July 1996.

sirability. Casual kisses, flirtations, and sexy displays would be taken more seriously in the real world outside the disco. In the disco they could be dismissed as inconsequential. Being inconsequential and anonymous was thus
a cover while one engaged in the important activities of erotic self-assessment
and self-appreciation.

Middle-aged men and women in the social dance hall also sought approval
in the sexual attentions of others, but the marital status and social backgrounds of participants made their interactions less showy. Many middle-aged
men in the social dance halls readily admitted to pursuing brief sexual li-
aisons as a form of "play." They disparagingly referred to their behavior as
"picking up cabbage leaves" (*jiancaipi*), meaning middle-aged women who
were not as desirable as "tender young things" (*xiaonennen*) but were considered more willing to have sex and to expect less from the man materially.
Middle-aged men who frequented dance halls were similarly disparaged by
women as "old gourds" or "old tortoises."

As for questions of marital fidelity, male informants in social dance halls
frequently replied that extramarital sex was all right as long as it was "playing around" and did not interfere with familial responsibilities. Married
women were more reluctant to take up the issue. When I asked one friend's
dance hall lover, a married factory worker, how she felt about dating men
other than her husband, she replied wryly, "I am really tough (*lihai*), right?
Anyway, I have no choice, I need to go out for myself. I need to do some
things for myself."

Not all descriptions of these affairs were benign. A conversation with a
middle-aged women entrepreneur (whose ex-husband had frequented dance
halls before their divorce) exemplified this negative view. She said:

> There are too many laid-off women now. They are all hanging out in these
> dance halls, not the really nice dance halls, but the really cheap ones some-
> times with only 10 or 15 people in them. They are just there looking for what-
> ever they can get. Most of them are thirty-something. They will come up to a
> man and say, "Oh, can I accompany you tonight." These unemployed women
> will do anything. They only get 100 to 200 rmb from the government. If they
> don't do this business, then what business can they do? This is different from
> a woman boss who might take a lover because her husband couldn't satisfy her.
> That would be a question of feelings. These [unemployed] women aren't in it
> for feelings. They want money. We call them "old cabbage leaves stirring glue."

This outsider's view marks some unemployed women as mercenary, but
also noticeably allows a space for extramarital relationships based on "feelings." The notion of "feelings" was often interpreted very loosely within the
dance hall to mean merely finding a partner attractive or likable. And although a women might expect a dinner and a taxi ride from a man she met
in the dance hall, actual exchanges of money like the one this woman described seemed the exception rather than the norm. Nonetheless, such out-

sider disapproval actually preserved the dance hall as a space for play. Descriptions of dance hall participants as "old cabbage leaves" or "old tortoises" made the erotic interactions in the dance hall seem less consequential by diminishing the seriousness of one's own actions and the judgments of other participants. Therefore, despite the general disapproval of earnest society, dance halls provided a semi-legitimate and clandestine space of everyday erotic freedom for many married women and men. Most Western studies describe working-class women's leisure as ending with marriage and childbearing.[18] In Shanghai many married men and women went alone to the dance hall for some extramarital eroticism (which sometimes led to dates outside the dance hall). When I asked women why they did not come with their husbands, they often answered with undisguised pleasure, "Who would take care of the child?" Men and women both gave this answer, indicating that some families accepted this arrangement, or merely that both men and women used the same pragmatic excuse.

THE SOCIAL BACKGROUNDS OF DANCE HALL PARTICIPANTS

While discos and social dance halls have many obvious similarities, they support very different forms of sociability. The sociability of the disco emphasizes desirability, coolness, and poise. The sexual culture of the disco is a culture of self-affirmation for youth faced with an uncertain world of sexual and social possibilities. The disco is a place to practice a desirable self-image, to imagine one's worth for oneself, especially one's sexual worth, in the mirror, in the eyes of the crown, and in playful interactions with strangers. The sociability of the social-class dance hall is more collegial. On the surface it is an orderly and humdrum working-class cultural backwater, a place for middle-aged people to engage in nondemanding physical exercise. Only after long participation does one notice the subtle eroticism of the dancers and the participants' winking acceptance of the extramarital dalliances of others.

The differences between the disco and social dance hall are clearly related to the different social and cultural backgrounds of their patrons, especially the most regular patrons who define the "feel" of a particular space. The most obvious difference is marital status. Disco-goers are typically unmarried and unsure of their status in the marriage market. They are more concerned with establishing their sexual "worth" than with seeking out a partner for casual intimacy. Social dancers, on the other hand, are usually married. If they engage in any intimacy at all, it is a little pleasure for immediate consumption. There is less need to establish their own worth in the eyes of others. By and large, they are not looking for new husbands and wives.

18. See Peiss 1986; McRobbie 1984.

These differences in disco and dance hall sociability also reflect the different relations of each age group to the market economy emerging in Shanghai. Their very different relationships to the labor market coincidentally mirrored their very different relations to the marriage market. In both markets youth had both greater expectations and greater uncertainty than the middle-aged people I met in the social dance halls.

A disproportionate number of disco regulars were young people who worked in the new service industries: hotels, restaurants, sales, hostessing, public relations, and a host of other new professions in which image and desirability were paramount. I interviewed several "cool" young men in their early twenties who visited the disco every day in their black unbuttoned shirts, gold chains, and striped suits. Few of them had steady jobs, and they found more status in the disco than in the jobs they occasionally did have in hotels and fast-food outlets. They also used the disco as a place to share their fantasies about the opportunities that might come their way. These ranged from meeting rich white-collar women in the disco, a fantasy several young guys revealed to me, to becoming professional dancers and making business connections.

These young disco regulars generally lived on the disorganized fringes of the new market economy, constantly looking for new opportunities. None of them had permanent jobs in state enterprises. For many of these serious regulars, the disco culture was a closed world of image competition in which they excelled. It was also a place to participate more fully in the image building they would need in their desired occupations in the market economy. For these participants the night life was mostly fantasy, but it was a fantasy that contained an element of possibility as well as pleasure: meeting a rich lover, making connections, or becoming well known.

At one disco I met a nineteen-year-old woman wearing black lipstick, a silver metallic miniskirt and halter-top, and a bright red bandanna, exotic attire for Shanghai. She enjoyed being asked about her costume, explaining her dress as a kind of rebellion: "We do this to break with tradition. If someone else is wearing a suit, does that mean I have to wear a suit? I wear what I want. Anyway that's me. We five friends have different personalities. One thing I really don't like is to wear jeans. Too many people wear them." This young woman's self-image in the disco was much more rewarding than her image at the hotel where she worked, where she described her pink costume with its white apron as the outfit of a "milkmaid." Like many young people in the fluid labor market of the service industry, she associated a more fashionable image with better life chances. She also interpreted the attentions of strangers as admiration, staking out a position of sexy coolness for herself directly opposed to the conventional jeans and business suits of students and "white collars."

The typical regular at the social dance hall had a very different relationship to the labor market. In general, people I met in social dance halls worked in stable jobs in the state sector. Even the minority who were entrepreneurs or unemployed almost all spent at least several years of their youth in the state sector, mostly as factory workers or low-level clerical employees. The shared culture of these middle-aged patrons was the socialist working-class culture of the work unit. Despite a generally glum view of their economic prospects, most dance hall regulars were not regularly engaged in self-promotion and self-marketing. Most of these middle-aged social dancers were flirting, enjoying the small pleasures that their circumstances permitted.

The social origins of this working-class dance hall sociability are indexed by the local Shanghai slang "stirring glue." "Stirring glue" means fooling around, but in an undemanding fashion. It means simply getting some small pleasure or benefit on the side. It was frequently used to describe the subdued affairs carried out in or begun in these social dance halls. Significantly, this expression was also used to describe the way people worked in state enterprises: taking their time, seeking out small benefits and small pleasures while not working too hard or risking too much. The eroticism of the dance hall was similarly one of limited expectations, routine attendance, and small stolen pleasures. Some middle-aged Shanghainese danced every day, even twice a day. According to one dance hall owner, some laid-off factory workers jokingly described their daily trips to the dance hall as "going to work."

The social origins of the youth disco sociability were similarly indexed by the local slang phrase "entering society," literally "stepping into society." Young people "entering society" are looking for jobs and for a mate. "Entering society" thus means entering an unpredictable market in life chances, and for most of these relatively unskilled young people the market was not an administrative career ladder in a state enterprise but a set of unpredictable possibilities that depended on how well they marketed themselves. Young people typically were allowed by parents to visit discos at the age of "entering society." Commercial discos were described as "in society"; admission to dance halls run by colleges and labor unions was controlled, excluding them from the chaos and freedom associated with commercial society. The following comment of a young woman illustrates this ambivalent concept of "society:" "In school [dance halls] you won't go out of bounds, you will control yourself. Outside in society, there is every kind of person. If you aren't careful, you will just be tricked into something," she said laughing. Like most people I met in discos, this woman began going to the discos "in society" when she herself entered society in a position as a "public relations girl," a job that put a high premium on her appearance and personal charm. It seemed, though, that after one had been "in society" for a few years, the disco began to seem boring and unattractive. One 27-year-old woman said: "I am already past 25, past the age of wanting to move so much. At the disco they are all 18, all very cute, peppy, and energetic. I have already been in society so long, I almost never feel like going out. In my heart I feel like I am already mature."

The young generation's entry into society was subjectively much more unpredictable than that of their parents, for whom jobs and courtship were more constrained by personal relationships. The new market society for the unskilled twenty-year-old is not a society of fixed ties. It is neither the gesellschaft of the bureaucratic socialist state nor the gemeinschaft of friends, family, and neighbors, but a chaotic market in life chances more alluring but also more perilous.

The "society" of the middle-aged informants in the social dance halls was clearly very different. The market society loomed as a great threat during the time of my study, but most of the social dancers had little direct experience with it. They experienced everyday life as a routine of work and household chores from which the dance floor was a welcome break but not a leap into an alternative world of glamorous possibilities. The sociability of the social dance hall was compatible with the predictable rhythms and small stolen pleasures of the state enterprise culture, offering an eroticized and pleasurable version of the same collegial routine.

IMPLICATIONS FOR UNDERSTANDING LEISURE CULTURE IN THE MARKET TRANSITION

Most studies examine the relationship between the market society and commercial leisure from one of two related perspectives that originated in critical theory: one looks at leisure activities for signs of "resistance" to the dominant market society,[19] and the other describes them as inextricably bound up in the ideology of consumption.[20]

Subcultural theory emphasizes the hegemony of commercial culture and resistance to it through appropriation and subversion by subaltern groups, including youth. In this vein, I did hear some poorly educated youth express resentment of those with better opportunities in the market economy. While they aspired to the wealth and style represented by the metropolitan disco, they felt they belonged to a different social group from the "white collars" they saw there but seldom interacted with. This resentment emerged when some of these young men met some women office workers at a dance party I held. In an altercation over a party game I had organized, a college-educated woman accused one unemployed young man of stealing her raffle ticket; he then complained to me: "They started talking to me in English; I don't understand English. It's like they look down on me. If I weren't think-

19. See Hebdige 1979; Martinez 1997.
20. See Bell 1976; Walsh 1993.

ing about your face, I would have smacked that girl. But I thought this is Mr. Liu's party, so I have to think about his face." (Liu was my Chinese name.) Still, these expressions of resentment did not represent rejection of the dominant market values. Rather, these young men continued to ask me to introduce them to white-collar women who could spend money on them, and they continued to consider the fancy metropolitan discos superior to any of their own local hangouts. For young men like these, the glamorous disco was a space in the market society in which their charm, appearance, and social skills were not immediately discounted because they lacked education and credentials. The disco allowed them a space to engage in games of one-upmanship, mixing shows of charm with displays of intimidating and occasionally misogynist toughness. One might have imagined that women felt threatened by such displays, but typically they dismissed them and used the disco themselves as a place to flirt with and poke fun at men.

Some recent studies of youth leisure have focused on the uses of music and dance for producing "alternative" identities in opposition to a "mainstream" of mass commercial youth culture.[21] Self-consciously alternative youth subcultures may emerge in Shanghai; however, except in expressions of resentment or the alternative fashion statements of some young women, I did not observe these outcomes during my fieldwork. Young women did resist criticism of their sexually daring clothing, dance, and behavior. They used the global standards of the commercial disco culture to oppose the judgments of the relational society of parents, neighbors, boyfriends, and coworkers. Their choices did not reflect resistance to the mass-market culture; rather, they embraced the anonymity of the disco to escape the limitations of their fixed social relations. Both young men and young women used the disco to play with the symbols and social relations of the new market society they were increasingly embedded in. Their aggressive claims and expressions might be understood as resistance or appropriation but are probably best understood as ways of "playing with society,"[22] in which the contents and symbols of the market-society youth are not questioned as much as their own places in this society and the freedom they have to engage in its new forms of expression and interaction.

A second popular perspective on leisure culture in the market economy explains it as part of a larger move from a culture of production to a culture of consumption, from a culture of discipline and self-control to a culture of consumerism and hedonism. This view originated in the work of Marcuse, Lasch, Bell, and other mid-twentieth-century critics of consumer culture, and most sociological studies still implicitly frame commercial leisure as hedo-

21. See Thornton 1996.
22. See Simmel 1971, p. 134.

nistic consumption encouraged by an ideology of consumerism: the "heart-less hedonism" of Bell's organizational man.[23]

What became obvious to me after spending several months in dis-cotheques and social dance halls is that simple "consumerism" is not the best description for the activities I observed. If anything, the disco, with its emphasis on desirability, is a place for selling the self, a place for "self-commodification." The cultural logic of the market for most of the young people I observed was neither the discipline of production nor the self-indulgence of consumption; rather it was the ordeal of selling themselves in the increasingly free and open life-chance markets, which to them included both labor markets and marriage markets. Entering these markets, "enter-ing society," was more perilous and required more cultural work than "learn-ing to labor" or "learning to consume." The logic of self-promotion was far less important to the social dancers than the logic of "passing days" (*guorizi*) in the state enterprise and stealing a few small pleasures along the way, or "stirring glue." I suggest that the differences between disco and dance hall sociability are thus partially explained by the generations' different relations to the labor market—which coincide with their different relations to the mar-riage market.

Different perspectives on the market are also embedded in the organi-zation of disco and dance hall markets. The disco market shows clear hier-archies of consumption, dominated by the metropolitan "disco plazas." Youth saw the emerging market society as both alluring and divided: divided into those who could afford to go regularly to fancy metropolitan discos and those who could only hang out in dingy local clubs. The middle-aged patrons of the social dance clubs, however, inhabited a world in which the "salaried classes" (*gongxinjieceng*) of state enterprise workers were still the great mid-dle class. The upper reaches of the market society were peopled by "big monies" with whom they had little in common. In their own dance hall cul-ture there were no steep hierarchies of consumption, no "New York's" and "L.A.'s" to aspire to. The social world of the social dance hall patrons was still embedded in the culture of the state enterprise, which defined the vast majority of Shanghainese as "petty urbanites" (*xiaoshimin*) or "salaried classes." Two social dance hall owners explained the popularity of this cul-tural form in exactly the same terms, saying simply, "Social dance is more suitable for the salaried classes."

CONCLUSION: DANCE AS A FORM OF PLAY

Thinking seriously about discos and dance halls is somewhat difficult because both Westerners and the Chinese consider dancing to be a leisure activity,

23. See Marcuse 1964; Lasch 1979; Stearns 1994; Bell 1976.

not a serious matter. I also think we can better understand the sexual ambiguities of both the disco and their dance hall if we thing of them as "play."[24] For casual customers who use dance as a means of demonstrating their sexual desirability or providing sexual comfort, the play-like quality of interactions provides deniability. Men and women often described the flirtations and indiscretions of the dance hall as "just playing around." Dancers could blame their actions on the heady atmosphere of dance. For those participants, the utility of dance relied on the deniability of the play form:[25] its separation from daily life, long-term relations, and the serious consequences of sexual play.

I contend, however, that the forms this play took were related to the external social worlds of the participants, that the forms of sociability in the disco and the dance hall can be considered, in Simmel's terminology, "play forms" of earnest activities. A play form is a form of sociability in which an instrumental form of conduct is used noninstrumentally. For instance, Simmel specifically frames flirting as the play form of courtship.[26] At the most general level, desirability and coolness in the disco can be interpreted as play forms of the market transaction. Being desirable corresponds to the sellers' making their goods as alluring as possible. Being cool corresponds to the buyers' feigned indifference as they try to lower the price. Similarly, the collegiality and "stirring glue" in the social dance hall are play forms of the collegial affability, perfunctory labor, and routinized cheating of "passing days" in the administrative socialist state.

For youth, the disco was a space apart from everyday life for work on the self. It was not a space to display who they were, but who they wanted to be. It allowed young people with no skills to pretend they were players, to pretend they were glamorous. The act was a fantasy, but it was also a fantasy with prospects, a rehearsal for the real selling of the self in the marketplace. For many young regulars—like the hotel maid and other service workers—their entire stock of human capital was their image. Image-building and display were therefore particularly rewarding and meaningful forms of play. Furthermore, the disco idealized and glamorized the market's best possibilities. Young Chinese patrons' enjoyment of the disco was partly the result of its deliberate engineering: a construction of Western glamour and mechanical sensuality that made self-display and flirtation as effortless, pleasurable, and successful as possible.

The disco as a contrived simulacrum of modernity, as a space for working on one's self-image, and as a reflection of and part of the marketplace in life chances was a cultural form that was especially useful for young peo-

24. See Huizinga 1950.
25. See Turner 1982.
26. See Simmel 1984, pp. 133–52.

ple "entering society" or entering the marketplace. Especially for young women, the disco was a safe site for exploring their sexual autonomy and desirability. Women did not have to be nice to people they met in discos. No obligations were incurred. According to this interpretation, disco attendance is best understood not as resistance to the market or as simple hedonistic consumption, but as "playing with" the market, enjoying the chaos and anonymity of the human marketplace, and exploring one's own desirability and marketability.

The Shanghai social dance hall was less a pure form of play in that much of what occurred there was simply an escape from the boring routine of work and family chores into an alternative but pleasurable routine of dance. Still the dance itself required a suspension of everyday norms simply because men and women embraced one another in what would normally be considered intimate ways. This suspension of ordinary norms against cross-sex embraces also served as a cover for the sexual playing around in the dance hall, the hand-holding and close embraces that could lead to greater degrees of intimacy if both partners desired it. That playing around was, however, usually low-key; there was little of the glamorous dress and cool self-promotion of the disco. Although I do not want to make too much of analogies between the routines of social dance and the predictable pace of work unit and family life, the routines of the social dance hall did fit in easily with the temporal routines of work-a-day Shanghai. Because the dance halls were open at all hours, factory workers could go before, after, or even during work—whenever it was convenient for them and their families. The dance hall was also a place where many ordinary workers could enjoy a bit of the disreputable pleasure that only the highest socialist party bosses were allowed under "high socialism." It is thus perhaps not too much of an exaggeration to describe the pleasures of social dance as a realization of the good life of twenty years earlier, an escape from but also an of eroticization of the everyday socialist routine replete with "revolutionary songs" from that period.

For purposes of explication, I also want to contrast both of these forms of sociability with other forms of Chinese sociability that have been discussed more often. The most important are the warmth, presumed sincerity, and ritual effusiveness of the banquet and karaoke rooms, the chosen leisure activities of businessmen and cadres. These forms of sociability center on the relationship between patron and client: making toasts at the banquet table, applauding the boss at the karaoke, showing generosity, accepting and receiving favors—or "patting the horse's butt" as the Chinese sometimes put it. This is the sociability of the relational society of long-term ties, and it could not be more different from the sexy coolness, flirtation, and displays of a desirable self in the disco or the collegial "exercise" and sly eroticism of the social dance floor. Different forms of sociability thus develop in different corners of the market economy, each grounded in a different concrete social figuration of actors, interests, and histories.[27]

I am thus tentatively suggesting that the dance hall and discotheque can be interpreted as sites of a fragmented cultural transition associated with the market transition in China. The transition from partnered to partnerless dance forms among youth is thus not simply a random change in fashion but a meaningful response to larger changes in social organization.[28] In particular, my description of disco culture resonates with descriptions of mid-twentieth-century American culture: a culture of narcissistic display, emotional coolness, and new forms of sociability based on short-term impressions.[29] The similarities with U.S. patterns are intriguing and point to what may be similar processes of cultural adjustment to a fully marketized society by Chinese youth, processes framed by cultural forms imported from the West.

Yet my suggestions for a methodological approach to these problems are different from those proposed by earlier U.S. studies. I do not ground a grand narrative of social change in fundamental changes in individual attitudes or values, but rather investigate the production of particular new forms of sociability in new social spaces. The reasons for this are simple. Outside the disco, the same individuals still are able to participate in older forms of sociability associated with the relational society of family, friends, and neighbors or with the administrative apparatus of the socialist state. To borrow Susman's language, an individual can have "character" at home and "personality" in the disco. (He can also be a "friend" at the bowling alley and a "boss" with cigarette-smoking buddies.)

Finally, it remains to be seen whether the current generation of disco-dancing youth will make the transition to social dance when they reach middle age. I think it is unlikely for all but those who are most closely tied through friends and family to the working-class culture of the social dance hall. At the time of this research the discotheque was a new space particularly attuned to the cultural logics of the increasingly free labor and marriage markets Shanghai youth were entering. Shanghai's social dance halls, however, were sites for middle-age people to enjoy some low-key eroticism within—but also behind the back of—the comfortable everyday world of work unit and family life.

Simmel supplies not only a definition of sociability as play but also normative standards by which to judge this play. According to Simmel, socia-

27. Elias 1978.
28. See Rust 1969.
29. See Marcuse 1964; Riesman, Glazer, and Denney 1969; Susman 1985; Bell 1976; and Lasch 1979.

bility can be adversarial, as it is in some of the examples I have mentioned, but it should allow an equality of pleasure in interactions. This democracy of pleasure was only partly achieved in dance hall interactions I observed. For instance, class prejudices and unequal and contradictory expectations of women's sexuality still pervaded dance hall interactions, but these inequalities and restrictive expectations were less rigid within the dance hall than in the opinions of people outside. Men and women, richer and poorer, came to dance because of a rough equality that permeated "fooling around," "showing off," and "stirring glue." Simmel also proposes an aesthetic standard for sociability. Sociability, like art, is deliberately separated from real life. However, like art, sociability can be vivid and meaningful when it comments on and reflects life, and when it does so in ways that are impossible in real life. Dance halls in Shanghai supported forms of sociability that allowed participants to play deeply with vital themes from everyday life. Although cynical outsiders may have seen only "old cabbage leaves stirring glue," the actual experience of dance sociability could be one of freedom and spontaneity and ironic reflections on the market and the family, allowing, in Simmel's language, "that simultaneous sublimation and dilution, in which the heavily freighted forces of reality are felt only as from a distance, their weight fleeting in a charm."[30]

30. Simmel 1971, pp. 139–40.

CHAPTER 11

Cultivating Friendship
through Bowling in Shenzhen

Gan Wang

In the summer of 1995, I went to the Shenzhen Special Economic Zone in southern China to do fieldwork for my dissertation. Shortly after I arrived, I was called by an old friend: "Did you say you wanted to know something about luxury consumption here? I am with a friend now who I think can help you on that. Can you come over? We'll wait for you in the cafe of the Shangri La Hotel." I went and was introduced to Mr. Z, a young business-man who, according to my friend, "has the knowledge and leisure to be a good informant." The next day I met Mr. Z again, and we talked over din-ner. After dinner, he asked if I had ever gone bowling in the United States. "Well," I said, "I've been to one alley in our city, but it was so crowded and smoky, and service people were really tough there, so we just left." He looked very surprised: "Really? Let's go bowling then."

When we entered the bowling alley, it was my turn to be surprised. I still re-member my first thought as I stepped in: "Oh, New Haven is such a small city, that's why the bowling alley there is so shabby. Look at this! This is Shenzhen!"

During my visit, bowling was at its peak in Shenzhen. Mainly a sport of the working class in the United States, bowling in Shenzhen at the time was a classy leisure activity among the elite. From 1994 to 1996, after the decline of song-and-dance halls and karaoke bars, bowling became another fad that the business strata in the city actively used in networking activities.

In this chapter, I use bowling to explore the significance of conspicuous consumption in shaping and reshaping interpersonal relationships in the business world in Shenzhen. As noted by Thomas Gold, instrumental net-work-building activities have proliferated.[1] Even during earlier decades of strong party-state efforts to promote a universalistic comradeship among all

---

1. Gold 1985; see also Yan 1996.

the citizens, particularistic personal relationships had survived and in fact gained importance in the latter stages of the Cultural Revolution (1966–76).[2] However, with the relaxation of the political atmosphere and the pervasive needs in marketization for access to scarce resources, personal connections became even more prominent.

The patron-client relationship between the bureaucracy and the growing private sector has attracted many researchers' attention, and there is a growing literature on the nature of these personal relationships, their forms and uses, as well as their significance for the relationship between the state and society.[3] In general, these researchers conclude that because the state still plays important roles in resource allocation and the market system is poorly regulated by the legal system, private entrepreneurs resort to personal relationships with bureaucrats for access to scarce resources and for protection. Solinger and Wank emphasize that the relationships between the bureaucracy and the private entrepreneurs today are of a symbiotic nature, each party pursuing long-term and enduring mutual help. Entrepreneurs use payoffs (cash payments, gifts, donations, etc.), offers of employment (to hire officials or their kin), and partnerships.[4]

I propose in this chapter that conspicuous consumption plays an important role in network-building by businesspeople in Shenzhen. "Consuming together" with "friends" is a significant way for entrepreneurs to accumulate social capital that can later be transformed into economic capital. Social capital as defined by Pierre Bourdieu "is the aggregate of the actual or potential resources which are linked to possession of a durable network of more or less institutionalized relationships of mutual acquaintance and recognition— or in other words, to membership in a group—which provides each of its members with the backing of the collectivity-owned capital, a 'credential' which entitles them to credit, in the various senses of the word."[5] According to Bourdieu, there are four basic forms of capital: economic capital, symbolic capital, social capital, and cultural capital. In certain circumstances, different forms of capital are mutually convertible.[6]

Social capital is extremely important for the rising economic elite in Shenzhen because of its potential for conversion into economic capital. Working outside the established state system, private entrepreneurs need networks to

2. See Vogel 1965. I thank Professor Sherman Cochran for bringing this article to my attention; see also M. Yang 1994.

3. See, e.g., Wank 1995; Bruun 1995; Solinger 1992; Pieke 1995; David Wank, "The Institutional Process of Market Clientelism: *Guanxi* and Private Business in a South China City," *China Quarterly* 147: 820–38.

4. See Wank 1995, pp. 166–71.

5. Bourdieu 1986, pp. 248–49.

6. See ibid. For a critique of Bourdieu's concepts of different forms of capital, especially social capital, see Smart 1993.

get access to scarce economic capital, either internally (often from the state) or externally (e.g., through foreign investment), and because the market is highly unregulated, they seek personal trust in economic transactions to reduce their risks.

In the first part of this chapter I place the bowling experience in the larger context of Shenzhen society. In the second part I discuss how bowling helped create new types of interpersonal relationships. Then drawing on the literature on gifts, *guanxi* (connections), and social capital, I explore how the conspicuous consumption of Shenzhen entrepreneurs facilitates the formation and maintenance of these new relationships. I argue that by "consuming together" businesspeople in Shenzhen transform distant, hierarchical relationships into close and more or less equalized ones. Although the goal of the relationship is instrumental, it is packaged as "friendship." Conspicuous consumption activities provide very good "wrappers" for this packaging process.

HOW BOWLING BECAME A FAD

Before 1994 there were only twenty bowling lanes in Shenzhen, and all were installed in four luxury hotels. Customers were foreigners, merchants from Taiwan or Hong Kong, and a few Chinese who had been exposed to the sport before. In July 1994 a Taiwanese merchant who had been doing business in China for years opened the first computerized twenty-lane professional bowling alley. Being an enthusiastic bowling fan himself, he had financially supported the training of professional bowlers in the city and had maintained a good relationship with the municipal government's sports commission. His first alley was a great success, and other investors soon copied his establishment. Fancy, brilliantly decorated bowling alleys opened one after another and became prestigious places for the wealthy strata of the city to meet their friends. By the end of 1995, Shenzhen had more than 40 bowling alleys with more than 700 lanes.[7] Advertisements occupied large spaces on newspaper pages, and huge bowling pins were erected on the sidewalk to attract public attention. The daily cash flow of bowling alleys peaked at the end of 1995 and then started to decline. Competition among alleys became so serious that many alleys had to lower their prices. Lower fees drew in more customers but also destroyed the aura of exclusivity that originally had attracted businessmen and their friends. By 1997 bowling alleys were no longer an appropriate venue for "rewrapping" economic capital.

The leisure activities of the Chinese people have changed dramatically

7. *Shenzhen tequbao* 1996; interview with director of the Shenzhen Bowling Association, Mr. Ke Zeming, November 13, 1996.

since the 1960s.[8] In the Maoist era leisure time was limited, and leisure activities were often organized by state-regulated work units. During the 1980s, leisure activities underwent processes of depoliticization, privatization, diversification, Westernization, commercialization, and polarization. The state no longer regulated all the activities in the leisure time of every citizen, and a variety of new multipriced leisure activities entered mainstream urban life. In that climate, bowling alleys mushroomed.

In Shenzhen bowling alleys, prices varied according to the time of day. A weekday game between 9 A.M. and 1 P.M. cost about 25 renminbi (rmb); between 1 P.M. and 5 P.M., about 35 rmb. In the evening and on weekends, one game cost 40 rmb. If two friends went bowling in the evening, each playing five games, they could easily spend 400 rmb. If they also rented shoes and bought drinks, they could spend nearly half the average monthly wage in Shenzhen on one night of bowling.[9] Therefore, shortly after emerging on Shenzhen's landscape, bowing alleys became another kind of luxury place frequented by businesspeople and their friends (see Table 11.1 for the cost of different leisure activities in Shenzhen in 1995–96).

As an indoor sport, bowling has some attractive features to the players. It can be played during any season of the year; because it is not very strenuous, people of any age, sex, and build can bowl; and especially important for businessmen seeking new networks of "friends," it takes only a few minutes for a new player to command some basic skills.

But for the businesspeople in Shenzhen, bowling as a fad had very special advantages in 1995–96. Mr. G, a private entrepreneur, told me that he took his official friends to bowling alleys to celebrate the Mid-Autumn Festival. He used to send moon cakes as gifts, the more expensive the better.(It is not a popular custom to tear off price tags before presenting gifts in Shenzhen.) But he doubted that those official friends ever ate the moon cakes because they received so many. Recipients of moon cakes could not even give them away because then others would know that they had accepted too many gifts. "But now," Mr. G said, "bowling can achieve the same result as moon cakes. And even better, it's something new, and my friends all love to try. And it's expensive. When I check out, they look at the bill, wow, 1,500 rmb. You spend so much for them and they think you are a friend indeed. You see, there's no gift, no bribery. We exercised our bodies and strengthened our friendship."

In local people's vocabulary, the phrase *xiaofei changsuo* literally means "consumption arena." It appears on newspaper and television, but people's

---

8. See S. Wang 1995.

9. In 1995 the average monthly income for Shenzhen residents was 926 rmb. *Shenzhen SEZ Daily*, January 28, 1996.

TABLE 11.1   Estimated Cost of Leisure Activities
in Shenzhen, 1995–1996

Movies	
University entertainment center	5 rmb
Ordinary cinema	15–30 rmb
Upscale cinema	40 rmb
Ticket to theme park	25–90 rmb
One hour of tennis	30–60 rmb
One hour of badminton	30–60 rmb
Ticket to disco	40–80 rmb
Ticket to song-and-dance hall	20–50 rmb
Rental of karaoke room (one night)	
Small room	400–500 rmb
Medium to large room	800–1,500 rmb
Golf (per round)	800–1,200 rmb

understanding of its meaning differs. Some people define it as "a place where you pay for the service," but they point out that stores are not included. Other people suggest that it is interchangeable with *yule changsuo*, or "place of entertainment," but they emphasize that restaurants should also be included. However, all agree on what should be included in the category *gaoji xiaofei changsuo* (high-class consumption arena): upscale restaurants, golf courses, bowling alleys, karaoke bars, song-and-dance halls, massage and sauna centers, bars and cafes in luxury hotels, etc. These are places where you pay high prices for services. But more important, you can meet and entertain people there.

The rise of bowling in Shenzhen followed the decline of karaoke bars and song-and-dance halls. First, it was something novel. Most of the entrepreneurs I met, both private and in state-owned enterprises, admitted that they spent at least three evenings every week socializing with "friends." Some bank managers could not find a single night for weeks to spend with their families. Their after-work time was always spent in "consumption arenas." After consecutive nights singing karaoke, people wanted a change, which bowling offered. Besides, the government began to regulate officials' participation in karaoke bars and song-and-dance halls, especially when prostitution in those places attracted public attention.

Bowling was also considered Western, healthy, and modern. Bowling alleys were generally bright, clean and tidy, and climate-controlled. The space was decorated with large plants and foreign posters that were unfamiliar to Chinese eyes. VCRs around the bar areas played tapes of bowling instructions and world bowling competitions. Light music and sometimes English songs floated in the air. The posters, the music, the computer scoreboards, the foreign-manufactured equipment, and foreign bowlers on television or on the scene all contributed to an atmosphere that the Chinese viewed as Western, tasteful, romantic, and classy. In comparison with the sultry evenings in the VIP rooms of karaoke bars and song-and-dance halls, bowling seemed healthful and refreshing. One of the a few women entrepreneurs I know in Shenzhen told me that she always said goodbye to her guests after dinner before her male assistant took the guests (most of them men) to karaoke bars. "When they call for three-accompanying-misses to the room, it's too embarrassing for a young woman to be there alone."[10] But she felt comfortable going to bowling alleys with her guests because the sexual overtones were absent there. Bowling especially appealed to younger people with higher education. Both my participant observations and a small survey I conducted in an alley support this view.

The changing fad also reflects the changing composition of the wealthy strata in Shenzhen. According to Dr. Shi Xianmin, immigrants to Shenzhen can be divided into three generations. The first generation arrived in early 1980s. Most were veterans and construction workers assigned by the central government to build a Special Economic Zone (SEZ) in the remote south. In the late 1980s, the second generation arrived. At the time, the city was growing, but the future of the SEZ was still unclear. Many of the new immigrants were adventurous individuals so dissatisfied with their lives at home that they had dared to leave and cope with the uncertainties of Shenzhen. Not until the early 1990s, especially after Deng's second southern trip, did large numbers of young people with more formal education and credentials move to the booming city to find their fortunes. It is this latest cohort, in their twenties and early thirties, who have brought new tastes to the city.[11]

The generational differences noted by Dr. Shi segment leisure activities. For example, karaoke fascinates people because it enables an ordinary person to sing like a real singer, thus fulfilling the individual's dream of being a star. But karaoke might have different meanings to those who were young during the Cultural Revolution, who constitute the first and to some extent the second generation of Shenzhen citizens. In their youth, leisure was highly politicized and monitored by a radical party-state. Life was monotonous and pale.[12] The stage at the time, however, played a paradoxical role. Although it was monopolized by the party-state and permeated by official ideology, it also facilitated young people's aesthetic pursuits, which were otherwise la-

10. In Shenzhen, hostesses are called *sanpei xiaojie*, which literally means "three-accompanying-misses." These are young girls who accompany the customers in drinking, singing, and dancing. Many of them are prostitutes.

11. Personal communication with Dr. Shi Xianmin, director of the Shenzhen Social Development Research Institute.

12. For a description and analysis of leisure in the Maoist era, see S. Wang 1995.

beled "petite bourgeois." And being on the stage was one of the few events for which women could put on makeup and wear bright-colored clothes. Singers and dancers in the "Mao Thought-Propaganda Teams" were very popular among their peers, and they subtly set the fashion of the time. Because they often appeared as revolutionary heroes and heroines on stage, imitating them was politically justified and relatively safe. Because of the monopoly of the official stage, people's fascination with it intensified even more.

For those who came of age during the Cultural Revolution and entered their forties in the 1990s, entertainment provided opportunities to get close to actors and actresses (in song-and-dance halls) and to get on stage themselves. In song-and-dance halls I saw middle-aged audience members present flowers to singers and then join them on stage. The stage reminded them of their past dreams and current successes. At the same time, songs and music of the past refreshed memories of their common experiences and emotionally bound them together.

But the younger generation, those in their thirties in the 1990s, have few fond memories of the past. Revolutionary songs do not interest college graduates, and fascination with popular singers from Hong Kong and Taiwan seems uncouth. They would rather display their sophistication with English songs. In 1995–96, the most popular English song in Shenzhen's karaoke bar was the theme song from the American movie *Ghost*. Others included "Edelweiss" from the musical *The Sound of Music* and a few pieces by the Carpenters, who were popular on Chinese college campuses in the 1980s. In a karaoke bar I once heard the song from *Ghost* sung three times in one hour, by two men and one woman sitting at different tables. But generally karaoke bars have few English song discs, and people are too busy to learn new songs. Therefore, many young businesspeople turned from karaoke to bowling.

Let's Go Bowling

To facilitate analysis, I run the risk of oversimplification and roughly divide Shenzhen bowlers into three categories: (1) private entrepreneurs; (2) the managerial personnel of state-owned enterprises; and (3) government officials. These categories are highly fluid not only because people move from one to another category easily in Shenzhen, but also because some individuals may operate in two or three capacities simultaneously.

Bowling was often used by the business groups in Shenzhen to entertain others as a way of showing gratitude or seeking help. They also entertained without any specific goal in mind besides establishing a good relationship that might be useful over the long run. Government officials were often invited to bowling alleys by businesspeople from private and state-owned enterprises. So were bank managers and middle-level clerks in charge of loan allocation. Private entrepreneurs invited managerial personnel from state-owned enterprises, and sometimes vice versa. People in every category might entertain their superiors in a bowling alley, especially in the state sectors. When the host and the guests were not well known to each other, the entertainment was conducted more formally, a process I elaborate on below.

The proposal of going bowling could be raised casually between two parties; if the parties had not had previous contact, a third party might act as an intermediary. The goal was often described as relaxation or physical exercise. And it was seen to be very natural for people to go bowling after dinner together to "improve digestion."

A person on his or her first visit to a bowling alley in Shenzhen could not help but notice that the dress of bowlers, both males and females, was quite formal. Many went to bowling alleys directly from work in their suits and bowled in shirts and ties. But even on weekends, few wore sportswear if they were going to entertain people they did not know well. Women bowlers almost always wore long tight skirts. This attire, considered appropriate for white-collar and professional women in public, obviously hindered their movement when they bowled. In contrast, bowling-alley attendants, who were usually young girls in their early twenties, wore bright-colored sportswear and on warmer days tennis skirts.

Many businesspeople who used bowling alleys as socializing places made it a point to know the manager and some attendants at their favorite alleys. Some companies had a monthly contract with bowling alleys. When the host accompanied the guests to the reception counter he often asked for the manager, who hurried to meet the guests and presented his or her name card. The host introduced the guests as "so-and-so *zong*" if they worked in business sectors, whether private or state-owned. The character *zong* means "chief" and is often used with other words, as in *zong bianji* (editor-in-chief) or *zong jingli* (general manager). But in recent years it has been used alone to refer to people of status in business, such as managers, vice-managers, chief financial officers, and department heads. Sometimes a host introduced a guest who worked in the government without specifying the guest's government department and later explained the guest's significance to the manager.

The group was then led to the lanes by the manager or an attendant. In some bowling alleys, customers picked up bowling shoes at the reception counter and returned them when they left. In others attendants delivered shoes to the lanes. When important guests visited, the host or the manager would always ask attendants to deliver shoes to the guests. But the manager never did it him/herself because shoes are often associated with lower status in Chinese culture. In bowling alleys where service was considered good, shoes were always delivered by attendants.

Usually the most important guest and the host played in the same lane, so they could chat while bowling. The conversation could become very personal, as the host and guest used discussion of sports, hobbies, health, and lifestyle to learn more about each other's backgrounds and preferences. Later these confidences could be used to build a closer relationship if desired.

The host paid great attention to improving his guests' skill in bowling. He might teach the guests himself, analyze their movements, applaud with the bowling attendants enthusiastically when the guests made progress, order drinks and cigarettes for them, and call the attendants to claim awards for them. In most alleys, customers received awards from the alley for three achievements: high scores, "auspicious scores," and strikes when a red pin appeared as the headpin. A bowler who scored 280, for example, might have won a microwave oven. Usually this kind of award only went to those who practiced often in bowling alleys. An "auspicious score" was 88 for women bowlers or 168 for anyone. Eight had become an auspicious number because its pronunciation resembles that of the Chinese character *fa*, the short form of *facai* (getting rich). And the number 168 sounds like the phrase "getting rich all along the way." Bowlers who received these awards were congratulated by friends on their good luck. When the red headpin appeared, the bowler was supposed to ask an attendant to watch him or her bowl. Bowlers who rolled strikes under such scrutiny were praised for their strong nerves.

When the host and the guests wanted to talk about serious things, such as business support or cooperation opportunities, they could find a suitable space in the bowling alley. Most bowling alleys had bars that served soft drinks, domestic or imported beers, some cocktails, and fast foods such as stir-fried rice and sandwiches. One bowling alley even boasted of self-brewed fresh beer on tap. Customers could have drinks when all the lanes were occupied or take a break between games. Bowling alleys also had VIP rooms. In some, these were small rooms next to the offices where the manager's friends and good patrons could talk or play cards with their friends. Other alleys set up VIP lanes that were screened from other bowlers. For an additional 10–15 rmb, bowlers could relax on comfortable couches and talk with their friends without being seen by other bowlers. One informant jokingly called these lanes "the bankers' lanes" because, she explained, enthusiastic bowlers working in state banks always used these VIP lanes when they came with entrepreneur friends. The private lanes allowed for quiet conversation and helped the bankers avoid charges of corruption.

The question of who paid the bill deserves attention. When the relationship between help-seeker and help-grantor was obvious, the help-seeker usually paid the bill. When this relationship was not obvious, several things needed to be considered. In some groups, individuals took turns paying and shared the expenses equally in the long run. In other groups the same member always paid, particularly if his income was high or his company would pick up the bill. The frequent payers were never government officials, who had lower nominal incomes, although they might treat their friends once or twice a year. The person who had the biggest company often volunteered to pay. The other thing to take into consideration was whether the money paid was from private pockets. State-owned enterprise managers with access to company expense accounts were often expected to pay. And in fact, a state official who entertained his supervisor or friends could cash in his receipts at his entrepreneur friend's company, or simply ask an entrepreneur friend to join them and pay the bill. In this way, state officials with low nominal incomes could host luxury leisure activities with financial help from their entrepreneur friends; the officials could later use their bureaucratic power to return the favor.

FRIENDS HELPING EACH OTHER

When I asked people with whom they went bowling, I always got the answer, "With friends." Only when I pressed further would they specify whether these friends were bank cadres or business partners. Later I began to pay attention to the term "friend" and the interpersonal relationship to which it refers.

In this section I first examine the relationship between "friends" and how friendship is initiated and maintained. I then discuss why conspicuous consumption became a major networking strategy for businesspeople in Shenzhen. Using bowling as an example, I compare the networking strategy of "consuming together" with gift-giving and consider why different situations call for different strategies.

As I described earlier, the circles of friends who went bowling and banqueting together were primarily state officials, private entrepreneurs, and managers of the state-owned enterprises. Each had resources the others might desire to advance a business endeavor or a career.

State officials can help both private and state-owned enterprises in many ways, and entrepreneurs make big efforts to build connections to seek help and protection from their friends in the state sectors.[13] First, the state still controls most of the scarce resources, and thus people working in the government, quasi-government agencies (such as banks), and state-owned enterprises can help their friends get access to scarce capital, raw materials, or land. Second, bureaucrats can reduce the scope of state regulation. They can help speed up bureaucratic procedures, cut through red tape, or use loopholes in regulations; they can also enlarge the revenue of private enterprises by lessening taxes or fines, directing entrepreneurs to appropriate documents, or even forging documents. Third, entrepreneurs need protection from state officials. In the gradual transition to a market economy, old rules no longer meet the needs of the changing environment, but they

13. See also Wank 1995, pp. 160–66.

still exist. Many people complain that they could never achieve anything without violating certain rules, but in doing so they take risks. If they are lucky and a new practice they introduce gets accepted, they become the "vanguards of the reform." But if they are not lucky, they can be punished as examples to all those who would violate the rules. Having friends in the government who can warn of upcoming campaigns to crack down on violators or even remove names from "blacklists" is especially important for some adventurous entrepreneurs.

But entrepreneurs are not the only ones with needs. State officials also have unmet desires. For some, networking with entrepreneurs allows them a lifestyle not permitted by their own salaries. For ambitious officials, financial success by enterprises within their jurisdiction advances bureaucratic careers now that cadres are evaluated on the basis of their ability to produce economic gain.[14]

Managers in state-owned enterprises are the third group in these circles of "friends." They may help entrepreneurs by providing scarce resources, market information, and opportunities. But they too need help from both entrepreneurs and government officials. Regulated by the reward system of the state, state managers often feel they are underpaid despite working as hard as private entrepreneurs. In their use of company expense accounts, they transfer public resources into personal social capital that can be of private use in the future.

Thus emerges an alliance among the three parties that is based on mutually beneficial cooperation. All three groups seek stability and long-term cooperation. In an era when many transactions take place outside official legal practice, individuals seek long-term, enduring relationships that will reduce their transaction costs. In these circumstances, "friends" became the right word to designate this kind of alliance.

Friends: A New Relationship

During my fieldwork in Shenzhen, I noticed some linguistic changes since the Maoist era. For example, within one company, businesspeople referred to their supervisor as *laoban* (the boss), their subordinates as *zhiyuan* (employees), and their equals as *dadang* ("partners"). *Tongshi* (colleague) was seldom used. Outside the company, they used *pengyou* (friends) or *shouren* (acquaintances). Terms such as *tongxue* (classmates), *tongxiang* (townsmen), or *gemer* (buddies) were later specified when necessary. The differences among these terms were very subtle.

14. See Meaney 1989.

Friends, Acquaintances, and Connections   One's "friends" are often of equal status with, or higher status than, oneself, while "acquaintances" have lower status. For example, a company manager told me that he could help me get data because he had official "friends" in municipal government and a clerk "acquaintance" working in the library.

In Mayfair Yang's ethnography of social connections before mid-1980s, *guanxi* (connections) could be bureaucrats as well as clerical and service workers who had control or easy access to scarce resources.[15] But in Shenzhen's business sector in the 1990s, this category was further divided into two subgroups: friends and acquaintances. Both words were used to refer to resourceful people who could help, but one's "friend" usually held a respectable position in society of similar status. People in one's personal network with lower status were referred to as "acquaintances" or simply "somebody I know," but not as "friends."

What if a person's status was not consistent with his or her resources, such as a low-ranking tax collector? According to my observations, a manager was very likely to pat the tax collector on the back and say "we are old friends," especially if he needed help from the latter. But he was unlikely to refer to the tax collector as his friend in front of his real friends. When he needed to entertain low-ranking government clerks, he sent his assistant or other employees out with them but did not go himself.

The terms "friends" and *guanxi* convey different degrees of instrumentality. In the 1970s and early 1980s, the term *guanxi* was castigated in official discourse and was notorious among many people.[16] The instrumental goal of the relationship was obvious and distasteful to many. After decades of politicization of interpersonal relationships in the Maoist era, "friends" took hold because it sounds more positive.

Friends, Classmates, Townsmen, and Buddies   The words "classmates" and "townsmen" reveal the origin of a relationship but give no information about the closeness between parties. "Buddies," however, refers to close, informal relationships without revealing the origin. Friends, with the connotation of mutual understanding and affection, can be closer than classmates and townsmen, but not as close as buddies. When classmates, townsmen, and buddies meet the status standard of friends, they are often introduced as friends first. When the closeness of the relationship between the two is concerned, further information might be provided. Why do these terms become secondary to "friends"?

A story I overheard helped me understand the popularity of "friends." A, B, and C were college classmates who now all work in Shenzhen. Once C

15. M. Yang 1994.
16. Ibid.

told B that he had a friend who had begun using the Internet, but when B asked who this person was, he only repeated: "A friend, a friend." Later B found out that this friend was A. Since disclosing the identity of this friend was not harmful and the three met often, A and B derided C, behind his back, for being pretentious and implying networking abilities he did not have.

The story reflects the tension in the minds of businesspeople when building up a social network. The term "friends" is preferred to other terms for several reasons. First, "friend" refers to an inclusive relationship that has the potential to be used on many occasions. Second, the connotation of affection emphasizes the potentiality of mutual help. Third, without specifying the origin of the relationship, the term mystifies and highlights the user's ability to network and thus suggests that leverage might be used in other interactions. As specified by Smart, this kind of image becomes symbolic capital that means a person has a reputation for having "networks that can be used to accomplish a great deal."[17] As a person becomes someone everybody would like to know, it becomes much easier for him or her to develop networks further.

"Now We Are Friends"

How was "friendship" initiated and maintained. Once, when I was chatting with Mr. Y, the manager of an advertising agency, I mentioned the name of Mr. J, a person working in the media whom I had met the previous evening. "Oh, I know, he's Shanghainese but grew up in the north," Mr. Y remarked. Because after so many years living in the north neither Mr. J's appearance nor his accent shows he's Shanghainese, I assumed that Mr. Y must be a good friend because he knew such details of Mr. J's personal history. But Mr. Y said, "No, we only have met each other once at a dinner to which we were both invited. We sat next to each other and talked for a while. This is a guy of quality. I would like to become his friend. Someday I'll invite him to bowling or something." He did so, and soon he began to refer to Mr. J as "a friend of mine."

During dinner table conversations, entrepreneurs often bragged about friendships with important people. Almost invariably they described some shared consumption activity as proof of the relationship. Likewise, one lost prestige if it became known that a VIP had never accepted one's invitation to consumption activities. Gradually, I came to realize how friendship is cultivated in Shenzhen's business world. When you have only conversed with someone in the office or in the street, even if you have been doing so for years, you are not friends yet. When both of you participate in some consumption activity together, such as dinner or karaoke, but on a third party's

17. See Smart 1993, p. 402.

expenses, strictly speaking you two are still not friends, although both of you may be friends with the third party, the host. Only when there is a direct host-guest relationship established between you, even if only once, can you refer to each other as friends.

Hosting consumption activities for someone establishes a relationship between the host and the guests that is different from the relationship among the rest of the guests. Certainly being invited to participate in a consumption activity with influential and important people is flattering because it suggests equal status. It also provides a chance for further interaction. But friendship is only established and stabilized through direct host-guest relationships. "Consuming together" is very important in the lives of businesspeople in Shenzhen. Through consuming together, they make friends and maintain these relationships. In this way, hosting and being hosted are the initiation ceremonies of friendship.

Why Consumption?

In the period I am discussing, many businesspeople went to bowling alleys to do networking. The bars, lounge areas, and especially attached VIP rooms symbolized the socializing function of bowling alleys. The customers' formal suits and business conversations revealed that going bowling was an extension of work, not a pure leisure activity. The participants understood this well, often complaining that activities after work were more exhausting than those in the office.

Why then did businesspeople choose to socialize in consumption arenas such as bowling alleys? First, they were places where personal interactions could be extensive and prolonged. People stayed for several hours, playing, eating, drinking, and above all, socializing. Going to these places night after night, people frequently met old friends who introduced them to new people. In this way, they maintained old connections and enlarged their networks in a short time. If they did not encounter people they wanted to see, they called them up and asked them to come. In these places one always heard men and women calling their friends on cellular phones: "I'm at such-and-such alley with some friends. I'd like you to meet them. Would you come over? Be quick!" An entrepreneur admitted that this was the major use of his cellular phone. With it, he was always "connected" to his friends, so he would have more chances to meet people and have more opportunities in business.

"Consuming together" is also valued as networking strategy because it provides an informal and relaxed environment in which people are believed to be more willing to reveal their true selves to others. Thus consuming together is a very important way to build mutual trust and enduring relationships.

The consumption arenas also grant the advantage to the businessman. In a government office, the businessperson is subordinate to government officials. Attempts to get closer to officials there seem awkward because the instrumental goal is too obvious. But relationships change subtly when people go together to consumption arenas. As frequent and welcome patrons, the business hosts are more at ease, more at home. The consumption arena becomes the place where they have superior authority and prestige. For example, in bowling alleys, the host, the businessperson, was usually more familiar with the environment and the sport than the government official. Through physical contact, warm encouragement, and friendly teasing, the social distance between them was quickly shortened. At the same time, because bowling was expensive, the financial advantages of the businessman remained highly visible. Only those with wealth could bowl frequently. Even the auspicious scores of 88 and 168 seemed to remind bowlers that in the 1990s being lucky was about accumulating riches; it was no longer about gaining political prestige, as it had been during the Mao years.

Gifts and "Consuming Together"

In building connections, gifts are preferred to cash.[18] In my observation, although gifts (and sometimes even cash in the form of gift certificates) were still presented, especially in dealing with lower-level state functionaries, going to consumption arenas became the major way for Shenzhen businesspeople to build up connections. Consumption was preferred over gift-giving for several reasons.

First, it is difficult for the gift-giver to choose something that will impress the recipient. As some of my informants complained: "Now the powerful guys have everything." With the development of the national economy, the living standard rises constantly. Even household durable goods do not always make impressive gifts. A television set is a welcome gift for someone who does not own one, but it is not appreciated if he already has more than one at home. As recipients get more picky about the gifts they are given, the gift-givers must compete among themselves to come up with more innovative and impressive gifts. Sometimes, the invitation to join in a fashionable new leisure activity is a welcome gift. In addition, in the relaxed atmosphere of the consumption arenas, a host can obtain personal preference information to guide subsequent gift purchases. One young entrepreneur wanted to show his gratitude to a senior official who had helped him before. But the older man refused to accept any gifts from him. Later he found out during dinner conversation that the official enjoyed fishing, so he asked a friend to buy a fishing rod for him in Japan. The gift was so welcome that he was invited to dinner at the official's home. Their relationship was strengthened significantly.

18. See, e.g., ibid., p. 400; Pieke 1995, p. 503.

Second, the state's efforts to curb rampant corruption among its officials has altered the available forms of bribery. Unlike durable goods and cash, consumption is "perishable," and money spent on activities in consumption arenas is hard to trace. Therefore, officials who dare not accept gifts might consider an invitation to bowling acceptable. When hosting banquets for officials was condemned by the state, networking moved to karaoke bars. Then when the presence of officials in karaoke bars was declared immoral by the state, bowling alleys became crowded. Paradoxically, the state policy contributes to rapidly changing fads in Shenzhen.

Third, compared with gift-giving, consuming together is claimed to be less embarrassing for both the host/giver and the guest/recipient. This "ease of embarrassment" claim can be analyzed from two sides. As observed by Smart: "For the gift to succeed as a gift, it must follow the social forms that usually prescribe that it be an unconditional offer of a presentation in which explicit recognition of instrumental goals is excluded from the performance."[19] In other words, successful gift-giving should subordinate instrumentality. Consumption, with the apparent goals of relaxation and exercise, serves well to subordinate instrumental goals. The fact that the hosts themselves participate in the consuming activities together with the guests apparently lessens the pressure on the guests to reciprocate. A commonly used expression to persuade a reluctant guest to go out for dinner is: "Anyway, I myself have to eat, so why don't you join me?" Shared leisure activity makes it easier for the hosts to initiate a connection and for the guests to accept the invitation. It is embarrassing for a recipient to accept a gift whose instrumental characteristics are too obvious, because doing so means that he or she can be easily bought off. But after the ritual of consuming together the two parties become friends, so the gift exchange turns into an expressive one that does not insult the morality of the recipient.[20]

Consumption activities are also preferred by hosts/givers. Some businesspeople, especially those who have previously worked in academia or government, would feel awkward giving a gift to a stranger whose help they needed. Doing so would disclose their lack of resources and power. But I noticed that those same people gracefully gave their guests cashmere underclothes in the consumption arena of the massage and sauna center, or bought them brand-name sneakers and T-shirts in a golf club. Prices in those places are double those at department stores, but the hosts are willing to pay extra money to alleviate the embarrassment and sense of inferiority created by purely instrumental gift-giving. Consumption activities not only subordinate instrumentality but also elevate the status of the hosts.

Bowling alleys provide another example. In the alley, the hosts asked the

19. See Smart 1993, p. 389.
20. For expressive and instrumental gift-giving in rural China, see Yan 1996.

manager to welcome the guests and the attendants to deliver shoes. Both the higher status of the manager and the attentive service of the attendants announced the importance of the guests and confirmed their high status. But both the manager and the attendants were at the command of the hosts, whose status was not lowered by their service. The fact that the hosts were not only being waited on but also in control elevated the status of the hosts. The status of the hosts and the guests was thus more or less equalized. The service as well as the importance of money in luxury consumption arenas contributed to the transformation. The enjoyment received by the guests is actually provided by the hosts. But since it is mediated by the service, the status of the host is not lowered as the giver. On the contrary, the hosts as the payers are highly respected in the luxury consumption arena. Conspicuous consumption enables them to forge a high-class identity that they share with their guests.

A host-guest relationship is necessary for consumption activities to become an initiation ceremony of friendship. There must be some mutual interest between the two parties who want to be friends. The high prices charged in luxury consumption arenas help businesspeople display resources in their control, which the guests do not have or cannot legitimately have. By being a generous host and sharing his resources with the guests, the entrepreneur both displays his resources and demonstrates his receptivity to possible exchange in the future.

Networking strategies also vary according to the level of the intended target. Wank found that for private entrepreneurs in Xiamen networking with lower-ranking officials was characterized by gift-giving, which was very time-consuming. Payments to higher officials, however, were made in more institutionalized forms such as salaries and dividends and were more efficient.[21] In Shenzhen, private entrepreneurs have different strategies. They often have employees send routine gifts to lower-level bureaucrats at festival times (such as lychee during the Lychee Festival or moon cakes during the Mid-Autumn Festival) or different forms of cash (shopping certificates, predeposited bank cards) at the New Year. But no matter how busy they are they always accompany higher-level guests in the consumption arena to demonstrate their respect and sincerity, or friendship.

According to Bourdieu, "the transformation of economic capital into social capital presupposes a specific labor, . . . which . . . has the effect of transfiguring the monetary import of the exchange and, by the same token, the very meaning of the exchange."[22] When the competition among businesspeople to build up connections with a useful source becomes severe, instrumentality should be carefully concealed in order to gain long-term fa-

21. See Wank 1995, pp. 172–73.
22. Bourdieu 1986, p. 253.

vor. To measure the time and labor attached to converting economic capital into social capital, we can construct a scale, ranging from cash to gifts to "consuming together." Cash takes the least time and labor but reveals the most instrumentality. At the other extreme, "consuming together" most successfully subordinates instrumentality but demands the most time and labor from the host/giver. Gifts fall in between, although a highly personalized gift (such as the fishing rod from Japan) can take even more time and labor and thus seem more sincere. So the higher the level of the guests, the less desirable it is to reveal instrumentality and the more time and labor are appreciated.

Clearly, partaking in conspicuous consumption activities is an important networking strategy by the businesspeople in Shenzhen. Using bowling as an example, I examined how it became a fad and then looked at the relationships between three groups of bowlers: state officials, managers of state-owned enterprises, and private entrepreneurs. Comparing these new relationships with *guanxi* and some other personal relationships, I further inquired into the nature of "friendship" and the way it is established and maintained. I found that although the goal of these relationships is fundamentally instrumental, they are packaged as friendship, which is more inclusive than other relationships and emphasizes personal commitment, equal status, and mutual help. Consuming together as a networking strategy is adopted by businesspeople because it can often successfully subordinate instrumentality. Conspicuous consumption activities can also help entrepreneurs transform a hierarchical relationship between the host and the guest into a more or less equal one, at least temporarily.

CHAPTER 12

Cigarettes and Domination in Chinese Business Networks

Institutional Change during the Market Transition

David L. Wank

Observers of communist social orders have long speculated on the institutional consequences of introducing market allocation of goods and services into redistributive economies. Ivan Szelenyi noted how the power of Hungary's communist officialdom rested on its administrative monopoly in the allocation of such daily necessities as housing. He hypothesized that the introduction of markets would serve the interests of nonofficials by opening up routes of access to commodities outside the purview of the administrative monopoly.[1] Many students of China's market transition follow the logic, explicitly or otherwise, of Szelenyi's hypothesis. They see access to goods and services in markets as enhancing the autonomy of activities and groups in society from local officialdom and the ideological projects of the party-state.

This chapter takes a different view. Despite the expansion of personal economic autonomy in production and consumption, China remains a politically authoritarian state. My broad concern is to explain how market-based consumption transforms institutions in ways that have no necessary consequences for state-society relations. I start with the assumption that daily-use

I would like to thank Deborah Davis for her comments on this paper. My fieldwork in Xiamen from 1988 to 1990 was supported by the Committee on Scholarly Communication with the People's Republic of China and sponsored in Xiamen by Lujiang College. The observations on the situation before marketization that I refer to occasionally, mostly in the footnotes, stem from two years of working at the Shanxi Agriculture College, Taigu county, Shanxi Province from 1980 to 1982. My stay there was made possible by a fellowship from the Oberlin Shansi Memorial Association.

1. Szelenyi 1978.

commodities are a form of social power: they reify inequalities and serve particular interests.[2] I show how the consumption of a daily-use item helps construct power relations in personal networks.

The commodity to be examined is premium cigarettes. Along with fine spirits and choice foodstuffs, premium cigarettes have long constituted a special category of goods in China with which citizens build and maintain personal networks (*guanxi*).[3] Before market reform, premium cigarettes were scarce and only available by using political capital or connections.[4] Citizens acquired premium cigarettes not for personal enjoyment but for their exchange value in influencing others, usually officials who had discretionary control over the allocation of centrally redistributed goods, services, and opportunities. This utility was reflected in popular idioms: a pack of cigarettes was "twenty rounds from a Mauser pistol," which, along with "hand grenades" (bottles of spirits) and "satchels of dynamite" (boxes of cake and pastry), were sufficient ammunition to storm any administrative barriers.

With market reform, all kinds of cigarettes are now readily available in

2. My assumption is in line with the views of Pierre Bourdieu, Arjun Appadurai, and others.

3. Kipnis 1977; Smart 1993; Wank 1998; Wilson 1997; Yan 1996; M. Yang 1994.

4. In the early 1980s when I was teaching in northern China, except in Beijing and Shanghai premium cigarettes were only available in Friendship Stores and at the overseas Chinese counters of department stores. These places were restricted to persons of high status who had special currencies such as foreign-exchange certificates (FECs, *waihuijuan*) and overseas Chinese certificates (*qiaohuijuan*). One day a friend asked me to buy him several cartons of premium Phoenix (*Fenghuang*) cigarettes that he wanted to use to influence the administration of a special cadre hospital to admit his father, a rural county cadre. Since the closest Friendship Store was in the provincial capital, Taiyuan, 40 miles away and I would need a travel permit to get there, I first tried the overseas Chinese counter in my town's main department store. Lacking overseas Chinese certificates, I was rebuffed. So I applied for a travel permit on the pretext of visiting foreign friends in Taiyuan. The reason for subterfuge was to prevent my college's Foreign Affairs Office functionaries from accompanying me to gain access to the store. Because I was a nonsmoker, they would surely have asked about the recipient of the cigarettes. A truthful answer would have gotten my friend in trouble for seeking favors from a foreigner, a fearsome charge for which he could have been persecuted. Refusal to answer would have upset the functionaries, causing them to be less cooperative in the myriad matters for which I depended on them. So a Foreign Affairs Office functionary dutifully wrote the report for official approval of my travel permit by university and county authorities. At the Friendship store the sales clerk said that I needed FECs to buy the cigarettes. I protested, waving my preferential treatment card (*youdaizheng*), which authorized me to buy domestic goods with the ordinary currency (renminbi) that I, as a cultural foreign expert (*wenjiao zhuanjia*), was paid in. Defeated, I went to my foreign friends for an FEC loan. Because it was late, I spent the night in their work unit's guest house. The next day I returned to the store. A new problem arose. The clerk would only sell three cartons in one transaction, ostensibly to prevent speculators from buying large lots for resale. So I bought three, went outside, and walked around the block. Returning to buy more, I found the door locked. I knocked for ten minutes until somebody told me the personnel were in their weekly political study session and that I should return the next day. The next morning I bought more cigarettes. Fortunately my effort paid off, and the friend's father was admitted to the hospital.

China: by the mid-1990s China had 350 million smokers who consumed 1.7 trillion cigarettes annually from over five hundred brands.[5] Yet premium cigarettes are expensive, and only the emerging middle class can afford to consume them regularly.[6] Just as premium brands once marked their bearers as members of the politically privileged cadre class, they now signify holders of commercial wealth, most visibly private businesspeople.[7] In this chapter I show that premium brands help construct the networks within which private business operates.

The insights of Pierre Bourdieu on institutional fields provide the analytic starting point. Institutional fields are constituted by relationships among persons and entities who, even as they compete with others, are bound by shared legitimate rules and codes of etiquette. Bourdieu likens a field to a game in which players bound by common rules but with distinct capital resources seek domination over others in pursuit of their interests.[8] He terms these resources "capital" to emphasize their convertibility into economic gain. Symbolic capital refers to prestige or status and can induce support through awe, respect, or deference. Social capital refers to the support and cooperation one can gain from others by manipulating the norms of reciprocity and obligation. Cultural capital refers to knowledge and skills that transcend mere educational credentials and indicates, for example, a grasp of etiquette in social relations. These capitals work in habituated social practices of partially unreflective deference and acquiescence to their possessors.[9]

Private business can be likened to an institutional field consisting of relations between entrepreneurial producers and distributors, regulatory

5. Frankel and Mufson 1996.

6. According to Cheng Li, the new middle class of the 1990s consisted of: urban private entrepreneurs; rural industrialists; speculators in the stock market; real estate and other business agents; managers in collective firms who earn profits through contracts; CEOs of large, state-owned enterprises; government officials made rich through corruption; Chinese representatives for foreign firms; Chinese executives in large joint ventures; sports stars and famous artists; Chinese who used to work abroad, especially in Japan and Australia, where they saved a great deal of money; smugglers; and professional call girls. See C. Li 1997, p. 23. To Li's middle class could be added Chinese employees of foreign financial, commercial, and service industries who are often paid significantly more than their counterparts in domestic industries, and even Chinese investors from Hong Kong and Taiwan who have purchased residences in China and live there for long periods of time.

7. The link between such cigarettes and cadre status can be seen in the exploits of Liang Heng, hero of the autobiography *Son of the Revolution*, during the mid-1970s. Liang Heng posed as the son of a high provincial official in order to frighten the stepbrother of Heng's female friend who was bullying her. His high-cadre disguise consisted of black corduroy shoes, wide blue pants, a huge army-style coast, a white face mask, white gloves, and pack of expensive cigarettes.

8. Bourdieu 1986.

9. Bourdieu and Wacquant 1992, pp. 97–101.

agencies, and labor oriented to the creation of commercial profit. I will show how premium cigarettes constitute capital that entrepreneurs use to enhance their business dealings with others. Following Bourdieu, cigarettes can be said to help constitute strategies of personal domination for entrepreneurs to appropriate others' support for profit.[10] These strategies are functional in a commercial system that lacks the institutions of a more established (i.e., ideal-typical) market economy, such as a juridical system, by enabling entrepreneurs to hold more stable expectations in dealings with others by recourse to habituated social practices.

Let me briefly describe the organization of this chapter. In the first section I provide an overview of the place of premium cigarettes in private business. In the second section I describe how premium cigarettes are used in strategies of personal domination in entrepreneurs' dealings with others. For comparative purposes, observations on premarket reform patterns of consumption in networks are located in footnotes. In conclusion, I juxtapose my findings with arguments about consumption contained in the state and society view. The data derive from almost two years of fieldwork conducted in Xiamen City from 1988 to 1990 and in 1995. My observations are taken from a sample of 100 operators of private trading companies. I interacted with entrepreneurs in many venues: formal interviews, social chats, and group functions, and as an interpreter between local entrepreneurs and foreign businessmen. As a participant observer, I also used premium cigarettes in many of the ways described herein.

Since market reforms were first adopted in the late 1970s, Xiamen, on the coast of Fujian Province, has become one of the most marketized cities in China. As a Special Economic Zone, Xiamen enjoys favorable policies such as low tariffs on imported goods, and large amounts of goods and money move through it.[11] Because of these favorable conditions, Xiamen has developed a thriving trading sector and is a hospitable environment for private commerce. By the 1990s there were two tiers in the private trading sector. On the lower tier were the traditional shopkeepers, the so-called *getihu*, who ranged from street vendors to proprietors of small stores and shops. They sold mostly in local retail markets and lacked connections to officialdom. On the upper tier was the capitalist sector, which included expansive wholesale trading companies (*maoyi gongsi*). Some were single firms with half a

---

10. Bourdieu 1977, pp. 183–97.

11. As early as 1982 the Xiamen city government permitted the operation of private collectives, called cooperatives (*minban jiti*), a full two years earlier than most other urban areas. It began licensing private enterprises (*siying qiye*) in 1987, a year earlier than elsewhere. And after the passage of the 1994 Company Law (*Gongsi Fa*), which established a legal framework for corporations, a local private firm was reputed to be the first in China allowed to make a public stock offering.

dozen employees, usually family members. They dealt in goods that required few official connections such as seafood, handicraft products, and light consumer appliances. Larger firms were business enterprise groups consisting of dozens of component firms linked by overlapping kinship and management ties. These firms traded inter-regionally and even internationally in more officially brokered commodities such as construction materials, raw minerals, and real estate and were diversifying into manufacturing and services. The discussion in this chapter focuses on this capitalist sector.

PREMIUM CIGARETTES IN THE BUSINESS COMMUNITY

Cigarettes are pervasive in interactions in the private business community. Almost all interactions beyond a fleeting encounter involve the pulling out of cigarette packs, tamping them to settle the tobacco, and then proffering cigarettes to others. So pervasive is cigarette smoking that many businesspersons have nicotine stains on their hands, which are seen almost as a professional symbol in itself, much as such stains were previously the mark of cadres who smoked heavily during long meetings. In the market economy, these stains mark entrepreneurs who spend long hours cutting deals and smoke to stay awake, to suppress appetite, and as described below, to facilitate personal deal-making. In one revealing comment an entrepreneur referred to a highly successful businessman who was so busy cutting deals that "his hands and teeth are dark from cigarettes." Given the propensity of businesspeople to smoke while making deals, it follows that one who cuts more deals will smoke more cigarettes and have deeper nicotine stains.

When I first arrived in Xiamen in 1988, a premium brand popular among entrepreneurs was Good Companion (*Liang You*), manufactured in Hong Kong with an American blend of tobacco and selling for around five renminbi (rmb) a pack. At the time it was being superseded by American-made brands flooding China's market as a result of American government pressure for China to reduce its trade imbalance with the United States. The most popular brand among the business community was Kent, followed by Winston and Marlboro, all of which sold for about 7 rmb a pack, many times the price of regular cigarettes, which could cost as little as 1 rmb. The desirability of foreign cigarettes lay less in their foreignness than in their expense and utility. As the most expensive readily available cigarettes they signified wealth, and their crush-proof boxes prevented the cigarettes from getting bent out of shape when stored in one's pocket. The popularity of these foreign brands was being superseded in the 1990s by domestic brands from Yunnan Province such as Red Pagoda Mountain (*Hong Ta Shan*) that have adopted crush-proof packages and are now twice as expensive as foreign cigarettes, which are heavily regulated and therefore have risen more slowly in price.

The smoking of high-grade cigarettes is a highly visible symbol of wealth that distinguishes businesspeople from other social groups. In the late 1980s a single pack of Kent cost around 7 rmb, which was the equivalent of the daily wage of a worker in a state enterprise. When I asked entrepreneurs why they had decided to go into business, which in the 1980s was still politically risky and ideologically suspect, a number answered using cigarettes. They held up a pack of Kent and said that if they were still working in a state enterprise they would be unable to smoke such cigarettes. One said, "Society is moving rapidly. If you want to enjoy the fruits of the good life you have to go into business. Otherwise you will be left behind and your daily wages will just amount to one pack of good cigarettes." Premium cigarettes are also a metaphor for the new social distance opening up between the wealthy and those in still in the public sector. One businessman who formerly worked in a factory said, "When I first came out [left the factory] and was just starting up, my friends from work often came by to encourage me. They would say, 'you are so brave to throw away your iron rice bowl.' But as my business became successful they stopped coming. I think they were embarrassed because I was now smoking Kent and they were still puffing on Front Gate (*Da Qian Men*). They could see how I was progressing as part of the new societal movement while they were being left behind."

Premium cigarettes also communicate status among the business group. I became aware of this after noticing that a small number of entrepreneurs smoked 555 State Express brand. I further noticed that such entrepreneurs tended to be successful managers in the larger companies and descendants of prerevolutionary bourgeois business families. When I commented on this to the businessmen, they remarked that 555 is an "old brand" (*laopaizi*) that had been marketed in China for a century.[12] Thus smoking 555 signified the symbolic capital of old-business family lineage, creating an aura of reliability and professionalism. Smoking 555 signified good breeding and background within the business community and thus evoked respect from others.[13] This became evident when I asked why I never saw shopkeepers or stall owners smoking the 555 brand. "He would be a joke (*cheng xiaohua*)," was

12. For the history of the British-American Corporation in China, see Cochran 1980.

13. There was also a hierarchy of premium cigarettes as expressions of privilege. The most difficult brand to obtain was *Zhonghua*, and I never found it in Shanxi Province, even at the Friendship Store in the capital. Even the party secretary at the school where I taught smoked only Peony (*Mudan*) a cigarette that was available in major departments stores in key urban areas such as Beijing and Shanghai. One of the few people I encountered who smoked *Zhonghua* was the son of a high-level cadre from Beijing who visited my school because he was writing a book on missionary schools in China. He visited the Shanxi Agricultural College from time to time and was always impeccably turned out in high-cadre style, including black leather shoes, a well-tailored *Zhongshan* suit, a gold pen, and, of course, *Zhonghua* cigarettes. His props clearly contrasted with the somewhat less prestigious ones of the cadres in the school and city administration.

one answer I received. The situation would be analogous to an upstart businessperson smoking cigarettes in a gold cigarette holder, appropriate for somebody of wealth and breeding but farcical for someone of lesser status. The only exceptions to the use of premium brands among private company operators were older entrepreneurs, who smoked cheap filterless brands of cigarettes that had been around for many years. For anybody else this would have appeared incongruous and even miserly, but for these entrepreneurs it conveyed unpretentiousness and honesty. For these individuals smoking cheap cigarettes that most entrepreneurs would not be caught dead puffing was almost a noble (*gaoshangde*) act.

I also used the symbolic value of cigarettes in my interactions with entrepreneurs. Since businessmen were always offering me cigarettes, it seemed impolite to refuse and polite to reciprocate. My assistant cautioned me to pay attention to the impression I would create by the kind of cigarette that I offered. He further suggested that I offer *Zhonghua*, which was about 1 rmb more expensive than Kent, 555, and other foreign brands favored by businesspersons. Because businesspeople judged people on their appearance of wealth, he felt I would gain respect if I carried the more expensive cigarettes. I am not sure that I enhanced my standing in their eyes, but I quickly realized a different utility, that of offering *Zhonghua* cigarettes as an icebreaker. One businessman commented in mock surprise that we were both unpatriotic because he smoked American and I smoked Chinese cigarettes. We chuckled over this joke, and I subsequently appropriated it into my interactions with other businesspersons. This gambit served me well until the student movement in June 1989, when patriotism was thrust to the fore by the state's accusation that foreign elements were behind the movement. After a tongue lashing by an entrepreneur I was having dinner with on how America was causing sedition in China, I decided to drop this joke from my repertoire.

Yet even as cigarettes mark distinct social spaces, they are also part of social practices that connect persons across social space in the business world. These social practices draw on a socially legitimate body of norms and practices to communicate meanings and expectations in personal interactions. For example, one can convey greater respect for another by offering a cigarette from a freshly produced pack. Others forms are more specific to business practices. For example, a polite way to refuse a cigarette is to place one's hand in front of one's chest with the palm facing inward and the fingers pointing sideways and waggle it up and down. A more direct way is to hold one's hand upright with the palm outward like a traffic policeman signaling cars to stop. This not only conveys refusal of the cigarette but also dashes expectations of future cooperation in other endeavors.

The use of premium cigarettes and other expensive props is, of course, standard business practice everywhere. The display and use of expensive goods can, if done properly, elicit awe, respect, and trust from others. However, this personalization assumes an intensified form in Chinese private business as it emerges from a centrally planned economy.[14]

CONSTRUCTING BUSINESS NETWORKS

In this section I describe how premium cigarettes help construct personal business ties. While the practices reflect general community and societal norms of reciprocity and patterns of etiquette, specific utilities and expectations inhere in specific types of interactions. This section first discusses how entrepreneurs use cigarettes in interactions among peers and then how they use them in dealing with officials and employees.

Enhancing Credit among Entrepreneurs

Entrepreneurs seek to enhance their credit—perceptions of trustworthiness—with other entrepreneurs. This is crucial in the business world where agreements are based on personal honor and courts of law are viewed as arbitrary and are to be avoided in seeking resolution of business disputes. Cigarettes can communicate that one is honorable and upright, or at least will not take undue advantage of others. For example, by communicating relative status within the business community, as described above, they can generate useful feelings of awe and respect. A businessperson who smokes 555 can signal that he is from a business family of long standing and therefore is more professional and trustworthy than less-experienced businesspersons.

Cigarettes enhance sociability in the business community. One entrepreneur said, "Cigarettes are part of doing business. I give you a cigarette. You give me a cigarette. No one thinks about it, but it creates feeling (*ganqing*) among us and it is easier to discuss matters." Much smoking is done during visits to nightclubs and restaurants and during spontaneous "drop in" (*chuanmen*) visits on entrepreneurs in their companies. Indeed since Xiamen, with a registered population of less than half a million, is a small city by Chinese standards, many of the businesspersons in the same age cohorts know each other well and socialized frequently to exchange views on market trends and rumors about new policies.

Actively proffering cigarettes conveys goodwill and willingness to engage in mutual give-and-take should problems arise. It conveys that one has a "broad bosom" (*xionghuai kuankuo*), or in other words, is generous and tolerant rather than stingy and petty. The importance of this aspect of cigarette exchange can be seen in an account of a Xiamen entrepreneur in his deal-

14. For a longer treatment of these points in Xiamen's private business community see Wank 1998.

ings with a Taiwan investor. He spent several days traveling with the investor to consider possible sites for a joint-venture factory. During the trip the investor never once offered the businessman a cigarette, but readily accepted those offered him. The businessman told me that this was the key reason he decided against doing business with the investor.

I witnessed two variations in social practices involving premium cigarettes among entrepreneurs. One was linked to business scale. Entrepreneurs running the smaller and less successful firms were more active givers. When I visited them at their firms, such businessmen were likely to show me respect by offering a cigarette from a fresh pack rather than an already opened one. Also, to demonstrate broad-mindedness, businesspersons scatter cigarettes to those in a room when they enter and push them across the table to those at the other end. If others do not pick up the cigarettes, the businessman receives the message that they do not value him highly. Businessmen are skilled in the art of cajoling others to accept cigarettes. To those who initially refuse they will say, "Take it to smoke later" or even insist, "Gift! Gift! (*yisi, yisi*)" as they thrust a cigarette forward. Such energetic assertions that the cigarette is a gift enhance the likelihood that the cigarette will be accepted, because the recipient would lose some face by not accepting a gift.

There are several reasons why such entrepreneurs are such insistent givers in their interactions with fellow businesspersons. One is because they lack the connections to officialdom of more successful entrepreneurs and therefore do not have a patron (*houtai laoban*) to intervene on their behalf in disputes. Thus they are constrained to ensure good personal relations with their colleagues. Second, many entrepreneurs rely on fellow entrepreneurs in the same business line for stock. They rarely keep large amounts on hand, and when they receive a large order they rush around to borrow the necessary amounts from fellow entrepreneurs with an agreement to repay by a certain date. The displays of generosity signified in proffering cigarettes are useful reminders of one's credit.

Wealthier entrepreneurs are less likely to push cigarettes on others.[15] In fact, in my observations, some even offered them almost as an afterthought after pulling one out for themselves. Wealthier entrepreneurs rely less on other entrepreneurs to solve business problems because they have tighter relations with officialdom and the state sector. Their disinclination to proffer cigarettes indicates that they have enough connections to officialdom to enable them to dispense with personalization strategies toward other entrepreneurs. Also, instead of offering cigarettes themselves, the wealthiest entrepreneurs have personal valets and gofers to do so. This is a powerful symbol of wealth and power.

15. For a discussion of the varied network strategies and political attitudes among private entrepreneurs, see Wank 1995.

The other variation is linked to gender. Only one out of the six women in my sample smoked. In contrast, all the men smoked, whether for enjoyment or out of a sense of business duty. This could reflect the perception that women in China generally do not smoke: urban women who smoke are considered to be coarse and low class or to have loose morals. Indeed, however, many of the women in the nightclub world that male entrepreneurs frequent do smoke. And even businesswomen who smoke may not do so while conducting business in order to maintain a sense of dignity. I once accompanied a businessman to an outlying county where he was trying reach an agreement with a collective township factory to produce export goods. He asked me to accompany him and pose as a foreign businessman in order to impress the township government officials. We met with half a dozen township officials from the local government's enterprise bureau; there was one woman in their midst. When the entrepreneur offered cigarettes all around, he did not proffer one to the female official, which turned out to be a sound decision since she did not smoke during our meeting or during the subsequent banquet with the bureau officials. On our drive back to Xiamen I commented that he had taken a gamble because, if she had turned out to be a smoker, she might have felt insulted at being excluded from the opening round of cigarette offerings. The businessman disagreed. He noted that even if she had been a smoker she would have appreciated his show of respect for her "femininity" by not offering her a cigarette. Offering her a cigarette would have suggested that the entrepreneur did not regard her highly and would have caused her to lose face.

The link between nonsmoking and perceptions of femininity was indicated in comments by another entrepreneur. He noted that I was clearly a nonsmoker despite the fact that I carried cigarettes with me, offered them to others, and puffed on them to be social. He said, "It is clear you do not really smoke. Your teeth are all white, just like a woman's."[16]

Perhaps women entrepreneurs may smoke less than men to enhance the symbolic capital of their femininity in creating trust.[17] As one such entrepreneur, a women in her early fifties said, "Because I am a woman people believe that I am less likely to do bad things. They have a feeling of safety. I give people the impression that my words are reasonable. I am not one of those fierce women who smokes cigarettes, talks in a loud voice, and is rude

16. Other foreign social scientists have told me that they also worried about how to conduct fieldwork in light of the pervasiveness of smoking among men. One researcher solved the problem by telling everyone that he was Muslim and did not smoke. Another carried cigarettes around and proffered them liberally to others but did not smoke them. People I talked to about this found the latter tactic amusing and commented about the foreigner who ran around with packs of cigarettes sticking out his pockets but did not smoke them himself.

17. Mayfair Yang also reports that women both eschewed more blatantly instrumental forms of *guanxi* while using their personal charm as a *guanxi* strategy. See M. Yang 1994, p. 128.

to others. So people feel safe in dealing with me." Thus it seems that businessmen use cigarette exchange to build relations, while businesswomen augment business through nonparticipation.

Influencing Officials

Discretionary support of officials in the lower bureaucracy furthers private business in several ways. One way is to enhance profit. Support gives entrepreneurs access to information across market segments as, for example, when an inland public unit has construction materials for sale or another public unit needs certain chemicals. Entrepreneurs also use connections with officials to obtain access to administratively mediated commodities. In the 1980s their focus was the two-tier price system, and in the 1990s it was more likely to be real estate. Another way is to enhance security. Economic reform has given officials a whole new range of power in the area of the regulation of private business in such matters as business licenses and taxation. Favorable decisions in these matters are more forthcoming when one has a network to call upon. Personalization also enhances security and protection. The judicial system is perceived as corrupt, and regulatory agencies administer laws and regulations haphazardly. To prevent harassment, entrepreneurs seek personal ties to officials in the government bureaus that supervise their business activities. For example, entrepreneurs dealing in grain may forge connections with the Grain Bureau; those in the trucking and the taxi business will establish connections with highway and transportation agencies. Officials from these bureaus can provide insider information to client entrepreneurs about upcoming policy changes and new regulations as well as head off harassment from other bureaus. In short, personalized strategies with power holders help entrepreneurs enforce their property rights through popular norms of reciprocity and obligation.

Cigarettes help maintain "warm human relations" (*ren he*) with officials. The practice of "dropping by" (*chuanmen*) to visit administrative officials at their offices for chatting and smoking is widespread in the business world. Entrepreneurs may use these visits to pick up useful bits of information about policy changes, market opportunities, and so on, but the visits are also intended to strengthen social relations. As one entrepreneur said, "I often go and visit the bureau to talk with them. Shoot the breeze, smoke some cigarettes. Sometimes I will just sit for several hours chatting about this and that. Sometimes they will talk about their families or some problem that I can help them with. They have much experience and I can learn a lot. If you sit with somebody long enough you develop feeling (*ganqing*)." Such contacts create a reservoir of goodwill that entrepreneurs can tap to deal with sudden problems.

Officials also drop in on entrepreneurs at their companies. This is common at the smaller firms that interact mostly with street-level officials. Officials come to provide information on policy and other regulatory matters and to express their intentions. To entertain them, entrepreneurs place packs of premium cigarettes on coffee tables in front of the sofas and chairs where visitors sit. As they chat, officials partake freely of the cigarettes. The power inequality is evident in that officials often help themselves to cigarettes without invitation from the entrepreneurs; employees and others would never take such liberties.

The offering of cigarettes can also exert influence through shared consumption. This was impressed upon me by a personal experience. Accompanied by a foreign affairs functionary from my sponsoring unit, I visited the Xiamen Industry and Commerce Bureau to conduct interviews with its officials. On the way there he stopped to buy a pack of Kent cigarettes. I knew he did not smoke and asked him why he was buying them. "It will lubricate things in there," he said nodding toward the Bureau. During an interview with an official, I noticed a stack of application forms for private business licenses on his desk. I asked if could see them and he nodded. The documents contained useful data on the entrepreneurs as well as official notations in the margin, so I began to copy them into my notebook. The official protested, saying that the applications were not public documents. I nervously sheathed my pen, fearful that the official would demand I hand them over. Then the foreign affairs functionary with me sprang into action. In a flash, he was offering a cigarette to the official and changed the topic of conversation. I spent the next 40 minutes scribbling madly as the functionary plied the official with cigarettes and engaged him in conversation.

Cigarettes can also be used by entrepreneurs to assess the character of officials during first encounters. During my research in the late 1980s, many purchasing agents of northern and inland public units came to Xiamen to purchase large orders of car parts for their units. At the time there were more than a hundred companies dealing in this commodity in Xiamen, and in the fierce competition kickbacks were generally necessary to obtain an order. Yet kickbacks (*huikou*) are deemed illegal by the state, and mentioning the subject requires some etiquette, particularly in dealing with first-time buyers. Yet cigarettes were often the opening round in a series of exchanges by which the entrepreneur advanced negotiations with these buyers.

Finally, cigarettes can be used to convey one's willingness to skirt the limits of the policy to engage in legally dubious but more lucrative trade such as sale of administratively priced items or smuggling items out of the Special Economic Zone without paying the duty tax. Businesspeople in Xiamen make use of smuggled cigarettes to see whether the other party is willing to deal. I became aware of this gambit while visiting an entrepreneur in his office. A buyer from a state public unit in Fuzhou came by whom the entrepreneur did not know. He introduced himself to the entrepreneur. The entrepreneur offered him a cigarette, saying jokingly, "Try one of my smuggled cigarettes." Packs of legally imported American cigarettes are stamped with such phrases as "Designated for sale in China (*Zhongguo zhuanxiao*), but smuggled cigarettes lack them. Many businessmen smoke smuggled cigarettes, which are widely available at the private kiosks: all one has to do is ask for "nonlabeled" (*bu dai biaoqian*) Kents or Winstons. The price is not necessarily cheaper, and crackdowns on smuggling can cause a sudden scarcity in this commodity and make smuggled cigarettes more expensive than legal imported ones.[18]

Later I asked the entrepreneur why he had said that, and he responded cryptically that it helped him understand (*liaojie*) the buyer. Exactly what he meant gradually became apparent as I came to understand the necessary role of kickbacks in landing purchase orders from state enterprises. Such comments let the entrepreneur test a buyer's willingness to receive kickbacks in exchange for placing orders. In an entrepreneur's eyes, a buyer who is put off by the fact that the cigarettes are smuggled or who hesitates does not have the flexible attitude necessary to enter into certain kinds of business transactions. Buyers who willingly accept a smuggled cigarette and make some joke or light comment in response show their loose sense of legality and willingness to deal. This kind of practice is especially prevalent in certain business lines such as car parts, which is extremely competitive.

During an entrepreneur's social "drop by" visits, an official can also communicate his intentions with cigarettes. He might accept a cigarette to indicate his willingness to receive further gifts from an entrepreneur and acquiesce to his wishes. Or he might politely refuse by waggling the back of his hand, an ambiguous response that communicates that any advances now are inconvenient but not categorically ruled out. Finally, he might bluntly refuse with palm outward, dashing expectations of future cooperation.

DISCIPLINING EMPLOYEES

Cigarettes are part of entrepreneurs' strategy for disciplining employees. They seek to ensure that employees work hard for them and do not steal or work halfheartedly. The strategy varies by economic activity and according to the bargaining positions of different employees. In commerce, where money passes through the hands of counter clerks and sales agents, entrepreneurs must ensure that clerks do not pilfer from the till and that sales agents do not under-report the volume of their transactions and skim profits

---

18. This raises the question of why businessmen smoke them. The usual answer they gave is that the labeled cigarettes use lower-quality tobacco and do not taste as good as the nonlabeled ones. However, neither I nor my friends could tell any difference, even in blind taste tests.

for their personal use. Also, employees in Xiamen are both local and from rural backgrounds. Locals are more urbane and better at interacting with customers and are preferred for such positions as sales agents, but precisely because they are locals any gossip they may have about the entrepreneur can find its way into the local community and the ears of local authorities. Also any reports they make to the authorities are more likely to be believed because they are locals. The problems such reports can create should not be underestimated. For example, one entrepreneur was charged with tax evasion because a former disgruntled employee made an anonymous report on a corruption hotline to the tax authorities.[19]

My observation was that entrepreneurs in commerce are much more likely to proffer cigarettes to employees than their counterparts in manufacturing and the service sector. For example, when an entrepreneur is talking to one of his sales agents he may pull out a cigarette and offer it and the two will share a smoke. Also, it is the practice of trading firms to make offerings to the God of Wealth (*Caishen*) on the second and sixteenth days of each month. Offerings of food and sometimes wine and cigarettes are laid out on a special table in the company on those days. At the appointed time all the firm employees gather for a meal. I attended some of these repasts and noticed that the entrepreneurs were solicitous on these occasions, referring to the personal lives of specific employees and mentioning their recent achievements. The meal was usually brought to a close when the entrepreneur produced packs of premium cigarettes, which he opened and distributed to employees. This practice helps builds loyalty to the firm through personal loyalty to its head and reduces discipline problems among the employees. As one entrepreneur said, "This way the employees feel like this is their family. They feel the affairs of the company are also their affairs and this lessens embezzlement and theft."

Manufacturing and service enterprises employ many people from the Xiamen hinterlands and further inland. Entrepreneurs in those sectors appeared somewhat less concerned about maintaining personal ties with their employees. Entrepreneurs do not have to worry about what kinds of rumors employees spread because nonlocals are unlikely to be believed. Also, because they come to Xiamen solely to make money, they want to avoid any trouble that would cause them to be blacklisted by employers. Entrepreneurs can simply fire problematic nonlocal employees. In manufacturing enterprises cigarette exchange is reversed when an employee offers a cigarette to his boss. At a factory that made bricks and house tiles, I witnessed an alter-

19. Corruption hotlines are modeled after the Hong Kong anticorruption hotlines that take anonymous complaints against officials. In Xiamen two kinds of hotlines were established in the late 1980s, one to report tax evasion and deviant practices by businesspersons and one to report corruption by officials.

cation between a foreman and entrepreneur. The entrepreneur was giving me a tour of his factory when he noticed a cracked mold. He became angry and shouted at the worker. The foreman intervened to defend the worker by saying that the mold had cracked from age, not from the worker's carelessness. The entrepreneur's anger abated, and their discussion shifted to production matters. The foreman pulled out a pack of cigarettes and offered one to the entrepreneur and to me. The entrepreneur initially pushed the offer aside with a backhand waggle but the foreman persisted, aided by the fact that I had accepted. The entrepreneur then accepted but put the cigarette behind his ear and walked off without smoking it in front of the foreman. I interpreted this cigarette play to be the entrepreneur's reluctant acceptance of the foreman's explanation.

In certain businesses that require team production rather than individual piecework, workers may also offer their foremen cigarettes. The car body repair business is a case in point. In private garages, workers are organized in small teams of three or four persons under a foreman. Together they undertake the repairs on a vehicle. It is up to the foreman to decide the specific contribution of each and to distribute the wages, which the foreman receives as a lump sum from the entrepreneur. To curry favor with the foreman, some workers compete by offering him cigarettes when they are chatting. I heard that some workers carried two kinds of cigarettes with them: inexpensive local brands for their own consumption and premium brands for offering to the foreman and the boss.

CONCLUSION

By way of conclusion, here I reflect on questions of institutional transformations in light of the preceding ethnography on cigarettes and networks. First, I consider studies that link the enhanced autonomy in production and consumption in the market transition era to changes in state-society relations. Then I sketch an alternative view of institutional changes that are occurring in networks and are decoupled from necessary shifts in the configuration of state and society.

State and Society Views

I can identify three overlapping views in extant studies of how autonomous production and consumption of commodities shapes institutional change. All posit a positive correspondence between greater economic autonomy and shifts in relations between state and society. Some emphasize that the rise of market allocation stimulates horizontal societal integration. For example, Victor Nee sees the market as allocating goods in horizontal transactions that bypass the state's vertical redistributive bureaucracy,[20] thereby undermining Maoist-era features at the state-society borders such as patron-client ties and stimulating the horizontal integration of society. However, my findings suggest that the circulation of market-allocated commodities is simultaneously embedded in various kinds of integration, including horizontal links among entrepreneurs, commercialized clientelism between officials and entrepreneurs, and ties of labor discipline between the entrepreneurs and the new working class. In short, deductive assumptions of positive correspondence between the increasing allocational autonomy and horizontal societal integration of society on the one hand and the decline of vertical lines of statist authority on the other hand are not borne out by this study of an "autonomously allocated" commodity. Instead we see these commodities helping to constitute the transformation of patron-client ties with officialdom, the emergence of new vertically oriented ties between entrepreneurs and employees, and ties of mutual aid among entrepreneurs.

Another view sees production and consumption as increasingly decoupled from state projects and ideologies to reflect local and private tastes and decisions, a process that suggests the emergence of a public sphere. Such decoupling is portrayed in Thomas Gold's study of Gangtai culture flows from Hong Kong and Taiwan into China. He maintains that "the Party has in effect yielded a 'zone of indifference' in the cultural realm to producers and consumers, where it will not intrude excessively as the costs outweigh the benefits,"[21] A similar view is suggested by Charlotte Ikels's account of changing lifestyles in Guangzhou, where consumers are left alone by the state and are free to define their personal tastes and lifestyles.[22] Such accounts portray the content of consumer production and consumption as no longer incorporated into state ideologies and projects but driven by private tastes, preferences, and wealth. This raises the question of what, if any, role the state plays in new patterns of consumption. According to institutional analysis, as the dominant authority in the realm states always pattern economic activity through both action and nonaction.[23]

There is still a considerable state presence in patterning consumption of premium cigarettes. Let me first describe how state inaction influences cigarette consumption in private business. The pervasiveness of cigarettes in private enterprise relations is due not only to private tastes and interests but

20. Victor Nee advances a concept called market-transition theory, which purports to validate Ivan Szelenyi's thesis. For Nee's earliest and clearest expression of the market-transition thesis, see Nee 1989.

21. Gold 1993, p. 921.

22. Ikels 1996.

23. This is the institutionalist view that because states always constitute economies questions of change center not on issues of degree but on the character of this constitution. See Block 1994; Polanyi 1957.

also to the "failure" of the state to erect an impartial juridical system to enforce legal rights to private property. The display and exchange of cigarettes help entrepreneurs enforce understandings in dealings with others. Thus utilities of cigarettes to private entrepreneurs reflect their economic interests in a *context heavily constrained by the state*. Next, let me describe an example of state action. The state has sought to define consumption behavior as part of incessant campaigns against corruption that target social practices involving cigarettes, food, and alcohol that are seen as stimulating illicit *guanxi* relations between officials and citizens. Such campaigns render suspect even the proffering of a single cigarette to an official. These negative campaigns are paralleled by more positive campaigns to instill professional ethics of legality and universalism in officials through codes of conduct issued for specific bureaus, and in businesspeople through meetings to teach them about "doing civilized business" (*wenming jingying*) and "cultivating a tax-paying consciousness" (*peiyang nashui yishi*). Thus, the very structure of the state (e.g., a haphazard juridical system) as well as its intended projects, can pattern consumption, belying the notion that market-based consumption is linked to the enhanced autonomy of society and retreat of the state.[24]

A third view on marketization, consumerism, and institutions is offered by Mayfair Yang.[25] Briefly, Yang sees *guanxi* as constituting a distinct Chinese-style public sphere that is constituted not by universal rights for individuals but by particularistic obligations in networks; she terms this social order a *minjian* (popular or "among the people") realm. It is constituted by social exchanges of premium cigarettes, fine spirits, and choice foodstuffs that embody values and interests independent of, and even subversive to, those promulgated by the state. In Yang's view, the market expands those networks into new kinds of consumer interest groups that will become part of a civil society once the state gives them legal recognition. But as Yang herself realizes, there is little internal drive within consumerism for the transformation of new market connections into a civil society because the key variable is the deus ex machina of state-promulgated legal rights. Moreover, my findings suggest that consumerism can also reinforce values of particularism that are inimical to the universalistic orientation and civic trust characteristic of civil society.[26] This is underscored by Richard Kraus's point in this volume that there is no necessary positive correspondence between a public sphere of individual tastes and opinions and a civil society of horizontally organized groups to promote and safeguard political rights.

24. For continuing state efforts to define citizens' use of leisure time see S. Wang 1995.

25. Mayfair Yang grapples with this same question and answers with the concept of a *minjian* order and its transformation through market reform (Yang 1994).

26. For a recent statement on the importance of civic trust in the function of civil society, see Putnam 1993.

Toward an Institutional View

Tracing the circulation of a single commodity in social relations reveals institutional changes in networks and relations of social power.[27] Clearly the greater availability of premium cigarettes has devalued their use in social strategies. Premium cigarettes are no longer only presented to others on special occasions but can now be smoked openly. Because they are now consumed by businesspersons they are no longer a mark only of bureaucratic rank but also of status distinctions among societal groups. This chapter's account of the circulation of cigarettes in the local business community suggests that social practices are becoming highly localized in specific fields and even unintelligible to those outside of them. In 1980, for example, anybody would have known that the smoker of a *Zhonghua* cigarette was a cadre, but in 1990 no one but a member of the business community would have known the difference in status between a smoker of 555 brand and Kent brand cigarettes. Although cigarette smoking still reflects broader societal conventions, it has been adapted to the practices of specific fields. These practices are frequently opaque to outside entities such as the central state, which seeks to regulate private business.

In the redistributive economy, the value of premium cigarettes lay in their ease of convertibility into social and political capital, which in turn could be used to enhance economic gain. Premium cigarettes could be stored for a considerable period, unlike food, and were light and therefore portable, unlike liquor. For these reasons, cigarettes approached commodity status as an exchange item. In the market economy single packs of cigarettes are now carried on one's person and can be used to project personal qualities such as trustworthiness. Yet devaluation notwithstanding, cigarettes are still proffered with expectations of reciprocity, although the expectations are quite altered. In the redistributive economy, premium cigarettes were primarily used as part of a strategy for influencing officials. The terms of exchange were clear cut in that the recipient often knew exactly what was expected in return. By contrast, cigarettes are increasingly proffered to elicit trust and enhance expectations of future but unspecified support. To generate more specific expectations, cigarettes have been replaced by cash and more valuable commodities such as televisions and other home appliances. Thus, the declining exchange value of premium cigarettes in negotiations with officials does not reflect the reduced need for connections to local government but rather the rising cost of obtaining officials' discretionary support. This suggests in turn that the capital of bureaucratic distributors in fields of intense commercial activity, such as private business, is increasing rather than declining in value in the emerging market economy.

27. Appadurai 1986.

Yet even as cigarettes have declined in exchange value, they can still be used to subvert state power. Because the value of premium cigarettes has declined, the link between cigarettes and social power is less sharply perceived. A premium cigarette is now more likely seen as a good smoke or a status symbol than as a bullet for a Mauser pistol with which to storm the fortress of the state bureaucracy. Yet as illustrated by my encounter with the official in the Xiamen business-licensing bureau, even a good smoke can break down barriers. Smoking together conveys the spirit of sociability rather than obligation and therefore is not be perceived as influence per se. Yet sociability is also highly effective in obtaining a favor. In fact, it could be said that the declining visibility of premium cigarettes as vehicles of influence has rendered them even more subversive in interactions with officials because they are no longer recognized as such. Also, in the command economy, citizens negotiated with officials for access to resources already marked for redistribution, whereas now they negotiate for access to items not so marked. For example, in 1981 my friend used cartons of cigarettes to obtain access to a bed at a cadre hospital (see footnote 7). From the vantage point of the state, the bed was already marked for allocation and it made no difference who filled it as long as the patient was sick and was a cadre of a certain rank. Almost a decade later I used cigarettes to see documents that were not intended for my eyes.

In sum, I have identified such institutional transformations as localization, changes in valuation, and shifting processes of subversion that are distinct from questions of societal autonomy and declines in state power. People use commodities available in markets to transform prior patterns of domination and construct new ones. In other words, the institutional consequences of expanded market-based consumption in China's redistributive economy are portrayed as changes in relational networks rather than in state and society. The institutional transformations linked to social practices of consumption of the emerging middle class could be occurring in either a democratic or an authoritarian context. This helps explain China's rapid marketization within an authoritarian one-party state.

CHAPTER 13

Public Monuments and Private Pleasures in the Parks of Nanjing

A Tango in the Ruins of the Ming Emperor's Palace

Richard Kraus

Time has not been kind to Nanjing's Imperial Palace since the Ming dynasty decamped for Beijing in 1421. Fire, conquest, and a 1911 English plunder of remaining statuary has left little but a grand gate, five stone bridges, and some broken columns set amidst a pleasantly wooded park in the south-eastern part of the city. The palace grounds today are the locus of typical urban park behavior: there are rides for children, pool tables, paintings for sale, a bookstore and a restaurant, vendors of trinkets and foodstuffs, citizens dressed to the nines to show off their new clothes, and dancers. The Ming ruins have two places where couples dance to recorded music, a democratic contrast to the spot's once awesome majesty (Figure 13.1).

The realms of public and private, of state and consumer are in constant juxtaposition in the public places of urban China: parks, memorials, and city squares. Using Nanjing as my primary example, I here examine the relationship between private consumer and public art and argue that, contrary to much recent writing on the question of civil society in China, China does indeed have a public sphere. I also argue that monuments and relics are highlighted, refurbished, rearranged, and invented by the state in its effort to adapt this sphere to the emergence of consumer society, and that this tacti-

I wrote an earlier draft of this paper while living in Nanjing between 1995 and 1997. I owe special thanks to Mary S. Erbaugh, Emily Honig, Cecily Hurst, Bruce Jacobs, Ellen J. Laing, Steven I. Levine, Milo Manley, Charles Musgrove, Yali Peng, Ron Scollon, and the participants in the 1997 Conference on Urban Consumption and the Emerging Consumer Culture of Chinese Cities, whose excellent suggestions I sometimes perversely disregarded. I must also acknowledge the invaluable (but unfortunately best kept anonymous) assistance of several Chinese colleagues and students at the Johns Hopkins University–Nanjing University Center for Chinese and American Studies.

FIGURE 13.1.   Dancers among the trees behind the great gate at the ruins of the Ming Palace (Photo by Richard Kraus)

cal flexibility masks a retreat of the state from its former easy assumption of ideological hegemony.

PUBLIC ART, PUBLIC SPHERE, CIVIL SOCIETY

The monuments, statues, murals, and other art works found in public spaces in urban China offer a way to discuss the thorny question of China's "public sphere." In the West, controversies over art in public places often remind us sharply how contested our own public sphere can be. Controversies about specific art works, deemed "public" either because they were state-funded or by their conspicuous placement, propelled the concept of public art into popular debate in recent decades. Disagreements are often sharp and center on the control of symbols that are ostensibly sponsored for the public but that critics sometimes charge only represent a part of a community. For instance, many middle-class residents of the Chicago suburb of Berwyn expressed outrage that their lives and values were being mocked by a cement tower embedded with washing machines and other appliances at the entrance to their Cermak Plaza shopping mall. More notorious was the rebellion of sophisticated New Yorkers against the placement of Richard Serra's *Tilted Arc* in the square in front of their office building, where the work created a new community united in opposition to its planned rust and "site-specific" conception.[1] And the politics that accompanied the selection of Maya Lin's

---

1. See "The Storm in the Plaza" 1985; and Storr 1989.

design for the Vietnam Memorial in Washington, D.C., have been extensively documented.[2]

Is there public art in China? One might answer no, because there is no popular involvement, no public controversy in the selection and construction of such art works that would conform to Western notions of a vital "public sphere." Although such an answer might be in the spirit of much of the discussion of whether China has ever had a public sphere, it would also lead to a nonsensical conclusion: if the art put in public places by the current Chinese state is not public, what is it? It is assuredly not private.

China has an older public art far richer than the United States: grand architecture, arches, and stone-carved calligraphy have long been placed by the state in public spots for the elevation of popular morality. To such state monuments we may add temples as another kind of nonofficial yet still public art. In the twentieth century, a Western-influenced public sculpture joined the relics of past dynasties, making China awash in public art.[3] Thus, while the name is new the practice is not. States have commissioned art works as long as there have been states—indeed, our popular indications of ancient states flows from the pyramids and other glorious tombs for dead rulers.[4]

Western discussion of China's public sphere often confuses by conflating two separate ideas: public sphere and civil society. This misstep has an easily identifiable origin. After centuries of disuse, the archaic phrase "civil society" was revived in order to explain the collapse of Communist regimes in Russia and Eastern Europe, as scholars searched for sources of power apart from the state.[5] Students of modern China understandably began to look for evidence that the civil society hypothesis might also apply to China. Historians, political scientists, and sociologists began a debate about whether one could identify signs of autonomous or potentially autonomous social groups. The debate has been inconclusive but valuable for raising consciousness of certain issues. Perhaps unavoidably, the China discussion took as its starting point what is probably the brainiest discussion of civil society in Europe, the work of Jürgen Habermas.[6] Habermas links civil society tightly to his notion of the public sphere, which he regards as the realm where pri-

2. For example, see Abramson 1996; Wagner-Pacifici and Schwartz 1991.

3. On management of relics, see Beijingshi wenwu shiye guanliju 1990; and Murphy 1995. One hundred examples of new monuments selected as exemplars for "patriotic education" are illustrated in Duoji Cairan 1997.

4. One must also recall, however, that the most precious symbols of the old elite included small and personal "superfluous things," exquisitely portable jades and porcelains that were far better insurance against political disaster than monuments were. See Clunas 1991.

5. See Gellner 1994. In one useful formation, civil society is "a sphere of non-state-dominated public activity, a vantage point from which it is possible to reject the state's claims to authority and legitimacy while, in this very act, reaffirming the value of alternative social organizations, units, networks, or rituals." Shue 1992, p. 164.

6. Habermas 1989.

vate individuals come together to debate the rules that govern privatized relations.[7] In Europe, where civil society grew as the public sphere was transformed, it makes sense to join the concepts. In China, where the depth of civil society is open to considerable doubt, it makes less sense. China scholars need not join Habermas in coupling them so tightly. All societies have a public sphere. Although many China scholars have cautioned that civil society and public sphere are distinct concepts, the two are still bound together, so the debate often shifts unintentionally from civil society, which is richly debatable, to the question of public sphere, which seems less controversial.[8] The idea of a public sphere surely embraces many state-society combinations, including both premodern and contemporary Chinese autocracies. The evidence for a Chinese civil society is contestable; the existence of a Chinese public sphere is questioned only because of the China field's unhelpful obsession with Habermas.

I emphasize this point because we should not lose sight of the fact that the Chinese Communist Party reorganized Chinese society precisely to create a public sphere over which it could hold hegemonic power. Although the party has often been intolerant of even small signs of personal autonomy, many understand that it has now made "room for the personal and the private in a public sphere monopolized by the state."[9] It is this state-hegemonic public sphere that is the realm of public art in China today. Not only is there public art in a public sphere, but there is also a presumptive public to which the regime responds as it shapes this art. This public is still amorphous because it lacks the clear edges given by the political organizations and movements of a civil society. Any political activities that directly challenge the Chinese state remain at high risk. Yet the consumer revolution of the 1990s each year embraced more urban Chinese within the domain of the commodity as it transformed their personal lives. This sometimes active, often passive and presumptive public takes much of its present shape from emerging consumer society, embracing a set of social activities that the state encourages but that follow a different logic from accustomed Communist politics.

NANJING AS A LAYERED ARRAY OF RELICS

Primarily because of Nanjing's strategic location, at a narrowing of the Yangzi River that commands the approach to the rich Jiangnan plain, the city has repeatedly served as capital of China: the Kingdom of Wu during the Three

7. Ibid., p. 27.

8. For caution that China's premodern concept of *gong* is public, but not an equivalent for civil society, see Rowe 1993 and Rankin 1993. See also Huang 1991.

9. M. Yang 1994, p. 48.For a sample of public sphere discussion, see also Wakeman 1993; Wagner 1995; Wasserstrom and Liu 1995; and Wang et al. 1995.

Kingdoms period, the early Ming dynasty, the Taiping Heavenly Kingdom, the Republic of China, and the Japanese puppet regime of Wang Jingwei are the most notable. Choice location and imperial status have also brought the city massive human and physical destruction, most recently in its conquest by the Taiping rebels in 1853, Zeng Guofan's destruction of the Taiping Heavenly Kingdom in 1864, and the Japanese rape of Nanjing in 1937–38.[10]

The political history of Nanjing in the People's Republic remains unwritten.[11] The victorious Communists seem to have regarded Chiang Kaishek's former base with initial suspicion and disdain, and the city's status certainly declined as it was demoted from national capital to capital of Jiangsu Province. Proud buildings housing national ministries were given over to officials managing the parochial affairs of Jiangsu—the once grand supreme court building of the Guomindang (Nationalist Party), for instance, now rather shabbily houses the Jiangsu Grain Department. Natives speak of Beijing with some combination of envy and resentment, and of Shanghai, East China's dominant economic center, with enthusiastic distaste. Such feelings are not just the consequence of metropolitan loss of status but also have a material foundation. Shanghai enjoys a cap on the proportion of its revenues that must be turned over to the central government. Jiangsu province does not, and officials in Nanjing believe they contribute a disproportionate share of Beijing's total revenues.[12] Xu Shiyou, the often brutal commander of the Nanjing Military Region, kept the city under tight control during the Cultural Revolution. The military presence remains conspicuous. When the Fuzhou Military Region was abolished in the early 1980s as a friendly gesture toward Taiwan, its responsibilities and territory were transferred to Nanjing, whose command now stretches from the Jiangnan to the Straits of Taiwan. Some claim that one-sixth of the city's land is controlled by the army, and many of the local industries have a military connection, such as the huge Panda Electronics firm. After the Cultural Revolution, economic reform came relatively slowly to Nanjing, although it has accelerated dramatically since the early 1990s. Currently, the entire city seems under reconstruction, building atop an economic foundation strong in electronics and petrochemicals.

Nanjing's public spaces reflect this past, in a way found only in Beijing or

10. I know of no general account of cultural destruction in Nanjing. Jonathan D. Spence describes the Taiping burning of Daoist and Buddhist temples and the smashing of religious images in *God's Chinese Son: The Taiping Heavenly Kingdom of Hong Xiuquan* (Spence 1996, p. 176). Guomindang and Communist regimes later destroyed additional religious relics in drives against feudal superstition. For background on the monuments and relics of Nanjing, I have relied upon Fan Yuxi 1995; Chen Ping 1995; and Jiang Yongcai and Di Shuzhi 1991.

11. See McCormick 1990; Crane 1994; Xu Kaifu 1995.

12. Conversation with Bruce Jacobs, Nanjing, November 1, 1996. It may be that Nanjing resentment is unjustified in this instance.

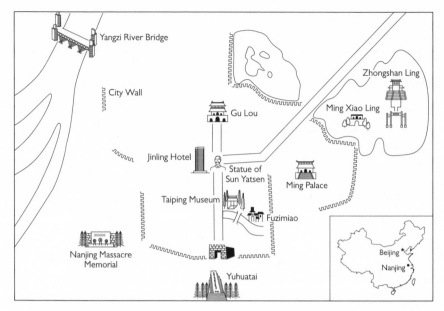

FIGURE 13.2.   Map of Nanjing, showing location of major relics, both old and new. (Map designed by Wang Haizhang)

Xi'an among China's great cities. One way of making visual and political sense of the city is through a fictive archaeological image in which the city's public monuments and parks form distinct strata. In this perspective, Nanjing consists of five layers of monuments. The first, representing imperial times, includes such relics as the tomb of the first Ming emperor, the ruins of his palace, and the Ming dynasty city wall. A second represents the short-lived Taiping Kingdom, which renamed the city "Tianjing" (Heavenly Capital), and whose chief marker is a museum in the former home of a Taiping general. The third stratum is the Republican era: the tomb of Sun Yat-sen, a monument to martyrs of the Northern Expedition, and Guomindang bureaucratic buildings scattered throughout the city. Fourth is the postrevolutionary city, which is symbolized by the stern revolutionary figures carved on the Nanjing bridge over the Yangzi and the martyr's monument at Yuhuatai. The newest and still living stratum is the reform period, which has produced a new statue of Sun Yat-sen at the city's commercial center of Xinjiekou (literally "the new intersection"), and high-rise commercial buildings that tower arrogantly over the relics of earlier eras (see Figure 13.2).

The array of relics is not just temporal, but spatial as well. A large amount of city space is given over to parkland, to be found in all six districts of the city. But the city's pride is Purple Mountain, an enormous public space on the eastern side of the city. Purple Mountain is a center for both relics and recreation, serving both as funeral ground for past rulers and as playground for contemporary citizens. Sun Quan of the Kingdom of Wu was the first monarch to be entombed there, in A.D. 252; the grandest tombs are for the Ming dynasty founder, Zhu Yuanzhang, and Sun Yat-sen. Nanjing is unusual among Chinese cities in having such easy access to a vast area for recreation, often a cooler spot in the city's notorious summer heat. The city center is laden with Republican-era architecture, as well as Ming and Qing relics. The major monuments erected in the Communist era are on the city's periphery, with the 1968 Yangzi River Bridge to the north, the Nanjing Massacre Memorial to the west, and the monument to 100,000 rebels executed by the Guomindang at Yuhuatai to the south (the east is blocked by Purple Mountain). It is as if the Communist government has enclosed Nanjing within a second city wall, this one of remembrances instead of bricks.

SORTING THE STONES OF MEMORY

At first view it appears that these public sites are historically determined. Yet state officials have considerable latitude in what they choose to celebrate and to ignore. The presentation of Nanjing's past is conscious: the state actively arranges the stones of memory. The public Nanjing of today is fashioned by four types of state action.

Highlighting Existing Relics

The state can favor one era over another in its representation of the glorious past. Nanjing's visual symbol is the blue-tiled tomb of Sun Yat-sen, which Chinese associate as readily with Nanjing as the Eiffel Tower with Paris or the Statue of Liberty with New York.[13] The tomb, located on a propitious site on the southern slope of Purple Mountain, was protected by the army during the Cultural Revolution, when radicals condemned the bourgeois Sun. Even though Purple Mountain is full of feudal relics, the tomb remained open. Yet the state took the precaution of covering the white-on-blue sun of the Guomindang, a symbol set repeatedly in the interior of the tomb. These coverings were removed after the Cultural Revolution as national policy toward Taiwan eased. Today, Nanjing plays a special ceremonial role in the protracted effort to reestablish links with Taiwan. Visitors from Taiwan are the most visible local tourists.

Similarly, the city wall of the Ming dynasty is being restored. Never very effective as a defensive structure, the 1366 wall is nonetheless visually impressive. Twenty-one of its original thirty-three kilometers remain; it is fourteen to twenty-six meters tall, and seven to fourteen meters wide at the top,

13. L. Wang 1996.

punctuated by several grand gates. Beijing destroyed its city wall during the Great Leap Forward, but Nanjing retained its wall and has restored places where it had been looted for building materials in recent years. Other relics have been recovered by easing out military and government offices. The Chaotiangong is a Ming dynasty palace built as a school to train young officials in court etiquette and was treasured by the public in the 1950s and 1960s, when it was open as a park. The People's Liberation Army occupied the palace during the Cultural Revolution, perhaps as much to enjoy as to protect its splendor. The army remained until 1986, when the city began restoration. Reopened in 1995, the palace has flourished anew as a public space; it is the weekend site of a busy sale of old books, curios, stamps, and Cultural Revolutionary memorabilia.

Here one should also note the state's highlighting of a relic that never was. Purple Mountain's greatest tombs are those of Sun Yat-sen and Ming founder Zhu Yuanzhang. Between them, in a spot no doubt redolent of cosmic geomancy (*fengshui*), is the place Chiang Kaishek selected for his own tomb, envisioning a glorious burial between two predecessors. Today there is an obscure trail up the mountainside to Chiang's would-be tomb, marked by no granite and only a simple sign that politely but condescendingly chronicles the defeated generalissimo's funerary fantasy.

Refurbishing Vanished Relics

The recreation of relics once destroyed is a second and closely related official strategy. The oldest part of Nanjing is the Confucian temple (*fuzimiao*) neighborhood in the southern part of the city, a district of shops, restaurants, and sellers of snacks and trinkets, where people go to hang out in their spare time. Although the neighborhood retains the remnant of an imperial examination hall, the Confucian temple, founded in 1034, was destroyed once during the Taiping struggles and burned again by the Japanese invaders. The Confucian temple district thus had no temple at its center until Nanjing began its newest reconstruction in 1986. Because this was not a high time in popular reverence for Confucius, it seems likely that its construction was aimed at appealing to tourists. The Disney-like interior of the temple reinforces such a view. It is not a true relic but a simulacrum of a relic, with performances of "Confucian" dances by students (including women, for a very un-Confucian touch), who resemble a kind of decorous Chinese cheerleading team. A similar neorelic is the statue of Confucius on the campus of Nanjing Teachers' University, donated by Taiwan in 1994 from its vast oversupply.

The newest refurbished relic is the Jinghai Temple where the Treaty of Nanjing was negotiated in 1842, ending the Opium War and opening China to Western trade. The temple, once home to Zheng He, the famous Ming admiral and explorer, was destroyed by fire in the 1930s. Reconstruction was impossible under wartime conditions, and the People's Republic was slow to deal with this symbol of China's past humiliation. But as Nanjing's contribution to the nationwide celebration over the return of Hong Kong, the old temple was reconstructed and outfitted with a new bell to ring the British from their Chinese colony in the summer of 1997. But it is a temple without gods or clergy, and its main hall is filled with an exhibition on the impact of imperialism on Nanjing.

Inventing New Relics

The state also actively creates new relics to fill new political needs. An obvious example of relic creation is the project launched in the early 1980s to create new urban sculpture that would symbolize the spirit of the post–Cultural Revolution era. I term these "maidens of modernization," because their most typical manifestation is a young woman questing for science and modernity. *Fine Arts* (*Meishu*), the official visual arts journal, devoted an entire issue to promoting outdoor urban sculpture, with illustrations from Warsaw to Rome and Mount Rushmore.[14] By 1984, seventeen provinces had set up leadership groups to plan new urban sculpture, as the reform regime sought to refurbish urban China with an uplifting set of new monuments.[15] In addition to symbolizing a change in political mood, the project was intended to add a quick bit of at least superficial beauty to China's cities, long deprived of new construction. Sculptors, as creators of relics, were especially enthusiastic about the project, which has left maidens of modernization scattered about the streets of Nanjing and all Chinese cities.

A still fresher example of a new relic is no maiden but a 5.75 meter bronze statue of Sun Yat-sen, unveiled on the 130th anniversary of his birth, November 12, 1996 (see Figure 13.3). Situated in the middle of the Xinjiekou traffic circle, the heart of Nanjing's commercial district, this statue is truly a relic, both in its nineteenth-century Western bronze realist appearance and in its ideological suggestion. The modern history of this public space is curious. This Sun Yat-sen replaces an earlier incarnation, which was cast by a Japanese sculptor and placed at the intersection by Wang Jingwei's puppet government in 1942. The Japanese statue lasted until it was removed for its own protection early in the Cultural Revolution; it now stands on Purple Mountain in front of a Sun Yat-sen museum. The Xinjiekou circle was empty for two decades, then graced with a modernist work in 1989, a set of abstract keys, perhaps to unlock the future or the heart of the city. These proved unsuccessful as an emblem for the heart of Nanjing, and the new cane-wielding Sun was ordered.

14. See "Rang diaosu yishu wei meihua chengshi fuwu" 1981 and the other articles in this issue.

15. Situ Zhaoguang and Cao Chunsheng 1984.

FIGURE 13.3.
This new statue of
Sun Yat-sen stands
in Nanjing's busiest
intersection, where
once the Japanese
puppet government
had installed another
statue of Sun. (Photo
by Richard Kraus)

Two monuments to China's complex interaction with Japan form an unconventional pair of new relics. One is the memorial to the 300,000 victims of the Nanjing massacre. This structure, part statue garden, part museum, is quite successful at capturing the horror of the rape of Nanjing. The predominantly abstract bas-relief of the memorial's walls is countered by a defiantly socialist-realist figure of a grieving and unforgiving mother (Figure 13.4). The latter figure is placed away from the wall in a way reminiscent of the American Vietnam Memorial's inclusion of realist figures of soldiers away from the nonrepresentational wall of names, and, like those American soldiers, was added after the completion of the original monument. The massacre memorial is alone among the monuments of Nanjing in not being in a park or other public space. It is in a light industrial neighborhood to the West of the city where thousands of civilians were killed, an unlikely destination for anyone except those commemorating a horrible event. Japanese friends

FIGURE 13.4.   A realist figure in the courtyard of the memorial to the victims of the Nanjing massacre. (Photo by Richard Kraus)

have told me of being taken somewhat unwillingly to this site. In contrast, prime Purple Mountain space next to the tomb of Zhu Yuanzhang has been allotted to a new (1992) forest of stele called the Yan Zhenqing garden, in memory of the great Tang dynasty calligrapher who is much emulated in Japan. The inscribed characters, all by Japanese calligraphers, are arranged before a statue of Yan; the garden is a quiet and lovely spot to celebrate Sino-Japanese cultural amity. These two monuments, both of which received Japanese funding, have quite obviously different uses as China shifts between its feelings of friendship and hostility toward its East Asian neighbor and rival.

FIGURE 13.5.   Wang Jingwei, who betrayed China to Japan, kneels in silent re-
pentance at the site of his former tomb on Nanjing's Purple Mountain. (Photo by
Richard Kraus)

A final new relic adds further complexity to the symbolic representation
of relations with Japan. Wang Jingwei, renegade Guomindang leader and
head of Japan's puppet government during the war, died in Japan in 1944.
His body was shipped back to China, where it was entombed on Purple
Mountain, near the graves of Sun Quan, Ming Taizu, Sun Yat-sen, and several Guomindang worthies. After Japan's defeat, outraged Guomindang
troops blew up Wang's grave. In 1989, Nanjing officials commissioned a
statue of Wang, who is depicted kneeling in shame (see Figure 13.5). A
highly realistic life-sized figure of Wang, dressed in glasses and the formal
Western clothes worn by Japanese politicians, kneels behind a fence, head
bowed. He faces the northeast—toward Tokyo—and is out of alignment with
the southern exposure of the mountain's geomancy (*fengshui*). A sign urges
visitors not to spit on the statue, which of course eggs them on. China's most
famous "Do not spit on the statue" sign is in Hangzhou, posted alongside
an image of Qin Gui, the Southern Song official who conspired against the
patriotic general Yue Fei. Over the centuries good patriots have displayed
their continuing hatred of Qin Gui by spitting on his statue in the Yue Fei
temple.

Demonumentalization

Finally, the Chinese state can either destroy relics or downplay their significance. Surprisingly few signs of the former Nationalist capital remain, and those that survive are not marked. Guomindang planners, inspired by thoughts of Paris and Washington, D.C., intended to rebuild Nanjing as a modern world city, escaping the *fengshui*-bound conventions of city planning found in Beijing.[16] They constructed a series of grand government buildings throughout the city, combining such modern construction materials as prestressed concrete and the big roofs associated with China's traditional architecture.[17] When writer Guo Moruo visited Nanjing in 1945, he viewed this new architecture with disdain, complaining of its disproportion to "the context of underdeveloped Nanjing." Amidst a low traditional cityscape and the desolation of wartime destruction "suddenly there emerge some enormously colossal, Chinese-Western combined palatial-style buildings."[18] Half a century of economic growth has now cut these "palatial-style buildings" down to size, as new highrise construction has turned them into odd little islands of tiled roofs.

Memories of the Taiping Heavenly Kingdom are relegated to one threadbare museum today. Yet the Communists once valued the Taipings as revolutionary precursors. The Taiping museum's displays still carry the now quaintly heroic language of muscular proletarianism and anti-imperialist indignation that formerly flourished in China's public spaces.[19] Other sites associated with the Taipings that could be celebrated are not. Nanjing bookstores are more likely to carry volumes about Zeng Guofan, who destroyed the rebellion and its capital, than about the Taiping emperor Hong Xiuquan.

Another major monument celebrating revolution is the Yangzi River Bridge, adorned with giant workers, peasants, and soldiers all captured in steely resolve in 1968. The bridge, once China's proudest construction achievement, may well be destroyed, not intentionally to efface its political message but because it is not high enough to permit the passage of 10,000-ton ships into the upper Yangzi after the completion of the Three Gorges Dam. Thus the expanding commodity economy will erase a now rather bumpy emblem of revolution.

Then there are the Mao statues. During the Cultural Revolution, Nanjing had two prominent Mao statues on the campuses of Dongnan and Hehai

16. Cody 1996; Musgrove 1996. On Beijing, see Wu Hung 1991.

17. For the continuing appeal of big roofs for Chinese architects, see Zha 1995, pp. 68–70.

18. Musgrove 1996, p. 34, translating Guo's *Nanjing yinxiang* [Impressions of Nanjing] (Litong chubanshe, n.d.), p. 3.

19. The Taiping exhibition was replaced in the summer of 1997 for a presumably temporary Hong Kong display.

FIGURE 13.6.   These semi-abstract dancing figures of welcome were demoted from a major traffic circle to a high-school courtyard. (Photo by Richard Kraus)

Universities. The erection of a Mao statue symbolized a peace in factional warfare, when contending sides could unite in a common project. Nanjing University never erected a Mao statue because its factional problems were so severe. The removal of the Mao statues in the 1980s dememorialized the Cultural Revolution, just as the earlier removal of lesser Guomindang statuary after 1949 symbolized the fall of that party.

The most recent subjects of demonumentalization are the maidens of modernization. After their introduction in the early 1980s, the statues became something of a plague upon the land, revealing a lack of imagination and often poor quality of materials, and now people seem to be a little tired of them.[20] Perhaps more fundamental is popular disinterest in what is often

20. Geremie Barmé describes some of the controversies over these statues in Barmé 1988.Sculptor Wang Keqing argued that new state funding for urban sculpture created greater demand than China's 500 trained sculptors could meet. He established a new "China Sculptural Arts Research Institute," which he pledged would help "in any way it can to prevent inferior sculptures from seeing the light of day." Zhong 1989.

Russian-inspired quasi-abstract art. The sculptor of the keys that preceded the new Sun Yat-sen statue in Xinjiekou traffic circle was chagrined; after a debate about the quality of his work, his keys were sold to a technical school in another Jiangsu city. Moreover, another of his works—an abstract group of shiny steel women dancing in a circle with joined hands—has been demoted from the center of a major traffic circle to the courtyard of a middle school (see Figure 13.6).[21] Many modernization maidens remain, but they seem unlikely to endure as symbols of Nanjing.

HEGEMONY LITE

Contemporary China is certainly not the first state to sort the stones of memory for political advantage. Nanjing has been built, destroyed, and rebuilt, often according to political plan, for two thousand years. Recent scholarship on Western cities shows a similar uncovering and concealing of layered historical spaces within the urban landscape. M. Christine Boyer describes "the city of collective memory" in which "different layers of historical time superimposed on each other or different architectural strata (touching but not necessarily informing each other) no longer generate a structural form to the city, but merely culminate in an experience of diversity."[22] The confusing juxtaposition of restoration projects

> forged a hybrid layering of architectural sites and a constant migration from one time period to another. This layering recoups many urban scenes for commercial or civil intent, situating the spectator between official narrations and more personal experiences or memories of city places. There is a constant oscillation established between any conventional and imaginary urban vision, a shimmering that produces both pleasurable and disturbing experiences.[23]

Dolores Hayden, in her study of Los Angeles, shows how an elite-dominated history of built space has excluded ordinary working people, but that such an unsettled and unsettling environment can facilitate the reclaiming of contested sites and memories.[24] China's public sphere is less dynamic, revealing less open controversy and debate. The state enforces at least the appearance of hegemony over public art, yet the situation is far from static; the divergent connotations of competing images elicit a "shimmering" that alternately pleases and unsettles.

By American standards, there is surprisingly little grumbling about unpopular works. Yet we know that Chinese can act out their feelings about

---

21. Interview with sculptor Zhang Jing, professor at Nanjing Arts College, May 28, 1996.
22. Boyer 1994, p. 19.
23. Ibid., p. ix.
24. Hayden 1995.

public art. Consider an episode from Hong Kong, a capitalist city perhaps understocked with monuments. On September 16, 1996, Poon Singlui attacked the four-meter statue of Queen Victoria in Victoria Park. After denting her nose with a hammer blow, he poured red paint over the statue. Victoria had sat in Hong Kong since 1887, surviving a near-death experience in an Osaka military scrap heap during World War II. After psychiatric evaluation, Poon served 28 days in jail. Poon is an artist, a graduate of Beijing's Central College of Arts and Crafts, and was a recent emigrant to Hong Kong. At the time of his vandalism, his proposed entry had been turned down by a major Hong Kong exhibition, although he had won (but did not yet know about) a generous fellowship from a French foundation. Poon seems to have misread the indifference of Hong Kong toward the departing British colonialists, because he justified his act as a blow against "colonial art." Victoria had in fact been vandalized with more convincing anti-imperialist sentiment in 1968 and 1978. This time, few were amused, and no one seemed convinced by his conscious likening of his act to patriotically spitting on the Hangzhou statue of Qin Gui.[25]

What is striking about Poon's act is that this kind of public art protest, familiar enough in the West, is nearly unknown in the People's Republic. Among the few recent exceptions are three Hunanese (including a 22-year-old artist) who were jailed for throwing ink-filled eggs at Mao Zedong's Tiananmen portrait in 1989 and Tibetan protestors who blew up a monument to Chinese road builders in 1995.[26] There are likely some other examples, but they are infrequent. The most common monument modifications have been official, such as the removal of Mao statues in the 1980s and the violent removal of Lin Biao's calligraphy from the plinths of these statues after his death and disgrace in 1971.[27] Nanjing's artists complain of being misunderstood, that officials are poorly educated in art, and that the state is more interested in designs for public toilets than public art, but their work is not physically attacked by a hostile public.[28]

Public passivity toward the state's chosen symbols is part of a greater avoidance of the political that runs deep in Chinese society and is felt especially powerfully in the aftermath of the 1989 Beijing massacre. Yet the state tries to avoid eliciting protest by avoiding unconventional art that might become a focus for discontent. The Chinese state has been more proactive in shaping its hegemony over the public sphere than we often imagine. The exam-

25. See Lo 1996; Moir and Lee 1996; Chin 1996a and 1996b; Wan 1996.

26. A Chinese monument to road builders in the western suburbs of Lhasa was bombed three times in 1995. See Tatlow 1996.

27. See Kraus 1991, pp. 111–12.

28. William Cohen, describes an era of "statumania" in which the left favored monuments to Rousseau and Voltaire and the right favored Jean d'Arc, while rival mobs destroyed symbols cherished by both sides. Cohen 1989.

ples I have introduced from contemporary Nanjing suggest that this hegemony is not cast in stone but constantly changing, precisely so that the state can deploy its symbols for changing political needs, such as policy toward Japan. There is also some limited responsiveness to public feelings, as in the removal of the Mao statues, the toning down of the cult of the Taiping Rebellion, the ongoing recycling of the unpopular maidens of modernization, and the state's decision, after consulting the masses, to turn the new Sun Yat-sen statue to face south instead of north.[29]

The relationship between public art and ideology is neither simple nor direct. The state deploys its monuments about the city, but one must not presume that bureaucrats are following a coherent plan as they erect new plinths and restore old walls. Instead, there is a quiet and ongoing negotiation as the state seeks to convince citizens that *its* monuments are *theirs*. If public art is to be successful as ideology, it should not be message art. The Chinese state seemingly wants to avoid upsetting citizens with public symbols that are radically out of harmony with their common-sense understanding of the world. For instance, there are no statues of model soldier Lei Feng, or exemplary bus conductors, or living political leaders, any of which might attract rude markings some night in the park.

The Chinese state imposes an official memory on Nanjing, but that is not identical to a public memory. Rubie Watson has described the private mourning that continues for the victims of still-controversial public events, such as the cultural revolution and the 1989 Beijing massacre.[30] The difference between a state-organized official memory and the memories shared by China's citizens suggests that the regime may no longer have the capacity to impose anything more than hegemony lite, the real thing having become too difficult to digest. To understand this, we must examine the activities of citizens in Nanjing's public spaces.

CONSUMING PUBLIC ART:
PUBLIC PURPOSES AND PRIVATE DESIRES

What does this system of art in public places have to do with China's new consumer society? Put another way, how does one consume a relic? Old or new, these monuments and structures are not consumer goods; China has yet to give rise to an entrepreneur of monuments like Christo. Indeed, monuments are the least commodified of arts products. They are dead, passive, conservative, and huge, in contrast to the living and active consumers. Monuments are

29. He faced north at first, apparently because Sun died before completing his Northern Expedition to unify the nation; in the end he faces south because traditional *fengshui* dictates that men of power should have homes, tombs, and apparently statues facing south.

30. R. Watson 1994.

designed to appeal to some higher purpose than shopping, one of the eternal verities such as national glory, revolutionary dedication, or religious faith.

Most of the new consumption of culture is done privately, at home: watching television, reading books, listening to music, painting. More public are concerts and dancing.[31] This brings us back to the dancers and why they tango in the ruins of the Ming Palace. Monuments enter the consumer economy indirectly; people must pay money to enter the parks around which these items are often built. Entrance fees vary, but may range between five mao and eight renminbi, neither a great expense nor a trivial amount, especially if one adds bus fare to reach a distant park. Just as in the class-riven consumer society outside the parks, not everyone in China can afford to "consume" relics.

Chinese citizens bring their consumption to the parks because their homes are small and lack privacy ("public" space may offer greater opportunity for confidential conversations than a crowded apartment), because the parks provide a convenient destination for group outings, and because Chinese have long enjoyed simply hanging out and observing society's spectacle (*kan renao*). The public purpose of these sites is secondary to private desires. One goes to Purple Mountain on a pretty Saturday or Sunday not because dead rulers are buried there but because the place is green, unpolluted, and pleasant. At best, the dead rulers lend the park prestige as a destination. On one outing, my hosts brought along an inflatable raft, which their daughter used in an artificial lake built during the Republican era. With campfires in the distance and the sounds of music wafting across the lake, the atmosphere was much like that in an American state park.[32]

Certainly other nearby spots reveal personal pleasures mixed with the state displays that provide their setting. At the reopened Meiling Villa, built by Chiang Kaishek for his wife, Song Meiling, an elderly woman posed in a colossal old American car for a photograph, her face beaming at her temporary occupation of the dictator's vehicle. At the statue of Wang Jingwei, teenage boys were the first to defy the posted request not to spit, as they made a game of their youthful patriotism.

It is to the parks that Chinese bring their consumer goods for display. Chinese dress up to go to public places. No one adopts the American-style camping look; one especially notices the women, many of whom wear elaborate

31. Wang Weiming (1996) discusses phenomena of the new consumer economy, including: hair salons, karaoke, fast food, up-market curio shops, pubs, karaoke TV, private clubs, exclusive addresses, foreign hotels, nightclubs, exercise machines, DHL, credit cards, pedigreed dogs, satellite television, Christmas cards, running shoes, children's toys, pop music, imported automobiles, etc. Most of these items are for private consumption, either in one's home or in a club or restaurant. Thomas Gold (1993) reminds us that the popular culture imported from Hong Kong and Taiwan stresses personal messages quite different from those of official culture.

32. An observation made by Steven Levine.

dresses and high heels, even when climbing Yellow Mountain in neighboring Anhui. Taking one's child or grandchild to the park is of course an escape, a loving outing, but it also represents an escalation in conspicuous consumption, as kiddies are treated to food, balloons, rides, and other material goodies.

One way of reading the relationship between public monument and private consumption is the metaphor of offerings to the gods. A feature of Chinese popular religion is food left by worshipers on the altars of the deities (or the burning of paper money and goods in effigy for the dead). The citizens of Nanjing bring their new consumer goods into the sacred precincts of the public to frolic before the monuments and to dance among the ruins. A tango in the faded splendor of the Ming Palace juxtaposes two displays, one a state-sanctioned commemoration of the past, the other a group of individuals delighting in their personal pleasures.

It is perhaps tempting to read this as popular celebration of the victory of joyous consumer society over dour collectivist state. But the relationship between state and consumer today is far less antagonistic than in the 1960s, when radicals warned their fellow citizens to be watchful of the subversive behavior of bad elements in parks, where one might find wearers of pointed shoes and other bourgeois fashions, idlers playing chess, and signs of illicit romance.[33] This officially sanctioned suspicion of parks persisted after the Cultural Revolution. It was not until nearly 1980 that officials felt comfortable removing the ubiquitous public address systems that had filled parks with martial music and newspaper editorials and further diminished the space for private activities within public spaces.[34] In contrast to the Maoist era, when the state's legitimacy rested in part on its promise to uphold revolutionary and socialist values, the Chinese state of the 1990s based its claim to rule on its success at increasing consumer goods and thus welcomed the dancers.

Many believe that nationalism has replaced collectivism as the core of the regime's ideology, pointing to the regime's manipulation of an image of a newly truculent and jingoistic China.[35] Yet in Nanjing, a city that has suffered from Japanese rape and looting as well as shelling by British and American gunboats, there is surprisingly little open display of nationalism. The abundance of relics from China's imperial and revolutionary heritage could eas-

33. For example, see the polemic by Red Guards of Beijing Mao Zedong-ism School 1967. Wang Shaoguang (1995) discusses the formerly dubious reputation of parks. For an account of more recent park activity, see Chen 1995.

34. I discuss this phenomenon in Kraus 1989, p. 183.

35. Note the popularity of *China Can Say No* (Song Qiang, Zhang Cangcang, and Qiao Bian 1996) and its imitators, readily available from street stalls throughout Nanjing and in other cities.

ily be used in support of openly nationalist sentiment. Nationalism might well be popular, but it is also difficult to control. The complexities of diplomacy compel the state to impose limits on nationalism amid the symbols of power. In 1996, for instance, Nanjing University students were warned not to demonstrate against Japan's occupation of the contested Diaoyudao (or Senkaku Islands).

An alternative to orchestrated nationalism is managed consumerism. Consumerism is also difficult for the state to control, but China's present leaders might easily prefer it to nationalism. Demonstrations against Japan or the United States might easily lead to broader social protest, but it is more difficult to imagine demonstrators demanding more imported televisions or the faster creation of new supermarkets. Consumerism's threat to state hegemony is long term, not sudden. With consumerism as an underlying ideology, the state's claim to legitimacy rests on a promise of economic performance similar to that of governments in Japan and the West.

Public space as a site for the popular celebration of consumption directly beneath the sober monuments of the state is a logical pairing, if initially an awkward one. Citizens, in entertaining themselves privately, reinforce the real new public foundation for the regime. The state's cost may be the loss of some dignity, since one space in urban China that can often be turned to commercial use is at the foot of a monument. Such loss of dignity only mirrors the problems faced by high culture at large in China today, but poses no threat to the political order.

In any event, it is not certain that consumerism will always triumph over monumentality. There is probably some core of the public monument experience that cannot be reduced to an aspect of commodity society. Many visitors to the martyr's shrine at Yuhuatai are teary-eyed, and a visit to the memorial to the Nanjing massacre cannot be turned into a lighthearted outing. A large number of Nanjing adults have memories of childhood visits to their city's solemn monuments as part of Youth League rituals. In the 1960s, for instance, Youth League members laid white flowers at the Yuhuatai martyr's monument—the place of mass graves of revolutionaries executed by the Guomindang. Such rituals may no longer seem important to them, but the sites are forever inscribed with memories more ardent and serious than tango dancing. Groups of pilgrims visit the tomb of Sun Yat-sen much as Americans tourists visit Mount Vernon or Lincoln's tomb on trips that are part frolic and part lesson in national heritage. The Chinese state encourages a solemn atmosphere within Sun's tomb, but with less success than at Mao Zedong's mausoleum in Beijing. The sober mood inside the tomb seems to be evidence that the state can inscribe its meaning in public places, although Sun Yat-sen is a popular figure not just because of state promotion of his cult—the cult may have been chosen because it would be popular. In any event, the mere presence of Sun's body may be enough in itself to quiet most crowds.

PUBLIC SQUARES AND PUBLIC SPHERES

There is a political affinity between the physical space of the public square and the metaphorical space of the public sphere. Nanjing's public spaces are the site of an ongoing yet quiet renegotiation of the relationship between state symbols and private desires. Parks and other public spaces are the spots under the strictest state supervision, the public face of the city where the state most wants to maintain its hegemony, yet where this state shares its most solemn monuments with the private activities of consuming citizens.

Ping-hui Liao, in an article on Taiwan's February 28 Incident (the 1947 massacre of perhaps 20,000 Taiwanese civilians by Chiang Kaishek's army), offers a helpful way out of the dilemma of the state's superficial control over the public sphere.[36] Liao suggests that it may be more helpful to look for multiple public spheres—one dominated by the government and at least superficially hegemonic, and alternative "counterpublic spheres." He argues that the political need to deal with the February 28 massacre is a part of a struggle to control the public sphere in Taiwan. It is possible that someday there may be a comparable process in the People's Republic of China because of a need to deal in public with the June 4, 1989, massacre in Beijing. But even without this kind of debate, it is helpful to consider the idea of multiple, flexible, and changing public spheres.[37] As in our conception of civil society, our concern for "a single, overarching public sphere" stems from Habermas, whom Nancy Fraser criticizes for not recognizing that "the proliferation of a multiplicity of publics" may be more democratic than "the institutional confinement of public life to a single, overarching public sphere."[38]

We can find indications of such institutional flux in Nanjing's public sphere. The public square was, like the rest of the public sphere, a realm for controversy in the 1980s. In that decade, cultural debate was in the air throughout China and made its way into new art of the public square. The quasi-abstract new monuments of that decade, which I have labeled maidens of modernization, were erected to symbolize the four modernizations as a break with the Maoist past. Artists and officials alike enjoyed greater confidence in the future and a newfound willingness to deal with at least limited controversy.[39] Contention accompanied these statues because they were abstract and also because their sculptors frequently employed nudity

36. Liao 1993.

37. Bryna Goodman argues that the public sphere / civil society discussion often introduced too passive a view of Chinese society during the Republican era and calls for a focus on "interpenetration and shifting strategic boundaries" instead of "oppositional forces and absolute notions of autonomy." Goodman 1996, p. 165.

38. N. Fraser 1992, p. 122.

39. Julia F. Andrews and Gao Minglu (1995) trace this daringness of the 1980s in oil painting.

to shock, to make names for themselves, and to show that they could break through barriers into a previously forbidden zone. Today the maidens look a bit shopworn, often because they were made with inferior materials. The newer public art is representational, safe, and boring. This is partly a matter of the times, of lying low in an era when "political stability" is prized above all public virtues.

But there is an aesthetic reason as well, if the experience of the West is any guide. Murray Edelman argues that modernist art contributed to the rise of skepticism in politics, undermining legitimacy in government. The decline of human-centered art meant a decline in the centrality of reason in aesthetics:

> In contrast to the optimism that was a dominant note in the nineteenth century, these judgments question the possibility of certain knowledge and the likelihood of progress, define the human subject as a peripheral construction rather than the center of the social world, see reason and instrumental intelligence as inherently flawed and look upon language as a form of action that can contribute to any kind of result rather than as a means to promote rationality. These developments are related as well to the marked disillusionment in public postures toward the state and other social institutions, and have helped to particularize and spread such disillusionment.[40]

If Edelman is correct, official suspicion of modernism in public art may be justified, if likely ineffectual. But by turning away from this one new direction in public art, the state has demonstrated the diminishing vitality of its chosen public symbols, in contrast again to the vigor of private consumption. What could be more dull and detached than a new statue of Sun Yatsen? It may well be that the Chinese state is simply too fearful and too exhausted to imagine and propagate meaningful public symbols. For all the *talk* of socialist ethics, visual expressions of the values of a socialist spiritual civilization are difficult to identify, thereby underscoring its shallow roots.

THE RECONFIGURATION OF PUBLIC SPACE

Another Nanjing development underscores the tentativeness of state hegemony in the public sphere. Wu Hung, in his fine analysis of Tiananmen Square as public space, reminds us that every Chinese city, however small, must have a public square.[41] Yet Nanjing has in fact destroyed its square. The former focal point for parades, official demonstrations, and popular protests was the Drum Tower. Until the early 1980s, there was a reviewing stand by the Drum Tower; but it vanished, along with much of the space, when city

40. Edelman 1995, p. 22.
41. Wu Hung 1991, p. 90.

officials built a vehicular tunnel under the Drum Tower traffic circle in 1995. A newly landscaped park may actually expand the total open space, but it is less welcoming to potential demonstrators, especially with the addition of a police station and the installation of video cameras for surveillance. One Nanjing intellectual commented that demonstrations could now be held in the Wutaishan sports stadium (originally a Guomindang project), and anyway, there were not so many demonstrations anymore. Demobilization of the populace is facilitated by making sure this public square will not become a part of anyone's counterhegemonic public sphere.

The relationship between public sphere and public square has become physical: the state's officials can rest comfortably only if they physically restrict public squares in order to ensure lack of protest of the hegemony lite that fills the public sphere. Public squares always occupy prime real estate, with new commercial uses challenging the no longer urgent public demand for them as places to hold meetings. Rising urban property values and a politics of demobilization combine to change the shape and sometimes reduce the physical size of the urban turf that once most symbolized Communist rule.

Is Nanjing representative? There will of course be local variations in the role public spaces play in sustaining and reinforcing the new ideology of consumption. In cities with long winters, the parks can be used for less of the year, whereas in Nanjing they are accessible year-round. Many cities lack the density of historical relics found in Nanjing, but other kinds of monuments can mark public space just as easily. Hints from other cities suggest that similar processes are under way elsewhere.

Shanghai's People's Square, once a British race track and then a parade ground for mass rallies after 1949, has been renovated. A new city office building has replaced the reviewing stand, and across the square stands the striking new Shanghai Museum; a performing arts center was completed in 1998. An underground shopping mall operates beneath the park, whose formerly open spaces have been replaced by benches, sinuous walks, and signs urging visitors to keep off the grass, which grows behind fences. It is a rather nice space, but no longer easily usable by demonstrators. Fuzhou's vast May First Square, where thousands protested in the spring of 1989 beneath a statue of Mao, a relic of the Cultural Revolution. Mao still stands, but the square has been planted with trees, creating a pleasant urban forest that makes protest nearly impossible. The city of Tianjin has gone a step further: Haihe Square, former seat of political demonstrations, was sold to a foreign company for property development in the early 1990s.

China's most celebrated and notorious public space, Beijing's Tiananmen Square, is under constant electronic surveillance, which may affect the public expression of private desires. The state has not yet dared to begin decommissioning Tiananmen Square, although there are hints of a changed

FIGURE 13.7. The yard of Nanjing's Sculpture World displays its diverse wares: abstract cubes, maidens of modernization, vigorous young workers, and lions that look suspiciously more like vestiges of the British than the Chinese empire. (Photo by Richard Kraus)

status. Foreign tour groups are now given lunch at the once sacred Great Hall of the People, and the part of the square before the Great Hall is now often turned into a temporary parking lot for high officials attending meetings. It is not difficult to imagine further encroachment on Tiananmen Square, the focal point of concentrated political and commercial pressure, from the installation of Mao's corpse in 1977 to the need to service tourists today. Beijing's "Democracy Wall," admittedly only a second choice for demonstrators in 1979 and never a sacred site of the revolution, now has a Pizza Hut where excited crowds once read big-character posters.

The retreat of the state is complemented by the extension of the private. One could argue that the real new monuments of Nanjing are the commercial and office towers that dwarf all else. When the Jinling Hotel was opened in 1987, it attracted rural visitors who just stood and gaped at this first high-rise building in a city dominated by horizontal structures. A decade later more sophisticated visitors visited the Golden Eagle Building, the most luxurious of new shopping emporia.

Another trend with a similar outcome is the appearance of private parks for the wealthy. The Nanjing Equestrian Academy offers horseback riding for the elite (I visited one fine spring day when the other guests were the entire party leadership of the neighboring city of Zhenjiang). Other cities have developed more private play areas, including theme parks and golf courses, but the impact is to create privatized spaces far outside the system that official monuments share with private consumption.

In contrast to the state's public-art monuments, there has emerged a curious species of private quasi-monumental art. Nanjing's Sculpture World is a private firm that sells large statues—Mao Zedong, Venus di Milo, Santa Claus, abstract black cubes atop bright red bases (labeled "modern" in English), and a variety of Roman-looking deities (see Figure 13.7). Some of these end up on private grounds, while others are placed on commercial buildings, thus blurring the distinction between the public and private spheres.

One Nanjing restaurant features a five-meter naked Roman deity staring down on the passing crowd. The Big Shot (*da renwu*) restaurant displays over its entrance a giant head of a sleek and mustachioed entrepreneur, truly a monument to consumer China. Initially I wondered if commercial advertising provided a private alternative to public monuments. But most citizens have learned to tune most of it out, just as Western citizens of consumer societies do, or for that matter just as Chinese had earlier developed a talent for tuning out political propaganda. These private neorelics are a different matter and echo the state's monuments in their scale and manufactured antiquity. Yet they are so obviously bogus and commercial, like the counterfeit Xi'an terra-cotta soldiers that guard still another restaurant, that their fantasy perhaps reminds citizens that the state's monuments are the real thing. This is the kind of uniquely urban ambiguity that M. Christine Boyer identified as "a shimmering." The spectator/participant simultaneously encounters official narratives and private sensations of the identical place. The experience is pleasurable to contemplate, yet obscure and sometimes disturbing to assess. The tango dancers cannot easily be brought into sharp focus through this shimmering; they move with private grace, but what is their offering to the graven deities of the state? Can we—or they—always tell the difference between dancers and demonstrators?

CHAPTER 14

Epilogue

The Second Liberation

Richard Madsen

In the historiographical vocabulary of the People's Republic of China, the victory of the Communists in 1949 is termed "the Liberation." The Communist Party's claim to legitimacy was at bottom a claim to have brought freedom to the Chinese people. This Liberation through political revolution had several dimensions. First, it brought the most fundamental freedoms—freedom from the violence of external aggression and internal political chaos and freedom from the hunger and preventable diseases that had plagued the Chinese people throughout the first half of the twentieth century. But Liberation brought not simply freedoms *from* but positive freedoms *for*—freedom for collective building of a strong and proud nation and freedom for personal fulfillment through an expansion of one's capacities for serving the people.

In the first few years of Communist rule, the freedoms promised by Liberation did indeed seem meaningful to many, perhaps most, Chinese. The imposition of order brought welcome relief to a population weary of war; a stabilized economy helped satisfy basic nutritional needs; incipient public health programs brought hope for further improvements in the physical quality of life. Moreover, China did indeed seem to be on the way to becoming a powerful nation that could demand the grudging respect of its competitors. Chinese troops helped fight the Americans to a standoff on the Korean peninsula. At the Bandung Conference of 1954, China emerged as one of the leaders of the nonaligned countries of the emerging Third World. And for many ordinary Chinese, the early 1950s brought personal agency as well. Many farmers had an opportunity to move from the countryside to the city to staff expanding government bureaucracies and industrial enterprises. In spite of tight political and ideological structures, many people felt the per-

sonal satisfaction of upward mobility and were able to assume broader responsibilities than they had ever dreamed of.

These new freedoms of course rested on a foundation of constraint. Freedom from insecurity and hunger for the majority was made possible by the
imposition of a totalitarian political system justified in part by the need to
carry out relentless class warfare on landlords, the bourgeoisie, and "coun-
terrevolutionaries." The Maoist mode of nation-building demanded the subordination of individual interests to the collective. Upward mobility was based
not so much on individual entrepreneurship as on the patronage of superiors in the political hierarchy.

Nonetheless, relative to the chaos, national humiliation, and personal
helplessness felt by many before Liberation, the new freedoms seemed genuine and important to many. There is indeed a relativity built in to all experience of freedom. There is no such thing as pure, absolute liberty. Living a coherent life in a complex society always entails constraints. The
experience of freedom entails leaving behind one set of constraints while
accepting another. The experience tends to be transitory. It often happens
that relentless political and economic logics tighten the constraints on
members of society. Moreover, the freshness of the experience of freedom
depends on novelty. What at first seems marvelously liberating eventually becomes taken for granted and finally banal. As this happens, one can feel the
constraints underlying one's freedom becoming more and more oppressive,
even if the objective level of constraint remains the same.

During the Maoist era, of course, the objective level of constraint continued to increase. Successive political campaigns targeted an ever wider array of victims. The bureaucratic apparatus expanded and ramified. Mega-
lomaniacal mismanagement led to the Great Leap Forward, which led to a
massive famine. Infighting at the top led to the chaos of the Cultural Revolution. By the end of the Maoist era, much of the Chinese population had
experienced new forms of starvation and anarchic violence; they were op-
pressed by a rigid, unaccountable government; and they were stifled by a static, stagnant economy. Even if the social structure and political processes of
the Maoist era had not nullified all of the aspects of liberation that had been
meaningful to people in the early 1950s, many Chinese might still have tired
of the kinds of freedom that would have been possible under the socialist
regime, even at its best. Mao, after all, claimed that mobilizing the nation's
youth for the Cultural Revolution was necessary because young people no
longer appreciated the values of socialist revolution.

By the beginning of Deng Xiaoping's era of "Reform and Opening" in
1979, most Chinese were indeed ready for a new liberation. Deng provided
it by making it possible for them, as Hanlong Lu puts it, to move toward a
life of "relative comfort" rather than "great equality." As Lu and the other

contributors to this volume have explained, many Chinese citizens of the late twentieth century indeed experienced a genuine liberation. Like the 1949 Liberation, the experience of freedom has several different dimensions within this new liberation of the consumer revolution. The chapters in this book can help us distinguish the various dimensions of this experienced freedom and understand the new kinds of constraints that have made it possible. Implicit in the book's content are also insights that could help us speculate on potential threats to this new experience of freedom: the ways in which the constraints that underlie it could get more oppressive, the ways in which the experience itself could gradually grow stale, and the ways in which it might be renewed.

First, like the Liberation of the political revolution, the consumer revolution has brought relative freedom from hunger and political chaos. Since 1979, China has had a steadily expanding economy, and in the early 1990s, the economic growth rate was truly spectacular. Even though inequality has grown, enough benefits have trickled down to all levels of the society to meet the most basic needs for nutrition and shelter. Although there do indeed continue to be political campaigns against "spiritual pollution" and "bourgeois liberalism," and there was the bloody crackdown against demonstrators around Tiananmen Square in 1989, the society seems peaceful and stable in contrast to the Maoist era. The political dissidents and religious leaders who are targets of government oppression are few relative to the Chinese population, and most people can be confident of staying out of trouble if they stay within defined limits. Although from the point of view of Western liberals this is inadequate, it feels like a comfortable freedom in contrast with memories of the Maoist era.

Besides the negative freedom from hunger and chaos, there are positive freedoms. Perhaps the most important in the experience of ordinary people is the freedom of consumer choice: the freedom to conveniently choose from a selection of wedding dresses, a variety of vegetables in the market, a menu of Big Macs and Quarter Pounders, an assortment of cigarettes, an array of dance halls. In China's expanding consumer society, the range of choices increases every day. The chapters in this book give abundant evidence of how meaningful it is for people who were once stuck in a gray, stagnant economy to have such a range of choice.

Another aspect of the new freedom is a capacity for personal expression. As described in the chapters by Kathleen Erwin and James Farrer, urban residents of China can now express, without much fear of legal sanction or even social recrimination, hitherto taboo feelings about passion and sex. Having expressed such feelings, they can explore a variety of intimate relationships, from extramarital affairs to new forms of friendship, sometimes mediated by a variety of "modern" greeting cards. One can imagine that listeners to the radio call-in shows described by Kathleen Erwin might be excited by the possibilities for more expressive, complex relationships, even when they themselves stay within conventional marriages.

A final aspect of the new freedom is the ability to live a private life among people who have chosen a similar lifestyle and to minimize association with people who are different from oneself. The luxury housing "oases" described by David Fraser are the fullest realization of the aspiration for this kind of private freedom; but redecorating one's apartment, as described by Deborah Davis in her introduction to this book, is a more affordable way to achieve similar ends.

All of these new freedoms are undergirded by powerful social and political constraints. They have depended first of all on the social stability made possible by a repressive state. They have also depended on the economic redistribution effected by still strong remnants of the socialist economy. For many urban workers, enjoyment of the freedoms of a consumer society has been made possible by underemployment in an inefficient system of state-owned enterprises that have limited individual mobility but provided basic salary, housing, and health benefits while a churning private economy produces dynamic economic growth. If the state-owned enterprises were to be dismantled quickly, there would be massive unemployment. One cannot well enjoy the thrills of consumer choice if one does not have a job.

A more subtle kind of constraint that gives order to the new consumer freedoms is peer pressure. A thick web of social norms determine what kinds of choices must be made: what kinds of cigarettes one must proffer if one is to be perceived as a successful entrepreneur, what kinds of expensive recreation (like bowling) one must take up if one is to make the right business contacts, what kinds of clothes one should wear if one wishes to seek a partner in a disco, what kinds of dress one should rent if one is getting married, what kind of toys one should buy if one is to properly raise one's child. Once one learns a few principles about stratification patterns in Chinese society, the choices made by most of the people described in this book seem very predictable.

As time goes on, these constraints could get more oppressive relative to the experience of liberation that Chinese people are feeling in the consumer revolution. If the Communist Party wishes to maintain its monopoly on power in the face of rising criticism about its corruption, it will have to maintain and probably increase its repressive apparatus and stifle groups that could offer a viable alternative. To maintain its export-led economic growth in a competitive global environment, especially one where East Asian countries are drastically devaluing their currencies in order to generate enough exports to satisfy their creditors, the Chinese state will have to continue to reduce the real wages of its working class through layoffs from state-run enterprises, reduction of social welfare benefits, and repression of worker unrest. As social-class differentiation continues, there may be increased pressure to settle into lifestyle enclaves associated with a particular class status—and an increased need for the privileged to defend themselves against less-privileged people, necessitating more walled "oases" and more repressive police forces.

But perhaps the most serious threats to the satisfactions of freedom in the Chinese consumer society may be more a matter of subjective expectation than external constraint. The novelty of the first stages of the consumer revolution will wear out. The freshness of consumer freedom is maintained by the constantly increasing production of new and different commodities. This leads, however, to constantly rising expectations, which may outstrip the capacity of the economy to deliver—or, if the economy does deliver, may induce moral and emotional anarchy that leads people to rethink the very value of consumerism.

Indeed, the consumer revolution has brought disappointment as well as satisfaction, and even its satisfactions appear fragile and contradictory. Consider the contrasts between two elderly men I interviewed for a study of Chinese Catholics.[1] Mr. Wang is a 70-year-old man living in a tiny two-room apartment off a narrow alley in Tianjin. The apartment is furnished only with a bed, a small hard bench, and some stools. Mr. Wang dresses in a blue Mao suit. Since he is a devout Catholic his walls are adorned with nicely framed pictures of Mary and Jesus. Though his life has had its share of troubles, he has a serenity, a feeling of happiness. He came from his village to the city 40 years ago and worked in a factory. He still keeps in touch, though, with his extended family in his home village. He makes the six-hour trip there frequently, and he knows about all the marriages, births, and deaths in his family. When his wife became bedridden with diabetes, he nursed her for ten years—given spiritual strength, he says, by his Catholic faith— until she died by his side while reciting the rosary (which, Mr. Wang is comforted to believe, meant that she probably went directly to heaven). He is happy that his children follow in his footsteps. He sees them frequently, and he is pleased that they are going to mass every Sunday and having their own children baptized. Mr. Wang was positively beaming with joy when I met him on the day that one of his grandsons was to be baptized.

One of his guiding principles in life is to protect what is important to him, especially his family, from being disturbed. He has developed quite an elaborate conviction about the need to preserve the natural environment. "If you try to change nature, all sorts of disasters will come. Who can change heaven and earth? I have been thinking a lot about this. I would even like to write a book about it if I had the cultural level."

"How can you have progress that way?" asks his friend Mr. Chen, who

1. Madsen 1998.

comes from the same village. Mr. Chen went to school with Mr. Wang—for both, their education stopped at the third grade. But Mr. Chen has made a lot more economic progress than Mr. Wang. The former lives close by, in an apartment roughly the same size, but much brighter and more colorful than Mr. Wang's. Mr. Chen has just acquired a telephone. He dresses in Western-style shirts and fake leather shoes rather than the cloth shoes that Mr. Wang prefers. The walls of his apartment are adorned with big posters of tropical beaches and pinup calendars of scantily clad women (as is common for people of his social status in northern China). Mr. Chen is a lapsed Catholic, and he does not go in for images of holy people. Unlike Mr. Wang, Mr. Chen has a strong entrepreneurial spirit. He came to Tianjin about the same time as Mr. Wang and worked in a similar kind of factory. But through various wheelings and dealings he managed to move into positions of some authority in the factory. This was a high-risk strategy that cost him considerably. He spent some time in prison camps because of suspect political and economic connections. Now, however, he has been able to take advantage of his entrepreneurial talent and has become the head of a small factory that is doing very active business in the new socialist market economy. Even Mr. Wang admits that Mr. Chen knows a lot more about Catholic doctrine than he. In fact, Mr. Chen likes to argue about theology with Mr. Wang. But Mr. Chen has lost his faith.

He has lost it, one suspects, because he saw in it the very qualities that made the Catholic faith so attractive to his friend Mr. Wang. The Catholic faith that both men learned celebrates a simple, stable, static way of life. Mr. Chen is a risk taker, an adventurer. He does not like the kind of life that Mr. Wang so admires. Though probably rooted in personality, the differences between the two men are deepened by the changing pattern of constraints and opportunities in their social context.

Even though Mr. Wang's aspirations were based in a traditionalist Catholic faith, they were oddly adapted to the anti-individualist, anticonsumerist ideology of the Maoist era. The fluidity of the new socialist market economy, however, encourages attitudes like Mr. Chen's. The wheeling and dealing required to succeed as an entrepreneur in the new society entails a repudiation of the idealized static rural life represented by traditional Catholicism and Maoist-style socialism. Those like Mr. Chen who are winners in the market will obviously be more favorably disposed to it. However, the market causes problems even for the winners. What Mr. Chen gains in embracing the new way of life is matched by losses. He gets more money, with which he can buy better decorations for his apartment, more stylish clothes, and appliances like his new telephone. But he has lost some domestic harmony. His wife, who comes from the same rural area that he does, is almost illiterate, she continues to wear peasant-style clothes, and she finds the new telephone frightening—its jangle makes her nervous and she is afraid to answer it. It is said that Mr. Chen's relationship with his wife is very sad. He does not love her, and they have little in common. Yet he is really too old and not wealthy enough to start a new family. The contrast with Mr. Wang's family life is clear. Shared hardship informed by shared faith kept Mr. Wang and his wife close. When faced with the tragedy of her lingering illness, he seems to have found a satisfying meaning in the unavoidable work of nursing her. Mr. Chen may find some solace in his new material possessions, but he does not seem to have enough to compensate for the frustrations he faces with his wife.

No less than for Mr. Wang, what seems important for Mr. Chen are not the things that money can buy, but the satisfactions of a way of life. Mr. Chen is curious and skeptical; he likes the excitement of taking on new endeavors and learning new things. His consumerism is not an end in itself but an adjunct to this way of life. His new telephone is necessary to further his business contacts. His clothes constitute the proper uniform for an entrepreneur. His paintings of tropical beaches and bathing beauties perhaps provide some relief in fantasy from the domestic frustrations that his lifestyle has brought him. But to an outside observer, it is not at all clear that Mr. Chen has had a more satisfying life than Mr. Wang.

Undoubtedly, there are many dialogues like that between Mr. Wang and Mr. Chen, and certainly not just among Catholics. It is common throughout China to hear ordinary people in circumstances similar to those of Mr. Wang and Mr. Chen voice disgust about the crazy rush after money, concern about the morals of their children, and even some nostalgia for the simpler life of the Maoist era—while they frantically seek to make a little extra money in order to buy the latest appliance or eat at the latest fast-food restaurant.

Someday perhaps, larger numbers of people in China will rise up in more systematic ways against some aspects of the consumer revolution. Perhaps the reactions of American social movements to consumerism in the second half of the twentieth century suggest the kinds of critiques Chinese will engage in at different stages of the consumer revolution. In the 1960s "age of affluence," the youthful counterculture, hungry for deeper experiences than those produced by shopping for commodities, embraced books like Herbert Marcuse's *One Dimensional Man*, which criticized (from a neo-Marxian point of view) the superficiality of freedom defined by commodity choices in a capitalist economy. By the late 1970s, as the American standard of living stagnated, the new fad among intellectuals was a critique of the "culture of narcissism"—an excessive focus on individual self-satisfaction that was self-defeating because we failed to recognize that we were living in "an age of limits." By the late 1990s, with vigorous economic growth resuming, but at the expense of widening income inequality, we were hearing more concerns about privatization (gated residential communities, for instance) and decreased capacity to deal with public problems.

In contemporary China, however, all of these stages of the development of a consumer economy seem to be present at once. In certain large regions, mainly on the southern coast, the socialist market economy has indeed produced an age of generalized affluence. But at the same time, the limits to growth are painfully present, especially in regions still dominated by state-run enterprises; and increasing inequality and its attendant quest for privatization seem pervasive. These problems may lead Chinese to express a full range of unfocused criticisms of the consumer revolution. The quest for new forms of liberation will not cease, but consensus on the meanings of liberation remains elusive at the present stage of development of China's consumer revolution.

CONTRIBUTORS

DEBORAH DAVIS is professor of sociology at Yale University. She is the author of *Long Lives: Chinese Elderly and the Communist Revolution* (1991), and coeditor of *Chinese Society on the Eve of Tiananmen* (1990) and *Urban Spaces in Contemporary China: The Potential for Autonomy and Community in Post-Mao China* (1995). Currently she is working on a book on family property and domestic space in Chinese cities entitled *A Home of Their Own*.

MARY S. ERBAUGH is associate professor in the Department of Chinese, Translation, and Linguistics at the City University of Hong Kong. She is the author of "Southern Chinese Dialects as a Medium for Political Reconciliation" (*Language and Society*, June 1995) and "The Secret History of the Hakkas: The Chinese Revolution as a Hakka Enterprise" (*China Quarterly*, December 1992). She is working on a book about the ideology of language in twentieth-century China.

KATHLEEN ERWIN received her Ph.D. in anthropology from the University of California, Berkeley, in 1998. She is working on a book, based on her dissertation, about transformations in sexuality, marriage, and family in Shanghai at the end of the millennium.

JAMES FARRER received his doctorate in sociology from the University of Chicago in 1998. He is now assistant professor of sociology in the Faculty of Comparative Culture at Sophia University in Tokyo. He is working on a book, based on his dissertation, tentatively titled *Opening Up: Sex and the Market in Shanghai*. His current research interests are sexuality, cultural globalization, and urban culture, and he has plans to conduct comparative work in Shanghai and Tokyo.

DAVID FRASER is a Ph.D. candidate in the Department of History at the University of California, Berkeley.

MARIS GILLETTE is assistant professor of anthropology at Haverford College. Her book *Between Mecca and Beijing: Modernization and Consumption among Urban Chinese Muslims* will be published by Stanford University Press in 1999.

RICHARD KRAUS is professor of political science at the University of Oregon. He is the author of *Class Conflict in Chinese Socialism* (1981), *Pianos and Politics in China: Middle-Class Ambitions and the Struggle over Western Music* (1989), *Brushes with Power: Modern Politics and the Chinese Art of Calligraphy* (1991), and coeditor of *Urban Spaces: Autonomy and Community in Contemporary China* (1995). He is currently writing about the changing organization of cultural life in China.

HANLONG LU is professor of sociology and director of the Institute of Sociology at the Shanghai Academy of Social Sciences. He is the author or editor of ten books, most recently *Modernisation and Community Development* (1996) and *Shanghai Society: 1978–1993* (1994). His publications have received awards from the Shanghai Academy of Social Sciences, the Sociology Society of China, and the Shanghai Municipal Government.

RICHARD MADSEN is professor of sociology at the University of California, San Diego. He is the author or coauthor of eight books on Chinese culture, American culture, and international relations. His works on China include *Chen Village* (1984, coauthored with Anita Chan and Jonathan Unger), *Morality and Power in a Chinese Village* (1984), and *China's Catholics: Tragedy and Hope in an Emerging Civil Society* (1998). His best-known works on American culture are those written with Robert Bellah, William Sullivan, Ann Swidler, and Steven Tipton: *Habits of the Heart* (1985) and *The Good Society* (1991).

ANN VEECK is an assistant professor of marketing at Western Michigan University. She completed her Ph.D. in business administration at Louisiana State University in 1997. Her ongoing research involves the changing patterns of household consumption in urban areas of China.

JULIA SENSENBRENNER is an independent scholar based in Maryland. She received her Ph.D. in sociology from The Johns Hopkins University in 1997. Her dissertation was titled "Rust in the Iron Rice Bowl: Labor Reforms in Shanghai's State Enterprises, 1992–1993." She is coauthor of "Embeddedness and Immigration: Notes on the Social Determinants of Economic Action" (1993) and has written a variety of articles for the *China Business Review.*

GAN WANG is a Ph.D. candidate in anthropology at Yale University. She received her bachelor's and master's degrees from Beijing University. Currently she is working on conspicuous consumption and the class-making processes of the new entrepreneurs in Shenzhen, China.

DAVID WANK is associate professor of sociology at Sophia University, Tokyo. He is the author of *Commodifying Communism: Business, Trust, and Politics in a Chinese City* (1998). He is currently conducting an ethnographic study of the revival movement of Buddhism in southeastern China.

YUNXIANG YAN is associate professor of anthropology at the University of California, Los Angeles. He is the author of *The Flow of Gifts: Reciprocity and Social Networks in a Chinese Village* (1996). He is currently working on a book about the transformation of private life in rural northern China from 1949 to 1998.

BIBLIOGRAPHY

Abramson, Daniel. 1996. "Maya Lin and the 1960s: Monuments, Time Lines, and Minimalism." *Critical Inquiry* 22, no. 4: 679–709.

Abu-Lughod, Lila. 1993. "Editorial Comment: On Screening Politics in a World of Nationals." *Public Sculpture* 5: 465–68.

Agence France-Presse. 1997. "Couples Look West for Latest Wedding Styles." *South China Morning Post*, December 6.

Agnew, Jean-Christophe. 1993. "Coming Up for Air: Consumer Culture in Historical Perspective." In *Consumption and the World of Goods*, edited by John Brewer and Roy Porter. London and New York: Routledge.

Anagnost, Ann. 1994. "The Politicized Body." In *Body, Subject and Power in China*, edited by Angela Zito and Tani E. Barlow. Chicago: University of Chicago Press.

———. 1992. "Social Ethics and the Legal System." In *Popular Protest & Political Culture in Modern China: Learning from 1989*, edited by Jeffrey Wasserstrom and Elizabeth J. Perry. Boulder, Colo.: Westview Press.

Anderson, Benedict. 1991. *Imagined Communities*. London: Verso.

Anderson, Eugene. 1988. *The Food of China*. New Haven, Conn.: Yale University Press.

Andrews, Julia F., and Gao Minglu. 1995. "The Avant-Garde's Challenge to Official Art." In *Urban Spaces: Autonomy and Community in Contemporary China*, edited by Deborah Davis, Richard Kraus, Barry Naughton, and Elizabeth J. Perry. Cambridge: Cambridge University Press.

Appadurai, Arjun. 1986. *The Social Life of Things: Commodities in Cultural Perspective*. Cambridge: Cambridge University Press.

———. 1981. "Gastro-Politics in Hindu South Asia." *American Ethnologist* 8, no. 3: 494–511.

Aronson, Sidney H. 1979. "The Sociology of the Telephone." In *Inter/media: Interpersonal Communication in a Media World*, edited by Gary Gumpert and Robert Cathcart. New York: Oxford University Press.

Barlow, Tani E. 1994. "Theorizing Woman: *Funü, Guojia, Jiating.*" In *Body, Subject and Power in China*, edited by Angela Zito and Tani E. Barlow. Chicago: University of Chicago Press.

Barlow, Tani. 1991. "Theorizing Women: Funü, guojia, jiating." *Genders* 10: 131–60.

Barmé, Geremie. 1995. "To Screw Foreigners Is Patriotic." *China Journal*, no. 34 (July): 209–38.

———. 1993. "Soft Porn, Packaged Dissent, and Nationalism: Notes on Chinese Culture in the 1990's." *Current History* 93: 584.

———. 1988. "Critics Now Chip Away at China's Concrete Eyesores." *Far Eastern Economic Review* (November 17): 54–56.

Beijingshi wenwu shiye guanliju, ed. 1990. *Wenwu gongzuo shouce* (Handbook on work with cultural relics). Beijing: Yanshan chubanshe.

Bell, Daniel. 1976. *The Cultural Contradictions of Capitalism*. New York: Basic Books.

Bi Yuhua. 1994. "Kuaicanye zhengshi chengwei xin de redianhangye" (Fast food officially becoming a new hot sector). *Shichang bao* (Market news), September 19.

Bian, Yanjie. 1994. *Work and Inequality in Urban China*. Albany: State University of New York Press.

Bian Yanjie et al. 1996. "Danweizhi yu zhufang shangpinhua" (The work-unit system and housing commercialization). *Shehuixue yanjiu* (Sociological research), no. 1.

Bian, Yanjie, and John Logan. 1996. "Market Transition and the Persistence of Power." *American Sociological Review* 61: 739–58.

Bian, Yanjie, John R. Logan, Hanlong Lu, Yunkang Pan, and Ying Guan. 1995. "Work Units and Housing Reform in Two Chinese Cities." In *The Danwei in Post-Maoist China*, edited by Xiaobo Lu and Elizabeth J. Perry. M. E. Sharpe.

Birch, Cyril, comp. 1965. *Anthology of Chinese Literature: From Early Times to the Fourteenth Century*. New York: Grove Press.

Block, Fred. 1994. "The Roles of the State in the Economy." In *The Handbook of Economic Sociology*, edited by Neil J. Smelser and Richard Swedberg. Princeton, N.J.: Princeton University Press.

Bourdieu, Pierre. 1991. *Language and Symbolic Power*, edited and introduced by John B. Thompson, translated by Gino Raymond and Matthew Adamson. Cambridge, Mass.: Harvard University Press.

———. 1986. "The Forms of Capital." In *Handbook of Theory and Research for the Sociology of Education*, edited by G. Richardson. New York: Greenwood Press.

———. 1984. *Distinction: A Social Critique of the Judgment of Taste*. Cambridge, Mass.: Harvard University Press.

———. [1972] 1977. *Outline of a Theory of Practice*. Cambridge: Cambridge University Press.

Bourdieu, Pierre, and Loic J. D. Wacquant. 1992. *An Invitation to Reflexive Sociology*. Chicago: University of Chicago Press.

Boyer, M. Christine. 1994. *The City of Collective Memory: Its Historical Imagery and Architectural Entertainments*. Cambridge, Mass.: MIT Press.

Brown, Penelope, and Stephen C. Levinson. 1987. *Politeness: Some Universals in Language Usage*. Cambridge: Cambridge University Press.

Bruun, Ole. 1995. "Political Hierarchy and Private Entrepreneurship in a Chinese Neighborhood." In *The Waning of the Communist State: Economic Origins of Political Decline in China and Hungary*, edited by Andrew G. Walder. Berkeley: University of California Press.

Brownell, Susan. 1995. *Training the Body for China: Sports in the Moral Order of the People's Republic*. Chicago: University of Chicago Press.

Butterfield, Fox. 1982. *China: Alive in the Bitter Sea*. New York: Bantam Books.

Chamberlain, Heath. 1993. "On the Search for Civil Society in China." *Modern China* 19, no. 2: 199–215.

Chang, Kwang-chih, ed. 1977. *Food in Chinese Culture: Anthropological and Historical Perspectives.* New Haven, Conn.: Yale University Press.

Charles, N., and M. Kerr. 1988. *Women, Food, and Families.* Manchester: Manchester University Press.

Chen, Nancy N. 1995. "Urban Spaces and Experiences of *Qigong*." In *Urban Spaces: Autonomy and Community in Contemporary China,* edited by Deborah Davis, Richard Kraus, Barry Naughton, and Elizabeth J. Perry. Cambridge: Cambridge University Press.

Chen Ping, ed. 1995. *Nanjing di wenwu* (Nanjing's cultural relics). Nanjing: Nanjing chubanshe.

Chen, Xiangming, and Xiaoyuan Gao. 1993. "Urban Economic Reform and Public-Housing Investment in China." *Urban Affairs Quarterly* 29, no. 1 (September): 117–45.

Chin, Michelle. 1996a. " 'Promising Artist' Accolade for Red-Paint Vandal." *South China Morning Post,* September 19.

———. 1996b. "Victoria's Painter to Suffer for Art with 28 Days Jail." *South China Morning Post,* October 10.

China: A Directory and Source Book. 1994. London: Euromonitor.

Clark, Gracia. 1991. "Colleagues and Customers in Unstable Market Conditions: Kumasi, Ghana." *Ethnology* 30, no. 1: 31–48.

Clear Thinking Agriculture Newsletter. 1997. (March).

Clunas, Craig. 1991. *Superfluous Things: Material Culture and Social Status in Early Modern China.* Urbana: University of Illinois Press.

Cochran, Sherman. 1992. "Inventing Nanjing Road: Advertising by the British-American Tobacco Company in Early Twentieth-Century China." Paper prepared for the conference "The Birth of a Consumer Society? Commerce and Culture in Shanghai, 1895–1937." Ithaca, N.Y.

———. 1980. *Big Business in China: Sino-Foreign Rivalry in the Cigarette Industry, 1890–1930.* Cambridge, Mass.: Harvard University Press.

Cody, Jeffrey W. 1996. "American Planning in Republican China, 1911–1937." *Planning Perspectives* 11: 339–77.

Cohen, William. 1989. "Symbols of Power: Statues in Nineteenth-Century Provincial France." *Studies in Comparative Society and History* 31: 491–513.

Cooper, Eugene. 1986. "Chinese Table Manners: You Are How You Eat." *Human Organization* 45: 179–84.

Cornue, Virginia. 1999. "Practicing NGO-ness and Relating Women's Space Publicly: The Women's Hotline and the State." In *Gender and Feminism in a Transnational Chinese Public,* edited by Mayfair M-H Yang. Minneapolis: University of Minnesota Press.

Crane, George T. 1994. "Collective Identity, Symbolic Mobilization, and Student Protest in Nanjing, China, 1988–1989." *Comparative Politics* 26, no. 4: 395–414.

Cressey, Paul G. 1932. *The Taxi-Dance Hall: A Sociological Study in Commercialized Recreation and City Life.* Chicago: University of Chicago.

Davis, Deborah. 1995. "Inequality and Stratification in the Nineties." In *China Review,* no. 19: 1–25, edited by Lo Chi Kin, Suzanne Pepper, and Tsui Kai Yuan. Hong Kong: Chinese University Press.

———. 1992. "Job Mobility in Post-Mao China." *The China Quarterly*, no. 132: 1062–85.

———. 1989. "My Mother's House." In *Unofficial China*, edited by Perry Link, Richard Madsen, and Paul Pickowicz. Boulder, Colo.: Westview Press.

Davis-Friedmann, Deborah. 1991. *Long Lives: Chinese Elderly and the Communist Revolution*. 2d ed. Stanford, Calif.: Stanford University Press.

Davis, Deborah, and Stevan Harrell, eds. 1993. *Chinese Families in the Post-Mao Era*. Berkeley: University of California Press.

Davis, Deborah, Richard Kraus, Barry Naughton, and Elizabeth Perry, eds. 1995. *Urban Spaces in Contemporary China: The Potential for Autonomy and Community in Post-Mao China*. Cambridge: Cambridge University Press.

Deleuze, Giles, and Felix Guattari. 1983. *Anti-Oedipus: Capitalism and Schizophrenia*. Minneapolis: University of Minnesota Press.

Deng Xiaoping wenxuan (Selected writings of Deng Xiaoping). 1983. Beijing: Renmin chubanshe.

Deng Zhanpei, chief ed. 1993. "Xinli rexian zixun (Psychological hotline inquiries)." Shanghai: Shanghai kexue jishu chubanshe.

Der Ling, Princess. 1929. *Kowtow*. New York: Dodd Mead.

DeVault, M. L. 1991. *Feeding the Family: The Social Organization of Caring as Gendered Work*. Chicago: University of Chicago Press.

Di Leonardo, Michaela. 1987. "The Female World of Cards and Holidays: Women, Families, and the Work of Kinship." *Signs: Journal of Women in Culture and Society* 23, no. 31: 440–53.

Ding Lu. 1995. "Shanghai xinli jiankang rexian saomiao (Scanning the Shanghai psychological health hotline)." *Kangfu* 5, no. 59: 6–8.

Dirlik, Arif. 1995. "Confucius in the Borderlands: Global Capitalism and the Reinvention of Confucianism." *Boundary* 2 22, no. 3 (Fall): 229–74.

Dong Fang. 1994. "Zhongguo chengshi xiaofei wuda redian" (The five hot points in Chinese urban consumption). *Jingji shijie*, no. 1.

Douglas, Mary. 1989. "Culture and Collective Action." In *The Relevance of Culture*, edited by Morris Freilich. South Hadley, Mass.: Bergin and Garvey.

———. 1984. "Standard Social Uses of Food: Introduction." In *Food in the Social Order: Studies of Food and Festivities in Three American Communities*, edited by Mary Douglas. New York: Russell Sage Foundation.

———. 1975. "Deciphering a Meal." In *Myth, Symbol, and Culture*, edited by Clifford Geertz. New York: W. W. Norton.

Douglas, Mary, and Baron Isherwood. 1979. *The World of Goods*. New York: Basic Books.

Duan Gang. 1991. "Kuaican quanji hanzhan jingcheng" (Fast food chickens are fighting with each other in Beijing). *Beijing Youth Daily*, April 2.

Duoji Cairan, ed. 1997. *Huaxia hun* (The soul of China). Shanghai: Shanghai jiaoyu chubanshe / Zhongguo shehui chubanshe.

Dwyer, F. Robert, Paul H. Schurr, and Sejo Oh. 1987. "Developing Buyer-Seller Relationships." *Journal of Marketing* 51 (April): 11–27.

Dyer, Richard. 1990. "In Defense of Disco." In *On Record: Rock, Pop, and the Written Word*, edited by Simon Frith and Andrew Goodwin. New York: Pantheon.

Edelman, Murray. 1995. *From Art to Politics: How Artistic Creations Shape Political Conceptions*. Chicago: University of Chicago Press.

Elias, Norbert. 1978. *The History of Manners: The Civilizing Process.* Translated by Edmund Jephcott. New York: Pantheon.

Ertong Shidai (Children's Epoch). 1979–1985.

Erwin, Kathleen. 1999. "White Women, Male Desires: A Televisual Fantasy of the Transnational Chinese Family." In *Gender and Feminism in a Transnational Chinese Public,* edited by Mayfair M-H Yang. Minneapolis: University of Minnesota Press.

———. 1998. *Liberating Sex, Mobilizing Virtue: Cultural Reconstructions of Gender, Marriage, and Family in Shanghai, China.* Ph.D. diss., University of California, Berkeley.

———. 1997. "Outward Bound in Shanghai: Gendered Strategies and Desires in Transnational Chinese Marriage." Paper presented at Center for Chinese Studies Annual Symposium, University of California, Berkeley, March.

Evans, Harriet. 1997. *Women and Sexuality in China.* New York: Continuum.

Faison, Seth. 1996. "It's a Lucky Day in May, and Here Come the Brides." *New York Times,* May 22.

Fan Yuxi, ed. 1995. *Nanjing di jianzhu* (Nanjing's architecture). Nanjing: Nanjing chubanshe.

Fantasia, Rick. 1995. "Fast Food in France." *Theory and Society* 24: 201–43.

Farb, Peter, and George Armelagos. 1980. *Consuming Passions: The Anthropology of Eating.* Boston: Houghton Mifflin Company.

Feng Tongqing. 1993. "Zou xiang shichang jingji de zhongguo qiye zhigong" (Trend of Chinese industrial workers as they go toward the market economy), *Zhongguo shehui kexue,* no. 3: 101–20.

Finkelstein, Joanne. 1989. *Dining Out: A Sociology of Modern Manners.* New York: New York University Press.

Finnane, Antonia. 1996. "What Should Chinese Women Wear? A National Problem." *Modern China* 22, no. 2: 99–131.

Fischler, Claude. 1980. "Food Habits, Social Change and the Nature/Culture Dilemma." *Social Science Information* 19, no. 6: 937–53.

Fitzgerald, Tricia. 1997. "Writer's Ties with Guerrillas Pay Off." *South China Morning Post,* July 28.

Formanek-Bunnell, Miriam. 1993. *Made to Play House: Dolls and the Commercialization of Girlhood 1830–1930.* New Haven, Conn.: Yale University Press.

Foucault, Michel. 1978. *History of Sexuality.* Volume 1: *An Introduction.* New York: Random House.

"4046765 Wei'er'fu Funü Ertong Xinli Rexian Jianjie" (4046765 Short Introduction to the Wei'er'fu Women's and Children's Psychological Hotline). N. d. Shanghai: Shanghai Training Center for Women and Children and the Wei'er'fu Company.

Frankel, Glenn, and Steven Mufson. 1996. "With 350 Million Smokers, China Is the World's Prize Market." *International Herald Tribune,* November 21: 2.

Fraser, David. 1994. "Smoking Out the Enemy: The Advertising of Nationalism in Republican China." Paper presented at the annual meeting of the Association for Asian Studies.

Fraser, Nancy. 1992. "Rethinking the Public Sphere." In *Habermas and the Public Sphere,* edited by Craig Calhoun. Cambridge, Mass.: MIT Press.

Friedman, Thomas. 1997. "The Globalutionaries." *New York Times,* July 24.

Frith, Simon, and Angela McRobbie. 1990. "Rock and Sexuality." In *On Record: Rock, Pop, and the Written Word,* edited by Simon Frith and Andrew Goodwin. New York: Pantheon.

Fung Yu-Lan. 1952. *A History of Chinese Philosophy,* translated by Derk Bodde, 2d ed. Princeton, N.J.: Princeton University Press.

Gaige daobao (Reform herald), no. 1 (1994), p. 34.

Gao Changli. 1992. "Woguo jiushi niandai chengxian duoyuanhua xiaofei qushi" (Consumption trends are diversified in China during the 1990s). *Shangpin pingjie* (Review of commodities), no. 10.

Geertz, Clifford. 1973. "Deep Play: Notes on the Balinese Cockfight." In *The Interpretation of Cultures.* New York: Basic Books.

Gellner, Ernest. 1994. *Conditions of Liberty: Civil Society and Its Rivals.* London: Hamish Hamilton.

Giddens, Anthony. 1984. *The Constitution of Society: Outline of the Theory of Structuration.* Berkeley: University of California Press.

Gillette, Maris Boyd. Forthcoming. *Between Mecca and Beijing.* Stanford, Calif.: Stanford University Press.

———. 1997. *Engaging Modernity: Consumption Practices among Urban Muslims in Northwest China.* Ph.D. diss., Harvard University.

Gladney, Dru. 1991. *Muslim Chinese: Ethnic Nationalism in the People's Republic.* Cambridge, Mass.: Council on East Asian Studies, Harvard University.

Gold, Thomas B. 1993. "Go with Your Feelings: Hong Kong and Taiwan Popular Culture in Greater China." *China Quarterly* 136 (December): 907–25.

———. 1990. "The Resurgence of Civil Society in *Journal of Democracy* 1, no. 1 (Winter): 18–31.

———. 1985. "After Comradeship: Personal Relations in China since the Cultural Revolution." *China Quarterly* 104: 657–75.

Goldman, Arieh. 1974. "Outreach of Consumers and the Modernization of Urban Food Retailing in Developing Countries." *Journal of Marketing* 38 (October): 8–16.

Goodman, Bryna. 1996. "Creating Civic Ground: Public Maneuverings and the State in the Nanjing Decade." In *Remapping China: Fissures in Historical Terrain,* edited by Gail Hershatter, Emily Honig, Jonathan N. Lipman, and Randall Stross. Stanford, Calif.: Stanford University Press.

Gu Bingshu. 1994. "Waican: dushi xin shishang" (Eating out: a new fashion in cities), *Xiaofeizhe,* no. 3: 14–15.

Gumpert, Gary, and Robert Cathcart, eds. 1979. *Inter/media: Interpersonal Communications in a Media World.* New York: Oxford University Press.

Guo Jianying. 1995. "Tantan kuaican de fuwu" (On service in the fast food sector). *Fuwu jingji* (Service economy), no. 2: 27–28.

Gusfield, Joseph. 1992. "Nature's Body and the Metaphors of Food." In *Cultivating Differences: Symbolic Boundaries and the Making of Inequality,* edited by Michele Lamont and Marcel Fournier. Chicago: University of Chicago Press.

Gustafson, Björne, and Li Shi. 1997. "Types of Income and Inequality in China." *Review of Income and Inequality* 43, no. 2 (June): 211–26.

Habermas, Jürgen. 1989a. *The Structural Transformation of the Public Sphere: An Inquiry into a Category of Bourgeois Society.* Translated by Thomas Burger and Frederick Lawrence. Cambridge, Mass.: MIT Press.

———. 1989b. "The Public Sphere." In *Jürgen Habermas on Society and Politics: A Reader*, edited by Steven Seidman. Boston: Beacon Press.

Han Shu. 1994. "M: changsheng jiangjun" (M [McDonald's]: the undefeated general). *Xiaofei zhinan* (Consumption guide), no. 2: 10–11.

Hankiss, Elemer. 1988. "The 'Second Society': Is There an Alternative Model Emerging in Contemporary Hungary?" *Social Research* 55, no. 1: 13–42.

Hanna, Judith Lynne. 1988. *Dance, Sex, and Gender: Signs of Identity, Defiance, and Desire.* Chicago: University of Chicago Press.

Harrell, Stevan, ed. 1995a. *Cultural Encounters on China's Ethnic Frontiers.* Seattle: University of Washington Press.

———. 1995b. "Introduction: Civilizing Projects and the Reaction to Them." *Cultural Encounters on China's Ethnic Frontiers.* Seattle: University of Washington Press.

Harris, Marvin. 1985. *Good to Eat: Riddles of Food and Culture.* New York: Simon and Schuster.

Hart, Dennis. 1990. "Advertising and the New Feminine Ideal: The Ideology of Consumption in South Korea." *Korea Journal* 30 (August): 18–26.

Harvey, David. 1989. *The Condition of Postmodernity.* Oxford: Basil Blackwell.

Havel, Vaclav. 1985. *Power of the Powerless.* Armonk, N.Y.: M. E. Sharpe.

Hayden, Dolores. 1995. *The Power of Place: Urban Landscapes as Public History.* Cambridge, Mass.: MIT Press.

He Yupeng. 1996. "Zuowei nuxin ripin de Beijing maidanglao" (McDonald's as feminine food in Beijing). Paper presented at the conference "Changing Diet and Foodways in Chinese Culture," Chinese University of Hong Kong, Hong Kong, June 12–14.

Hebdige, Dick. 1979. *Subculture: The Meaning of Style.* London: Methuen.

Heisley, Deborah D., and Sidney J. Levy. 1991. "Autodriving: A Photoelicitation Technique." *Journal of Consumer Research* 18 (December): 257–72.

Heng, Geraldine, and Janadas Devan. 1995. "State Fatherhood: the Politics of Nationalism, Sexuality and Race in Singapore." In *Bewitching Women, Pious Men*, edited by A. Ong and M. Peletz. Berkeley: University of California Press.

Heng, Liang, and Judith Shapiro. 1982. *Son of the Revolution.* New York: Vintage Books.

Hershatter, Gail. 1997. *Dangerous Pleasures: Prostitution and Modernity in Twentieth-Century Shanghai.* Berkeley: University of California Press.

———. 1996. "Sexing Modern China." In *Remapping China: Fissures in Historical Terrain*, edited by Gail Hershatter, Emily Honig, Jonathan Lipman, and Randall Stross. Stanford, Calif.: Stanford University Press.

———. 1994. "Modernizing Sex, Sexing Modernity: Prostitution in Early Twentieth-Century Shanghai." In *Engendering China: Women, Culture and the State*, edited by Christina Gilmartin et al. Cambridge, Mass.: Harvard University Press.

Hirschman, Elizabeth C. 1984. "Experience Seeking: A Subjectivist Perspective of Consumption." *Journal of Business Research* 12 (March): 115–36.

Hirshey, Gerri. 1995. "Happy [] Day to You." *New York Times Magazine*, July 2: 20–27, 43–46.

Honig, Emily, and Gail Hershatter. 1988. *Personal Voices: Chinese Women in the 1980's.* Stanford, Calif.: Stanford University Press.

"Honggaoliang yuyan zhongshi kuaican da qushi" (The red sorghum predicts the trend of Chinese fast food). 1996. *Zhongguo jingyingbao* (Chinese business). June 11.

Hochschild, Arlie. 1979. "Emotion Work, Feeling Rules, and Social Structure." *American Journal of Sociology* 85: 551–75.

Hsu, Francis L. K. 1948. *Under the Ancestors' Shadow: Chinese Culture and Personality.* New York: Columbia University Press.

Hu Jin and Zhao Pinghe, eds. 1995. *Funü ertong xinli zixun 100 li.* Shanghai: Xuelin chubanshe.

Hu, Zhenhua, ed. 1993. *China's Hui (Zhongguo huizu).* Yinchuan: Ningxia People's Publishing House.

Hua Li and Xiao Ding. 1996. *"Yangzhou au di si jia di xia shi pin chang"* (Yangzhou shuts down four illegal food factories." *Yangzi wanbao* (Yangtze evening news), January 16: 3.

Huang, Philip C. C. 1991. "The Paradigmatic Crisis in Chinese Studies." *Modern China* 17, no. 3 (July): 299–341.

———, ed. 1993. " 'Public Sphere'/Civil Society' in China?: Paradigmatic Issues in Chinese Studies III." *Modern China,* Special Issue 19, no. 2 (April).

Huang Shengbing. 1995. "Kuaican xiaofie xingwei de bijiao yanjiu" (Comparative study of fast food consumption behavior). *Xiaofei jingji,* no. 5: 33–34.

Huang Zhijian. 1994. "Yi ge juda de qingnian xiaofei shichang" (A huge market of youth consumers). *Zhongguo qingnina yanjiu* (China youth studies), no. 2: 12–16.

Huizinga, Johan. 1950. *Homo Ludens: A Study of the Play Element in Culture.* Boston: Beacon Press.

Humphreys, Caroline. 1995. "Creating a Culture of Disillusionment: Consumption in Moscow, a Chronicle of Changing Times." In *Worlds Apart: Modernity through the Prism of the Local,* edited by Daniel Miller. London: Routledge, 1995.

Ikels, Charlotte. 1996. *The Return of the God of Wealth: The Transition to a Market Economy in Urban China.* Stanford, Calif.: Stanford University Press.

Jerome, N. W., ed. 1980. *Nutritional Anthropology: Contemporary Approaches to Diet and Culture.* New York: Redgrave.

Ji Jianlin et al. 1995. "Dianhua xinli zixun de yingyong ji pinggu" (Use and analysis of telephone counseling). *Zhongguo xinli weisheng zazhi* (China mental health journal) 9, no. 1: 24–26.

Jian Feng. 1992. "Zhongshi kuaican, na chu ni de mingpai" (Chinese fast food, show your best brand). *Shichang bao,* November 10.

Jiang Yongcai and Di Shuzhi, eds. 1991. *Nanjing zhi zui* (The most of Nanjing). Nanjing: Nanjing chubanshe.

K'ang Yu-wei. 1958. *Ta Tung Shu: The One-World Philosophy of K'ang Yu-wei.* Translated by Laurence G. Thompson. London: George Allen and Unwin.

Kaynak, Erdener. 1985. "Global Spread of Supermarkets: Some Experiences from Turkey." In *Global Perspectives in Marketing,* edited by Erdener Kaynak. New York: Praeger.

Kaynak, Erdener, and Cavusgil S. Tamer. 1982. "The Evolution of Food Retailing Systems: Contrasting the Experience of Developed and Developing Countries." *Journal of the Academy of Marketing Science* 10, no. 3 (Summer): 249–69.

Kernen, Antoine, and Jean-Louis Rocca. 1998. *La reforme des entreprises publiques en Chine.* Paris: Les Etudes de Ceri.

Khan, Azizur Rahman, et al. 1992. "Household Income and Its Distribution in China." *China Quarterly,* no. 132: 1029–61.

Kinney, Anne Behnke. 1995. *Chinese Views of Childhood.* Honolulu: University of Hawaii Press.

Kipnis, Andrew. 1977. *Producing Guanxi: Sentiment, Self, and Subculture in a North China Village.* Durham, N.C.: Duke University Press.

Kleinman, Arthur. 1988. *The Illness Narratives.* New York: Basic Books.

Kleinman, Arthur, and Joan Kleinman. 1996. "The Appeal of Experience: Dismay of Images: Cultural Appropriations of Suffering in Our Times." *Daedalus* 125, no. 1: 1–24.

Kondo, Dorinne. 1992. "The Aesthetics and Politics of Japanese Identity in the Fashion Industry." In *Remade in Japan,* edited by Joseph Tobin. New Haven, Conn.: Yale University Press.

Kottak, Conrad. 1978. "Rituals at McDonald's." *Journal of American Culture* 1: 370–86.

Kraus, Richard Curt. 1991. *Brushes with Power: Modern Politics and the Chinese Art of Calligraphy.* Berkeley: University of California Press.

———. 1989. *Pianos and Politics in China: Middle-Class Ambitions and the Struggle over Western Music.* New York: Oxford University Press.

Kristoff, Nicholas. 1993. "Chinese Find Voice: Radio Call-ins." *New York Times,* April 26.

Lam, Willy Wo-Lap. 1998. "Liberals' Role Thwarts Assessment of Reform." *South China Morning Post,* December 23.

Lamont, Michele, and Marcel Fournier. 1992. *Cultivating Differences.* Chicago: University of Chicago Press.

Lasch, Christopher. 1979. *Culture of Narcissism: American Life in an Age of Diminishing Expectations.* New York: Warner.

Lawrence, Susan V. 1993. "Dr. Ruth, Beijing Style." *U.S. News and World Report,* May 17: 16.

Lears, T. J. Jackson. 1994. *Fables of Abundance: A Cultural History of Advertising in America.* New York: Basic Books.

———. 1983. "From Salvation to Self-Realization: Advertising and the Therapeutic Roots of the Consumer Culture, 1880–1930." In *The Culture of Consumption: Critical Essays in American History 1880–1980,* edited by Richard Wightman Fox and T. J. Jackson Lears. New York: Pantheon.

Lechner, Frank. 1991. "Simmel on Social Space." *Theory, Culture and Society* 8: 195–201.

Lee, Benjamin. 1993. "Going Public." *Public Culture* 5, no. 2: 165–78.

Leiss, William, Stephen Kline, and Sut Jhally. 1986. *Social Communication in Advertising: Persons, Products, and Images of Well-Being.* New York: Methuen.

Lester, David. 1977. "The Use of the Telephone in Counseling and Crisis Intervention." In *The Social Impact of the Telephone,* edited by Ithiel de Sola Pool. Cambridge, Mass.: MIT Press.

Lévi-Strauss, Claude. 1983. *The Raw and the Cooked.* Chicago: University of Chicago Press.

Li, Cheng. 1997. *Rediscovering China: Dynamics and Dilemmas of Reform.* Lanham, Md.: Rowman and Littlefield.

Li Dingqiang. 1996. "*Shi chang ye cai jia ge da fu hui luo* (Price of wild vegetables drops in Nanjing market)." *Yangzi wanbao* (Yangtze evening news), March 28: 13.

Li Ki. 1885. *Sacred Books of the East.* Vols. 27 and 28. Translated by James Legge. Oxford: Clarendon Press.

Li Lulu. 1995. "Shehui ziben yu siying qiyejia" (Social capital and private entrepreneurs). *Shehuixue yanjiu* 6: 46–58.

Li Qiang. 1997. "Zhengzhi fenceng yu jingji fenceng" (Political strata and economic strata). Manuscript.

———. 1995. "Woguo shehui de jieceng shouru chazu fenxie (Analysis of income of Chinese social groups). *Keji daobao,* no. 11 (1995): 61–64.

Li, Rongxia. 1998. "Urban Housing." *Beijing Review* (May 18–24): 14–16.

Li Xinjia. 1992. "Xiaofeishehuixue de jige zhongyao wenti (Several important questions about the sociology of consumption), *Qiujia,* no. 9: 15–18

Li, Xingjian. 1990. "Mental Counseling: Budding in Beijing." *Beijing Review* 33, no. 10 (March 5–11): 11–12.

Li, Yan. 1996. "China Buys Christmas Craze." *China Daily,* December 22–28.

Li Yongqiao. 1995. "Lun dangqian zhongguo dabi de pinfu chaju (Discussion of growing gap between rich and poor). *Xinbao caijing yuekan* no. 217 (April): 3–14.

Li Yu. 1994. "Shanghai shimin shouru zhuangkuang," (Situation of Shanghai urban income). *Shehuixue,* no. 1: 13–19.

Li, Yuning, ed. 1992. *Chinese Women through Chinese Eyes.* New York: East Gate / M. E. Sharpe.

Liao, Ping-hui. 1993. "Rewriting Taiwanese National History: The February 28 Incident as Spectacle." *Public Culture* 2, no. 3: 281–96.

Ling Dawei. 1996. "Nuli ba zhongshi kuaican gao shang qu" (Endeavor to develop Chinese fast food). *Zhongguo pengren,* no. 6: 4–5.

———. 1995. "Zhongxi kuaican jingzheng zhi wo jian" (My views on the competition between Chinese and Western fast foods). *Xinshiji zhoukan* (New century weekly), November.

Lipman, Jonathan. 1998. *Familiar Strangers: A Muslim History in China.* Seattle: University of Washington Press.

———. 1987. "Hui-Hui: An Ethnohistory of the Chinese-Speaking Muslims." *Journal of South Asian and Middle Eastern Studies* 11, nos. 1 and 2: 112–30.

Liu Fen and Long Zaizu. 1986. "Jing, jin, hu chi shenmo?" (What are people eating in Beijing, Tianjin, and Shanghai?). *People's Daily* (overseas edition), August 9.

Liu Guiqiu. 1986. "Gudai de 'ming tie' (Ancient name cards)." In <Wen Shi Zhishi> *bianzhuan bu,* eds., Vol. 2: *Gudai lishi fengsu mantan* (An informal discussion of courteous customs of ancient times). Beijing: Xinhua Shudian.

Liu Guoguan, ed. 1988. *Zhongguo jingji tizhi gaige de moshi yanjiu* (Studies in models of economic institutional reform in China). Beijing: Zhongguo shehuikexueyuan chubanshe.

Liu Guoyue. 1996. "Shenzhen kuaican shichang jiqi fazhan" (The fast food market in Shenzhen and its development). *Zhongguo pengren,* no. 8: 20–22.

Liu Ming. 1992. "Guoji kuaicancheng de meili" (The charming international fast food city). *Zhongguo shipinbao* (Chinese food newspaper), July 13.

Liu Ying and Xue Suzhen, eds. 1987. *Zhongguo hunyin jiating yanjiu* (Chinese marriage and family research). Beijing: Social Science Publishing House.

Lo, Clifford. 1996. "Red menace puts her majesty's nose out of joint," *South China Morning Post,* September 17.

Love, John. 1986. *McDonald's: Behind the Arches*. New York: Bantam Books.

Lu Hanchao. 1991. *The Workers and Neighborhoods of Modern Shanghai, 1911–1949.* Ph.D. diss., University of California at Los Angeles.

Lu Hanlong. 1997. "Jumin shouru fenpei" (Personal income distribution). In *Jiuwu qijian shehui fazhan wenti sikao* (Reflections on problems of social development at the turn of the century), edited by Zhuo Zuejin. Shanghai: Shanghai shehuikexueyuan chubanshe.

———. 1990. "Laizi geti de baogao" (A report from individuals). *Shehuixue yanjiu* (Sociological research), no. 1: 83–95.

Lu, Yang. [1966] 1969. "How Should the Wedding Be Arranged?" *Chinese Sociology and Anthropology* 1, no. 3: 32–36.

Luk, Veronica. 1997. "Cards of Compassion." *Sunday Young Post (South China Morning Post)*. April 20.

MacNeil, Ian R. 1980. *The New Social Contract: An Inquiry into Modern Contractual Relations*. New Haven, Conn.: Yale University Press.

McCormick, Barrett L. 1990. *Political Reform in Post-Mao China: Democracy and Bureaucracy in a Leninist State*. Berkeley: University of California Press.

McCracken, Grant. 1988. *Culture and Consumption: New Approaches to the Symbolic Character of Consumer Goods and Activities*. Bloomington: Indiana University Press.

McGranahan, Carole. 1996. "Miss Tibet, or Tibet Misrepresented? The Trope of Woman-as-Nation in the Struggle for Tibet." In *Beauty Queens on the Global Stage*, edited by Colleen Cohen, Richard Wilk, and Beverly Stoeltje. New York: Routledge.

McKendrick, Neil, John Brewer, and J. H. Plumb. 1982. *The Birth of Consumer Society*. Bloomington: Indiana University Press.

McKhann, Charles. 1995. "The Naxi and the Nationalities Question." In *Cultural Encounters on China's Ethnic Frontiers*, edited by Stevan Harrell. Seattle: University of Washington Press.

McNiel, Theresa, and Kirstin Nilsson. 1994. "The Food Chain." *China Business Review* (November/December): 34–36.

McRobbie, Angela. 1994. "Shut Up and Dance: Youth Culture and Changing Modes of Femininity." In *Postmodernism and Popular Culture*. New York: Routledge.

———. 1984. "Dance and Social Fantasy." In *Gender and Generation*, edited by Angela McRobbie and Mica Nava. London: Macmillan.

Madsen, Richard. 1998. *China's Catholics: Tragedy and Hope in an Emerging Civil Society*. Berkeley: University of California Press.

———. 1993. "The Public Sphere, Civil Society and Moral Community: A Research Agenda for Contemporary China Studies." *Modern China* 19, no. 2: 183–98.

Marchand, Roland. 1985. *Advertising the American Dream: Making Way for Modernity, 1920–1940*. Berkeley: University of California Press.

Marcuse, Herbert. 1964. *One-Dimensional Man*. Boston: Beacon Press.

Martinez, Theresa A. 1997. "Popular Culture as Oppositional Culture: Rap as Resistance." *Sociological Perspectives* 40, no. 2: 265–86.

Matisoff, James A. 1996. Review of *Cross-cultural Pragmatics: The Semantics of Human Interaction,* by Anna Wierzbicka. *Language* 72, no. 3: 624–30.

———. 1979. *Blessings, Curses, Hopes, and Fears: Psycho-ostensive Expressions in Yiddish*. Philadelphia: Institute for the Study of Human Issues.

Meaney, Constance S. 1989. "Market Reform in a Leninist System: Some Trends in the Distribution of Power, Status, and Money in Urban China." *Studies in Comparative Communism* 22: 203–20.

Meckel, Mary V. 1995. *A Sociological Analysis of the California Taxi-Dancer: The Hidden Halls.* Lewiston, N.Y.: Edwin Mellen.

Messer, Ellen. 1984. "Anthropological Perspectives on Diet." *Annual Review of Anthropology* 13: 205–49.

Mian Zhi. 1993. "Xishi kuaican fengmi jingcheng; zhongshi kuaican zemmaban?" (Western fast food is the fashion; what about Chinese fast food?). *Lianai, hunyin, jiating* (Love, marriage, and family), no. 6: 10–11.

Mihalca, Matai. 1992. "Eating Bitterness: Youths Set Out for Beidahuang." In *Far Eastern Economic Review* 155, no. 2: 28–29.

Miller, Daniel. 1995. "Consumption as the Vanguard of History." In *Acknowledging Consumption*, edited by Daniel Miller. London: Routledge.

———. 1992. "The Young and the Restless in Trinidad: A Case of the Local and the Global in Mass Consumption." In *Consuming Technologies: Media and Information in Domestic Space*, edited by Roger Silverstone and Eric Hirsch. London: Routledge.

———. 1987. *Material Culture and Mass Consumption.* London: Basil Blackwell.

Mintz, Sidney. 1993. "The Changing Role of Food in the Study of Consumption." In *Consumption and the World of Goods*, edited by John Brewer and Roy Porter. London: Routledge.

Moir, James, and Vivian Lee. 1996. "Art Attack Dismissed as 'Sour Grapes,' " *South China Morning Post*, September 18.

Mukerji, Chandra. 1983. *From Graven Images.* New York: Columbia University Press.

Mungham, Geoff. 1976. "Youth in Pursuit of Itself." In *Working Class Youth Culture*, edited by Geoff Mungham and Geoff Peterson. London: Routledge.

Murphy, Christopher. 1986. "Piety and Honor: The Meaning of Muslim Feasts in Old Delhi." In *Food, Society, and Culture*, edited by R. S. Khare and M. S. A. Rao. Durham, N.C.: Carolina Academic Press.

Murphy, J. David. 1995. *Plunder and Preservation: Cultural Property Law and Practice in the People's Republic of China.* Hong Kong: Oxford University Press.

Musgrove, Charles D. 1996. "Building a Dream: Constructing Government Buildings in the Guomindang's Model Capital at Nanjing." Paper presented at University of California, San Diego, conference "Beyond Shanghai," September 7–9.

Naughton, Barry. 1995. *Growing Out of the Plan.* Cambridge: Cambridge University Press.

Nee, Victor. 1989. "A Theory of Market Transition." *American Sociological Review*, no. 54: 663–81.

Ni, Yang. 1994. "Longqi: Dragon Prays." Translated by Norman Walling, S.J. *Tripod.* 14 (July–August): 82.

Nonini, Donald. 1997. "Shifting Identities, Positioned Imaginaries: Transnational Traversals and Reversals by Malaysian Chinese." In *Ungrounded Empires: The Cultural Politics of Chinese Transnationalism*, edited by A. Ong and D. Nonini. New York, Routledge.

Nonini, Donald, and Aihwa Ong. 1997. "Introduction: Chinese Transnationalism as an Alternative Modernity." In *Ungrounded Empire: The Cultural Politics of Chinese Transnationalism*, edited by A. Ong and D. Nonini. New York: Routledge.

"140m Telephone Lines Nation's Goal by 2000." 1995. *Shanghai Star* (Xinhua News Agency), May 19: 7.

"1m Phone Lines Plug in This Year." 1995. *Shanghai Star* (Xinhua News Agency), May 15: 4.

Ong, Aihwa. 1997. "Chinese Modernities: Narrative of Nation and of Capitalism." In *Ungrounded Empires: The Cultural Politics of Chinese Transnationalism,* edited by Aihwa Ong and Donald M. Nonini. Berkeley: University of California Press.

———. 1995. "Women Out of China: Traveling Tales and Traveling Theories in Postcolonial Feminism. In *Women Writing Culture,* edited by R. Behar and D. A. Gordon. Berkeley: University of California Press.

———. 1993. "On the Edge of Empires: Flexible Citizenship among Chinese in Diaspora." *Positions* 1, no. 3: 743–78.

Ong, Aihwa, and Donald M. Nonini, eds. 1997. *Ungrounded Empires: The Cultural Politics of Chinese Transnationalism.* New York: Routledge Press.

Pan Yunkang et al. 1995. *Jingi gaige de shehuiguan* (Social perspectives on economic reform). Tianjin: Tianjin renmin chubanshe.

Peiss, Kathy. 1986. *Cheap Amusements: Working Women and Leisure in Turn-of-the-Century New York.* Philadelphia: Temple University Press.

———. 1989. " 'Charity Girls' and City Pleasures: Historical Notes on Working-Class Sexuality, 1980–1920." In *Passion and Power: Sexuality in History,* edited by Kathy Peiss and Christina Simmons. Philadelphia: Temple University Press.

Pellow, Deborah. 1993. "No Place to Live, No Place to Love: Coping in Shanghai." In *Urban Anthropology in China,* edited by Greg Guldin and Adam Southall. New York: E. J. Brill.

Pian Ming. 1994. "Jingcheng qingnian qingxin gaojia shangpin" (Beijing youth are keen on expensive commodities). *Zhonghua gongshang shibao* (China industrial and commercial times), July 16.

Pieke, Frank. 1995. "Bureaucracy, Friends and Money: The Growth of Capital Socialism in China." *Comparative Studies in Society and History* 37, no. 3: 494–518.

Pillsbury, Barbara. 1978. "Being Female in a Muslim Minority in China." *Women in the Muslim World,* edited by Lois Beck and Nikki Keddie. Cambridge, Mass.: Harvard University Press.

———. 1975. "Pig and Policy: Maintenance of Boundaries between Han and Muslim Chinese." *Minorities: A Text with Readings in Intergroup Relations,* edited by B. Eugene Griessman. Hinsdale, Ill.: Dryden Press.

Polanyi, Karl. [1944] 1957. *The Great Transformation.* Boston: Beacon Press.

Polhemus, Ted. 1993. "Dance, Gender, and Culture." In *Dance, Gender, and Culture,* edited by Helen Thomas. New York: St. Martin's Press.

Pool, Ithiel de Sola, ed. 1977. *The Social Impact of the Telephone.* Cambridge, Mass.: MIT Press.

Putnam, Robert D. 1993. *Making Democracy Work: Civic Traditions in Modern Italy.* Princeton, N.J.: Princeton University Press.

Qu Huahan and Yuanshen Wu. 1996. "Pu kou cai nong fan yin mai cai nan (Peasants in Pukou districts complain of difficulty selling their vegetables)." *Yangzi wanbao* (Yangtze evening news), March 30: 13.

"Rang diaosu yishu wei meihua chengshi fuwu" (Let the art of statuary serve urban beautification). 1981. *Meishu* (Fine arts) 7: 6–8.

Rankin, Mary. 1993. "Some Observations on a Chinese Public Sphere." *Modern China* 19, no. 2: 158–82.

Redhead, Steve, Derek Wynne, and Justin O'Conner. 1997. *The Subcultures Reader: Readings in Popular Cultural Studies.* Oxford: Basil Blackwell.

Richardson, Miles. 1982. "Being-in-the-Market versus Being-in-the-Plaza: Material Culture and the Construction of Social Reality in Spanish America." *American Ethnologist* 19, no. 2: 421–36.

Riesman, David, with Nathan Glazer and Reuel Denney. 1969. *The Lonely Crowd: A Study of the Changing American Character.* Abridged ed. New Haven, Conn.: Yale University Press.

Ritzer, George. 1993. *The McDonaldization of Society.* Newbury Park, Calif.: Pine Forge.

Rofel, Lisa. 1994a. "Yearnings: Televisual Love and Melodramatic Politics in Contemporary China." *American Ethnologist* 21, no. 4 (November): 700–22.

———. 1994b. "Liberation Nostalgia and a Yearning for Modernity." *Engendering China,* edited by Christina Gilmartin, Gail Hershatter, Lisa Rofel, and Tyrene White. Cambridge, Mass.: Harvard University Press.

Rowe, William. 1993. "The Problem of 'Civil Society' in Late Imperial China." *Modern China* 19, no. 2: 139–57.

Rust, Frances. 1969. *Dance in Society: An Analysis of the Relationship between the Social Dance and Society in England from the Middle Ages to the Present Day.* London: Routledge.

Saari, Jon. 1990. *Legacies of Childhood.* Cambridge, Mass.: Harvard University Press.

Sack, Robert David. 1992. *Place, Modernity, and the Consumer's World.* Baltimore: Johns Hopkins University Press.

Sahlins, Marshall. 1976. *Culture and Practical Reason.* Chicago: University of Chicago Press.

Sayer, Andrew. 1985. "The Difference That Space Makes." In *Social Relations and Spatial Structures,* edited by Derrek Gregory and John Urry. London: Macmillan.

Schmidt, Leigh Eric. 1995. *Consumer Rites.* Princeton, N.J.: Princeton University Press.

Schurr, Paul H., And Julie L. Ozanne. 1985. "Influences on Exchange Processes: Buyer's Preconceptions of a Seller's Trustworthiness and Bargaining Toughness." *Journal of Consumer Research* 11 (March): 939–53.

Schwarcz, Vera. 1996. "The Pane of Sorrow: Public Use of Personal Grief in Modern China." *Daedalus* 125, no. 1: 119–48.

Scott, James C. 1990. *Domination and the Arts of Resistance.* New Haven, Conn.: Yale University Press.

Seiter, Ellen. 1993. *Sold Separately: Children and Parents in Consumer Culture.* New Brunswick, N.J.: Rutgers University Press.

Shanghai shehui 15 nian (Shanghai society after 15 years of reform). 1994. Shanghai: Shanghai Academy of Social Sciences.

Shelton, Allen. 1990. "A Theater for Eating, Looking, and Thinking: The Restaurant as Symbolic Space." *Sociological Spectrum* 10: 507–26.

Shenzhen tequbao (Shenzhen special economic zone daily), 1996. January 8.

Sherry, John F., Jr. 1990. "A Sociocultural Analysis of a Midwestern American Flea Market." *Journal of Consumer Research* 17 (June): 13–30.

Shih, Shu-mei. 1997. "Nationalist Patriarchy and Gendered Minoritization in the Global Context." Paper presented at Center for Chinese Studies Annual Symposium, U.C. Berkeley, March.

Shue, Vivienne. 1992. "China: Transition Postponed." *Problems of Communism* 41, no. 1–2: 157–69.

Silber, Cathy. 1994. "From Daughter to Daughter-in-Law in the Women's Script of Southern Hunan." In *Engendering China: Women, Culture, and the State,* edited by Christina K. Gilmartin, Gail Hershatter, Lisa Rofel, and Tyrone White. Cambridge, Mass.: Harvard University Press.

Simmel, Georg. 1984. *George Simmel: On Women, Sexuality, and Love.* Translated by Guy Oakes. New Haven, Conn.: Yale University Press.

———. 1971. "Sociobility." In *Georg Simmel on Individuality and Social Forms: Selected Writings,* edited by Donald N. Levine. Chicago: University of Chicago Press.

———. [1904] 1957. "Fashion." *American Journal of Sociology* 62, no. 6 (May): 541–58.

Simoons, Frederick, J. 1991. *Food in China: A Cultural and Historical Inquiry.* Boca Raton, Fla.: CRC Press.

Situ Zhaoguang and Cao Chunsheng. 1984. "Rang woguo changshi diaosu geng jiankangdi fazhan" (Let our country's urban sculpture develop even more healthily). *Meishu* (Fine arts) 7: 15.

Siu, Helen. 1993. "Reconstituting Dowry and Brideprice in South China." In *Chinese Families in the Post-Mao Era,* edited by Deborah Davis and Stevan Harrell. Berkeley: University of California Press.

Smart, Alan. 1993. "Gifts, Bribes, and Guanxi: A Reconsideration of Bourdieu's Social Capital." *Cultural Anthropology* 8, no. 3: 388–408.

Solinger, Dorothy. 1994. "China's Urban Transients in the Transition from Socialism and the Collapse of the Communist Urban Public Goods Regime." *Comparative Politics* (January): 127–47.

———. 1992. "Urban Entrepreneurs and the State: The Merger of State and Society." In *State and Society in China: The Consequences of Reform,* edited by Arthur Rosenbaum. Boulder, Colo. Westview Press.

Somers, Margaret. 1993. "Citizenship and the Place of the Public Sphere." *American Sociological Review* 58, no. 5: 587–620.

Song Qiang, Zhang Cangcang, and Qiao Bian. 1996. *Zhongguo keyi shuo bu* (China can say no). Beijing: Zhonghua gongshang lianhe chubanshe.

Song, Shunfeng. 1992. "Policy Issues Involving Housing Commercialization in the People's Republic of China." *Socio-Economic Planning Science* 26, no. 3: 213–22.

Spence, Jonathan D. 1996. *God's Chinese Son: The Taiping Heavenly Kingdom of Hong Xiuquan.* New York: W. W. Norton.

State Statistical Bureau and East-West Population Center. 1993. *Survey of Income and Expenditure of Urban Households in China in 1986.* Honolulu: University of Hawaii.

Stearns, Peter N. 1994. *American Cool: Constructing a Twentieth-Century Emotional Style.* New York: New York University Press.

Stephenson, Peter. 1989. "Going to McDonald's in Leiden: Reflections on the Concept of Self and Society in the Netherlands." *Ethos* 17, no. 2: 226–47.

"The Storm in the Plaza." 1985. *Harper's Magazine* (July): 28–33.

Storr, Robert. 1989. "Tilted Arc: Enemy of the People?" In *Art in the Public Interest,* edited by Arlene Raven. Ann Arbor, Mich.: UMI Research Press.

Susman, Warren. 1985. *Culture as History: The Transformation of American Society in the Twentieth Century*. New York: Pantheon.

Swain, Margaret. 1990. "Commoditizing Ethnicity in Southwest China." *Cultural Survival Quarterly* 14, no. 1: 26–29.

Swetman, John. 1990. "Migratory Patterns of Vendors in a Guatemalan Market." *Ethnology* 29, no. 4: 261–73.

Szelenyi, Ivan. 1978. "Social Inequalities in State Socialist Redistributive Economies: Dilemmas for Social Policy in Contemporary Socialist Societies of Eastern Europe." *International Journal of Comparative Sociology* 19, nos. 1–2: 63–87.

Tabakoff. 1998. "Prankster Scores Star Sports Own Goal." *South China Morning Post*. December 22.

Tang Wing-Shing and Alan Jenkins. 1990. "Urbanisation: Processes, Policies, and Patterns." In *The Geography of Contemporary China: The Impact of Deng Xiaoping's Decade*, edited by Terry Cannon and Alan Jenkins. London: Routledge.

Tannen, Deborah, and Piyale Comert Oztek. 1977. "Health to Our Mouths: Formulaic Expressions in Turkish and Greek." In *Proceedings of the 10th Annual Meeting of the Berkeley Linguistic Society*, edited by Kenneth Whistler et al. Berkeley, Calif.: Berkeley Linguistic Society.

Tao Wentai. 1996. "Guanyu zhongwai yinshi wenhua bijiao de ji ge wenti" (Issues in comparing Chinese and foreign culinary cultures). *Zhongguo pengren*, no. 8: 26–28.

Tatlow, Didi Kirsten. 1996. "Police Hot on Trail of Bombers." *Eastern Express*, February 3–4.

Taylor, William R. 1991. *Inventing Times Square: Commerce and Culture at the Crossroads of the World*. New York: Russell Sage Foundation.

Thornton, Sarah. 1996. *Club Cultures Music, Media, and Subcultural Capital*. Hanover, N.H.: Wesleyan University Press.

Tong, Zhong Yi, and R. Allen Hays. 1996. "The Transformation of the Urban Housing System in China." *Urban Affairs Review* 31, no. 5 (May): 625–58.

Tu, Wei-ming. 1996. "Destructive Will and Ideological Holocaust: Maoism as a Source of Social Suffering in China." *Daedalus* 125, no. 1: 149–80.

Turner, Victor. 1982. *From Ritual to Theater: The Human Seriousness of Play*. New York: Performing Arts Journal Publications.

Urry, John. 1985. "Social Relations, Space and Time." In *Social Relations and Spatial Structures*, edited by Derek Gregory and John Urry. London: Macmillan.

Vogel, Ezra. 1965. "From Friendship to Comradeship: The Change in Personal Relations in Communist China." *China Quarterly*, no. 21: 46–60.

Wagner, Rudolf. 1995. "The Role of the Foreign Community in the Chinese Public Sphere." *China Quarterly*, no. 142: 423–43.

Wagner-Pacifici, Robin, and Barry Schwartz. 1991. "The Vietnam Veterans Memorial: Commemorating a Difficult Past." *American Journal of Sociology* 97, no. 2: 376–420.

Wakeman, Frederic, Jr. 1995. *Policing Shanghai 1927–1937*. Berkeley: University of California Press.

———. 1993. "The Civil Society and Public Sphere Debate: Western Reflections on Chinese Political Culture." *Modern China* 19, no. 2: 108–38.

Walder, Andrew G. 1991. "Workers, Managers, and the State." *China Quarterly*, no. 127: 467–92.

————. 1990. "Economic Reform and Income Distribution in Tianjin, 1876–1986." In Chinese Society on the Eve of Tiananmen," edited by Deborah Davis and Ezra Vogel. Cambridge, Mass.: Harvard University Press.

————. 1986. *Communist Neo-Traditionalism: Work and Authority in Chinese Industry.* Berkeley: University of California Press.

————, ed. 1995. *The Waning of the Communist State.* Berkeley: University of California Press.

Walsh, David. 1993. "Saturday Night Fever: An Ethnography of Disco Dancing." In *Dance, Gender, and Culture,* edited by Helen Thomas. New York: St. Martin's Press.

Wan, Marianna. 1996. "The Artist Who Saw Red." *South China Morning Post,* October 10.

Wang Chunzhen, ed. 1995. *Woguo jumin shouru fenpei wenti* (Problems of income distribution in China). Beijing: Zhongguo jihua chubanshe.

Wang, Feng. 1997. "Invisible Walls within Cities." Paper prepared for Conference on Social Consequences of Chinese Economic Reform, Harvard University, May 23–24.

Wang, Hui, and Leo Ou-fan Lee, with Michael M. J. Fischer. 1994. "Is the Public Sphere Unspeakable in Chinese? Can Public Spaces (*gonggong kongjian*) Lead to Public Spheres?" *Public Culture,* no. 6: 597–605.

Wang Jinhai, with Pan Yadi, Qian Chunlan, Yu Zhiwei, Gan Zulin, Xie Zhenhua, Bei Runpu, Zou Liyang, and Yan Hanxiang, eds. 1987. *Nuxing zhishi shouce* (A women's information handbook). Chengdu: Sichuan kexue zhishu chuban she.

Wang, Liping. 1996. "Creating a National Symbol: The Sun Yatsen Memorial in Nanjing," *Republican China* 21, no. 2: 23–63.

Wang, Shaoguang. 1995. "The Politics of Private Time: Changing Leisure Patterns in Urban China." In *Urban Spaces in Contemporary China: The Potential for Autonomy and Community in Post-Mao China,* edited by Deborah Davis, Richard Kraus, Barry Naughton, and Elizabeth J. Perry. Cambridge: Cambridge University Press.

Wang Weiming. 1996. *Yuwang de chengshi* (City of longing). Shanghai: Wenhui chuban she.

Wang, Ya Ping, and Alan Murie. 1996. "The Process of Commercialisation of Urban Housing in China." *Urban Studies* 33, no. 6: 971–89.

Wang Yong and Zhi Long. 1996. "*Nanjing zhui da de shi lei ning mao shi chang kai zhang* (Nanjing's biggest indoor food market opens)." *Yangzi wanbao* (Yangtze evening news), January 29: 6.

Wank, David L. Forthcoming. "Social Networks and Property Rights: Enforcement, Expectations, and Efficiency in the Urban Nonstate Sector." In *Property Rights and Economic Reform in China,* edited by Jean C. Oi and Andrew G. Walder. Stanford, Calif.: Stanford University Press.

————. 1998. *Commodifying Communism: Markets, Trust, and Politics in a South China City.* Cambridge: Cambridge University Press.

————. 1995. "Bureaucratic Patronage and Private Business: Changing Networks of Power in Urban China." In *The Waning of the Communist State: Economic Origins of Political Decline in China and Hungary,* edited by Andrew G. Walder. Berkeley: University of California Press.

————. 1993. "The Institutional Process of Market Clientelism." *China Quarterly,* no. 147: 820–38.

Ward, Andrew H. 1993. "Dancing in the Dark: Rationalism and the Neglect of Social Dance." In *Dance, Gender, and Culture*, edited by Helen Thomas. New York: St. Martin's Press.

Wasserstrom, Jeffrey N., and Liu Xinyong. 1995. "Student Associations and Mass Movements." In *Urban Spaces: Autonomy and Community in Contemporary China*, edited by Deborah Davis, Richard Kraus, Barry Naughton, and Elizabeth J. Perry. Cambridge: Cambridge University Press.

Watson, James. 1997. "Introduction: Transnationalism, Localization, and Fast Foods in East Asia." In *Golden Arches East: McDonald's in East Asia*, edited by James Watson. Stanford, Calif.: Stanford University Press.

———. 1987. "From the Common Pot: Feasting with Equals in Chinese Society." *Anthropos* 82: 389–401.

———, ed. 1997. *Golden Arches East: McDonald's in East Asia*. Stanford University Press.

Watson, Rubie S. 1994. "Making Secret Histories: Memory and Mourning in Post-Mao China." In *Memory, History, and Opposition under State Socialism*, edited by Rubie S. Watson, ed. Santa Fe, N.M.: School of American Research Press.

———. 1986. "The Named and the Nameless: Gender and Person in Chinese Society." *American Ethnologist* 13, no. 4: 619–31.

"Wei'er'fu rexian xinxi" (Wei'er'fu hotline news). 1995. Pamphlet.

Weller, Robert P. 1994. "Resistance, Chaos and Control in China: Taiping Rebels." *Taiwanese Ghosts and Tiananmen*. Seattle: University of Washington Press.

Whyte, Martin K. 1993. "Wedding Behavior in Chengdu." In *Chinese Families in the Post-Mao Era*, edited by Deborah Davis and Stevan Harrell. Berkeley: University of California Press.

Whyte, Martin K., and S. Z. Gu. 1987. "Popular Response to China's Fertility Transition." *Population and Development Review* 13, no. 3 (September).

Whyte, Martin K., and William L. Parish. 1984. *Urban Life in Contemporary China*. Chicago: University of Chicago Press.

Wierzbicka, Anna. 1992. *Semantics, Culture, and Cognition: Universal Human Concepts in Culture-Specific Configurations*. New York: Oxford University Press.

Wiest, Jean-Paul. 1988. *Maryknoll in China*. Armonk, N.Y.: M. E. Sharpe.

Wilder, Laura Ingalls. [1941] 1971. *Little Town on the Prairie*. New York: Harper and Row.

Wilk, Richard. 1994. "Consumer Goods as Dialogue about Development: Colonial Time and Television Time in Belize." In *Consumption and Identity*, edited by Jonathan Friedman. Chur, Switzerland: Harwood Academic Publishers.

Williamson, Judith. 1978. *Decoding Advertisements*. London: Marion Boyars.

Willis, Paul. 1984. *Learning to Labor: How Working-Class Kids Get Working-Class Jobs*. New York: Columbia University Press.

Wilson, Scott. 1977. "The Cash Nexus and Social Networks: Mutual Aid and Gifts in Contemporary Shanghai Villages." *China Journal* 37 (January): 91–112.

Wolf, Margery. 1972. *Women and Family in Rural Taiwan*. Stanford, Calif.: Stanford University Press.

Wood, Denis. 1992. *The Power of Maps*. New York: Guilford Press.

Wong, Yu. 1996, 1997. "Beijing-Speak: Beijing's 168 Hotlines." *Far Eastern Economic Review* (December and January): 106–7.

World Resources Institute. 1994. *World Resources, 1994–1995: A Guide to the Global Environment.* New York: Oxford University Press.

Wu, Hung. 1995. "Private Love and Public Duty." In *Chinese Views of Childhood,* edited by Anne Kinney. Honolulu: University of Hawaii Press.

——— 1991. "Tiananmen Square: A Political History of Monuments." *Representations* 35: 84–117.

Xiao Hua. 1993. "Da ru Zhongguo de yangkuaican" (The invasion of Western fast food), *Jianting shenghuo zhinan* (Guidance of family life), no. 5.

Xiao Yan. 1994. "Xiaofei guannian xin qingxie" (New orientations of consumption perception). *Zhongguo xiaofeizhe bao* (China consumer news), September 12.

Xiaonian bao (Children's news). 1995–1996.

Xie Dingyuan. 1996. "Pengren wangguo mianlin tiaozhan" (The kingdom of cuisine is facing a challenge). *Zhongguo pengren,* no. 2: 27–29.

Xie, Xiaolin, Lawrence Weinstein, and William Meredith. 1996. "Hotline in China: One Way to Help Chinese People." *Psychological Reports* 78 (February): 1–90.

" 'Xingwei yishujia' xiayue tixun jiang renzui" ('Performance artist' will enter plea next month). 1996. *Dongfang ribao,* September 19.

Xu Anqi. 1995. "Tongju fen shi, yijia liangzhu: Sha sandai tongtang jiating xin quxiang" (Living together, eating apart; one house, two masters: new trends in three generations). *Wen hui bao,* March 7.

Xu, Binglan. 1995–96. "New Year Cards Cheapest at Stalls." *China Daily,* December 31—January 6.

Xu Chengbei. 1994. "Kuaican, dacai, yu xinlao zihao" (Fast food, formal dishes, and the new and old restaurants). *Jingji ribao* (Economic daily), September 17.

———. 1993. "Cong Maidanglao kan shijie" (Seeing the world from McDonald's). *Zhongguo pengren,* no. 8.

———. 1992. "Maidanglao de faluu" (McDonald's law). *Fazhi ribao* (Legal system daily), September 9.

Xu Kaifu. 1995. *Xu Shiyou di wannian suiyue* (The last years of Xu Shiyou). Nanjing: Jiangsu renmin chubanshe.

Xu Wangsheng. 1995. "Zhongxi yinshi wenhua de qubie" (The differences between Chinese and Western culinary cultures). *Zhongguo pengren,* no. 8: 28–30.

Yan, Yunxiang. 1997a. "McDonald's in Beijing: The Localization of Americana." In *Golden Arches East: McDonald's in East Asia,* edited by James Watson. Stanford, Calif.: Stanford University Press.

———. 1997b. "The Triumph of Conjugality: Structural Transformation of Family Relations in a Chinese Village." *Ethnology* 36, no. 3: 191–212.

———. 1996. *The Flow of Gifts: Reciprocity and Social Networks in a Chinese Village.* Stanford, Calif.: Stanford University Press.

———. 1994. "Dislocation, Reposition and Restratification: Structural Changes in Chinese Society." In *China Review 1994,* edited by Maurice Brosseau and Lo Chi Kin. Hong Kong: Chinese University Press.

Yan Zhenguo and Liu Yinsheng. 1992a. "Yangkuaican chongjipo hou de chensi" (Pondering thoughts after the shock wave of Western fast food). *Shoudu jingji xinxibao* (Capital economic information news), December 3.

———. 1992b. "Zhongguo kuaican shichang shu zhu chenfu?" (Who will control the fast food market in China?). *Shoudu jingji xinxibao,* December 8.

Yang, Ch'ing-ch'u. 1981. "Born of the Same Roots." In *Born of the Same Roots,* translated by Thomas Gold and edited by Vivian Hsu. Bloomington: Indiana University Press.

Yang, Mayfair M-H., ed. 1999. *Gender and Feminism in a Transnational Chinese Public.* Minneapolis: University of Minnesota Press.

———. 1997. "Mass Media and Transnational Subjectivity in Shanghai: Notes on (Re)Cosmopolitanism in a Chinese Metropolis." In *Ungrounded Empires: The Cultural Politics of Modern Chinese Transnationalism,* edited by Aihwa Ong and Donald Nonini. New York: Routledge.

———. 1994. *Gifts, Favors, and Banquets: The Art of Social Relationships in China.* Ithaca, N.Y.: Cornell University Press.

———. 1993. "Of Gender, State Censorship and Overseas Capital: An Interview with Zhang Yimou." *Public Culture* 5, no. 2: 297–316.

Yavas, Ugur, Erdener Kaynak, and Eser Borak. 1981. "Retailing Institutions in Developing Countries: Determinants of Supermarket Patronage in Istanbul, Turkey." *Journal of Business Research* 9: 367–79.

Ye Nange. 1992. "Jiangsu Chengxiang zhumin shenghuo zhiliang" (Quality of domestic consumption by Jiangsu urban and suburban residents). *Zhongguo shehui kexue,* no. 2: 135–48.

Ye Xianning. 1993. "Jingcheng kuaican yi pie" (An overview of fast food in Beijing). *Fuwu jingji,* no. 4.

Yi Qiang and Wang Yi. 1996. *"Nan Jing jie ri zhu fu shi pin gon yin cong zu"* (Adequate supplies of staple and nonstaple foods for the holiday period in Nanjing Markets). *Yangzi wanbao* (Yangtze evening news), February 11: 14.

You Zi. 1994. "Jingcheng zhongshi kuaican re qi lai le" (Chinese fast food has become hot in Beijing). *Jingji shijie* (Economic world), no. 6: 60–61.

Yu Bin. 1996. "Zhongwai kuaican zai jingcheng" (Chinese and foreign fast foods in Beijing). *Zhongguo shangbao* (Chinese commercial news), June 20.

Yu Weize. 1995. "Shanghai Ronghuaji kuaican liansuo de jingying zouxiang" (The management directions of the Shanghai Ronghua Chicken fast food chain). *Zhongguo pengren* (Chinese culinary art), no. 9: 19–20.

Yu Wenxue and Zhang Lehe. 1988. *Zhongguo gudai wenhua zhishi baiti (Topics in ancient Chinese culture).* Beijing: Xinhua shuju.

Zelizer, Viviana. 1987. *Pricing the Priceless Child.* New York: Basic Books.

Zha, Jianying. 1995. *China Pop: How Soap Operas, Tabloids, and Bestsellers Are Transforming a Culture.* New York: New Press.

Zhan, Kaidi. 1992. *Strategies of Politeness in the Chinese Language.* Berkeley: Institute of East Asian Studies, University of California.

Zhang Guoyun. 1995. "Zhongshi kuaican, dengni dao chuntian" (Chinese fast food, waiting for you in the spring). *Xiaofei jingji* (Consumer economy), no. 3: 54–56.

Zhang Yubin. 1992. "Xishi kuaican jishi lu" (Inspirations from Western fast food). *Zhongguo shipinbao* (Chinese food newspaper), September 4.

Zhang Zhaonan. 1992a. "Gan yu yangfan bi gaodi" (Dare to challenge the foreign fast food). *Beijing wanbao* (Beijing evening news), September 13.

———. 1992b. "Kuaicanye kai jin Zhongguo budui" (The "Chinese troops" entering the fast food sector). *Beijing wanbao,* October 9.

Zhang Zhigang. 1966. "The New Daughter-in-Law Breaks Away from Old Practices." Translated in *Survey of Chinese Mainland Magazines,* no. 515 (March 14).

Zhao Huanyan. 1995. "Shilun fandian yingxiao zhong de wenhua dingwei" (On the cultural position of the restaurant business). *Fuwu jingji* (Service economy), no. 8: 10–11.

Zhong, Hua. 1989. "Poor Sculptures Shunned?" *China Daily,* January 31.

Zhong Zhe. 1993. "Meishi kuaican—gongfu zai shi wai" (American fast food—something beyond foods). *Xiaofeizhe* (Consumers), no. 2.

Zhou Dengge. 1993. "Lun shicheng jingji xiade chengshi fupin wenti" (Discussion of problem of urban poor in market economy). *Shehu kexue,* no. 7: 46–49.

Zhou, Min, and John R. Logan. 1996. "Market Transition and the Commodification of Housing in Urban China." *International Journal of Urban and Regional Research* 20, no. 3 (September): 400–21.

Zhou Yiling. 1996. "Xian Zuo Xian Mai Huo Guo Pi Liao Zhou Qiao" (Ready-to-cook materials for hot pot become popular). *Yangzi wanbao* (Yangtze evening news), February 1: 2.

Zhu Gongbing. 1996. "Nanjing shi jia kuai shi le nong mao shi chang jian she" (Nanjing speeds up the construction of indoor food markets). *Yangzi wanbao* (Yangtze evening news), March 24: 2.

Zu Qingfang. 1992. *Shehui zhibiao de yingyong* (Application of social indicators). Beijing: Zhongguo tongji chubanshe.

YEARBOOKS

Beijing tongji nianjian 1996 (Beijing statistical yearbook). Beijing: Zhongguo tongji chubanshe.

Chongqing tongji nianjian 1996 (Chongqing statistical yearbook). Beijing: Zhongguo tongji chubanshe.

Guangzhou tongji nianjian 1996 (Guangzhou statistical yearbook). Beijing: Zhongguo tongji chubanshe.

Harbin tongji nianjian 1996 (Harbin statistical yearbook). Beijing: Zhongguo tongji chubanshe.

Nanjing tongji nianjian 1996 (Nanjing statistical yearbook). Beijing: Zhongguo tongji chubanshe.

Shanghai jiating buzhi yibaili 1995 (100 designs for renovating Shanghai homes). Shanghai: Shanghai renmin meishu chubanshe.

Shanghai jingji nianjian 1996. (Shanghai economic yearbook). Shanghai: Shanghai jingji nianjian chubanshe.

Shanghai jingji nianjian 1993 (Shanghai economic yearbook). Shanghai: Shanghai jingji nianjian chubanshe.

Shanghai tongji nianjian 1997 (Shanghai statistical yearbook). Shanghai: Shanghai Zhongguo tongji chubanshe.

Shanghai tongji nianjian 1996 (Shanghai statistical yearbook). Beijing: Zhongguo tongji chubanshe.

Shanghai tongji nianjian 1993 (Shanghai statistical yearbook). Beijing: Zhongguo tongji chuban she.

Shanghai tongji nianjian 1995. (Shanghai statistical yearbook). Beijing: Zhongguo tongji chubanshe.

Shanghai tongji nianjian 1986 (Shanghai statistical yearbook). Beijing: Zhongguo tongji chubanshe.

Shanghai zhuzhai 1993 (Shanghai housing). Shanghai: Shahai kexue puji chubanshe.

Shenyang tongji nianjian 1996 (Shenyang yearbook). Beijing: Zhongguo tongji chubanshe.

Shenyang tongji nianjian 1992 (Shenyang yearbook). Beijing: Zhongguo tongji chubanshe.

Shenzhen tongji nianjian 1996 (Shenzhen statistical yearbook). Beijing: Zhongguo tongji chubanshe.

Tianjin tongji nianjian 1996 (Tianjin statistical yearbook). Beijing: Zhongguo tongji chubanshe.

Wuhan tongji nianjian 1996 (Wuhan statistical yearbook). Beijing: Zhongguo tongji chubanshe.

Xi'an tongji nianjian 1996 (Xian statistical yearbook). Beijing: Zhongguo tongji chubanshe.

Xi'an tongji nianjian 1994 (Xian statistical yearbook). Beijing: Zhongguo tongji chubanshe.

Zhongguo chengshi tongji nianjian 1995 (Chinese urban statistical yearbook). 1995. Beijing: Zhongguo tongji xinxi zixun fuwu zhongxin / Zhongguo jianshe chubanshe.

Zhongguo chengshi tongji nianjian 1993–1994 (Chinese urban statistical yearbook). 1995. Beijing: Zhongguo tongji chubanshe.

Zhongguo chengshi tongji nianjian 1987 (Chinese urban statistical yearbook). Beijing: Zhongguo tongji chubanshe.

Zhongguo chengzhen zhumin jiating shouzhu diaochaziliao (Survey materials on Chinese city residents family income and expenditures). 1991. Beijing: Zhongguo tongji chubanshe.

Zhongguo fangdichan shichang 1995 (China's real estate market). Beijing: Qiye guanli chubanshe.

Zhongguo renkou tongji nianjian 1993 (Chinese population statistical yearbook). Beijing: Zhongguo tongji chubanshe.

Zhongguo tongji nianjian 1996 (Chinese statistical yearbook). Beijing: Zhongguo tongji chubanshe.

Zhongguo tongji nianjian 1995 (Chinese statistical yearbook). Beijing: Zhongguo tongji chubanshe.

INDEX

acquaintances *(shouren)*, contemporary
use of term, 260–61
action figures (toys), 68
address, terms of, on Chinese greeting
cards, 189–90
advertising, 9, 28–29, 32n, 70, 193, 196;
for cigarettes and insecticides in 1920s,
46; for housing in 1990s, 26–29, 31–
42, 44–53; of products for infants
and children, 54–57, 63, 70, 72; for
Shenzhen bowling alleys, 252; use of
nin (honorific "you"), 189–90
affairs. *See* infidelity
affluence. *See* wealth
age, 19–20; generational differences in
leisure activities, 255–56; generational
differences at Shanghai dance halls and
discos, 14, 19, 227, 231–32, 239–43; of
hotline callers, 155–56, 156 table 7.2;
of women at time of marriage, 194
agents of the state (bureaucrats; government
officials), 1, 2–3, 11–12, 16; efforts to
curb corruption among, 265, 279–80,
281, 281n, 284; networking with, 21–22,
267; networking with by private entrepreneurs, 251–52, 259–63, 276, 278–80; as
Shenzhen bowlers, 256–59
Agnew, Jean-Christophe, 180, 196
agricultural status *(nongye hukou)*, 2n2
agriculture, 107; farmers as vendors in Nanjing food markets, 113, 113n; products
traded for grain coupons, 130

ahongs (Muslim religious specialists): role
in Hui weddings, 80–81, 87, 89, 90 fig.
4.2, 97; Western-style wedding attire
censured by, 101–2
Aifeng (Xue's mother), 84, 91, 100
air conditioners, 4 table 1.1, 32n, 61 table
3.3, 74, 134 table 6.3, 136, 137 table 6.4,
222
alcohol consumption, prohibited in
McDonald's, 217, 219
alley apartments *(shikumen)*, 41–42
Americana, Western-style fast-food restaurants as symbol of, 211, 214–15, 221
American Greetings, 197, 198
amusement arcades, 76
amusement parks, 75, 254 table 11.1, 311
Anagnost, Ann, 166n54, 168n58
angels, on Christmas cards, 178, 178n
anonymity: of disco, 244; in forms of public
speech, 13; offered by romantic greeting
cards, 195; in use of hotlines, 147, 157,
167
Anqi, Xu, 163n
apartments, 10, 20, 28n2, 36–37; advertisements for, 26–29, 31–35, 38–42, 44–53;
allocation of in 1970s, 3; floor space, 34,
35n, 36; purchase of, 8–10, 61 table 3.3
Appadurai, Arjun, 15n28
appliances, 2, 4 table 1.1, 18, 32n, 118–19,
131, 134 table 6.3, 136, 137 table 6.4
architecture, 289, 299
art, public. *See* public art

Text:	10/12 Baskerville
Display:	Baskerville
Composition:	Integrated Composition Systems, Inc.
Printing and binding:	Thomson-Shore

DATE DUE

MAR 2 4 2005	
MAY 1 7 2007	
OCT 0 1 2008	